THE BILL OF RIGHTS

Original Arguments and Fundamental Documents

Edited by

Gordon Lloyd
Margie Lloyd

University Press of America,® Inc.
Lanham • New York • Oxford

University Press of America,® Inc.
4501 Forbes Boulevard, Suite 200
Lanham, Maryland 20706

12 Hid's Copse Rd.
Cummor Hill, Oxford OX2 9JJ

Printed in the United States of America
British Library Cataloging in Publication Information Available

Library of Congress Cataloging-in-Publication Data

The essential Bill of Rights : original arguments and fundamental documents / edited by Gordon Lloyd, Margie Lloyd
p. cm.
Includes bibliographical references and index.
1. United States. Constitution. 1st-10th Amendments.—Sources. 2. Civil rights—United States.—History—Sources. 3. Constitutional history—United States—Sources. I. Lloyd, Gordon. II. Lloyd, Margie
KF4744 1998 342.73'085—dc21 98-12804 CIP

ISBN 0-7618-1075-7 (cloth: alk. ppr.)
ISBN 0-7618-1076-5 (pbk: alk. ppr.)

∞™ The paper used in this publication meets the minimum requirements of American National Standard for information Sciences—Permanence of Paper for Printed Library Materials, ANSI Z39.48—1984

Contents

Preface

Our objective is to encourage an intelligent conversation between the contemporary reader and the authors of essential historical texts pertaining to the origin of the Bill of Rights. We want readers to engage in a discussion with writers of seventeenth and eighteenth century articles, books, letters, and pamphlets concerning the relationship between private rights and the public good, as well as analyze and evaluate original constitutional documents that were consciously framed to protect rights.

Our purpose is to provide an accessible and authentic collection of original arguments and fundamental documents. We aim to provide the reader with a concise yet reliable account of the creation of the Bill of Rights. In short, we want to make the essential story available. To that end, we do our best to keep out of sight as much as possible. We have focused our intrusions into this vital discourse to bibliographically-oriented headnotes for each entry and jargon-free commentaries at the beginning of each chapter. From time to time, however, we have added explanatory footnotes to help the reader understand the context in which the conversation or document appeared, to provide definitions of now unfamiliar words and phrases, or to show the differences between scholarly reproductions of the same argument or document. To assist the reader, we have also provided sectional breakdowns to lengthy texts that were continuous in the original version. Due to the length of some of the commentaries, we have found it necessary to edit those that are less "essential" to the story, but without which the richness of the account would be missing.

Otherwise, we ask the contemporary reader to engage the original text on its own terms. Accordingly, we have not made an editorial decision to modernize the form in which the original conversations appeared. Instead, we have been careful to reproduce the grammatical style, spelling, and syntax found in the original sources. We have retained, for example, an author's use of italics--prevalent in works that were originally given as speeches--and the earlier reliance on the upper case. As a result of our decision to provide verbatim representations, readers will note an absence of uniformity in style as they journey through our reproductions of the original texts.

We have also retained the larger philosophical and political context within which the discussion about rights took place over a period of two hundred years. Thus we invite the reader to recover the discussion between enlightenment thinkers and skeptical traditionalists over the nature and origin of rights, to explore the efforts of practical Americans to apply and adapt the traditional understanding of rights to a new federal and republican situation, as well as to evaluate the exchange between the Federalists and Antifederalists in the ratification period over how rights are best secured. Finally, the correspondence between Thomas Jefferson and James Madison presents a fascinating picture of the multidimensional nature of the original conversation over the essential rights of the people.

Many of the early American charters, constitutions, declarations, and pamphlets have, over the years, been reproduced in a variety of configurations and contradictory formats. This is also true of the extensive correspondence that occurred between prominent Americans of the founding era as well as the published work of practical commentators and political theorists. The quest for the authentic text has been difficult and time-consuming. In the end, we have relied on Congressionally-authorized versions of the original documents such as those generated by Sol Bloom, Jonathan Elliot, James Richardson, Charles Tansill, and Francis Thorpe, and on Congressionally-authorized versions of the correspondence and debates that took place in various assemblies and conventions during the 1770s and 1780s. We have tried, where possible, to reproduce the earliest available edition of an author's work unless guided by the author to a later corrected version.

We wish to neither compete with nor replace such multi-volume research sources as Linda De Pauw's *Documentary History of the First Federal Congress*; Jonathan Elliot's *Debates in the Several State Conventions*; Herbert Storing's *The Complete Anti-Federalist*; Philip Kurland and Ralph Lerner's *The Founders Constitution*; Merrill Jensen and John Kaminski's *Documentary History of the Ratification*; Charles Hyneman and Donald Lutz's *American Political Writing*; or Bernard Schwartz's *The Roots of the Bill of Rights*. In fact, in our headnotes, we encourage the reader to consult these works, along with others mentioned in the bibliography, because they are the major sources for original scholarship. But they are not readily available to college students, public officials, or concerned citizens. This is unfortunate because the contemporary discourse about the Constitution is largely a discourse about rights and sooner or later the discussion turns on an appeal to, or rejection of, the arguments and documents of the founding era. Our aim is to overcome this discrepancy by providing the contemporary reader with a one-volume source book that contains the essential original arguments and documents pertaining to the adoption of the Bill of Rights.

Our own conversation with the original texts has been enhanced by our association with The Huntington Library, San Marino, California, where we are fortunate to be readers. We thank the Huntington for giving us access to their vast authentic collection. We have checked every entry for accuracy against the extensive collection of original manuscripts and early editions generously made available to us and have noted discrepancies where relevant. Special thanks to Paul Zall of the Huntington Library for his encouragement and insight.

Gordon Lloyd thanks the many University of Redlands students who endured early drafts and the Hewlett Foundation and the Morlan Fund for financial support.

Margie Lloyd thanks Steve Ealy of Liberty Fund, and Donald Lutz of the University of Houston, for providing the opportunity to discuss America's constitutional heritage with scholars from across the world.

Finally, we both thank Lynnae Pattison for her technical advice and editorial assistance.

G. L. and M. L.
Pasadena

Chapter One

The Common Law and Covenanting Traditions

Chapter One focuses on the contributions made to the development of the Bill of Rights by two separate but related traditions. First, the British common law tradition provides the foundation for the due process of law, the right to petition, and constitutional restraints on monarchy. Second, the American colonial experience articulates the right to self-government within a covenanting tradition.

The Magna Carta

Despite the presence of words such as "scutage," and "wapenstakes," which locate the Great Charter squarely in the feudal era, the spirit of the document speaks to subsequent generations. The Magna Carta is more than a practical document specifically designed to solve feudal difficulties. True, King John was forced at gun point to recognize the existence of the traditional rights of the barons, but there are a set of principles which inform the sixty-three chaptered document signed in Runnymede in 1215 and reaffirmed by subsequent British monarchs. The principles extend beyond the often recognized origin of the no taxation without representation doctrine in chapter 12 and the due process clause of chapter 39. The concepts of trial by jury and no cruel punishments are present in chapter 21; and the confrontation clause of the Sixth Amendment is anticipated in chapters 38, 40, and 44. Moreover, chapters 1 and 63 show that the British defended both the free exercise of religion and the existence of an established English church. But the most important contribution of the Magna Carta is the claim that there is a fundamental set of principles which even the King must respect. Above all else, Magna Carta makes the case that the people have a "right" to expect "reasonable" conduct by the monarch. These rights are to be secured by the principle of representation outlined in the longest chapter.

The Virginia Charter

Nearly four hundred years later, another monarch was faced with the same issue: to provide appropriate recognition for the rights of Englishmen. This time the issue emerged under far more amicable conditions, for no one was accusing the king of unreasonable conduct. Mutual negotiation, rather than concentrated force, produced a document that secured mutual advantage for both the king and his subjects. The quandary in the seventeenth century was how to apply the traditional rights under completely novel conditions. To be specific: were Englishmen who emigrated still entitled to the rights of Englishmen? The answer was, "yes," for inhabitants of overseas territories under the explicit jurisdiction of the crown. In 1606, King James I granted, willingly, the first colonial charter to English settlers who occupied Virginia. The colonists were expected to advance the king's glory, bring Christianity to the "savages," and provide him with revenue. The king, in return, committed himself, and his heirs, to recognize "forever" certain individual rights of Englishmen.

Like the Magna Carta, this Charter does not contain an extensive list of the rights to be secured, nor does it anticipate the twentieth-century notion that declared rights are only "enforceable" by courts empowered with the authority of judicial review. Instead, the colonists relied on a council form of government--a system of local self-government--to secure their "Liberties, Franchises, and Immunities." This right to limited self-government went beyond the traditional rights of Englishmen. In fact, the emphasis of the document is on the right to self-rule. To this end, the Charter establishes a local legislature that can pass laws subject to the veto of the monarch.

The Mayflower Compact

A decade later, in 1620, King James I authorized another political founding, this time by Puritans in the northern parts of America. Sixty-five days after leaving Plymouth, the 102 passengers on the Mayflower landed at Cape Cod in Massachusetts. An unidentified number invoked the authority of the "Virginia patent" under which they traveled and threatened to go their own way once on shore. Passenger William Bradford, who left an extensive diary on the Plymouth

Plantation from 1620 to 1646 and was later the second governor of the colony, noted that the "covenant" was written and signed with the expectation that it "might be as firm as any patent, and in some respect more sure." This gave birth to the American tradition of "combining" and "framing" just and equal laws. It is significant to note that this American tradition of framing good government preceded by eight years the petition of King Charles by the English Parliament. Even more significantly, the covenanting tradition began some seventy years *before* the 1689 contract between Parliament and the Monarchy in Britain, as well as the publication of John Locke's *Second Treatise* in which the enlightenment version of the contract theory of government receives its full articulation. The importance of the Mayflower Compact for understanding the development of American politics and culture was not lost on Alexis de Tocqueville. According to Tocqueville, the Mayflower Compact illustrates that "Democracy more perfect than any of which antiquity had dared to dream sprang full-grown from and fully armed from the midst of the old feudal society."

The Petition of Right

The 1628 Petition of Right is the second of the three British documents that provided a strong common law component to the development of the American Bill of Rights. The authors of the statute consciously invoke the memory of the rule of law heritage of the Magna Carta: they insist that the monarchy honor and respect rights to which Englishmen have been accustomed for centuries. In the thirteenth century, the nobles petitioned the King to abandon his arbitrary and tyrannical policies; four centuries later, it was the commoners who petitioned the King to adhere to the principles of reasonable government bequeathed by the English tradition. Under the leadership of Sir Edward Coke, a legal scholar-turned-practical politician, Parliament petitioned Charles I--son of the recently deceased King James I--to uphold the traditional rights of Englishmen. Among the customary "divers rights and liberties of the subjects" listed were no taxation without consent, "due process of law," the right to habeas corpus, no quartering of troops, the respect for private property, and the imposition of no cruel punishment.

To be sure, King Charles did not consider himself bound by the petition; in fact he disregarded it. Nevertheless, it would be wrong to underestimate the importance of the document. On the one hand, it reaffirmed the right to petition as a fundamental right that can be invoked legitimately against a monarch who has strayed from traditional principles. Moreover, Coke's argument still had considerable appeal over one hundred years later on the other side of the Atlantic. During the 1760s, the American colonists articulated their grievances against

King George in terms reminiscent of Coke's petition to uphold the rights of Englishmen. On the other hand, King Charles's rejection of the appeal shows the inherent limitations of the right to petition.

The Fundamental Orders of Connecticut

In 1635, immigrants from Massachusetts settled near Hartford, Connecticut and by 1639 had created "Fundamental Orders" for the governance of Connecticut. The settlers followed the covenanting tradition of the Mayflower Compact and made mutual promises to associate with each other under "an orderly and decent Gouernment established according to God." But the Connecticut founders went beyond their Puritan ancestors, for the British monarch was neither the initiator nor authorizing agent of the document. In fact, there is no mention of the monarch anywhere in the agreement. True, the Fundamental Orders of Connecticut did not contain a formal listing of guaranteed individual rights. Nevertheless, it does list one of the most fundamental rights of all--and one that was *not* an Englishman's right--the right to create the form of government under which one shall live. The settlers established this political right along with provisions for annual elections, the secret ballot, rotation in office, and the "liberty of spech" for elected representatives.

The Massachusetts Body of Liberties

The Massachusetts Body of Liberties, adopted in December 1641, was the first attempt in Massachusetts to restrain the power of the elected representatives by an appeal to a document that lists the rights, and duties, of the people. The document, drafted and debated over several years, combines the American covenanting tradition with an appeal to the common law tradition. Containing ninety-eight sections, it covers the rules concerning judicial proceedings (sections 18-57); "liberties more peculiarly concerning the free man" (sections 58-78); and the rights of women (79-80), children (sections 81-84), servants (85-88), foreigners (89-91), and animals (92-93). Section 94 provides biblical justification supporting the death penalty in twelve cases, and Section 95 contains eleven liberties given by "the Lord Jesus...to the Churches." The most enduring part of the Body of Liberties are the preamble and the first seventeen sections, which contain the essential rights of the common law tradition. Of particular importance are references to what by now were traditional on the American side of the Atlantic: the equal treatment of all persons under laws passed by the legislature, just compensation for property taken for public use, the right to petition government for redress of grievances, the right to trial by jury, the right to travel, and lastly, the right to trade.

The Toleration Act

The 1649 Maryland Act Concerning Religion--also known popularly as the Toleration Act--is a good example of the paradoxical relationship in America between the establishment of religion and the free exercise of religion. This paradox emerged during the colonial experience--both the public establishment of religion and the individual right of conscience were supported simultaneously at various times among the colonies--and attained its controversial character in the 1780s.

The first two thirds of the act establishes the importance of the public recognition of the Christian religion for "a well governed" commonwealth. In fact, the freemen and the governor expressly state the "serious" causal connection between the promotion of political virtue and respect for established religion. To that end, provision is made for the punishment of a series of violations ranging from death in the case of blaspheming God to a fine for profaning the Sabbath. The 1649 act establishes the public centrality of Christianity without designating preferential treatment for one Christian sect. When Lord Baltimore's property became a royal colony in 1702, the establishment portion of the paradox acquired an additional dimension. The Church of England became the established sect in 1702.

The last third of the act recognizes the theological and political importance of religious toleration, including severe penalties to be levied against individuals who violate the free exercise of religion clause. These include reparations to be paid by the wrong doer to the person whose individual right to freedom of conscience has been violated. The Maryland Act not only explicitly uses the phrase, "free exercise" of religion, but it does so at least one hundred years before the enlightenment argument that the free exercise of religion was a natural right.

The Fundamental Laws of West New Jersey

The "great charter" of New Jersey, 1677, done in the name of the "Proprietors, Freeholders, and Inhabitants of the said Province," was modeled on the Rhode Island Charter. The New Jersey framers also attempted to secure the potentially conflicting goals of local self government and adherence to enduring principles. The first twelve chapters of the forty-four chapter charter concern the selection and duties of Commissioners, the encouragement of land ownership, and provision for the construction of public highways. Chapters 24-44 cover relations with the Indians, wills and testaments, and taxes and assessments. The critical middle eleven sections cover the "common law or fundamental rights and priviledges of West New Jersey." Among the rights to be protected are the rights to the free exercise of religion; due process of law, trial by jury, and to confront witnesses in an open court of law. Finally, the government is obligated to ensure that every person shall "be free from oppression and slavery."

The Pennsylvania Frame of Government

In 1681, King Charles II granted Quaker William Penn ownership of the "Province of Pennsilvania." The 1682 Frame of Government was designed "for the good Government thereof" and included a "grant" of "divers Liberties, Franchises and Properties." This document is unique to the seventeenth-century American experience; the authorizing, or granting, agent was neither the English monarch nor the people. Penn, as lone founder, "did grant and confirm unto" the inhabitants certain individual rights. And yet, scholars are surely correct to note that this 1682 document ranks among "the most influential of the Colonial documents protecting individual rights," against the abuse of governmental powers.

There is both a constitutional and legalistic tone to the document. First, a preamble announcing the purposes of government and declaring that the rule of "good laws," supported by a wise and virtuous people, is to be chosen over "the rule of one, few, and many" magistrates in a country inhabited by "a loose and depraved people." This is followed by a "Frame," containing twenty-four sections guaranteeing the right of participation and outlining the powers and responsibilities of government officials. Finally, there is an extensive itemization of civil and criminal rights and expectations. The list not only includes the familiar common law right to fair trial by a jury of one's peers, but also detailed provisions for the careful handling of such specific matters as court fees, fines, and documents.

The document also addresses the American religious paradox. On the one hand, Section XXXV declares that inhabitants "shall, in no ways, be molested or prejudiced for their religious persuasion, or practice, in matters of faith and worship, nor shall they be compelled, at any time, to frequent or maintain any religious worship, place or ministry whatever." On the other hand, specific provision is made in Section XXXVI for the observance of "the Lord's day," and punishments are indicated in Section XXXVII for "offences against God." There is a political, as well as a theological, reason for itemizing twelve offences of "uncleanness," eight offences of "violence," and eleven offences productive of "rudeness, cruelty, looseness, and irreligion." These thirty-one "offences against God" are examples of the "wildness and looseness of the people" that, in turn, "provoke the indignation of God against a country."

The English Bill of Rights

The third British contribution to the development of the American Bill of Rights is the 1689 English Bill of Rights. The "Convention Parliament" of 1689 declared an end to the three-year reign of James II--formerly the Duke of York--and passed an Act to secure "the Kingdom from Popery and Arbitrary Power." To that end, Parliament listed twelve indictments against him and issued a declaration of the rights and liberties of the subject. Never again, declared the agreement between the Parliament and the newly enthroned monarchs--King William of Orange and Queen Mary, daughter of dethroned King James II--must the "Religion, Laws, and Liberties" of the Realm "be in danger of being subverted." To that end, several ancient rights of Englishmen are reaffirmed: the right to petition government for the redress of grievances, the expectation that governmental policy shall confirm to the rule of law, that standing armies in peace time without the consent of Parliament is illegal, and "that Excessive Bail ought not to be required, nor Excessive Fines imposed; nor cruel and unusual Punishments inflicted." Parliament also declared that henceforth it was going to be a major political actor; the representatives of the people shall be guaranteed the freedom of speech and debate and that there were to be frequently held elections. Not included, however, in the declaration of rights that Englishmen have are the right to the free exercise of religion and the right to choose their form of government.

The Pennsylvania Charter of Privileges

The final document in this chapter, the 1701 Pennsylvania Charter of Privileges, was the last and, perhaps, "the most famous of all colonial constitutions." This charter, also written by William Penn, replaced the original 1682 document as the fundamental law of the colony. (The necessary "Six parts of Seven of the Freemen" requested an amendment to the 1682 Frame of Government.) The new charter, which remained in force for the next one hundred and seventy five years, was designed to be more "suitable to the present Circumstances of the Inhabitants." The most important structural changes are the provisions for annual county-based elections to a unicameral General Assembly and an enhanced political role for the legislature. Enhanced protection is also given to freedom of conscience. For example, the free exercise of religion clause is placed first, and is unamendable, and religious qualification for holding office is limited to belief in Jesus Christ. Moreover the "offences against God" section of the 1682 charter are absent. Finally, Penn included the right of criminals to have "the same Privileges of Witness and Council as their prosecutors."

I.

MAGNA CARTA, 1215

Two of the four original copies of the Magna Carta are in the British Museum, the third is in the Lincoln Cathedral, and the fourth is in Salisbury Cathedral. For a reproduction of one of the extant versions see Bernard Schwartz, editor, *The Roots of the Bill of Rights*, 1980 (1: 4-16). For one which attempts to "convey the sense rather than the precise wording of the original Latin," see Sir Ivan Jennings, *Magna Carta and Its Influence in the World Today* (London, 1965). Another version with the same purpose is in G. R. C. Davis, *Magna Carta* (London, 1963). We have relied on the Lincoln Cathedral copy reproduced in Sol Bloom's *History of the Formation of the Union Under the Constitution* (Washington, DC, 1943, esp. 511-518), but retained the now-established practice of dividing the Magna Carta into sixty-three paragraphs and added our own footnotes.

~

JOHN, by the grace of God King of England, Lord of Ireland, Duke of Normandy and of Aquitaine, and Earl[1] of Anjou: To the Archbishops, Bishops, Abbots, Earls, Barons, Justiciaries, Foresters, Sheriffs, Reeves,[2] Ministers,[3] and all Bailiffs and others, his faithful subjects,[4] Greeting. Know ye that We, in the presence of God, and for the health of Our soul, and the souls of Our ancestors and heirs, to the honour of God, and the exaltation of Holy Church, and amendment of Our kingdom, by the advice of Our reverend fathers...and others,[5]

---

[1]Both Davis and Schwartz use "Court."

[2]Like Bloom, Schwartz uses "reeves" while Davis uses "stewards."

[3]Davis uses "servants."

[4]Davis uses "to all his officials and legal subjects." Schwartz uses "men."

[5]Here are the others listed by Bloom: "Stephen, Archbishop of Canterbury, Primate of all England and Cardinal of the Holy Roman Church; Henry, Archbishop of Dublin; William of London: Peter of Winchester, Jocelin of Bath and Glastonbury, Hugh of Lincoln, Walter of Worcester, William of Coventry, Benedict of Rochester, Bishops; and Master Pandulph, the Pope's subdeacon and familiar; Brother Aymeric, Master of the Knights of the Temple in England; and the noble persons, William Marshal, Earl of Pembroke; William, Earl of Salisbury; William, Earl of Warren; William, Earl of Arundel; Alan de Galloway, Constable of Scotland; Warin Fitz-Gerald, Hubert de Burgh, Seneschal of Poictou, Peter Fitz-Herbert, Hugo de Neville, Matthew Fitz-Herbert, Thomas Basset, Alan Basset, Philip Daubeney, Robert do Roppelay, John Marshal, John Fitz-Hugh, and

1. Our liegemen, have, in the first place granted to God, and by this Our present Charter have confirmed for Us and Our heirs for ever--That the English Church shall be free and enjoy all her rights in their integrity and her liberties untouched. And that We will this so to be observed appears from the fact that We of our own mere and free will, before the outbreak of the dissensions between Us and Our Barons, granted, confirmed and procured to be confirmed by Pope Innocent III., the freedom of elections which is considered most important and necessary to the English Church, which Charter We will both keep Ourself and will it to be so kept by Our heirs for ever. We have also granted to all the free men of Our kingdom, for Us and our heirs for ever, all the liberties underwritten, to have and to hold to them and their heirs of Us and Our heirs.

2. If any of Our Earls, Barons, or others who hold of Us in chief by Knight's service shall die, and at the time of his death his heir shall be of full age and owe a relief, he shall have his inheritance by ancient relief; to wit, the heir or heirs of an Earl of an entire Earl's Barony, £100, the heir or heirs of a Baron of an entire Barony, £100; the heir or heirs of a Knight of an entire Knight's fee, 100*s.* at the most; and he that oweth less shall give less, according to the ancient custom of fees.

3. If, however, the heir of any such shall be under age and in ward, he shall, when he comes of age, have his inheritance without relief or fine.

4. The guardian of the land of any such heir so under age shall take therefrom reasonable issues and customs and services only, and without destruction and waste of men or property; and if We shall have committed the custody of any such land to the sheriff or any other person who ought to be answerable to Us for its issues thereof he commit destruction or waste upon the ward-lands, We will take an emend from him, and the land shall be committed to two lawful and discreet men of that fee, who shall be answerable for the issues to Us or to whomever We shall have assigned them. And if We shall give or sell the wardship of any such land to any one, and he commit destruction or waste upon it, he shall lose wardship, which shall be committed to two lawful and discreet men of that fee, who shall, in like manner, be answerable unto Us as hath been aforesaid.

5. But the guardian, so long as he shall have the custody of the land, shall keep up and maintain the houses, parks, fish ponds, pools, mills, and other things pertaining thereto, out of the issues of the same, and shall restore the whole to the heir when he comes of age, stocked

---

others...." Davis lists all of the names, including Hubert de "Burgh senenschal of Pointou." He also drops all hyphens.

with ploughs and wainage,[6] according as the season may require and the issues of the land can reasonably bear.

6. Heirs shall be married without disparagement,[7] to which end the marriage is made known to the heir's nearest of kin before it be contracted.

7. A widow, after the death of her husband, shall immediately and without difficulty have her marriage portion and inheritance, nor shall she give anything for her marriage portion, dower, or inheritance which inheritance her husband and her held on the day of his death; and she may remain in her husband's house for forty days after his death, within which her dowry shall be assigned to her.

8. No widow shall be distrained[8] to marry so long as she has a mind to live without a husband; provided, however, that she give security that she will not marry without Our assent if she holds of Us, or that of the Lord of whome she holds, if she holds of another.

9. Neither We nor Our bailiffs[9] shall seize any land or rent for any debt so long as the debtor's chattels are sufficient to discharge the same; nor shall the debtor's sureties be distrained so long as the chief debtor hath sufficient to pay the debt, and if he fail in the payment thereof, not having wherewithal to discharge it, then the sureties shall answer it, and, if they will, shall hold the debtor's lands and rents until satisfaction of the debt which they have paid for him be made them, unless the chief debtor can show himself to quit thereof against them.

10. If any one shall have borrowed money from the Jews, more or less, and die before the debt satisfied, no interest shall be taken upon such debt so long as the heir be under age, of whomsoever he may hold; and if the debt shall fall into Our[10] hands We will only take the chattel mentioned in the Charter.[11]

11. And if any one die indebted to the Jews his wife shall have her dower and pay nothing on that debt; and if the children of the said deceased be left under age they shall have necessities provided for them according to the condition of the deceased, and the debt shall be paid out of the residue, saving the Lord's service; and so shall it be done with regard to debts owed to others than Jews.

---

[6]Schwartz uses "produce" while Davis utilizes "implements of husbandry."

[7]Davis's copy reads as "heirs may be given in marriage but not to someone of lower social standing."

[8]Schwartz uses "forced."

[9]Schwartz uses "officers."

[10]Davis substitutes "Crown" for "Our."

[11]Davis uses "bond" instead of "Charter."

12. No scutage or aid shall be imposed in Our kingdom unless by the common council thereof, except to ransom Our person, make Our eldest son a Knight, and once to marry Our eldest daughter, and for this a reasonable aid only shall be paid so shall it be with regard to aids from the City of London[.]

13. [And] the City of London shall have all her ancient liberties and free customs, both by land and water. Moreover we will and grant that all the other cities, boroughs, towns, and ports shall have all their liberties and free customs.

14. And for obtaining the common council of the kingdom concerning the assessment of aids other than in the three cases aforesaid of scutage, We will cause to be summoned, severally by our letters the Archbishops, Bishops, Abbots, Earls and great Barons; and in addition, We will also cause to be summoned, generally, by Our Sheriffs and bailiffs, all those who hold of Us in chief, to meet at a certain day, to wit, at the end of forty days at least, and at a certain place; and in all letters of such summons We will explain the cause thereof, and the summons being thus been made the business shall proceed on the day appointed, according to the advice of those who shall be present, notwithstanding that the whole number of persons summoned shall not have come.

15. We will not, for the future, grant permission to any man to levy an aid upon his freemen, except to ransom his person, make his eldest son a Knight, and once to marry his eldest daughter, for which a reasonable aid only shall be levied.

16. No man shall be distrained to perform more service for a knight's fee or other free tenement than is due therefrom.

17. Common pleas[12] shall not follow our Court, but be beholden in some definite place.

18. Recognisances of Novel Disseisin, Mort d'Ancestor, and Darrein Presentment shall be taken in their proper countries only, and in this wise;--We Ourself, or, if We be absent from the realm, Our Chief Justiciary, shall send two justiciaries through each county four times a year; who, together with four knights elected out of each shire by the people thereof, shall hold the said assizes on the day and in the place aforesaid.

19. And if the said assizes cannot be held on the day appointed, so as many of the knights and free holders as shall have been present thereat on that day shall remain as will be sufficient for the administration of justice, according as the business to be done be greater or less.

---

[12]Davis uses "ordinary lawsuits."

20. A free man shall not be amerced[13] for a small fault, but according to the measure thereof; and for a great crime according to its magnitude, in proportion to his degree; and in a like manner a merchant in proportion to his merchandise, and a villein[14] in proportion to his wainage[15] if he should fall under Our mercy; and none of the said amercements shall be imposed unless by the oath of honest men of the venue.

21. Earls and Barons shall only be amerced by their peers, in proportion to the measure of the offence.

22. No clerk[16] shall be amerced for his lay tenement, except after the manner of the other persons aforesaid, and not according to the value of his ecclesiastical benefice.

23. Neither shall any vill[17] or person be distrained to make bridges over rivers, but they who are bound to do so by ancient custom and law.

24. No sheriff, constable, coroners, or other Our bailiffs shall hold pleas of Our Crown.

25. All counties, hundreds, tithings and wapentakes[18] shall stand at the old farms, without any increased rent, except Our demesne manors.

26. If any one dies holding a lay fee of Us, and the sheriff or Our bailiff show Our letters patent of summons touching the debt due to Us from the deceased, it shall be lawful to such sheriff or bailiff to attach and register the chattels of the deceased found in the lay fee to the value of that debt, so that, by view of lawful men, so that nothing be removed therefrom until Our whole debt be paid; and the residue shall be given up to the executors to carry out the will of the deceased. And if there be nothing is due from him to Us, all his chattels[19] shall remain to the deceased, saving to his wife and children their reasonable shares.

---

[13]Amerce means to inflict a discretionary or arbitrary penalty.

[14]According to Davis, "husbandman."

[15]Davis uses "husbandry."

[16]Schwartz uses "clergyman;" Davis says "clerk in holy orders."

[17]Davis uses "town."

[18]According to the 1933 *Shorter Oxford English Dictionary* (p. 2383), a wapentake is "a subdivision of certain English shires, corresponding to the 'hundred' of other counties" or "the judicial court of such a subdivision." The word derives from weapon and "tak" or the act of taking. Examples of such a division are "Yorkshire, Derbyshire, Notts, Lincolnshire, Northhamptonshire, and Leicestershire, all of which have a large Danish element in the population." (p. 2383) Future references to this source will be cited as OED.

[19]Davis uses "property."

27. If any free man shall die intestate his chattels[20] shall be distributed by the hands of his nearest kinfolk and friends by view of the Church saving to every one the debts due to him from the deceased.[21]

28. No constable or other Our bailiff shall take corn or other chattels[22] of any man without immediate payment for the same, unless he hath a voluntary respite of payment from the seller.

29. No constable shall distrain any knight to give money for castle-guard, if he will perform it either in his proper person or some other fit man, if he himself be prevented from doing so by reasonable cause; and if We lead or send him into the army, he shall be quit[23] of castle-guard for the time he shall remain in the army by Our command.

30. No sheriff or other Our bailiff or any other man, shall take the horses or carts of any free man for carriage[24] except with his consent.

31. Neither shall We or Our bailiffs take another man's timber for Our castles or other uses, unless with the consent of the owner thereof.

32. We will only retain the lands of persons convicted of felony for a year and a day, after which they shall be restored to the lords of the fees.

33. From henceforth, all weirs[25] shall be entirely removed from the Thames and Medway, and throughout England, except upon the seacoast.

34. The writ called "Praecipe" shall not for the future issue to any one of any tenement whereby a freeman may lose his court.[26]

35. There shall be one measure of wine throughout Our entire kingdom, and one of ale; and one measure of corn, to wit, the London

---

[20]Davis uses "movable goods."

[21]Davis renders this as "The rights of his debtors are to be preserved."

[22]Again, Davis uses the term "movable goods."

[23]Davis uses "excused."

[24]Davis uses "transport."

[25]Both Davis and Schwartz use "fish-weirs."

[26]Davis interprets this paragraph thusly: "The writ call *precipe* shall not in future be issued to anyone in respect of any holding of land, if a free man could thereby de deprived of the right of trail in his own lord's court." The *OED* (p. 1560) notes that the word praecipe derives from the Latin to admonish or enjoin (see "precept"), as in the opening word of the writ *praecipe quod reddat* (enjoin him that render). In legal terms, a praecipe is a writ requiring something to be done, or demanding a reason for its non-performance; it may also be a note containing particulars of a writ which must be filed with the officer of the court from which the writ issues, by the party asking for the writ, or by his solicitor. (*OED*, p. 1848.)

quarter, and one breadth of dyed cloth, russetts, and haberjects,[27] to wit, two ells within the lists.[28] And as with measure, so shall it be also with weights.

36. From henceforth nothing shall be given for a writ of inquisition upon life or limbs, but it shall be granted gratis, and shall not be denied.

37. If any one hold of Us by fee-farm, socage or burgage,[29] and hold land of another by Knight's service, We will not have the wardship of his heir, or the land which belongs to another man's fee, by reason of that fee-farm, socage or burgage; nor will We have the wardship of such fee-farm, socage, or burgage, unless such fee-farm owe Knight's service. We will not have the wardship of any man's heir, or the land which he holds of another by Knight's service, by reason of any petty serjeanty which he holds of Us by service of rendering Us daggers, arrows, or the like.

38. No bailiff shall for the future put any man to trial upon his simple accusation without producing credible witnesses to the truth thereof.

39. No freeman shall be taken, imprisoned, disseised,[30] outlawed, banished, or in any way destroyed, nor will We proceed against or prosecute him except by lawful judgment of his peers or the law of the land.

---

[27]Russet (from the Old French *rousset*) is "a course homespun woollen cloth of a reddish-brown, grey, or neutral color, formerly used for the dress of peasants and country-folk." Other definitions of the word are the garments of such cloth, or the eating of an apple of the same color. (*OED*, p.1771.) Davis replaces the word "haberject" with the word "hauberk." A "hauberk" is "a piece of defensive armour, originally for neck and shoulders; but early developed into a long military tunic, usually of ring or chain mail." (*OED*, p. 871). A "habergeon" is a smaller version of a hauberk. (*OED*, p. 849.)

[28]Schwartz renders the last part of this sentence as "two yards between the borders." Davis substitutes "selvedges" for "borders."

[29]According to the *OED* (p. 1935), socage is "the tenure of land by certain determinate services other than Knight-service." Its 1464 version meant an "estate held in socage;" in 1859, it meant a "payment made to the superior by one holding land in socage." Burgage is a legal term whose 1502 A.D. usage meant "a tenure whereby lands or tenements in cities and towns were held of the lord, for a certain yearly rent." The 1827 version was "a freehold property in a borough; also a house etc., held by burgage tenure."

[30]The *OED* (p. 535) defines disseise as "to put out of actual seisin or possession; to dispossess a person of his estates, usually wrongfully or by force; to oust." In other words, seize.

40. To no one will We sell, to none will We deny or defer[31] right or justice.

41. All merchants shall have safe conduct to go and come out of and into England, and to stay in and travel through England by land and water for purchase or sale without maltolt, [32] by ancient and just customs, except in time of war or if they belong to a country at war with Us. And if any such be found in Our domain at the outbreak of war, they shall be attached,[33] without injury to their persons or goods, until it be known to Us or Our Chief Justiciary, after what sort Our merchants are treated who shall be found at that time in the country at war with Us, and if they be safe there then these shall be also with Us.

42. It shall be lawful in future, unless in time of war, for any one to leave and return to Our kingdom safely and securely by land and water, saving his fealty to Us, for any short period, for the common benefit of the realm, except prisoners and outlaws according to the law of the land, people of the country at war with Us, and merchants who shall be dealt with as is aforesaid.

43. If any one die holding of any escheat [34] as of the honour of Wallingford, Nottingham, Boulogne, Lancaster, or other escheats which are in Our hands and are baronies, his heir shall not give any relief or do any service to Us other than he would owe to the baron if such barony should have been in the hands of a baron, and We will hold it in the same manner in which the baron held it.

44. Persons dwelling without the forest shall not for the future come before Our justiciaries of the forest by common summons, unless they are be impleaded or are bail for any person or persons attached[35] for breach of forest-laws.

45. We will only appoint such men to be justiciaries, constables, sheriffs, or bailiffs as know the law of the land and will keep it well.

46. All barons, founders of abbies, by charters of English Kings or ancient tenure, shall have the custody of the same during vacancy[36] as is due.

47. All forests which have been afforested in Our time shall be forthwith disafforested, and so shall it be done with regard to rivers which have been placed in fence in Our time.

---

[31]Davis and Schwartz use "delay."

[32]Davis interprets "without maltolt" as "free from all illegal exactions." Perhaps the word is closer to "maltort" or even "maltreat."

[33]Schwartz uses "arrested," while Davis uses "detained."

[34]Escheat means to confiscate.

[35]Davis uses "seized," while Schwartz uses "arrested."

[36] Davis interprets this as "when there is no abbot."

48. All evil customs concerning forest and warrens, foresters, warreners, sheriffs, and their officers, rivers and their conservators, shall be immediately inquired into in each county by twelve sworn knights of such shire, who must be elected by honest men thereof, and within forty days after making the inquisition they shall be altogether and irrevocably abolished, the matter having been previously brought to Our knowledge or that of Our Chief Judiciary if We Ourself, shall not be in England.

49. We will immediately given up all hostages and charters delivered to Us by the English for the security of peace and the performance of loyal service.

50. We will entirely remove from their bailiwicks the kinsmen of Gerard de Atyes, so that henceforth they shall hold no bailiwick in England, Engelard de Cygoyney, Andrew, Peter and Gyon de Cancelles, Gyon de Cygoyney, Ralph de Martiny and his brothers, Philip Marc and his brothers, and his grandson Ralph, and all their followers[.][37]

51. and directly after the restoration of peace We will dismiss out of our kingdom all foreign soldiers, bowmen, serving men,[38] and mercenaries, who come with horses and arms to the nuisance thereof.

52. If any one have been disseised or deprived by Us without the legal judgment of his peers, of his lands, castles, liberties, or rights, We will instantly restore the same, and if a dispute shall arise thereupon, the matter shall be decided by judgment of the twenty-five barons, mentioned below for the security of peace. With regard to all those things, however, whereof any person shall have disseised or deprived without the legal judgment of this peers, by King Henry Our Father, or by Our Brother King Richard, and which remain in Our hands or are held by others under Our warranty, We will have respite thereof till the term commonly allowed to the crusaders, except as to those matters on which a plea shall have arisen, or an inquisition have been taken by Our command prior to Our assumption of the Cross,[39] and immediately after Our return from Our pilgrimage, or if by chance We should remain behind from it We will do full justice therein.

53. We will likewise have the same respite and in like manner shall justice be done with respect to forests to be disafforested or let alone, which Henry Our Father or Richard Our Brother afforested, and to wardships of lands belonging to another's fee, which We have hitherto

[37]Both Davis and Schwartz translate these names as follows: " Gerard d'Athée, Engelard de Cigogné, Peter and Guy and Andrew de Chanceaux, Guy de Cigogné, Geoffrey de Martigny and his brothers, Philip Marc and his brothers and his nephew Geoffrey."

[38]While Schwartz uses "serjeants," Davis uses "bowmen's attendants."

[39]In other words, as Davis notes, they became Crusaders.

held by reason of the fee which some person has held of Us by Knight's service, and to abbies founded in another's fee than Our own, and whereto the lord of that fee asserts his right. And when We return from Our pilgrimage, or if We remain behind therefrom, We will forthwith do full justice to the complainants in these matters.

54. No one shall be taken or imprisoned upon a woman's appeal for the death of any other person than her husband.

55. All fines unjustly and unlawfully made with Us, and all amercements levied unjustly and against the law of the land, shall be entirely condoned or the matter settled by judgment of the twenty-five barons of whom mention is made below; for the security of peace,[40] or the majority of them, together with the aforesaid Stephen, Archbishop of Canterbury, if he himself can be present, and any others whom he may wish to summon for the purpose, and if he cannot be present the business shall nevertheless proceed without him. Provided that if any one or more of the said twenty-five barons be interested in a plaint of this kind, he or they shall be set aside, as to this particular judgment, and another or others elected and sworn by the rest of the said barons for this purpose only be substituted in his or their stead.

56. If We have disseised or deprived the Welsh of lands, liberties, or other things without legal judgment of their peers in England or Wales, they shall be instantly be restored to them, and if a dispute arise thereon, the questions shall be determined on the Marches by judgment of their peers according to the law of England with regard to English tenements, the law of Wales respecting Welsh tenements, and the law of the Marches as to tenements in the March. The same shall the Welsh do to Us and Ours.

57. But with regard to all those things whereof any Welshman shall have been disseised or deprived without legal judgment of his peers by King Henry Our Father or Our Brother King Richard, and which We hold in Our hands or others hold under Our warranty. We will have respite thereof till the term commonly allowed to the crusaders, except as to those matters whereon a plea shall have risen or an inquisition have been taken by Our command prior to Our assumption of the Cross, and immediately after Our return from Our pilgrimage, or if by chance We should remain behind from it We will do full justice therein, according to the laws of the Welsh and the parts aforesaid.

58. We will immediately give up the son of Lewelyn[41] and all the Welsh hostages, and the charters which were delivered to Us for the security of peace.

---

[40]Davis refers to section 61 at this point.

[41]Schwartz uses "Llewelyn," while Davis prefers "Llywelyn."

59. We will do the same with regard to Alexander, King of the Scots, in the matter of giving up his sisters and hostages, and of his liberties and rights, as We would with regard to Our other barons of England, unless it should appear by the charters which We hold of William his father, late King of the Scots, that it ought to be otherwise, and this shall be done by judgment of his peers in Our court.

60. All which customs and liberties aforesaid, which We have granted to be enjoyed, as far as in Us lies, by Our people throughout our kingdom, let all Our subjects, clerks and laymen, observe, as far as in them lies, toward their dependents.[42]

61. And whereas We, for the honour of God, and the amendment of Our realm, and in order the better to allay the discord arisen between Us and Our barons, have granted all these things aforesaid, We, willing that they be for ever enjoyed wholly and in lasting strength, do give and grant to Our subjects the following security; to wit, that the barons shall elect any twenty-five barons of the kingdom at will, who shall, with their utmost power, keep hold, and cause to be holden the peace and liberties which We have granted unto them, and by this Our present Charter confirmed, so that, for instance, if We Our Justiciary, bailiffs or any of Our ministers,[43] offend in any respect against any man, or shall transgress any of these articles of peace or security, and the offense be brought before four barons of the said five and twenty barons, those four barons shall come before Us, or Our Chief Justiciary if We are out of the kingdom, declaring the offence, and shall demand speedy amends for the same. And if We, or in case of Our being out of the Kingdom, Our chief Judiciary, fair to afford redress within the space of forty days from the time the case was brought before Us or Our Chief Judiciary, or to the aforesaid four barons shall refer the matter to the rest of the twenty-five barons, who, together with the commonality of the whole country, shall distrain and distress Us to the utmost of their power, to wit, by capture of Our castles, lands, possessions, and all other possible means, until compensation be made according to their own decision, saving Our person and that of Our Queen and children, and as soon as that be done they shall return to their former allegiance. Any one whatsoever in the kingdom may take oath that, for the accomplishment of the aforesaid matters, he will obey the orders of the said twenty-five barons, and distress Us to the utmost of his power; and We give public and free leave to every one wishing to take such oath to do so, and to none will We deny the same. Moreover, We will compel all such of Our subjects who shall decline to swear to, and together with the said

---

[42]Davis uses "own men."

[43]Davis uses "Chief Justice, our officials or any of our servants."

twenty-five barons, to distrain and distress of their own free will and accord, to do so by Our command as is aforesaid. And if any one of the twenty-five barons shall die or leave the country, or be in any way hindered from executing the said office, the rest of the said twenty-five barons shall choose another in his stead at their discretion, who shall be sworn in as the others. And in all the cases referred to the twenty-five barons to execute, and in which a difference shall arise among them, supposing them all to be present, or that all who have been summoned are unwilling or unable to appear, the verdict of the majority shall be considered as firm and binding as if the whole number should have been of one mind. And the aforesaid twenty-five shall swear to keep faithfully all the aforesaid articles, and, to the best of their power, neither of Ourself cause them to be kept by others. And we will not procure, either by Ourself or any other, anything from any man whereby any of the said concessions or liberties may be revoked or abated; and if any such procurement be made let it be null and void; it shall never be made use of either by Us or any other.

62. We have also wholly remitted and condoned all ill-will, wrath, and malice which have arisen between Us and Our subjects, clerk and laymen, during the disputes, to and with all men; as WE have moreover fully remitted, and as far as in Us lies, wholly condoned to and with all clerks and layman of the said disputes from Easter in the sixteenth year of Our reign[44] till the restoration of peace; and, over and above this, we have caused to be made in their behalf letters patent by testimony of Stephen, Archbishop of Canterbury, Henry, Archbishop of Dublin, the Bishops above mentioned, and Master Pandulph[45] upon the security and concession aforesaid.

63. Wherefore We will, and firmly charge, that the English Church be free, and that all men in Our Kingdom have and hold all the aforesaid liberties, rights, and concessions, well and peaceably freely, quietly, fully and wholly, to them and their heirs, of Us and Our heirs, in all things and places for ever, as is aforesaid. It is, moreover sworn, as well on Our part as on the part of the Barons, that all these matters aforesaid shall be kept in good faith and without malengine. Witness the above-mentioned Prelates and Nobles and many others. Given by Our hand in the meadow which is called Runnymede between Windsor and Staines, on the Fifteenth day of June in the Seventeenth year of Our reign.

---

[44]Davis adds "(i.e. 1215)."

[45]Both Schwartz and Davis use "Pandulf." His identity is not known.

II.

FIRST CHARTER OF VIRGINIA, 1606

The following entry, with minor editorial changes, relies on Hening's *Statutes at Large* (I: 57-66). We have excluded Hening's sidebar summary commentaries, but have retained the breakdown of the text into twenty sections. The footnotes have been added. See also Thorpe (VII: 3783-3789), who cites Hening as his source, but makes significant stylistic changes. See Schwartz (I: 54-61) for another version of this Charter.

~

I. JAMES, by the Grace of God, King of England, Scotland, France and Ireland, Defender of the Faith, &c. WHEREAS our loving and well-disposed Subjects, Sir Thomas Gates, and Sir George Somers, Knights, Richard Hackluit, Clerk, Prebendary of Westminster, and Edward-Maria Wingfield, Thomas Hanham, and Ralegh Gilbert, Esqrs. William Parker, and George Popham, gentlemen, and divers others of our loving subjects, have been humble Suitors unto us, that we would vouchsafe unto them our licence, to make Habitation, Plantation, and to deduce a colony of sundry of our People into that part of America commonly called Virginia, and other parts and territories in America, either appertaining unto us, or which are not now actually possessed by any christian prince or people, situate, lying, and being all along the sea coasts, between four and thirty degrees of Northerly latitude from the Equinoctial line, and five and forty degrees of the same latitude, and in the main land between the same four and thirty and five and forty degrees, and the Islands thereunto adjacent, or within one hundred miles of the coast thereof.

II. And to that end, and for the more speedy accomplishment of their said intended plantation and habitation there, are desirous to divide themselves into two several colonies and companies; the one consisting of certain knights, gentlemen, merchants, and other adventurers, of our city of London and elsewhere, which are, and from time to time shall be, joined unto them, which do desire to begin their plantation and habitation in some fit and convenient place, between four and thirty and one and forty degrees of the said latitude, alongst the coasts of Virginia, and the coasts of America aforesaid; and the other consisting of sundry knights, gentlemen, merchants, and other adventurers, of our cities of Bristol and Exeter, and of our town of Plimouth, and of other places, which do join themselves unto that Colony, which do desire their Plantation and habitation in some fit and convenient place, between eight and thirty degrees and five and forty degrees of the said latitude, all alongst the said coasts of Virginia and America, as that coast lyeth.

III. We greatly commending and graciously accepting of, their desires for the furtherance of so noble a work, which may, by the providence of Almighty God, hereafter tend to the glory of his divine Majesty, in propagating of Christian religion to such people, as yet live in darkness and miserable ignorance of the true knowledge and worship of God, and may in time bring the infidels and savages, living in those parts, to human civility, and to a settled and quiet government; Do, by these our letters pattents, graciously accept of, and agree to, their humble and well-intended desires;

IV. And do therefore, for us, our heirs and successors, grant and agree, that the said Sir Thomas Gates, Sir George Somers, Richard Hackluit, and Edward-Maria Wingfield, adventurers of and for our city of London, and all such others, as are, or shall be joined unto them of that colony, shall be called the first Colony; and they shall and may begin their said first plantation and habitation, at any place upon the said coast of Virginia or America, where they shall think fit and convenient, between the said four and thirty and one and forty degrees of the said latitude; And that they shall have all the lands, woods, soil, grounds, havens, ports, rivers, mines, minerals, marshes, waters, fishings, commodities, and hereditaments, whatsoever, from the said first seat of their Plantation and Habitation by the space of fifty miles of English statute measure, all along the said coast of Virginia and America, towards the west and south-west, as the coast lyeth, with all the islands within one hundred miles directly over against the same sea coast; and also all the lands, soil, grounds, havens, ports, rivers, mines, minerals, woods, waters, marshes, fishings, commodities, and hereditaments, whatsoever, from the said place of their first plantation and habitation for the space of fifty like English miles, all alongst the said coasts of Virginia and America, towards the east and north-east, or towards the north, as the coast lyeth, together with all the islands within one hundred miles, directly over against the said sea coast; and also all the lands, woods, soils, grounds, havens, ports, rivers, mines, minerals, marshes, waters, fishings, commodities, and hereditaments, whatsoever, from the same fifty miles every way on the sea coast, directly into the main land by the space of one hundred like English miles; and shall and may inhabit and remain there; and shall and may also build and fortify within any the same for their better safeguard and defence, according to their best discretion, and the discretion of the council of that colony; and that no other of our subjects shall be permitted, or suffered to plant or inhabit behind, or on the backside of them, towards the main land, without the express license or consent of the council of that colony, thereunto in writing first had and obtained.

V. And we do likewise, for us, our heirs, and successors, by these presents, grant and agree, that the said Thomas Hanham, and Ralegh Gilbert, William Parker, and George Popham, and all others of the town of Plimouth in the county of Devon, or elsewhere, which are, or shall be, joined unto them of that colony, shall be called the second colony; and that they shall and may begin their said Plantation and seat of their first abode and habitation, at any place upon the said coast of Virginia and America, where they shall think fit and convenient, between eight and thirty degrees of the said latitude, and five and forty degrees of the same latitude; and that they shall have all the lands, soils, grounds, havens, ports, rivers, mines, minerals, woods, marshes, waters, fishings, commodities, and hereditaments, whatsoever, from the first seat of their plantation and habitation by the space of fifty like English miles, as is aforesaid, all alongst the said coasts of Virginia and America, towards the west and south-west, or towards the south, as the coast lyeth, and all the Islands within one hundred miles, directly over against the said sea coast; and also all the lands, soils, grounds, havens, ports, rivers, mines, minerals, woods, marshes, waters, fishings, commodities, and hereditaments, whatsoever, from the said place of their first plantation and habitation for the space of fifty like miles, all alongst the said coast of Virginia and America, towards the east and north-east, or towards the north, as the coast lyeth, and all the Islands also within one hundred miles directly over against the same sea coast; and also all the lands, soils, grounds, havens, ports, rivers, woods, mines, minerals, marshes, waters, fishings, commodities, and hereditaments, whatsoever, from the same fifty miles every way on the sea coast, directly into the main land, by the space of one hundred like English miles; and shall and may inhabit and remain there; and shall and may also build and fortify within any the same for their better safeguard, according to their best discretion, and the discretion of the council of that colony; and that none of our subjects shall be permitted, or suffered, to plant or inhabit behind, or on the back of them, towards the main land, without express licence of the council of that colony, in writing thereunto first had and obtained.

VI. Provided always, and our will and pleasure herein is, that the plantation and habitation of such of the said colonies, as shall last plant themselves, as aforesaid, shall not be made within one hundred like English miles of the other of them, that first begin to make their plantation, as aforesaid.

VII. And we do also ordain, establish, and agree, for us, our heirs, and successors, that each of the said colonies shall have a council, which shall govern and order all matters and causes, which shall arise, grow, or happen, to or within the same several colonies, according to such laws, ordinances, and instructions, as shall be, in that behalf, given and signed with our hand or sign Manuel, and pass under the privy seal of our realm of England; each of which councils shall consist of thirteen persons, to be ordained, made, and removed, from time to time, according as shall be directed and comprised in the same instructions; and shall have a several seal, for all matters that shall pass or concern the same several councils; each of which seals, shall have the king's arms engraven on the one side thereof, and his portraiture on the other; and the seal of the council of the said first colony shall have engraven round about, on the one side, these words: *Sigillum Regis Magnæ Britanniæ, Franciæ, & Hiberniæ:* [46] on the other side this inscription round about; *Pro Concilio primæ Coloniæ Virginiæ.* And the seal for the council of the said second colony shall also have engraven, round about the one side thereof, the aforesaid words: *Sigillum Regis Magnæ Britanniæ, Franciæ, & Hiberniæ;* and on the other side; *Pro Concilio secunoæ Coloniæ, Virginiæ:*

VIII. And that also there shall be a Council, established here in England, which shall, in like manner, consist of thirteen persons, to be, for that purpose, appointed by us, our heirs and successors, which shall be called our Council of Virginia; and shall, from time to time, have the superior managing and direction, only of and for all matters that shall or may concern the government, as well of the said several colonies, as of and for any other part or place, within the aforesaid precincts of four and thirty and five and forty degrees abovementioned; which council shall, in like manner, have a seal, for matters concerning the council or colonies, with the like arms and portraiture, as aforesaid, with this inscription, engraven round about on the one side; *Sigillum Regis Magnæ Britanniæ, Franciæ, & Hiberniæ,* and round about on the other Side, *Pro Concillio suo Virginiæ.*

IX. And moreover, we do grant and agree, for us, our heirs and successors; that the said several councils, of and for the said several colonies, shall and lawfully may, by virtue hereof, from time to time, without any interruption of us, our heirs or successors, give and take order, to dig, mine, and search for all manner of mines of gold, silver, and copper, as well within any part of their said several colonies, as of the said main lands on the backside of the same colonies; And to have and enjoy the gold, silver, and copper, to be gotten thereof, to the use and behoof of the same colonies, and the plantations thereof; yielding therefore to us, our heirs and successors, the fifth part only of all the same gold and silver, and the fifteenth part of all the same copper, so to be gotten or had, as is aforesaid, without any other manner of profit or

---

[46]Loosely translated: "the Seal of the King of Great Britain, France, and Ireland."

account, to be given or yielded to us, our heirs, or successors, for or in respect of the same:

X. And that they shall, or lawfully may, establish and cause to be made a coin, to pass current there between the people of those several colonies, for the more ease of traffick and bargaining between and amongst them and the natives there, of such metal, and in such manner and form, as the said several councils there shall limit and appoint.

XI. And we do likewise, for us, our heirs, and successors, by these presents, give full power and authority to the said Sir Thomas Gates, Sir George Somers, Richard Hackluit, Edward-Maria Wingfield, Thomas Hanham, Ralegh Gilbert, William Parker, and George Popham, and to every of them, and to the said several companies, plantations, and colonies, that they, and every of them, shall and may at all and every time and times hereafter, have, take, and lead in the said voyage, and for and towards the said several plantations, and colonies, and to travel thitherward, and to abide and inhabit there, in every the said colonies and plantations, such and so many of our subjects, as shall willingly accompany them, or any of them, in the said voyages and plantations; with sufficient shipping, and furniture of armour, weapons, ordnance, powder, victual, and all other things, necessary for the said plantations, and for their use and defence there: Provided always, that none of the said persons be such, as shall hereafter be specially restrained by us, our heirs, or successors.

XII. Moreover, we do, by these presents, for us, our heirs, and successors, give and grant licence unto said Sir Thomas Gates, Sir George Somers, Richard Hackluit, Edward-Maria Wingfield, Thomas Hanham, Ralegh Gilbert, William Parker, and George Popham, and to every of the said colonies, that they, and every of them, shall and may, from time to time, and at all times forever hereafter, for their several defences, encounter, expulse, repel, and resist, as well by sea as by land, by all ways and means whatsoever, all and every such person and persons, as without the especial licence of the said several colonies and plantations, shall attempt to inhabit within the said several precincts and limits of the said several colonies and plantations, or any of them, or that shall enterprise or attempt, at any time hereafter, the hurt, detriment, or annoyance, of the said several colonies or plantations:

XIII. Giving and granting, by these presents, unto the said Sir Thomas Gates, Sir George Somers, Richard Hackluit, Edward-Maria Wingfield, and their associates of the said first colony, and unto the said Thomas Hanham, Ralegh Gilbert, William Parker, and George Popham, and their associates of the said second colony, and to every of them, from time to time, and at all times forever hereafter power and authority to take and surprise, by all ways and means whatsoever, all and every person and persons, with their ships, vessels, goods, and other furniture, which shall be found trafficking, into any harbour or harbours, creek or creeks, or place, within the limits or precincts of the said several colonies and plantations, not being of the same colony, until such time, as they, being of any realms, or dominions under our obedience, shall pay, or agree to pay, to the hands of the treasurer of that colony, within whose limits and precincts they shall so traffick, two and a half upon every hundred, of any thing, so by them trafficked, bought, or sold; and being strangers, and not subjects under our obeysance, until they shall pay five upon every hundred, of such wares and merchandises, as they shall traffick, buy, or sell, within the precincts of the said several colonies, wherein they shall so traffick, buy, or sell, as aforesaid; which sums of money, or benefit, as aforesaid, for and during the space of one and twenty years, next ensuing that date hereof, shall be wholly emploied to the use, benefit, and behoof of the said several plantations, where such traffick shall be made; and after the said one and twenty years ended, the same shall be taken to the use of us, our heirs, and successors, by such officers and ministers as by us, our heirs, and successors, shall be thereunto assigned or appointed.

XIV. And we do further, by these presents, for us, our heirs and successors, give and grant unto the said Sir Thomas Gates, Sir George Somers, Richard Hackluit, and Edward-Maria Wingfield, and to their associates of the said first colony and plantation, and to the said Thomas Hanham, Ralegh Gilbert, William Parker, and George Popham, and their associates of the said second colony and plantation, that they, and every of them, by their deputies, ministers, and factors, may transport the goods, chattels, armour, ammunition, and furniture, needful to be used by them, for their said apparel, food, defence, or otherwise in respect of the said plantations, out of our realms of England and Ireland, and all other our dominions, from time to time, for and during the time of seven years, next ensuing the date hereof, for the better relief of the said several colonies and plantations, without any customs, subsidy, or other duty, unto us, our heirs, or successors, to be yielded or payed for the same.

XV. Also we do, for us, our heirs, and successors, declare, by these presents, that all and every the persons being our subjects, which shall dwell and inhabit within every or any of the said several colonies and plantations, and every of their children, which shall happen to be born within any of the limits and precincts of the said several colonies and plantations, shall have and enjoy all liberties, franchises, and immunities, within any of our other dominions, to all intents and purposes, as if they had been abiding and born, within this our realm of England, or any other of our said dominions.

XVI. Moreover, our gracious will and pleasure is, and we do, by these presents, for us, our heirs, and successors, declare and set forth, that if any person or persons, which shall be of any of the said colonies and plantations, or any other, which shall traffick to the said colonies and plantations, or any of them, shall, at any time or times hereafter, transport any wares, merchandises, or commodities, out of any of our dominions, with a pretence to land, sell, or otherwise dispose of the same, within any the limits and precincts of any the said colonies and plantations, and yet nevertheless, being at sea, or after he hath landed the same within any of the said colonies and plantations, shall carry the same into any other foreign country, with a purpose there to sell or dispose of the same, without the licence of us, our heirs, and successors, in that behalf first had and obtained; that then, all the goods and chattels of such person or persons, so offending and transporting, together with the said ship or vessel, wherein such transportation was made, shall be forfeited to us, our heirs, and successors.

XVII. Provided always, and our will and pleasure is, and we do hereby declare to all Christian kings, princes, and states, that if any person or persons, which shall hereafter be of any of the said several colonies and plantations, or any other, by his, their, or any of their licence and appointment, shall, at any time of times hereafter, rob or spoil, by sea or land, or do any act of unjust and unlawful hostility, to any the subjects of us, our heirs, or successors, or any the subjects of any king, prince, ruler, governor, or state, being then in league or amity with us, our heirs, or successors, and that upon such injury, or upon just complaint of such prince, ruler, governor, or state, or their subjects, we, our heirs, or successors, shall make open proclamation, within any of the ports of our realm of England, commodious for that purpose, that the person or persons, having committed any such robbery[47] or spoil, shall, within the term to be limitted by such proclamations, make full restitution or satisfaction of all such injuries done, so as the said princes, or others, so complaining, may hold themselves fully satisfied and contented; and that, if the said person or persons, having committed such Robbery or spoil, shall not make, or cause to be made, satisfaction accordingly, within such time so to be limited, that then it shall be lawful to us, our heirs, and successors, to put the said person or persons, having committed such robbery or spoil, and their procurers, abetters, and comforters, out of our allegiance and protection; and that it shall be lawful and free for all Princes and others, to pursue with hostility the said offenders, and every of them, and their

[47]Editors' note: Hening uses the upper case later in the section.

and every of their procurers, aiders, abetters, and comforters, in that behalf.

XVIII. And finally, we do for us, our heirs, and successors, grant and agree, to and with the said Sir Thomas Gates, Sir George Somers, Richard Hackluit, Edward-Maria Wingfield, and all others of the said first colony, that we, our heirs and successors, upon petition in that behalf to be made, shall, by letters, patent under the great seal of England, given and grant unto such persons, their heirs and assigns, as the council of that colony, or the most part of them, shall, for the purpose nominate and assign, all the lands, tenements, and hereditaments, which shall be within the precincts limited for that colony, as is aforesaid, to be holden of us, our heirs and successors, as of our manor at East-Greenwich in the County of Kent, in free and common soccage only, and not in Capite:[48]

XIX. And do, in like manner, grant and agree, for us, our heirs and successors, to and with the said Thomas Hanham, Ralegh Gilbert, William Parker, and George Popham, and all others of the said second colony, that we, our heirs, and successors, upon petition in that behalf to be made, shall, by letters patent, under the great seal of England, give and grant unto such persons, their heirs and assigns, as the council of that colony, or the most part of them, shall, for that purpose, nominate and assign, all the lands, tenements, and hereditaments, which shall be within the precincts limited for that colony, as is aforesaid, to be holden of us, our heirs, and successors, as of our manor of East-Greenwich in the colony of Kent, in free and common Soccage only, and not in Capite.

XX. All which lands, tenements, and hereditaments, so to be passed by the said several letters patent, shall be sufficient assurance from the said patentees, so distributed and divided amongst the undertakers for the plantation of the said several colonies, and such as shall make their plantations in either of the said several colonies, in such manner and form, and for such estates, as shall be ordered and set down by the council of the said colony, or the most part of them, respectively, within which the same lands, tenements, and hereditaments shall lye or be; although express mention of the true yearly value or certainty of the premises or any of them, or of any other gifts or grants, by us or any of our progenitors or predecessors, to the aforesaid Sir Thomas Gates, knight, Sir George Somers, knight, Richard Hackluit, Edward-Maria Wingfield, Thomas Hanham, Ralegh Gilbert, William Parker, and George Popham, or any of them, heretofore made, in these presents, is not made; or any statute, act, ordinance, or provision, proclamation, or

---

[48]According to the *OED* (p. 261), capite is the "name of a tenure by which land was held immediately of the king or of the crown."

restraint, to the contrary hereof had, made, ordained, or any other thing, cause, or matter whatsoever, in any wise notwithstanding. In witness whereof, we have caused these our letters to be made patents; witness ourself at Westminster, the tenth day of April, in the fourth year of the reign of England, France, and Ireland, and of Scotland the nine and thirtieth.

Lukin
Per breve de privato Sigillo

III.

THE MAYFLOWER COMPACT, 1620

In the original copy of the Mayflower Compact, William Bradford did not name the signers. Colonial commentator Nathaniel Morton compiled a list of forty-one signers in 1669, based on the passenger list found in Bradford's diary. We have followed the tradition, begun by Morton, of listing the names of the presumed signers at the end of the covenant. We have relied on F. N. Thorpe, *The Federal and State Constitution,* 1909 (III: 1841). Also see Henry Steele Commager, *Documents of American History,* 1968 (I: 15-16).

~

AGREEMENT BETWEEN THE SETTLERS AT NEW PLYMOUTH
November 11, 1620

IN THE NAME OF GOD, AMEN. We, whose names are underwritten, the Loyal Subjects of our dread Sovereign Lord King *James*, by the Grace of God, of *Great Britain, France,* and *Ireland*, King, *Defender of the Faith,* &c. Having undertaken for the Glory of God, and Advancement of the Christian Faith, and the Honour of our King and Country, a Voyage to plant the first Colony in the northern Parts of *Virginia*; Do by these Presents, solemnly and mutually, in the Presence of God and one another, covenant and combine ourselves together into a civil Body Politick, for our better Ordering and Preservation, and Furtherance of the Ends aforesaid: And by Virtue hereof do enact, constitute, and frame, such just and equal Laws, Ordinances, Acts, Constitutions, and Offices,[49] from time to time, as shall be thought most meet and convenient for the general Good of the

[49]Thorpe's version says "officers," but we believe "offices" to be correct.

Colony; unto which we promise all due Submission and Obedience. IN WITNESS whereof we have hereunto subscribed our names at *Cape Cod* the eleventh of *November*, in the Reign of our Sovereign Lord King *James* of *England, France*, and *Ireland*, the eighteenth, and of *Scotland*, the fifty-fourth, *Anno Domini*, 1620.

Mr. John Carver,
Mr. William Bradford,
Mr. Edward Winslow,
Mr. William Brewster,
Isaac Allerton,
Myles Standish,
John Alden,
John Turner,
Francis Eaton,
James Chilton,
John Craxton,[56]
John Billington,
Joses Fletcher,[59]
John Goodman,
Mr. Samuel Fuller,
Mr. Christopher Martin,
Mr. William Mullins,[50]
Mr. William White,
Mr. Richard Warren,
John Howland,
Mr. Stephen Hopkins,
Digery Priest,[53]
Thomas Williams,
Gilbert Winslow,
Edmund Margesson,[57]
Peter Brown,[58]
Richard Bitteridge,[60]
George Soule
Edward Tilly,
John Tilly,
Francis Cooke,
Thomas Rogers,
Thomas Tinker,
John Ridgdale,[51]
Edward Fuller,[52]
Richard Clarke,[54]
Richard Gardiner,[55]
Mr. John Allerton,
Thomas English,
Edward Doten,
Edward Liester.

---

[50]Mullines in Bradford's version.

[51]Rigdale in Bradford's version. Commager refers to Ridgate.

[52]Commager leaves out Fuller.

[53]Digerie Priest in Bradford's version.

[54]Clark in Bradford's version.

[55]Gardenar in Bradford's version.

[56]Crakston in Bradford's version.

[57]Margeson in Bradford's version.

[58]Browne in Bradford's version.

[59]Moyes Fletcher in Bradford's version.

[60]Betterigein Bradford's version.

IV.

PETITION OF RIGHT, 1628

The following text of the eleven-part Petition of Right is based on the version reproduced in the *Statutes at Large, From the First year of the Reign of King James the First To The Tenth Year of the Reign of King William the Third,* London, MDCCLXIII. See I: 123-124 (3 Char. I. c.1). Sol Bloom (519-521) relies on an 1811 printing of the *Statutes at Large*. The sixteen-part enumeration in Roman numerals are in the original 1763 version. So too are the Arabic numerals, in parentheses, in the main body of the text. See also Schwartz (I: 19-24) who relies on *Statutes of the Realm*. The Schwartz reproduction does not include the breakdown of the petition into twelve parts. The Petition was passed by Parliament in 1627 and agreed to, reluctantly, by King Charles I on June 7, 1628. See *The Petition of Right* (London, 1642, printed for M. Walbancke and L. Chapman), for a reproduction of the two negative, and final affirmative, responses of King Charles. The manuscript is available at the Huntington Library.

~

TO THE King's Most Excellent Majesty.

HUMBLY shew unto our Sovereign Lord the King, the Lords Spiritual and Temporal, and Commons, in Parliament assembled, That whereas it is declared and enacted by a Statute made in the time of the Reign of King *Edward* the First, commonly called *Statutum de Tallagio non concedendo*, that no Tallage[61] or Aid shall be laid or levied by the King or his Heirs in this Realm, without the good Will and Assent of the Archbishops, Bishops, Earls, Barons, Knights, Burgesses and other the Freemen of the Commonalty of this Realm; and by the Authority of Parliament holden in the Five and twentieth Year of the Reign of King *Edward* the Third, it is declared and enacted, that from thenceforth no Person should be compelled to make any Loans to the King against his Will, because such Loans were against Reason and the Franchise of the Land; and by other Laws of this Realm it is provided, that none should be charged by any Charge or Imposition, called a Benevolence, nor by such like Charge; by which the Statutes before mentioned, and other the good Laws and Statutes of this Realm, Your Subjects have inherited this Freedom, that they should not be compelled to contribute to any Tax, Tallage, aid, or other like Charge not set by Common Consent in Parliament.

---

[61]Tallage is a compulsory tax levied on feudal dependents by Norman and Angevin (of the Anjou region in France) lords.

II. Yet nevertheless, of late divers Commissions directed to sundry Commissioners in several Counties, with Instructions, have issued; by means wherof Your People have been in divers Places assembled, and required to lend certain Sums of Money unto Your Majesty, and many of them, upon their Refusal so to do, have had an Oath administered unto them not warrantable by the Laws or Statutes of this Realm; and have been constrained to become bound to make Appearance and give Attendance before Your Privy Council and in other Places; and others of them have been therefore imprisoned, confined, and sundry other Ways molested and disquieted; and divers other Charges have been laid and levied upon Your People in several Counties by Lord Lieutenants, Deputy Lieutenants, Commissioners for Musters, Justices of Peace and others, by Command or Direction from Your Majesty, or Your Privy Council, against the Laws and Free Customs of this Realm.

III. And where also by the Statute called *The Great Charter of the Liberties of England,* it is declared and enacted, That no Freeman may be taken or imprisoned, or be disseised of his Freehold or Liberties, or his Free Customs, or be outlawed or exiled, or in any manner destroyed, but by the lawful Judgment of his Peers, or by the Law of the Land.

IV. And in the Eight and twentieth Year of the Reign of King *Edward* the Third, it was declared and enacted by Authority of Parliament, that no Man of what Estate or Condition that he be, should be put out of his Land or Tenements, nor taken, nor imprisoned, nor disherited, nor put to Death, without being brought to answer by due Process of Law:

V. Nevertheless against the Tenor of the said Statutes, and other the good Laws and Statutes of Your Realm to that End provided, divers of Your Subjects have of late been imprisoned without any Cause shewed; and when for their Deliverance they were brought before your Justices by your Majesty's Writs of *Habeas Corpus,* there to undergo and receive as the Court should order, and the Keepers commanded to certify the causes of their Detainer, no Cause was certified, but that they were detained by Your Majesty's special Command, signified by the Lords of Your Privy Council, and yet were returned back to several Prisons, without being charged with any Thing to which they might make Answer according to the Law.

VI. And wheras of late great Companies of Soldiers and Mariners and been dispersed into divers Counties of the Realm, and the Inhabitants against their Wills have been compelled to receive them into their Houses, and there to suffer them to sojourn, against the Laws and Customs of this Realm, and to the great Grievance and Vexation of the People:

VII. And wheras also by Authority of Parliament, in the Five and twentieth Year of the Reign of King *Edward* the Third, it is declared and enacted, that no Man shall be forejudged of Life or Limb against the Form of the Great Charter and the Law of the Land; and by the said Great Charter and other the Laws and Statutes of this Your Realm, no Man ought to be adjudged to death but by the Laws established in this Your Realm, either by the Customs of the same Realm, or by Acts of Parliament: And whereas no Offender of what Kind soever is exempted from the Proceedings to be used, and Punishments to be inflicted by the Laws and Statutes of this Your Realm: Nevertheless of late times divers Commissions under Your Majesty's Great Seal have issued forth, but which certain Persons have been assigned and appointed Commissioners, with Powers and Authority to proceed within the Land, according to the Justice of Martial Law, against such Soldiers and Mariners, or other dissolute Persons joining with them, as should commit any Murther, Robbery, Felony, Mutiny, or other Outrage or Misdemeanour whatsoever, and by such summary Course and Order as is agreeable to Martial Law, and as is used in Armies in Time of War, to proceed to the Trial and Condemnation of such Offenders, and them to cause to be executed and put to Death according to the Law Martial:

VIII. By Pretext whereof some of Your Majesty's Subjects have been by some of the said Commissioners put to death, when and where, if by the Laws and Statutes of the Land they had deserved death, by the same Laws and Statutes also they might, and by no other ought to have been adjudged and executed:

IX. And also sundry grievous Offenders, by colour thereof claiming an Exemption, have escaped the Punishments due to them by the Laws and Statutes of this Your Realm, by reason that divers of your Officers and Ministers of Justice have unjustly refused or forborn to proceed against such Offenders according to the same Laws and Statutes, upon Pretence that the said Offenders were punishable only by Martial Law, and by Authority of Such Commissions as aforesaid: which Commissions, and all other of like nature, are wholly and directly contrary to the said Laws and Statutes of this Your Realm.

X. They do therefore humbly pray Your most excellent Majesty, that no Man hereafter be compelled to make or yield any Gift, Loan, Benevolence, Tax or such charge, without Common Consent by Act of Parliament; and that none be called to make Answer, or take such Oath, or to give Attendance, or be confined, or otherwise molested or disquieted concerning the same, or for Refusal thereof; and that no Freeman, in any such Manner as is before mentioned, be imprisoned or detained; and that Your Majesty would be pleased to remove the said Soldiers and Mariners; and that Your People may not be so burthened in time to come; and that the aforesaid Commissions for proceeding by Martial Law, may be revoked and annulled; and that hereafter no Commissions of like Nature may issue forth to any Person or Persons whatsoever to be executed as aforesaid, lest by Colour of them any of Your Majesty's Subjects be destroyed, or put to death contrary to the Laws and Franchise of the Land.

XI. All which they most humbly pray of Your most excellent Majesty as their Rights and Liberties, according to the Laws and Statutes of this Realm; and that Your Majesty would also vouchsafe to declare, that the Awards, Doings and Proceedings, to the Prejudice of Your People in any of the Premises shall not be drawn hereafter into Consequence or Example; and that Your Majesty would be also graciously please, for the further comfort and Safety of Your People, to declare your Royal Will and Pleasure, that in the Things aforesaid all your Officers and Ministers shall serve You according to the Laws and Statutes of this Realm, as they tender the Honour of Your Majesty, and the Prosperity of this Kingdom.

V.

FUNDAMENTAL ORDERS OF CONNECTICUT, 1638-39

We have retained the original seventeenth-century spelling used by the framers of the Fundamental Orders of Connecticut. This is the official title for the compact agreed to by the freemen of the towns of Windsor, Hartford, and Wethersfield in 1638-1639. We follow Thorpe, *The Federal and State Constitution* (I: 519-526) who reproduces Hazard's *State Papers* (I: 437-441). The Arabic numerals are in the original text. See also Schwartz (I: 62-66) who relies on Thorpe's version, as well as Commager, *Documents* (I: 22-24), and MacDonald, *Documentary Source Book* (36-39) for an edited version of the oldest written constitution in America.

~

FORASMUCH as it hath pleased the Allmighty God by the wise disposition of his diuyne pruidence so to Order and dispose of things that we the Inhabitants and Residents of Windsor, Harteford and Wethersfield are now cohabiting and dwelling in and vppon the River of Conectecotte and the Lands thereunto adoiyneing; And well knowing where a people are gathered togather the word of God requires that to mayntayne the peace and vnion of such a people there should be an orderly and decent Gouerment established according to God, to order and dispose of the affayres of the people at all seasons as occation shall require; doe therefore assotiate and conioyne our selues to be as one Publike State or Comonwelth; and doe, for our selues and our Successors and such as shall be adioyned to vs att any tyme hereafter, enter into Combination and Confederation togather, to mayntayne and p^{r}searue the liberty and purity of the gospell of our Lord Jesus wch we now p^{r}fesse, as also the disciplyne of the Churches, wch according to the truth of the said gospell is now practised amongst vs; As also in or Ciuell Affaires to be guided and gouerned according to such Lawes, Rules, Orders and decrees as shall be made, ordered & decreed, as followeth:

1. It is Ordered, sentenced and decreed, that there shall be yerely two generall Assemblies or Courts, the on the second thursday in Aprill, the other the second thursday in September, following; the first shall be called the Courte of Election, wherein shall be yerely Chosen fro tyme to tyme soe many Magestrats and other publike Officers as shall be found requisitte: Whereof one to be chosen Gouernour for the yeare ensueing and vntill another be chosen, and noe other Magestrate to be chosen for more then one yeare; p^{r}uided allwayes there be sixe chosen besids the Gouernour; wch being chosen and sworne according to an Oath recorded for that purpose shall haue power to administer iustice according to the Lawes here established, and for want thereof according to the rule of the word of God; wch choise shall be made by all that are admitted freemen and haue taken the Oath of Fidellity, and doe cohabitte wthin this Jurisdiction, (hauing beene admitted Inhabitants by the maior p^{r}te of the Towne wherein they liue,) or the mayor p^{r}te of such as shall be then p^{r}sent.

2. It is Ordered, sentensed and decreed, that the Election of the aforesaid Magestrats shall be on this manner: euery p^{r}son p^{r}sent and quallified for choyse shall bring in (to the p^{r}sons deputed to receaue the) one single pap^{r} wth the name of him written in yt whom he desires to haue Gouernour, and he that hath the greatest nuber of papers shall be Gouernor for that yeare. And the rest of the Magestrats or publike Officers to be chosen in this manner: The Secretary for the tyme being shall first read the names of all that are to be put to choise and then shall seuerally nominate them distinctly, and euery one that would haue the p^{r}son nominated to be chosen shall bring in one single paper written vppon, and he that would not haue him chosen shall bring in a blanke and euery one that hath more written papers than blanks shall be a Magistrat for that yeare; wch papers shall be receaued and told by one or more that shall be then chosen by the court and sworne to be faythfull therein; but in case there should not be sixe chosen as aforesaid, besids the Gouernor, out of those wch are nominated, then he or they wch haue the most written pap^{r}s shall be a Magestrate or Magestrats for the ensueing yeare, to make vp the aforesaid nuber.

3. It is Ordered, sentenced and decreed, that the Secretary shall not nominate any p^{r}son, nor shall any p^{r}son be chosen newly into the Magestracy wch was not p^{r}pownded in some Generall Courte before, to be nominated the next Election; and to that end yt shall be lawfull for ech of the Townes aforesaid by their deputyes to nominate any two who they conceaue fitte to be put to election; and the Courte may ad so many more as they iudge requisitt.

4. It is Ordered, sentenced and decreed that noe p^{r}son be chosen Gouernor aboue once in two yeares, and that the Gouernor be always a meber of some approved congregation, and formerly of the Magestracy wthin this Jurisdiction; and all the Magestrats Freemen of this Comonwelth: and that no Magestrate or other publike officer shall execute any p^{r}te of his or their Office before they are seuerally sworne, wch shall be done in the face of the Courte if they be p^{r}sent, and in case of absence by some deputed for that purpose.

5. It is Ordered, sentenced and decreed, that to the aforesaid Courte of Election and seu^{r}all Townes shall send their deputyes, and when the Elections are ended they may p^{r}ceed in any publike searuice as at other Courts. Also the other Generall Courte in September shall be for makeing of lawes, and any other publike occation wch conserns the good of the Comonwelth.

6. It is Ordered, sentenced and decreed, that the Gou^{r}nor shall, ether by himselfe or by the secretary, send out sumons to the Constables of eu^{r} Towne for the cauleing of these two standing Courts, on month at lest before their seu^{r}all tymes: And also if the Gou^{r}nor and the gretest p^{r}te of the Magestrats see cause vppon any spetiall occation to call a generall Courte, they may giue order to the secretary soe to doe wthin fowerteene dayes warneing; and if vrgent necessity so require, vppon a shorter notice, giueing sufficient grownds for yt to the deputyes when they meete, or els be questioned for the same; And if the Gou^{r}nor and Mayor p^{r}te of Magestrats shall ether neglect or refuse to call the two Generall standing Courts or ether of the, as also at other tymes when the occations of the Comonwelth require, the Freemen thereof, or the Mayor p^{r}te of them, shall petition to them soe to doe: if then yt be ether denyed or neglected the said Freemen or the Mayor p^{r}te of them shall haue power to giue order to the Constables of the seurall Townes to doe the same, and so may meete togather, and chuse to themselues a Moderator, and may p^{r}ceed to do any Acte of power, wch any other Generall Courte may.

7. It is ordered, sentenced and decreed that after there are warrants giuen out for any of the said Generall Courts, the Constable or Constables of ech Towne shall forthwth give notice distinctly to the inhabitants of the same, in some Publike Assembly or by goeing or sending fro howse to howse, that at a place and tyme by him or them lymited and sett, they meet and assemble the selues togather to elect and chuse certen deputyes to be att the Generall Courte then following to agitate the afayres of the comonwelth; wch said Deputyes shall be chosen by all that are admitted Inhabitants in the seu^{r}all Townes and haue taken the oath of fidellity; p^{r}uided that non be chosen a Deputy for any Generall Courte wch is not a Freeman of this Comonwelth.

The a-foresaid deputyes shall be chosen in a manner following: euery p^{r}son that is p^{r}sent and quallified as before exp^{r}ssed, shall bring the names of such, written in seu^{r}rall papers, as they desire to haue chosen for that Imployment, and these 3 or 4, more or lesse, being the nuber agreed on to be chosen for that tyme, that haue greatest nuber of papers written for the shall be deputyes for that Courte; whose names shall be endorsed on the backe side of the warrant and returned into the Courte, wth the Constable or Constables hand vnto the same.

8. It is Ordered, sentenced and decreed, that Wyndsor, Hartford and Wethersfield shall haue power, ech Towne, to send fower of their freemen as deputyes to euery Generall Courte; and whatsoeuer other Townes shall be hereafter added to this Jurisdiction, they shall send so many deputyes as the Courte shall judge meete, a reasonable p^{r}portion to the nuber of Freemen that are in the said Townes being to be attended therein; wch deputyes shall have the power of the whole Towne to giue their voats and alowance to all such lawes and orders as may be for the publike good, and unto wch the said Townes are to bownd.

9. It is ordered and decreed, that the deputyes thus chosen shall haue power and liberty to appoynt a tyme and a place of meeting togather before any Generall Courte to aduise and consult of all such things as may concerne the good of the publike, as also to examine their owne Elections, whether according to the order, and if they or the gretest p^{r}te of them find any election to be illegall they may seclud such for p^{r}sent fro their meeting, and returne the same and their resons to the Courte; and if yt proue true, the Courte may fyne the p^{r}ty or p^{r}tyes so intruding and the Towne, if they see cause, and giue out a warrant to goe to a newe election in a legall way, either *in whole or* in p^{r}te. Also the said deputyes shall haue power to fyne any that shall be disorderly at their meetings, or for not coming in due tyme or place according to appoyntment; and they may returne the said fynes into the Courte if yt

be refused to be paid, and the tresurer to take notice of yt, and to estreete or levy the same as he doth other fynes.

10. It is Ordered, sentenced and decreed, that euery Generall Courte, except such as through neglecte of the Gou^{r}nor and the greatest p^{r}te of Magestrats the Freemen themselves doe call, shall consist of the Gouernor, or some one chosen to moderate the Court, and 4 other Magestrats at lest, wth the mayor p^{r}te of the deputyes of the seuerall Townes legally chosen; and in case the Freemen or mayor p^{r}te of the through neglect or refusall of the Gouernor and mayor p^{r}te of the magestrats, shall call a Courte, that y^{t} shall consist of the mayor p^{r}te of Freemen that are p^{r}sent or their deputyes, wth a Moderator chosen by the: *In wch said Generall Courts shall consist the supreme power of the Comonwelth,* and they only shall haue power to make laws or repeale the, to graunt leuyes, to admitt of Freemen, dispose of lands vndisposed of,, to seuerall Townes or p^{r}sons, and also shall haue power to call ether Courte or Magestrate or any other p^{r}son whatsoeuer into question for any misdemeanour, and may for just causes displace or deale otherwise according to the nature of the offence; and also may deale in any other matter that concerns the good of this comon welth, excepte election of Magestrats, wch shall be done by the whole boddy of Freemen: In wch Courte the Gouernour or Moderator shall haue power to order the Courte to giue liberty of spech, and silence vnceasonable and disorderly speakeings, to put all things to voate, and in case the vote be equall to haue the casting voice. But non of these Courts shall be adiorned or dissolued wthout the consent of the maior p^{r}te of the Court.

11. It is ordered, sentenced and decreed, that when any Generall Courte vppon the occations of the Comonwelth haue agreed vppon any sume or somes of mony to be leuyed vppon the seuerall Townes wthin this Jurisdiction, that a Comittee be chosen to sett out and appoynt w^{t} shall be the p^{r}portion of euery Towne to pay of the said leuy, p^{r}vided the Comittees be made vp of an equall nuber out of each Towne.

14th January, 1638, the 11 Orders abouesaid are voted.

THE OATH OF THE GOU^{r}NOR, FOR THE [P^{r}SENT]

I, N. W. being now chosen to be Gou^{r}nor wthin this Jurisdiction, for the yeare ensueing, and vntil a new be chosen, doe sweare by the greate and dreadfull name of the everliueing God, to p^{r}mote the publicke good and peace of the same, according to the best of my skill; as also will mayntayne all lawfull priuiledges of this Comonwealth; as also that all wholsome lawes that are or shall be made by lawfull authority here established, be duly executed; and will further the execution of Justice according to the rule of Gods word; so helpe me God, in the name of the Lo: Jesus Christ.

THE OATH OF A MAGESTRATE, FOR THE PRSENT

I, N. W. being chosen a Magestrate wthin this Jursidiction for the yeare ensueig, doe sweare by the great and dreadfull name of the euerliueing God: to p^{r}mote the publike good and peace of the same, according to the best of my skill, and that I will mayntayne all the lawfull priuiledges thereof according to my vnderstanding, as also assist in the execution of all such wholsome lawes as are made or shall be made by lawfull authority heare established, and will further the execution of Justice for the tyme aforesaid according to the righteous rule of Gods word; so helpe me God, etc.

VI.

THE MASSACHUSETTS BODY OF LIBERTIES, 1641

The first seventeen sections of the ninety-eight part Massachusetts Body of Liberties are reproduced below. The numbered paragraphs are in the original. The complete version can be found in W. H. Whitemore, *The Colonial Laws of Massachusetts*, 1889 (33-46). We have followed Whitemore's reproduction, as have Kurland and Lerner (I: 428-429), and Schwartz (I: 71-84). Mortimer Adler, *The Annals of America* (I: 163-169) modernizes the spelling.

~

The free fruition of such liberties Immunities and priveledges as humanitie, Civilitie, and Christianitie call for as due to every man in his place and proportion without impeachment and Infringement hath ever bene and ever will be the tranquillitie and Stabilitie of Churches and Commonwealths. And the deniall or deprivall thereof, the disturbance if not the ruine of both.

We hould it therefore our dutie and safetie whilst we are about the further establishing of this Government to collect and expresse all such freedomes as for present we foresee may concerne us, and our posteritie after us, And to ratify them with our sollemne consent.[62]

---

[62] According to Kurland and Lerner (I: 428): "with out sollemne consent."

Wee doe therefore this day religiously and unanimously decree and confirme these following Rites, liberties and priveledges concerneing our Churches, and Civill State to be respectively impartiallie and inviolably enjoyed and observed throughout our Jurisdiction for ever.

1. No mans life shall be taken away, no mans honour or good name shall be stayned, no mans person shall be arested, restrayened, banished, dismembered, nor any wayes punished, no man shall be deprived of his wife or children, no mans goods or estaite shall be taken away from him, nor any way indammaged under colour of law or Countenance of Authoritie, unlesse it be by vertue or equitie of some expresse law of the Country waranting the same, established by a generall Court and sufficiently published, or in case of the defect of a law in any parteculer case by the word of God. And in Capitall cases, or in cases concerning dismembring or banishment according to that word to be judged by the Generall Court.

2. Every person within this Jurisdiction, whether Inhabitant or forreiner shall enjoy the same justice and law, that is generall for the plantation, which we constitute and execute one towards another without partialitie or delay.

3. No man shall be urged to take any oath or subscribe any articles, covenants or remonstrance, of a publique and Civill nature, but such as the Generall Court hath considered, allowed, and required.

4. No man shall be punished for not appearing at or before any Civill Assembly, Court, Councell, Magistrate, or Officer, nor for the omission of any office or service, if he shall be necessarily hindred by any apparent Act or providence of God, which he could neither foresee nor avoid. Provided that this law shall not prejudice any person of his just cost or damage, in any civill action.

5. No man shall be compelled to any publique worke or service unlesse the presse be grounded upon some act of the generall Court, and have reasonable allowance therefore.

6. No man shall be pressed in person to any office, worke, warres or other publique service, that is necessarily and suffitiently exempted by any naturall or personall impediment, as by want of yeares, greatnes of age, defect of minde, fayling of sences, or impotencie of Lymbes.

7. No man shall be compelled to goe out of the limits of this plantation upon any offensive warres which this Commonwealth or any of our freinds or confederats shall volentarily undertake. But onely upon such vindictive and defensive warres in our owne behalfe or the behalfe of our freinds and confederats as shall be enterprized by the Counsell and consent of a Court generall, or by authority derived from the same.

8. No mans Cattel or goods of what kinde soever shall be pressed or taken for any publique use or service, unlesse it be by warrant grounded

upon some act of the generall Court, nor without such reasonable prices and hire as the ordinairie rates of the Countrie do afford. And if his Cattle or goods shall perish or suffer damage in such service, the owner shall be suffitiently recompenced.

9. No monopolies shall be granted or allowed amongst us, but of such new Inventions that are profitable to the Countrie, and that for a short time.

10. All our lands and heritages shall be free from all fines and licenses upon Alienations, and from all hariotts, wardships, Liveries, Primer-seisins, yeare day and wast, Escheates, and forfeitures, upon the deaths of parents or Ancestors, be they naturall, casuall or Juditiall.

11. All persons which are of the age of 21 yeares, and of right understanding and meamories, whether excommunicate or condemned shall have full power and libertie to make there wills and testaments, and other lawfull alienations of theire lands and estates.

12. Every man whether Inhabitant or fforreiner, free or not free shall have libertie to come to any publique Court, Councel, or Towne meeting, and either by speech or writeing to move any lawfull, seasonable, and materiall question, or to present any necessary motion, complaint, petition, Bill or information, whereof that meeting hath proper cognizance, so it be done in convenient time, due order, and respective manner.

13. No man shall be rated here for any estaite or revenue he hath in England, or in any forreine partes till it be transported hither.

14. Any Conveyance or Alienation of land or other estaite what so ever, made by any woman that is married, any childe under age, Ideott or distracted person, shall be good if it be passed and ratified by the consent of a generall Court.

15. All Covenous or fraudulent Alienations or Conveyances of lands, tenements, or any heriditaments, shall be of no validitie to defeate any man from due debts or legacies, or from any just title, clame or possession, of that which is so fraudulently conveyed.

16. Every Inhabitant that is an howse holder shall have free fishing and fowling in any great ponds and Bayes, Coves and Rivers, so farre as the sea ebbs and flowes within the presincts of the towne where they dwell, unlesse the free men of the same Towne or the Generall Court have otherwise appropriated them, provided that this shall not be extended to give leave to any man to come upon others proprietie without there leave.

17. Every man of or within this Jurisdiction shall have free libertie, notwithstanding any Civill power remove both himselfe, and his familie at their pleasure out of the same, provided there be no legall impediment to the contrarie.

VII.

MARYLAND ACT CONCERNING RELIGION, 1649

The Act was passed by the Assembly on 21 April 1649, and confirmed by the Lord Proprietary, on 26 August 1650. We have followed the spelling and grammar found in the original 1649 version of the Act. See Archives of Maryland: *Proceedings and Acts of the General Assembly of Maryland, 1637-1664* (Baltimore, Maryland Historical Society, 1883 (I: 244-247). See Schwartz (I: 91-94) and Kurland and Lerner (V: 49-50) who reproduce the Act as one continuous paragraph. We have provided a six-paragraph breakdown of the text, shown by means of Arabic numerals in square parentheses. The first four paragraphs emphasize the centrality of the Christian religion to a well-governed commonwealth. The last two paragraphs provide protection for the "free exercise" of religion.

~

[1] Afforasmuch as in a well governed and Xpian Comon Weath matters concerning Religion and the honor of God ought in the first place to bee taken, into serious consideracon and endeavoured to bee settled. Be it therefore ordered and enacted by the Right Hoble Cecilius Lord Baron of Baltemore absolute Lord and Proprietary of this Province with the advise and consent of this Generall Assembly. That whatsoever pson or psons within this Province and the Islands thereunto belonging shall from henceforth blaspheme God, that is Curse him, or deny our Saviour Jesus Christ to bee the sonne of God, or shall deny the holy Trinity the ffather sonne and holy Ghost, or the God-head of any of the said Three psons of the Trinity or the Vnity of the Godhead, or shall use or utter any reproachfull Speeches, words or language concerning the said Holy Trinity, or any of the said three psons thereof, shalbe punished with death and confiscaton or forfeiture of all his or her lands and goods to the Lord Proprietary and his heires, [2] And bee it also Enacted by the Authority and with the advise and assent aforesaid. That whatsoever pson or psons shall from henceforth use or utter any reproachfull words or Speeches concerning the blessed Virgin Mary the Mother of our Saviour or the holy Apostles or Evangelists or any of them shall in such case for the first offence forfeit to the said Lord Proprietary and his heirs Lords and Proprietaries of this Province the sume of ffive pound Sterling or the value thereof to be Levyed on the goods and chattells of every such pson soe offending, but in case such Offender or Offenders, shall not then have goods and chattells sufficient for the satisfyeing of such forfeiture, or that the same bee not otherwise speedily satisfyed that then such Offender or

Offenders shalbe publiquely whipt and bee ymprisoned during the pleasure of the Lord Proprietary or the Leivet of cheife Governor of this Province for the time being. And that every such Offender or Offenders for every second offence shall forfeit tenne pound sterling or the value thereof to bee levyed as aforesaid, or in case such Offender or Offenders shall not then haue goods and chattells within this Province sufficient for that purpose then to bee publiquely and severely whipt and imprisoned as before is expressed. And that every psons or psons before mentioned offending herein the third time, shall for such third Offence forfeit all his lands and Goods and bee for ever banished and expelled out of this Province. [3] And be it also further Enacted by the same authority advise and assent that whatsoever pson or psons shall from henceforth vppon any occasion of Offence or otherwise in a reproachful manner or Way declare call or denominate any pson or psons whatsoever inhabiting residing traffiqueing trading or comerceing within this Province or within any Ports, Harbors, Creeks or Havens to the same belonging an heritick, Scismatick, Idolator, puritan, Independent, Prespiterian popish prest, Jesuite, Jesuited papist, Lutheran, Calvenist, Anabaptist, Brownist, Antinomian, Barrowist, Roundhead, Sepatist, or any other name or terme in a reproachfull manner relating to matter of Religion shall for every such Offence forfeit and loose the some or terne shillings sterling or the value thereof to bee levyed on the goods and chattells of every such Offender and Offenders, the one half thereof to be forfeited and paid unto the pson and psons of whom such reproachfull words are or shalbe spoken or vttered, and the other half thereof to the Lord Proprietary and his heires Lords and Proprietaries of this Province, But if such pson or psons who shall at any time vtter or speake any such reproachfull words or Language shall not have Goods or Chattells sufficient and overt within this Province to bee taken to satisfie the penalty aforesaid or that the same bee not otherwise speedily satisfyed, that then the pson or psons soe offending shalbe publickly whipt, and shall suffer imprisonmt without baile or maineprise vntill hee shee or they respectively shall satisfy the party soe offended or grieved by such reproachfull Language by asking him or her respectively forgivenes publiquely for such his Offence before the Magistrate or cheife Officer or Officers of the Towne or place where such Offence shalbe given. [4] And be it further likewise Enacted by the Authority and consent aforesaid That every pson or psons within this Province that shall at any time hereafter pphane the Sabbath or Lords day called Sunday by frequent swearing, drunkennes or by any uncivill or disorderly recreacon, or by working on that day when absolute necessity doth not require it shall be every such first offence forfeit 2s. 6d sterling or the value thereof, and for the second offence 5s sterling or the value thereof, and for the third offence and soe for every time he shall offend in like manner afterwards 10s sterling or the value thereof. And in case such offender and offenders shall not have sufficient goods or chattells within this Province to satisfy any of the said Penalties respectively hereby imposed for prophaning the Sabbath or Lords day called Sunday as aforesaid, That in Every such case the ptie soe offending shall for the first and second offence in that kinde be imprisoned till hee or shee shall publickly in open Court before the cheife Commander Judge or Magistrate, of that County Towne or precinct where such offence shalbe committed acknowledg the Scandall and offence he hath in that respect given against God and the good and civill Government of this Province And for the third offence and for every time after shall also bee publickly whipt. And whereas the inforceing of the conscience in matters of Religion hath frequently fallen out to be of dangerous Consequence in those commonwealthes where it hath been practised, And for the more quiett and peaceable governemt of this Province, and the better to pserve mutuall Love and amity amongst the Inhabitants thereof. [5] Be it Therefore also by the Lo: Proprietary with the advise and consent of this Assembly Ordeyned & enacted (except as in this psent Act is before Declared and sett forth) that noe person or psons whatsoever within this Province, or the Islands, Ports, Harbors, Creekes, or havens thereunto belonging professing to beleive in Jesus Christ, shall from henceforth bee any waies troubled, Molested or discountenanced for or in respect of his or her religion nor in the free exercise thereof within this Province or the Islands thereunto belonging nor any way compelled to the beleife or exercise of any other Religion against his or her consent, soe as they be not unfaithfull to the Lord Proprietary, or molest or conspire against the civill Governemt established or to bee established in this Province vnder him or his heires. And that all & every pson and psons that shall presume Contrary to this Act and the true intent and meaning thereof directly or indirectly either in pson or estate willfully to wrong disturbe trouble or molest any person whatsoever within this Province professing to beleive in Jesus Christ for or in respect of his or her religion or the free exercise thereof within this Province other than is provided for in this Act that such pson or psons soe offending, shalbe compelled to pay trebble damages to the party soe wronged or molested, and for every such offence shall also forfeit 20s sterling in money or the value thereof, half thereof for the vse of the Lo: Proprietary, and his heires Lords and Proprietaries of this Province, and the other half for the vse of the party soe wronged or molested as aforesaid, Or if the ptie soe offending as aforesaid shall refuse or bee vnable to recompense the party soe wronged, or to satisfy such ffyne or forfeiture, then such Offender shalbe severely punished by publick whipping & imprisonmt during the pleasure of the Lord Proprietary, or his Leivetenat or cheife

Governor of this Province for the tyme being without baile or maineprise. [6] And bee it further alsoe Enacted by the authority and consent aforesaid That the Sheriff or other Officer or Officers from time to time to bee appointed & authorized for that purpose, of the County Towne or precinct where every particular offence in this psent Act conteyned shall happen at any time to bee committed and wherevppon there is hereby a fforfeiture ffyne or penalty imposed shall from time to time distraine and seise the goods and estate of every such pson soe offending as aforesaid against this psent Act or any pt thereof, and sell the same or any part thereof for the full satisfaccon of such forfeiture, ffine, or penalty as aforesaid, Restoring vnto the ptie soe offending the Remainder or overplus of the said goods or estate after such satisfaccon soe made as aforesaid.

The ffreemen haue assented. Tho: Hatton
Enacted by the Governor Willm Stone

VIII.

THE CHARTER OR FUNDAMENTAL LAWS OF WEST NEW JERSEY, AGREED UPON, 1676

The complete title of the document in which the more-popularly referred to "Fundamental Laws" appears is "The Concessions and Agreements of the Proprietors Freeholders & Inhabitants of the Province of West New Jersey in America." The core of the document are chapters XIII to XXIII which we have reproduced below. We have followed Thorpe's version (V: 2548-2551). See also Kurland and Lerner (I: 429-431) and Schwartz (I: 125-129) for slightly different grammatical versions. The entire forty-four chapters can be found in Julian P. Boyd, editor, *Fundamental Laws and Constitutions of New Jersey,* Princeton: Van Nostrand, 1964 (XVII: 72-104).

~

CHAPTER XIII

THAT THESE FOLLOWING CONCESSIONS ARE THE COMMON LAW, OR FUNDAMENTAL RIGHTS, OF THE PROVINCE OF WEST NEW JERSEY

That the common law of fundamental rights and priviledges of West New Jersey, are individually agreed upon by the Proprietors and freeholders thereof, to be the foundation of the government, which is not to be altered by the Legislative authority, or free Assembly hereafter mentioned and constituted, but that the said Legislative authority is constituted according to these fundamentals, to make such laws as agree with, and maintain the said fundamentals, and to make no laws that in the least contradict, differ or vary from the said fundamentals, under what pretence or alligation soever.

CHAPTER XIV

But if it so happen that any person or persons of the said General Assembly, shall therein designedly, willfully, and maliciously, move or excite any to move, any matter or thing whatsoever, that contradicts or any way subverts, any fundamentals of the said laws in the Constitution of the government of this Province, it being proved by seven honest and reputable persons, he or they shall be proceeded against as traitors to the said government.

CHAPTER XV

That these Concessions, law or great charter of fundamentals, be recorded in a fair table, in the Assembly House, and that they be read at the beginning and dissolving of every general free Assembly: And it is further agreed and ordained, that the said Concessions, common law, or great charter of fundamentals, be writ in fair tables, in every common hall of justice within this Province, and that they be read in solemn manner four times every year, in the presence of the people, by the chief magistrates of those places.

CHAPTER XVI

That no men, nor number of men upon earth, hath power or authority to rule over men's consciences in religious matters, therefore it is consented, agreed and ordained, that no person or person whatsoever within the said Province, at any time or times hereafter, shall be any ways upon any pretence whatsoever, called in question, or in the least punished or hurt, either in person, estate, or privilege, for the sake of his opinion, judgment, faith or worship towards God in matters of religion. But that all and every such person, and persons, may from time to time, and at all times, freely and fully have, and enjoy his and their judgments, and the exercises of their consciences in matters of religious worship throughout all the said Province.

CHAPTER XVII

That no proprietor, freeholder or inhabitant of the said Province of West New Jersey, shall be deprived or condemned of life, limb, liberty, estate, property or any ways hurt in his or their privileges, freedoms or franchises, upon any account whatsoever without a due tryal, and judgment passed by twelve good and lawful men of his neighborhood first had: And that in all causes to be tryed, and in all tryals, the person or persons, arraigned may except against any of the said neighborhood, without any reason rendered, (not exceeding thirty five) and in case of any valid reason alleged, against every person nominated for that service.

CHAPTER XVIII

And that no Proprietor, freeholder, freedenison, or inhabitant in the said Province , shall be attached, arrested, or imprisoned, for or by reason of any debt, duty, or thing whatsoever (cases felonious, criminal, and treasonable excepted) before he or she have personal summon or summons, left at his or her last dwelling place, if in the said Province, by some legal authorized officer, constituted and appointed for that purpose, to appear in some court of judicature for the said Province, with a full and plain account of the cause or thing in demand, as also the name or names of the person or persons at whose suit, and the court where he is to appear, and that he hath at least fourteen days time to appear and answer the said suit, if he or she live or inhabit within forty miles English of the said court, and if at a further distance, to have for every twenty miles, two days time more, for his and their appearance, and so proportionably for a larger distance of place.

That upon the recording of the summons, and non-appearance of such person and persons, a writ of attachment shall or may be issued out to arrest, or attach the person or person of such defaulters, to cause his or their appearance in such court, returnable at a day certain, to answer the penalty or penalties, in such suit or suits; and if he or they shall be condemned by legal tryal and judgment, the penalty or penalties shall be paid and satisfied out of his or their real or personal estate so condemned, to lie in execution till satisfaction of the debt and damages be made. *Provided always*, if such person or persons so condemned, shall pay and deliver such estate, goods, and chattles which he or any other person hath for his or their use, and shall solemnly declare and aver, that he or they have not any further estate, goods or chattles wheresoever to satisfy the person or persons, (at whose suit, he or they are condemned) their respective judgments, and shall also bring and produce three other persons as compurgators, who are well known and of honest reputation, and approved of by the commissioners of that division, where they dwell or inhabit, which shall in such open court, likewise solemnly declare and aver, that they believe in their consciences, such person and persons so condemned, have not werewith further to pay the said condemnation or condemnations, he or they shall be thence forthwith discharged from their said imprisonment, any law or custom to the contrary thereof, heretofore in the said Province, notwithstanding. And upon such summons and default of appearance, recorded as aforesaid, and such person and persons not appearing within forty days after, it shall and may be lawful for such court of judicature to proceed to tryal, of twelve lawful men to judgment, against such defaulters, and issue forth execution against his or their estate, real and personal, to satisfy such penalty or penalties, to such debt and damages so recorded, as far as it shall or may extend.

CHAPTER XIX

That there shall be in every court, three justices or commissioners, who shall sit with the twelve men of the neighborhood, with them to hear all causes, and to assist the said twelve men of the neighborhood in case of law; and that they the said justices shall pronounce such judgment as they shall receive from, and be directed by the said twelve men in whom only the judgment resides, and not otherwise.

And in case of their neglect and refusal, that then one of the twelve, by consent of the rest, pronounce their own judgment as the justices should have done.

And if any judgment shall be past, in any case civil or criminal, by any other person or persons, or any other way, then according to this agreement and appointment, it shall be held null and void, and such person or persons presuming to give judgment, shall be severely fin'd, and upon complaint made to the General Assembly, by them be declared incapable of any office or trust within this Province.

CHAPTER XX

That in all matter and causes, civil and criminal, proof is to be made by the solemn and plain averment, of at least two honest and reputable persons; and in case that any person or persons shall bear false witness, and bring in his or their evidence, contrary to the truth of the matter as shall be made plainly to appear, that then every such person or persons, shall in civil causes, suffer the penalty which would be due to the person or persons he or they bear witness against. And in case any witness or witnesses, on the behalf of any person or persons, indicted in a criminal case cause, shall be found to have borne false witness for fear, gain, malice or favour, and thereby hinder the due execution of the law, and deprive the suffering person or persons of their due satisfaction, that then and in all other cases of false evidence, such person or persons, shall be first severely fined, and next that he or they shall forever be disabled from being admitted in evidence, or into any public office, employment, or service within this Province.

CHAPTER XXI

That all and every person and persons whatsoever, who shall prosecute or prefer any indictment or information against others for any personal injuries, or matter criminal, or shall prosecute for any other criminal cause, (treason, murther, and felony, only excepted) shall and may be master of his own process, and have full power to forgive and remit the person or persons offending against him or herself only, as well before as after judgment, and condemnation, and pardon and remit the sentence, fine and punishment of the person or persons offending, be it personal or other whatsoever.

CHAPTER XXII

That the tryals of all causes, civil and criminal, shall be heard and decided by the virdict or judgment of twelve honest men of the neighborhood, only to be summoned and presented by the sheriff of that division, or propriety where the fact or trespass is committed; and that no person or persons shall be compelled to fee any attorney or councillor to plead his cause, but that all persons have free liberty to plead his own cause, if he please: And that no person nor persons imprisoned upon any account whatsoever within this Province, shall be obliged to pay any fees to the officer or officers of the said prison, either when committed or discharged.

CHAPTER XXIII

That in all publick courts of justice for tryals of causes, civil or criminal, any person or persons, inhabitants of the said Province may freely come into, and attend the said courts, and hear and be present, at all or any such tryals as shall be there had or passed, that justice may not be done in a corner nor in any covert manner, being intended and resolved, by the help of the Lord, and by these our Concessions and Fundamentals, that all and every person and persons inhabiting the said Province, shall, as far as in us lies, be free from oppression and slavery.

IX.

PENNSYLVANIA FRAME OF GOVERNMENT, 1682

For a version that uses extensively the upper case and italics, as well as varying font sizes and types, see the copy of the 1682 original in the Huntington Library. We have relied on the spelling found in the original but followed Thorpe's usage of the lower case and plain text (V: 3052-3063). Unlike Thorpe, however, we have consistently italicized the word

"God." Schwartz (I: 132-144) reproduces Thorpe with minor punctuation and grammatical changes. The parentheses in the text are from the original as are the Roman numerals that identify the separate clauses in the document. Reproduced below are the Preface and Laws Agreed Upon.

~

The frame of the government of the province of Pensilvania, *in* America: *together with certain laws agreed upon in* England, *by the Governor and divers freemen of the aforesaid province. To be further explained and confirmed there, by the first provincial Council, that shall be held, if they see meet.*

THE PREFACE

When the great and wise *God* had made the world, of all his creatures, it pleased him to chuse man his Deputy to rule it: and to fit him for so great a charge and trust, he did not only qualify him with skill and power, but with integrity to use them justly. This native goodness was equally his honour and his happiness; and whilst he stood here, all went well; there was no need of coercive or compulsive means; the precept of divine love and truth, in his bosom, was the guide and keeper of his innocency. But lust prevailing against duty, made a lamentable breach upon it; and the law, that before had no power over him, took place upon him, and his disobedient posterity, that such as would not live comformable to the holy law within, should fall under the reproof and correction of the just law without, in a judicial administration.

This the Apostle teaches in divers of his epistles: "The law (says he) was added because of transgression;" In another place, "Knowing that the law was not made for the righteous man; but for the disobedient and ungodly, for sinners, for unholy and prophane, for murderers, for whoremongers, for them that defile themselves with mankind, and for man-stealers, for lyers, for perjured persons," &c., but this is not all, he opens and carries the matter of government a little further: "Let every soul be subject to the higher powers; for there is no power but of *God*. The powers that be are ordained of *God*: whosoever therefore resisteth the power, resisteth the ordinance of *God*. For rulers are not a terror to good works, but to evil: wilt thou then not be afraid of the power? Do that which is good, and thou shalt have praise of the same." "He is the minister of *God* to thee for good." "Wherefore ye must needs be subject, not only for wrath, but for conscience sake."

This settles the divine right of government beyond exception, and that for two ends: first, to terrify evil doers: secondly, to cherish those that do well; which gives government a life beyond corruption, and makes it as durable in the world, as good men shall be. So that government seems to me a part of religion itself, a thing sacred in its institution and end. For, if it does not directly remove the cause, it crushes the effects of evil, and is as such, (though a lower, yet) an emanation of the same Divine Power, that is both author and object of pure religion; the difference lying here, that the one is more free and mental, the other more corporal and compulsive in its operations: but that is only to evil doers; government itself being otherwise as capable of kindness, goodness and charity, as a more private society. They weakly err, that think there is no other use of government, than correction, which is the coarsest part of it: daily experiences tell us, that the care and regulation of many other affairs, more soft, and daily necessary, make up much of the greatest part of government; and which must have followed the peopling of the world, had Adam never fell, and will continue among men, on earth, under the highest attainments they may arrive at, by the coming of the blessed *Second Adam*, the *Lord* from heaven. Thus much of government in general, as to its rise and end.

For particular *frames* and *models*, it will become me to say little; and comparatively I will say nothing. My reasons are:

First. That the age is too nice and difficult for it; there being nothing the wits of men are more bury and divided upon. It is true, they seem to agree to the end, to wit, happiness; but in the means, they differ, as to divine, so to this human felicity: and the cause is much the same, not always want of light and knowledge, but want of using them rightly. Men side with their passions against their reason, and their sinister interests have so strong a bias upon their minds, that they lean to them against the good of the things they know.

Secondly. I do not find a model in the world, that time, place, and some singular emergences have not necessarily altered: nor is it easy to frame a civil government, that shall serve all places alike.

Thirdly. I know what is said by the several admirers of *monarchy, aristocracy* and *democracy*, which are the rule of one, a few, and many, and are the three common ideas of government, when men discourse on the subject. But I chuse to solve the controversy with this small distinction, and it belongs to all three: *Any government is free to the people under it* (whatever be the frame) *where the law rules, and the people are a party to those laws*, and more than this is tyranny, oligarchy, or confusion.

But, lastly, when all is said, there is hardly one frame of government in the world so ill designed by its first founders, that, in good hands, would not do well enough; and story tells us, the best, in ill ones, can do nothing that is great or good; witness the *Jewish* and *Roman* states. Governments, like clocks, go from the motion men give them; and as governments are made and moved by men, so by them they are ruined too. Wherefore governments rather depend upon men, than men upon governments. Let men be good, and the government cannot be bad; if it be ill, they will cure it. But, if men be bad, let the government be never so good, they will endeavor to warp and spoil it to their turn.

I know some say, let us have good laws, and no matter for the men that execute them: but let them consider, that though good laws do well, good men do better: for good laws want good men, and be abolished or evaded[63] by ill men; but good men will never want good laws, nor suffer ill ones. It is true, good laws have some awe upon ill ministers, but that is where they have not power to escape or abolish them, and the people are generally wise and good: but a loose and depraved people (which is the question) love laws and an administration like themselves. That, therefore, which makes a good constitution, must keep it, *viz*: men of wisdom and virtue, qualities, that because they descend not with worldly inheritances, must be carefully propagated by a virtuous education of youth; for which after ages will owe more to the care and prudence of founders, and the successive magistracy, than to their parents, for their private patrimonies.

These considerations of the weight of government, and the nice and various opinions about it, made it uneasy to me to think of publishing the ensuing frame and conditional laws, farseeing both the censures, they will meet with, from men of differing humors and engagements, and the occasion they may give of discourse beyond my design.

But, next to the power of necessity, (which is a solicitor, that will take no denial) this induced me to a compliance, that we have (with reverence to *God*, and good conscience to men) to the best of our skill, contrived and composed the *frame* and *laws* of this government, to the great end of all government, *viz: To support power in reverence with the people, and to secure the people from the abuse of power*; that they may be free by their just obedience, and magistrates honourable, for their just administration: for liberty without obedience is confusion, and obedience without liberty is slavery. To carry this evenness is partly owing to the constitution, and partly to the magistracy: where either of these fail, government will be subject to convulsions: but where both are wanting, it must be totally subverted: then where both meet, the government is like to endure. Which I humbly pray and hope *God* will please to make the lot of this of *Pensilvania*. Amen.

WILLIAM PENN.

---

63 Both Thorpe (I: 3054) and Schwartz (I: 133) place the following at this point in the text: "[invaded in Franklin's print] ."

LAWS AGREED UPON IN ENGLAND, &c.[64]

I. That the charter of liberties, declared, granted and confirmed the five and twentieth day of the second month, called April, 1682, before divers witnesses, by *William Penn*, Governor and chief Proprietor of *Pensilvania*, to all the freemen and planters of said province, is hereby declared and approved, and shall be for ever held for fundamental in the government thereof, according to the limitations mentioned in the said charter.

II. That every inhabitant in the said province, that is or shall be, a purchaser of one hundred acres of land, or upwards, his heirs and assigns, and every person who shall have paid his passage, and taken up one hundred acres of land, at one penny an acre, and have cultivated ten acres thereof, and every person, that hath been a servant, or bonds-man, and is free by his service, that shall have taken up his fifty acres of land, and cultivated twenty thereof, and every inhabitant, artificer, or other resident in the said province, that pays scot and lot to the government; shall be deemed and accounted a freeman of the said province: and every such person shall, and may, be capable of electing, or being elected, representatives of the people, in provincial Council, or General Assembly, in the said province.

III. That all elections of members, or representatives of the people and freemen of the province of *Pensilvania*, to serve in provincial Council, or General Assembly, to be held within the said province, shall be free and voluntary: and that the elector, that shall receive any reward or gift, in meat, drink, monies, or otherwise, shall forfeit his right to elect; and such person as shall directly or indirectly give, promise, or bestow any such reward as aforesaid, to be elected, shall forfeit his election, and be thereby incapable to serve as aforesaid: and the provincial Council and General Assembly shall be the sole judges of the regularity, or irregularity of the elections of their own respective Members.

IV. That no money or goods shall be raised upon, or paid by, any of the people of this province by way of public tax, custom or contribution, but by a law, for that purpose made; and whoever shall levy, collect, or pay any money or goods contrary thereunto, shall be held a public enemy to the province and a betrayer of the liberties of the people thereof.

V. That all courts shall be open, and justice shall neither be sold, denied nor delayed.

---

[64]The original 1682 version reads thus: "as agreed upon in England by the Governour and Divers of the Free-Men of Pennsilvania, To be further Explained and Conformed there by the first Provincial Council and General Assembly that shall be held in the said Provinces, if they see meet."

VI. That, in all courts all persons of all persuasions may freely appear in their own way, and according to their own manner, and there personally plead their own cause themselves; or, if unable, by their friends: and the first process shall be the exhibition of the complaint in court, fourteen days before the trial; and that the party, complained against, may be fitted for the same, he or she shall be summoned, no less than ten days before, and a copy of the complaint delivered him or her, at his or her dwelling house. But before the complaint of any person be received, he shall solemnly declare in court, that he believes, in his conscience, his cause is just.

VII. That all pleadings, processes and records in courts, shall be short, and in *English*, and in an ordinary and plain character, that they may be understood, and justice speedily administered.

VIII. That all trials shall be by twelve men, and as near as may be, peers or equals, and of the neighborhood, and men without just exception; in cases of life, there shall be first twenty-four returned by the sheriffs, for a grand inquest, of whom twelve, at least, shall find the complaint to be true; and then the twelve men, or peers, to be likewise returned by the sheriff, shall have the final judgment. But reasonable challenges shall be always admitted against the said twelve men, or any of them.

IX. That all fees in all cases shall be moderate, and settled by the provincial Council, and General Assembly, and be hung up in a table in every respective court; and whosoever shall be convicted of taking more, shall pay twofold, and be dismissed his employment; one moiety of which shall go to the party wronged.

X. That all prisons shall be work-houses, for felons, vagrants, and loose and idle persons; whereof one shall be in every county.

XI. That all prisoners shall be bailable by sufficient sureties, unless for capital offences, where the proof is evident, or the presumption great.

XII. That all persons wrongfully imprisoned, or prosecuted at law, shall have double damages against the informer, or prosecutor.

XIII. That all prisons shall be free, as to fees, food and lodging.

XIV. That all lands and goods shall be liable to pay debts, except where there is legal issue, and then all the goods, and one-third of the land only.

XV. That all wills, in writing, attested by two witnesses, shall be of the same force as to lands, as other conveyances, being legally proved within forty days, either within or without the said province.

XVI. That seven years quiet possession shall give an unquestionable right, except in cases of infants, lunatics, married women, or persons beyond the seas.

XVII. That all briberies and extortion whatsoever shall be severely punished.

XVIII. That all fines shall be moderate, and saving men's contenements, merchandize, or wainage.

XIX. That all marriages (not forbidden by the law of God, as to nearness of blood and affinity by marriage) shall be encouraged; but the parents, or guardians, shall be first consulted, and the marriage shall be published before it be solemnized; and it shall be solemnized by taking one another as husband and wife, before credible witnesses, and a certificate of the whole, under the hands of parties and witnesses, shall be brought to the proper register of that county, and shall be registered in his office.

XX. And, to prevent frauds and vexatious suits within the said province, that all charters, gifts, grants, and conveyances of and (except leases for a year or under) and all bills, bonds, and specialities above five pounds, and not under three months, made in the said province, shall be enrolled, or registered in the public enrolment office of the said province, within the space of two months next after the making thereof, else to be void in law, and all deeds, grants, and conveyances of land (except as aforesaid) within the said province, and made out of the said province, shall be enrolled or registered, as aforesaid, within six months next after the making thereof, and settling and constituting an enrolment office or registry within the said province, else to be void in law against all persons whatsoever.

XXI. That all defacers or corrupters of charters, gifts, grants, bonds, bills, wills, contracts, an conveyances, or that shall deface or falsify any enrolment, registry or record, within this province, shall make double satisfaction for the same; half whereof shall go the party wronged, and they shall be dismissed of all places of trust, and be publicly disgraced as false men.

XXII. That there shall be a register for births, marriages, burials, wills, and letters of administration, distinct from the other registry.

XXIII. That there shall be a register for all servants, where their names, time, wages, and days of payment shall be registered.

XXIV. That all lands and goods of felons shall be liable, to make satisfaction to the party wronged twice the value; and for want of lands or goods, the felons shall be bondmen to work in the common prison, or work-house, or otherwise, till the party injured be satisfied.

XXV. That the estates of capital offenders, as traitors and murderers, shall go, one-third to the next of kin to the sufferer, and the remainder to the next of kin to the criminal.

XXVI. That all witnesses, coming, or called, to testify their knowledge in or to any matter or thing, in any court, or before any lawful authority, within the said province, shall there give or deliver in their evidence, or testimony, by solemnly promising to speak the truth, the whole truth, and nothing but the truth, to the matter, or thing in questions. And in case any person so called to evidence, shall be convicted of wilful falsehood, such person shall suffer and undergo such damage or penalty, as the person, or persons, against whom he or she bore false witness, did, or should, undergo; and shall also make satisfaction to the party wronged, and be publicly exposed as a false witness, never to be credited in any court, or before any Magistrate, in the said province.

XXVII. And, to the end that all officers chosen to serve within this province, may, with more care and diligence, answer the trust reposed in them, it is agreed, that no such person shall enjoy more than one public office at one time.

XXVIII. That all children, within this province, of the age of twelve years, shall be taught some useful trade or skill, to the end none may be idle, but the poor may work to live, and the rich, if they become poor, may not want.

XXIX. That servants be not kept longer than their time, and such as are careful, be both justly and kindly used in their service, and put in fitting equipage at the expiration thereof, according to custom.

XXX. That all scandalous and malicious reporters, backbiters, defamers and spreaders of false news, whether against Magistrates, or private persons, shall be accordingly severely punished as enemies to the peace and concord of this province.

XXXI. That for the encouragement of the planters and traders in this province, who are incorporated into a society, the patent granted to them by *William Penn*, Governor of the said province, is hereby ratified and confirmed.

XXXII. * * *[65]

XXXIII. That all factors or correspondents in the said province, wronging their employers, shall make satisfaction, and one-third over, to their said employers: and in case of the death of any such factor or correspondent, the committee of trade shall take care to secure so much of the deceased party's estate as belongs to his said respective employers.

XXXIV. That all Treasurers, Judges, Masters of the Rolls, Sheriffs, Justices of the Peace, and other officers and persons whatsoever, relating to courts, or trials of causes, or any other service in the government; and all Members elected to serve in provincial Council and General Assembly, and all that have right to elect such Members, shall be such as possess faith in Jesus Christ, and that are not convicted of ill fame,

---

[65] Absent in both Thorpe and in the 1682 version.

or unsober and dishonest conversation, and that are of one and twenty years of age, at least; and that all such so qualified, shall be capable of the said several employments and privileges, as aforesaid.

XXXV. That all persons living in this province, who confess and acknowledge the one Almighty and eternal *God*, to be the Creator, Upholder and Ruler of the world; and that hold themselves obliged in conscience to live peaceably and justly in civil society, shall, in no ways, be molested or prejudiced for their religious persuasion, or practice, in matters of faith and worship, nor shall they be compelled, at any time, to frequent or maintain any religious worship, place or ministry whatever.

XXXVI. That, according to the good example of the primitive Christians, and the case of the creation, every first day of the week, called the Lord's day, people shall abstain from their common daily labour, that they may the better dispose themselves to worship *God* according to their understandings.

XXXVII. That as a careless and corrupt administration of justice draws the wrath of *God* upon magistrates, so the wildness and looseness of the people provoke the indignation of *God* against a country: therefore, that all such offences against *God*, as swearing, cursing, lying, prophane talking, drunkenness, drinking of healths, obscene words, incest, sodomy, rapes, whoredom, fornication, and other uncleanness (not to be repeated) all treasons, misprisons, murders, duels, felony, seditions, maims, forcible entries, and other violences, to the persons and estates of the inhabitants within this province; al prizes, stage-plays, cards, dice, May-games, gamesters, masques, revels, bull-baitings, cock-fightings, bear-baitings, and the like, which excite the people to rudeness, cruelty, looseness, and irreligion, shall be respectively discouraged, and severely punished, according to the appointment of the Governor and freemen in provincial Council and General Assembly; as also all proceedings contrary to these laws, that are not here made expressly penal.

XXXVIII. That a copy of these laws shall be hung up in the provincial Council, and in public courts of justice: and that they shall be read yearly at the opening of every provincial Council and General Assembly, and court of justice; and their assent shall be testified, by their standing up after the reading thereof.

XXXIX. That there shall be, at no time, any alteration of any of these laws, without the consent of the Governor, his heirs, or assigns, and six parts of seven of the freemen, met in provincial Council and General Assembly.

XL. That all other matters and things not herein provided for, which shall, and may, concern the public justice, peace or safety of the said province; and the raising and imposing taxes, customs, duties, or prudence and determination of the Governor and freemen, in provincial Council and General Assembly, to be held, from time to time, in the said province.

Signed and sealed by the Governor and freemen aforesaid, the fifth day of the third month, called *May*, one thousand six hundred and eighty-two.

X.

ENGLISH BILL OF RIGHTS, 1689

Several versions of the English Bill of Rights are available. See Kurland and Lerner (I: 433-434), Bloom (526-528), Dumbauld (166-169), and Schwartz (I: 40-46) for the available textual variations. We follow the format in *Statutes at Large,* (III: 440-441) published in 1763. The Act contains six sections. We have followed scholarly custom and omitted the last three sections dealing with the response of their majesties and the formal announcement of the Act. We have also deleted the third section which contains the oaths of allegiance, but retained the second section declaring William and Mary to be King and Queen. The first section is the critical one dealing with the issue of tyranny and liberty. The numerical listing of the twelve indictments against King James is in the original as is the numerical declaration of thirteen rights of Englishmen.

~

Anno Regni GULIELMI & MARIÆ primo,

CAP. II (36.)
An Act declaring the Rights and Liberties of the Subject, and settling the Succession of the Crown.

WHEREAS the Lords Spiritual and Temporal, and Commons, assembled at *Westminster*, lawfully, fully, and freely representing all the Estates of the People of this Realm, did upon the thirteenth Day of *February* in the Year of our Lord one thousand six hundred eighty-eight, present unto their Majesties, then called and known by the Names and stile of *William* and *Mary*, Prince and Princess of *Orange*, being present in their proper Persons, a certain Declaration in Writing, made by the said Lords and Commons, in the Words following; *viz.*

WHEREAS the late King *James* the Second, by the Assistance of divers evil Counsellors, Judges, and Ministers employed by him, did endeavour to subvert and extirpate the Protestant Religion, and Laws and Liberties of this Kingdom.

1. By assuming and exercising a Power of dispensing with and suspending of Laws, and the Execution of Laws, without Consent of Parliament.

2. By committing and prosecuting divers worthy Prelates, for humbly petitioning to be excused from concurring to the said assumed Power.

3. By issuing and causing to be executed a Commission under the Great Seal for erecting a Court called *The Court of Commissioners for Ecclesiastical Causes.*

4. By levying Money for and to the Use of the Crown, by Pretence of Prerogative, for other Time, and in other Manner, than the same was granted by Parliament.

5. By raising and keeping a Standing Army within this Kingdom in Time of Peace, without Consent of Parliament, and quartering Soldiers contrary to Law.

6. By causing several good Subjects, being Protestants, to be disarmed, at the same Time when Papists were both armed and employed, contrary to Law.

7. By violating the Freedom of Election of Members to serve in Parliament.

8. By Prosecutions in the Court of King's Bench, for Matters and Causes cognizable only in Parliament; and by divers other arbitrary and illegal Courses.

9. And whereas of late Years, partial, corrupt, and unqualified Persons, have been returned and served on Juries in trials, and particularly divers Jurors in Trials for High Treason, which were not Freeholders.

10. And excessive Bail hath been required of Persons committed in criminal Cases, to elude the Benefit of the Laws made for the Liberty of the Subjects.

11. And excessive Fines have been imposed; and illegal and cruel punishments inflicted.

12. And several Grants and Promises made of Fines and Forfeitures, before and Conviction or Judgment against the Persons, upon whom the same were to be levied.

All which are uttely and directly contrary to the known Laws and Statutes, and Freedom of this Realm.

And whereas the said late King *James* the Second having abdicated the Government, and the Throne being thereby vacant, his Highness the Prince of *Orange* (who it hath pleased Almighty God to make the glorious Instrument of delivering this Kingdom from Popery and arbitrary Power) did (by the Advice of the Lords spiritual and Temporal, and divers principal Person of the Commons) cause Letters to be written to the Lords Spiritual and Temporal, being Protestants; and other Letters to the several Counties, Cities, Universities, Boroughs, and Cinque-ports, for the choosing of such Persons to represent them,as were of right to be sent to Parliament, to meet and sit at *Westminster* upon the two and twentieth Day of *January* in this Year one thousand six hundred eighty and eight, in order to such an Establishment, as that their Religion, Laws, and Liberties might not again be in Danger of being subverted: Upon which Letters, Elections having been accordingly made,

And thereupon the said Lords Spiritual and Temporal, and Commons, pursuant to thei respective Letters and Elections, being now assembled in a full and free Representative of this Nation, taking into their most serious Consideration the gest Means for attaining the Ends aforesaid; do in the first Place (as their in like Case have usually done) for the vindicating and asserting their ancient Rights and Liberties, declare;

1. That the pretended Power of suspending of Laws, or the Execution of Laws, by regal Authority, without Consent of Parliament, is illegal.

2. That the pretended Power of dispensing with Laws, or the Execution of Laws, by regal Authority, as it hath been assumed and exercised of late, is illegal.

3. That the Commission for erecting the late Court of Commissioners for Ecclesiastical Causes, and all other Commissions and Courts of like Nature, are illegal and pernicious.

4. That levying Money for or to the Use of the Crown, by Pretence of Prerogative, without Grant of Parliament, for longer Time, or in other Manner than the same is or shall be granted, is illegal.

5. That it is the Right of the Subjects to petition the King, and all Commitments and Presecutions for such petitioning are illegal.

6. That the raising or keeping a Standing Army within the Kingdom in Time of Peace, unless it be with Consent of Parliament, is against Law.

7. That the Subjects which are Protestants, may have Arms for their Defence suitable to their Conditions, and as allowed by Law.

8. That Election of Members of Parliament ought to be free.

9. That the Freedom of Speech, and Debates or Proceedings in Parliament, ought not to be impeached or questioned in any Court or Place out of Parliament.

10. That excessive Bail ought not to be required, nor excessive Fines imposed; nor cruel and unusual Punishments inflicted.

11. That Jurors ought to be duly impanelled and returned, and Jurors which pass upon Men in Trials for High Treason ought to be Freeholders.

12. That all Grants and Promises of Fines and Forfeitures of particular Persons before Conviction, are illegal and void.

13. And that for Redress of all Grievances, and for the amending, strengthening, and preserving of the Laws, Parliaments ought to be held frequently.

And they do claim, demand, and insist upon all and singular the Premisses, as their undoubted Rights and Liberties; and that no Declarations, Judgements, Doings, or Proceedings, to the Prejudice of the People in any of the said Premisses, ought in any wise to be drawn hereafter into Consequence or Example.

To which Demand of their Rights they are particularly encouraged by the Declaration of his Highness the Prince of *Orange*, as being the only Means for obtaining a full Redress and Remedy therein.

Having therefore an entire Confidence, That his said Highness the Prince of *Orange* will perfect the Deliverance so far advanced by him, and will still preserve them from the Violation of their Rights, which they have here asserted, and from all other Attempts upon their Religion, Rights, and Liberties.

II. The said Lords Spiritual and Temporal, and Commons, assembled at *Westminster*, do resolve, That *William* and *Mary* Prince and Princess of *Orange* be, and be declared, King and Queen of *England, France, and Ireland*, and the Dominions thereunto belonging, to hold the Crown and Royal Dignity of the said Kingdoms and Dominions to them the said Prince and Princess during their Lives, and the Life of the Survivor of them; and that the sale and full Exercise of the Regal Power be only in, and executed by the said Prince of *Orange*, in the Names of the said Prince and Princess, during their joint Lives; and after the Deceases, the said Crown and Royal Dignity of the said Kingdoms and Dominions to be to the Heirs of the Body of the said Princess; and for default of such Issue to the Princess *Anne* of *Denmark*, and the Heirs of her Body; and for Default of such Issue to the Heirs of the Body of the said Prince of *Orange*. And the Lords Spiritual and Temporal, and Commons, do pray the said Prince and Princess to accept the same accordingly.

XI.

PENNSYLVANIA CHARTER OF PRIVILEGES, 1701

We have relied on Thorpe (V: 3076-3081). See also Schwartz (I: 170-175) who relies on Thorpe. The numerical breakdown of the Charter is in the original. The Huntington Library has a 1725 publication of the 1701 Charter of Privileges that includes a useful sidebar summary. It also contains an extensive use of the uppercase and italics. See the eight-paged, *The Charter of Privileges* (Philadelphia: Samuel Keimer, 1725).

~

William Penn, Proprietary and Governor of the Province of Pensilvania and Territories thereunto belonging, To all to whom these Presents shall come, sendeth Greeting. Whereas King Charles the Second, by His Letters Patents, under the Great Seal of England, bearing Date the Fourth Day of March, in the Year One Thousand Six Hundred and Eighty-one, was graciously pleased to give and grant unto me, and my Heirs and Assigns for ever, this Province of Pensilvania, with divers great Powers and Jurisdictions for the well Government thereof.

And whereas the King's dearest Brother, James Duke of York and Albany, &c. by his Deeds of Feoffment,[66] under his Hand and Seal duly perfected, bearing Date the Twenty-Fourth Day of August, One Thousand Six Hundred Eighty and Two, did grant unto me, my Heirs and Assigns, all that Tract of Land, now called the Territories of Pensilvania, together with Powers and Jurisdictions for the good Government thereof.

And Whereas for the Encouragement of all the Freemen and Planters, that might be concerned in the said Province and Territories, and for the good Government thereof, I the said William Penn, in the Year One Thousand Six Hundred Eighty and Three, for me, my Heirs and Assigns, did grant and confirm unto all the Freemen, Planters and Adventurers therein, divers Liberties, Franchises and Properties, as by the said Grant, entituled, The Frame of the Government of the Province of Pensilvania, and Territories thereunto belonging, in America, may appear; which Charter or Frame being found in some Parts of it, not so suitable to the present Circumstances of the Inhabitants, was in the Third Month, in the Year One Thousand Seven Hundred, delivered up to me, by Six Parts of Seven of the Freemen of this Province and

[66]A feoff is a large land grant.

Territories, in General Assembly met, Provision being made in the said Charter, for that End and Purpose.

And Whereas I was then pleased to promise, That I would restore the said Charter to them again, with necessary Alterations, or in lieu thereof, give them another, better adapted to answer the present Circumstances and Conditions of the said Inhabitants; which they have now, by the Representatives in General Assembly met at Philadelphia, requested me to grant.

Know ye therefore, That for the further Well-being and good Government of the said Province, and Territories; and in Pursuance of the Rights and Powers before-mentioned, I the said William Penn do declare, grant and confirm, unto all the Freemen, Planters and Adventurers, and other Inhabitants of this Province and Territories, these following Liberties, Franchises and Privileges, so far as in me lieth, to be held, enjoyed and kept, by the Freemen, Planters and Adventurers, and other Inhabitants of and in the said Province and Territories thereunto annexed, for ever.

I

Because no People can be truly happy, though under the greatest Enjoyment of Civil Liberties, if abridged of the Freedom of their Consciences, as to their Religious Profession and Worship: And Almighty God being the only Lord of Conscience, Father of Lights and Spirits; and the Author as well as Object of all divine Knowledge, Faith and Worship, who only doth enlighten the Minds, and persuade and convince the Understandings of People, I do hereby grant and declare, That no Person or Persons, inhabiting in this Province or Territories, who shall confess and acknowledge One almighty God, the Creator, Upholder and Ruler of the World; and profess him or themselves obliged to live quietly under the Civil Government, shall be in any Case molested or prejudiced, in his or their Person or Estate, because of his or their conscientious Persuasion or Practice, nor be compelled to frequent or maintain any religious Worship, Place or Ministry, contrary to his or their Mind, or to do or suffer any other Act or Thing, contrary to their religious Persuasion.

And that all Persons who also profess to believe in Jesus Christ, the Saviour of the World, shall be capable (notwithstanding their other Persuasions and Practices in Point of Conscience and Religion) to serve this Government in any Capacity, both legislatively and executively he or they solemnly promising, when lawfully required, Allegiance to the King as Sovereign, and Fidelity to the Proprietary and Governor, and taking the Attests as now established by the Law made at New-Castle, in the Year One Thousand and Seven Hundred, entitled, An Act directing the Attests of several Officers and Ministers, as now amended and confirmed this present Assembly.

II

For the well governing of this Province and Territories, there shall be an Assembly yearly chosen, by the Freemen thereof, to consist of Four Persons out of each County, of most Note for Virtue, Wisdom and Ability, (or of a greater number at any Time, as the Governor and Assembly shall agree) upon the First Day of October for ever; and shall sit on the Fourteenth Day of the same Month, at Philadelphia, unless the Governor and Council for the Time being, shall see Cause to appoint another Place within the said Province or Territories: Which Assembly shall have the Power to chuse a Speaker and other their Officers; and shall be Judges of the Qualifications and Elections of their own Members; sit upon their own Adjournments; appoint Committees; prepare Bills in order to pass into Laws; impeach Criminals, and redress Grievances; and shall have all other Powers and Privileges of an Assembly, according to the Rights of the free-born Subjects of England, and as is usual in any of the King's Plantations in America.

And if any County or Counties, shall refuse or neglect to chuse their respective Representatives as aforesaid, or if chosen, do not meet to serve in Assembly, those who are so chosen and met, shall have the full Power of an Assembly, in as ample Manner as if all the Representatives had been chosen and met, provided they are not less than Two Thirds of the whole Number that ought to meet.

And that the Qualifications of Electors and Elected, and all other Matters and Things related to Elections of Representatives to serve in Assemblies, though not herein particularly expressed, shall be and remain as by a Law of this Government, made at New-Castle in the Year One Thousand Seven Hundred, entitled, An Act to ascertain the Number of Members of Assembly, and to regulate the Elections.

III

That the Freemen in each respective County, at the Time and Place of Meeting for Electing their Representatives to serve in Assembly may as often as there be Occasion, chuse a double Number of Person to present to the Governor for Sheriffs and Coroners to serve for Three Years, if so long they behave themselves well; out of which respective Elections and Presentments, the Governor shall nominate and commissionate one for each of the said Offices, the Third Day after such Presentment, or else the First named in such Presentment, for each Office as aforesaid, shall stand and serve in that Office for the Time before respectively limited; and in Case of Death or Default, such Vacancies shall be supplied by the Governor, to serve to the End of the said Term.

Provided always, That if the said Freemen shall at any Time neglect or decline to chuse a Person or Persons for either or both the aforesaid Offices, then and in such Case, the Persons that are or shall be in the respective Offices of Sheriffs or Coroners, at the Time of Election, shall remain therein, until they shall be removed by another Election as aforesaid.

And that the Justices of the respective Counties shall or may nominate and present to the Governor Three Persons, to serve for Clerk of the Peace for the said County, when there is a Vacancy, one of which the Governor shall commissionate within Ten Days after such Presentment, or else the First nominated shall serve in the said Office during good Behavior.

IV

That the Laws of this Government shall be in this Stile, viz. By the Governor, with the Consent and Approbation of the Freemen in General Assembly met; and shall be, after Confirmation by the Governor, forthwith recorded in the Rolls Office, and kept at Philadelphia, unless the Governor and Assembly shall agree to appoint another Place.

V

That all Criminals shall have the same Privileges of Witnesses and Council as their Prosecutors.

VI

That no Person or Persons shall or may, at any Time hereafter, be obliged to answer any Complaint, Matter or Thing whatsoever, relating to Property, before the Governor and Council, or in any other Place, but in ordinary Course of Justice, unless Appeals thereunto shall be hereafter by law appointed.

VII

That no Person within this Government, shall be licensed by the Governor to keep an Ordinary, Tavern or House of Publick Entertainment, but such who are first recommended to him, under the Hands of the Justices of the respective Counties, signed in open Court; which Justices are and shall be hereby impowered, to suppress and forbid any Person, keeping such Publick-House as aforesaid, upon their Misbehaviour, on such Penalties as the Law doth or shall direct; and to recommend others from time to time, as they shall see Occasion.

VIII

If any Person, through Temptation or Melancholy, shall destroy himself; his Estate, real and personal, shall notwithstanding descend to his Wife and Children, or Relations, as if he had died a natural Death; and if any Person shall be destroyed or killed by Casualty or Accident, there shall be no Forfeiture to the Governor by reason thereof.

And no Act, Law or Ordinance whatsoever, shall at any Time hereafter, be made or done, to alter, change or diminish the Form or Effect of this Charter, or of any Part or Clause therein, contrary to the true Intent and Meaning thereof, without the Consent of the Governor for the Time being, and Six Parts of Seven of the Assembly met.

But because the Happiness of Mankind depends so much upon the Enjoying of Liberty of their Consciences as aforesaid, I do hereby solemnly declare, promise and grant, for me, my Heirs and Assigns, That the First Article of this Charter relating to Liberty of Conscience, and every Part and Clause therein, according to the true Intent and Meaning thereof, shall be kept and remain, without any Alteration, inviolably for ever.

And lastly, I the said William Penn, Proprietary and Governor of the Province of Pensilvania, and Territories thereunto belonging, for myself, my Heirs and Assigns, have solemnly declared, granted and confirmed, and do hereby solemnly declare, grant and confirm, That neither I, my Heirs or Assigns, shall procure or do any Thing or Things whereby the Liberties in this Charter contained and expressed, nor any Part thereof, shall be infringed or broken: And if any thing shall be procured or done, by any Person or Persons, contrary to these Presents, it shall be held of no Force or Effect.

In witness whereof, I the said William Penn, at Philadelphia in Pensilvania, have unto this present Charter of Liberties, set my Hand and broad Seal, this Twenty-eighth Day of October, in the Year of Our Lord One Thousand Seven Hundred and One, being the Thirteenth Year of the Reign of King William the Third, over England, Scotland, France and Ireland, &c. And the Twenty-First Year of my Government.

And notwithstanding the Closure and Test of this present Charter as aforesaid, I think fit to add this following Proviso thereunto, as Part of the same, That is to say, That notwithstanding any Clause or Clauses in the above-mentioned Charter, obliging the Province and Territories to join together in Legislation, I am content, and do hereby declare, that if the Representatives of the Province and Territories shall not hereafter agree to join together in Legislation, and that the same shall be signified unto me, or my Deputy, in open Assembly, or otherwise from under the Hands and Seals of the Representatives, for the Time being, of the Province and Territories, or the major Part of either of them, at any Time within Three Years from the Date hereof, that in such Case, the Inhabitants of each of the Three Counties of this Province, shall not have less than Eight Persons to represent them in Assembly, for the Province; and the Inhabitants of the Town of Philadelphia (when the said Town is incorporated) Two Persons to represent them in Assembly; and the Inhabitants of each County in the Territories, shall have as many Persons to represent them in a distinct Assembly for the Territories, as shall be by them requested as aforesaid.

Notwithstanding which Separation of the province and Territories, in Respect of Legislation, I do hereby promise, grant and declare, That the Inhabitants of both Province and Territories, shall separately enjoy all other Liberties, Privileges and Benefits, granted jointly to them in this

Charter, any Law, Usage or Custom of this Government heretofore made and practised, or any law made and passed by this General Assembly, to the Contrary hereof, notwithstanding.

William Penn

This Charter of Privileges being distinctly read in Assembly; and the whole and every Part thereof, being approved of and agreed to, by us, we do thankfully receive the same from our Proprietary and Governor, at Philadelphia, this Twenty-Eighth Day of October, One Thousand Seven Hundred and One. Signed on Behalf, and by Order of the Assembly.

per Joseph Growdon, Speaker

Edward Shippen, Griffith Owen,
Phineas Pemberton, Caleb Pusey,
Samuel Carpenter, Thomas Story,
Proprietary and Governor's Council

Chapter Two

Elementary Books of Public Right

In this chapter, we examine the reflective dimension of the conversation pertaining to the origin of the Bill of Rights. Four related, but separate, "schools of thought" can be identified during the roughly one hundred years from the adoption of the English Bill of Rights in 1689 to the Declaration of Independence in 1776.

The first is the revolutionary school within which we can locate the work of John Locke and Algernon Sidney. They emphasize the importance of the original social contract, agreed to voluntarily by individuals, for understanding the purposes and limits of government. When rulers undermine the contract, the people have a right to alter or abolish government. The second is the petition school associated with Cato. It is the right of the people, says Cato, to "meddle with Government" when those in power betray the public trust. When magistrates deceive and oppress the people, they have the right to invoke the principles of 1689 and "petition for redress of grievance." The third is the obligation school. William Blackstone and David Hume criticize the contractarians and the petitioners as misguided reformers or utopian speculators. They substitute common sense for abstract reflection and urge an adherence to the common--but positive--law tradition. The fourth, or institutional school, is presented by Baron de Montesquieu. Americans of the late eighteenth century found Montesquieu appealing because he discussed liberty within the context of such institutional arrangements as federalism and the separation of powers.

John Locke

John Locke's *Second Treatise* (1689) has been the subject of scholarly controversy for three hundred years. Was Locke an apologist for the emerging industrial class? Did Locke write to justify the Glorious Revolution of 1688-1689? Or was Locke part of an underground movement connected with the earlier Commonwealthmen? Regardless of the answers to these, and other, questions, Locke's *Second Treatise* had a profound impact on the subsequent understanding of the origin of individual rights, the defense of the rule of law and representative government, and the right to revolution. Locke argued that the natural condition of humans is one of perfect freedom and perfect equality. By nature, each individual is endowed with the right to life, liberty, and property (§4, 6-7, 13-15). However, the state of peace, which exists in this original state of nature, becomes a state of war. In order to protect life, liberty, and property, on which political and economic improvement depends, individuals leave the state of nature and create a social contract: they relinquish certain "executive and judicial" rights in exchange for the certainty of a known law to secure the right to property and to settle political disputes (§32-34, 87-90, 99, 123-131, 142). Finally, Locke argues that when the government becomes tyrannical, it is the right and duty of the people to alter or abolish such government (§222-230, 240-241, 243).

Algernon Sidney

Algernon Sidney is hardly a household name today. But the American revolutionaries held him in the same high esteem as they did Locke. John Adams, for example, in *Thoughts on Government* (1771), urged his readers to consult the writings of "Sidney, Harrington, Locke, Milton..." And in a letter to Henry Lee (1825), Thomas Jefferson explained that the Declaration of Independence relies on such "elementary books of public right, as Aristotle, Cicero, Locke, Sidney, etc." Although published posthumously in 1698, the *Discourses Concerning Government* was written in the 1680s as a challenge to Robert Filmer's divine right of kings argument found in his *Patriarcha* (1680). Like Locke, he argued that the people have a right to resist unjust rule and to institute such government as shall provide for their safety and happiness. Unlike the "judicious" Locke, who went into exile, Sidney was charged with treason and executed in 1683.

Trenchard and Gordon

John Trenchard and Thomas Gordon wrote a series of weekly letters for the opposition *London Journal* in the early 1720s under the pseudonym "Cato." The immediate purpose was to criticize the symbiotic relationship between the South Sea Company and the leading ministers of the British government. But as often happens in political commentary, they grounded their coverage of the financial crisis, known as the "South Sea Bubble," on a comprehensive theory of politics. Cato elevates the year 1689, and the Bill of Rights agreed to by Parliament and the Monarchy, to a privileged position; it expresses both the traditional rights of Englishmen and the enlightenment doctrine of natural rights found in Locke and Sydney. Cato argues that it is the right and "business" of the people "to meddle with government." The honest ploughman, like a sentinel, protects the "glorious Principles of liberty" from entrenched "court" leaders corrupted by power and wealth. This notion that the objective of revolutionary "country" republicanism was to restore established principles, was very influential in America during the 1760s.

Baron de Montesquieu

Montesquieu was "justly celebrated" for his contribution to the creation of constitutional government in four areas.

First, Montesquieu identified the "principle" of democratic government to be virtue. Accordingly, "when virtue is banished, ambition invades the minds of those who are disposed to receive it, and avarice possesses the whole community." Retracing the arguments of ancient historians, Montesquieu claimed that when "manufacture, commerce, finances, opulence, and luxury" become the focus of attention, popular government is in on the verge of collapse. His warning influenced both the framers of the state constitutions and Antifederalist opponents to the 1787 United States Constitution.

Second, Montesquieu argued that republican government must operate within a confined orbit. The Antifederalists appealed to Montesquieu's claim that "in an extensive republic the public good is sacrificed to a thousand private views; it is subordinate to exceptions, and depends on accidents. In a small one, the interest of the public is more obvious, better understood, and more within the reach of every citizen; abuses have less extent, and, of course, are less protected."

Montesquieu's third contribution is his argument that "a confederate republic" would enable a republic to remain small for domestic purposes but become temporarily large in order to defend itself in a despotic world. A confederate republic is a form of government "by which several petty states agree to become members of a larger one which they intend to establish. It is a kind of assemblage of societies, that constitute a new one, capable of increasing by means of further associations, till they arrive at such a degree of power as to be able to provide for the security of the whole body." His views on the advantages of confederating for limited purposes was received favorably in revolutionary America.

With independence, each of the former colonies faced the task of creating republican governments at the state level. Montesquieu's commentary on the separation of powers--his fourth contribution--was of central importance to those who drafted new constitutions. In fact, one of the most cited passages in the conversation over how best to secure rights is the following from Montesquieu: "When the legislative and executive powers are united in the same person, or in the same body of magistrates, there can be no liberty; because apprehensions may arise, lest the same monarch or senate should enact tyrannical laws, to execute them in a tyrannical manner." His argument that the rights of the citizen were secure only when careful attention was paid to the structure of the government was central to the discussion over what form of government would best secure the right to life, liberty, and the pursuit of happiness.

David Hume

David Hume wrote, and revised, twenty-seven Political Essays between 1741 and 1776. "That Politics may be reduced to a Science," and "Of Parties in General" have received considerable attention, especially since they are deemed to have influenced James Madison's *Federalist* 10. But also important is his less-popular observations on the origin of the social contract. "Of the Original Contract" is his twelfth essay on politics. Hume criticizes both Locke's "original contract" theory and Cato's constitutional theory. Hume relies on experience and common sense, not a collective "act of the mind," to justify founding and maintaining a government. (He believes that Plato, as well as the contractarians, produced models that are "plainly imaginary." See his "Idea of a Perfect Commonwealth," Essay XII in *Political Discourses*.) He argues that experience shows that every government has come into existence by means of force or accident, rather than by mutual consent and voluntary agreement. Even the "revolution" of 1689 deviated from the ideals of popular consent and constitutional discourse. It follows, says Hume, that experience alone can provide the ground for the establishment of rights and duties. Experience teaches that "society cannot possibly be maintained without the authority of magistrates, and that this authority must soon fall into contempt where exact obedience is not paid to it."

William Blackstone

Although Blackstone acknowledged the theoretical validity of the doctrine of natural right--humans are endowed by nature with the capacity to "know good from evil, and with power of choosing those measures which are usually summed up in one general appellation"--he reserves the practical application of this doctrine to "extraordinary" situations. Whenever there are "unconstitutional oppressions"--such as the tyrannical actions of James II--"experience" indicates that the people will appeal to the extraconstitutional foundation of individual rights. But, Blackstone warns, it is inappropriate to appeal to this foundation as a normal and regular mode of settling disputes. In "ordinary" circumstances--as existed in eighteenth century Britain--Blackstone endorses an appeal to the rule of civil laws passed by parliament, executed by the monarch, and interpreted by the courts. An appeal to the "over-zealous republican" doctrine of abstract rights is unnecessary and dangerous. Moreover, the idea of petitioning the king and parliament to "redress" grievances presumes that the king and parliament can make mistakes. But they "can do no wrong."

XII.

JOHN LOCKE, *SECOND TREATISE,* 1694

There are a number of editions of *The Second Treatise* available. See, for example, the widely-used edition by Peter Laslett who makes a conscious effort to recover the "authentic" Locke. Kurland and Lerner (I: 42-46, 82-87) have followed Laslett. We have avoided breaking down the text into chapters, but instead have organized the text around five themes and followed Locke's system of dividing his argument into paragraphs. The numbered sections are in the original. For a thorough coverage of Locke's political thought, see Richard Ashcraft, *Revolutionary Politics and Locke's Two Treatises of Government* (Princeton: Princeton University Press, 1986). We have used the second edition published by A. and J. Churchill (London, 1694).

~

[1] The State of Nature

§4. To understand Political Power aright, and derive it from its Original, we must consider what State all Men are naturally in, and that is, a State of perfect Freedom to order their Actions, and dispose of their Possessions, and Persons as they think fit, within the bounds of the Law of Nature, without asking leave, or depending upon the Will of any other Man.

A State also of Equality, wherein all the Power and Jurisdiction is reciprocal, no one having more than another, there being nothing more evident, than that Creatures of the same species and rank promiscuously born to all the same advantages of Nature, and the use of the same faculties, should also be equal one amongst another without Subordination or Subjection, unless the Lord and Master of them all, should by any manifest Declaration of his Will set one above another, and confer on him by an evident and clear appointment an undoubted Right to Dominion and Sovereignty.

§6. But though this be a State of Liberty, yet it is not a State of Licence, though Man in that State have an uncontroleable Liberty, to dispose of his Person or Possessions, yet he has not Liberty to destroy himself, or so much as any Creature in his Possession, but where some nobler use, than its bare Preservation calls for it. The State of Nature, has a Law of Nature to govern [it][1] which obliges every one, and Reason, which is that Law, teaches all Mankind, who will but consult it; That being all equal and independent, no one ought to harm another in his Life, Health, Liberty, or Possessions; for Men being all the Workmanship of one Omnipotent, and infinitely wise maker; All the Servants of one Sovereign Master, sent into the World by his order and about his business, they are his Property, whose Workmanship they are, made to last during his, not one anothers Pleasure. And being Furnished with like Faculties, sharing all in one Community of Nature, there cannot be supposed any such Subordination among us, that may Authorize us to destroy one another, as if we were made for one anothers uses, as the inferior ranks of Creatures are for ours, every one as he is bound to preserve himself, and not to quit his Station willfully; so by the like reason when his own Preservation comes not in competition, ought he as much as he can to preserve the rest of Mankind, and may not unless it be to do Justice on an offender, take away, or impair the life, or what tends to the Preservation of the Life, Liberty, Health, Limb or Goods of another.

§7. And that all Men may be restrained from invading others Rights, and from doing hurt to one another, and the Law of Nature be observed, which willeth the Peace and Preservation of all Mankind, the Execution of the Law of Nature is in that State, put into every Mans hands, whereby everyone has a right to punish the transgressors of that Law to such a Degree, as may hinder its Violation. For the Law of Nature would as all other Laws that concern Men in this World be in vain, if there were no body that in the State of Nature, had a Power to Execute that Law, and thereby preserve the innocent and restrain offenders, and if any one in the State of Nature may punish another, for any evil he has done, every one may do so. For in that State of perfect Equality, where naturally there is no superiority or jurisdiction of one, over another, what any may do in Prosecution of that Law, every one must needs have a Right to do.

§13. To this strange Doctrine, viz. That in the State of Nature, every one has the Executive Power of the Law of Nature, I doubt not

---

[1] Laslett (311), and Kurland and Lerner (I: 43), insert [it] here.

but it will be objected; That it is unreasonable for Men to be Judges in their own Cases, that self-love will make Men partial to themselves and their Friends. And on the other side, that Ill Nature, Passion and Revenge will carry them too far in punishing others. And hence nothing but Confusion and Disorder will follow, and that therefore God hath certainly appointed Government to restrain the partiality and violence of Men. I easily grant, that Civil Government is the proper Remedy for the Inconveniences of the State of Nature, which must certainly be Great, where Men may be Judges in their own Case, since 'tis easie to be imagined, that he who was so unjust as to do his Brother an Injury, will scarce be so just as to condemn himself for it: But I shall desire those who make this Objection, to remember that Absolute Monarchs are but Men, and if Government is to be the Remedy of those Evils, which necessarily follow from Mens being Judges in their Own Cases, and the State of Nature is therefore not to be endured, I desire to know what kind of Government that is, and how much better it is than the State of Nature, where one Man commanding a multitude, has the Liberty to be Judge in his own Case, and may do to all his Subjects whatever he pleases, without the least question or controle those who Execute his Pleasure? And in whatsoever he doth, whether led by Reason, Mistake or Passion, must be submitted to? Which men in the State of Nature are not bound to do one to another; And if he he that Judges, Judges amiss in his own, or any other Case, he is answerable for it to the rest of Mankind.

§14. 'Tis often asked as a mighty Objection, Where are, or ever were, there any Men in such a State of Nature? To which it may suffice as an answer at present; That since all Princes and Rulers of *Independent* Governments all through the World, are in a State of Nature, 'tis plain the World never was, nor never will be, without Numbers of Men in that State. I have named all Governors of *Independent* Communities, whether they are, or are not, in League with others; For 'tis not every Compact that puts an end to the State of Nature between Men, but only this one of agreeing together mutually to enter into one Community, and make one Body Politick; other Promises and Compacts, Men may make one with another, and yet still be in the State of Nature. The Promises and Bargains for Truck, &c. between the two Men in the Desert Island, mentioned by *Garcilasso De la vega*, in his History of *Peru*, or between a *Swiss* and an *Indian*, in the Woods of *America*, are binding to them, though they are perfectly in a State of Nature, in reference to one another. For Truth and keeping of Faith belongs to Men, as Men, and not as Members of Society.

§15. To those that say, There were never any Men in the State of Nature; I will not only oppose the Authority of the Judicious *Hooker, Eccl. Pol. Lib. I. Sect 10*...But I moreover affirm, That all Men are naturally in that State, and remain so, till by their own Consents they make themselves Members of some Politick Society; And I doubt not in the Sequel of this Discourse, to make it very clear.

[2] The Right to Private Property

§32. But the chief matter of Property being now not the Fruits of the Earth, and the Beasts that subsist on it, but the Earth it self; as that which takes in and carries with it all the rest: I think it is plain, that Property in that too is acquired as the former. As much Land as a Man Tills, Plants, Improves, Cultivates, and can use the Product of, so much is his Property. He by his Labour does, as it were, inclose it from the Common. Nor will it invalidate his right to say, Every body else has an equal Title to it; and therefore he cannot appropriate, he cannot inclose, without the Consent of all his Fellow-Commoners, all Mankind. God, when he gave the World in common to all Mankind, commanded Man also to labour, and penury of his Condition required it of him. God and his Reason commanded him to subdue the Earth, *i.e.* improve it for the benefit of Life, and therein lay out something upon it that was his own, his labour. He that in Obedience to this Command of God, subdued, tilled and sowed any part of it, thereby annexed to it something that was his *Property*, which another had no Title to, nor could without injury take from him.

§33. Nor was this appropriation of any parcel of Land, by improving it, any prejudice to any other Man, since there was still enough, and as good left; and more than the yet unprovided could use. So that in effect, there was never the less left for others because of his inclosure for himself. For he that leaves as much as another can make use of, does as good as take nothing at all. No Body could think himself injur'd by the drinking of another Man, though he took a good Draught, who had a whole River of the same Water left him to quench his thirst. And the Case of Land and Water, where there is enough of both, is perfectly the same.

§34. God gave the World to Men in Common; but since he gave it them for their benefit, and the greatest Conveniencies of Life they were capable to draw from it, it cannot be supposed he meant it should always remain common and uncultivated. He gave it to the use of the Industrious and Rational, (and Labour was to be his Title to it;) not to the Fancy or Covetousness of the Quarrelsom and Contentious. He that had as good left for his Improvement, as was already taken up, needed not complain, ought not to meddle with what was already improved by another's Labour: If he did, 'tis plain he desired the benefit of another's Pains which he had no right to, and not the Ground which God had given him in common with others to labour on, and whereof there was as good left, as that already possessed, and more than he knew what to do with, or his Industry could reach to.

§36. The measure of Property, Nature has well set, by the Extent of Mens Labour, and the Conveniency of Life: No Man's Labour could subdue, or appropriate all; nor could his Enjoyment consume more than a small part; so that it was impossible for any Man, this way, to intrench upon the right of another, or acquire, to himself, a Property, to the Prejudice of his Neighbour, who would still have room, for as good, and as large a Possession (after the other had taken out his) as before it was appropriated, which measure did confine every Man's Possession, to a very moderate Proportion, and such as he might appropriate to himself, without Injury to any Body, in the first Ages of the World, when Men were more in danger to be lost, by wandering from their Company, in the then vast Wilderness of the Earth, than to be straitned for want of room to plant in. And the same measure may be allowed still, without prejudice to any Body, as full as the World seems. For supposing a Man, or Family, in the state they were at first peopling of the World by the Children of *Adam*, or *Noah*; let him plant in some in-land, vacant places of *America*, we shall find that the *Possessions* he could make himself upon the measures we have given, would not be very large, nor, even to this day, prejudice the rest of Mankind, or give them reason to complain, or think themselves injured by this Man's Incroachment, though the Race of Men have now spread themselves to all the corners of the World, and do infinitely exceed the small number [2] was at the beginning. Nay, the extent of Ground is of so little value, without labour, that, I have heard it affirmed, that in *Spain* it self, a Man may be permitted to plough, sow, and reap, without being disturbed, upon Land he has no other Title to, but only his making use of it. But, on the contrary, the Inhabitants think themselves beholden to him, who, by his Industry on neglected, and consequently waste Land, has increased the stock of Corn, which they wanted. But be this as it will, which I lay no stress on; this I dare boldly affirm, That the same Rule of Propriety, (*viz.*) that every Man should have as much as he could make use of, would hold still in the World, without straitning any body, since there is Land enough in the World to suffice double the Inhabitants, had not the Invention of Money, and the tacit Agreement of Men, to put a value on it, introduced (by Consent) larger Possessions, and a Right to them; which, how it has done, I shall, by and by, shew more at large.

§37. This is certain, That in the beginning, before the desire of having more than Man needed, had altered the intrinsick value of

---

[2] Laslett inserts [which] here.

things, which depends only on their usefulness to the Life of Man; or [3] had agreed, that a little piece of yellow Metal, which would keep without wasting or decay, should be worth a great piece of Flesh, or a whole heap of Corn; though Men had a Right to appropriate, by their Labour, each one to himself, as much of the things of Nature, as he could use: Yet this could not be much, nor to the Prejudice of others, where the same plenty was still left, to those who would use the same Industry.[4]

[3] Origin of Political Society

§87. Man being born, as has been proved, with a Title to perfect Freedom, and an uncontrouled enjoyment of all the Rights and Priviledges of the Law of Nature, equally with any other Man, or Number of Men in the World, hath by Nature a Power, not only to preserve his Property, that is, his Life, Liberty and Estate, against the Injuries and Attempts of other Men; but to judge of, and punish the breaches of that Law in others, as he is perswaded the Offence deserves, even with Death it self, in Crimes where the heinousness of the fact, in his Opinion, requires it. But because no Political Society can be, nor subsist without having in it self the Power to preserve the Property, and in order thereunto punish the Offences of all those of that Society: There, and there only is Political Society, where every one of the Members hath quitted this natural Power, resign'd it up into the hands of the Community in all cases that exclude him not from appealing for Protection to the Law established by it. And thus all private judgment of every particular Member being excluded, the Community comes to be Umpire, by settled standing Rules, indifferent, and the same to all Parties; And by Men having Authority from the Community, for the execution of those Rules, decides all the differences that may happen between any Members of that Society, concerning any matter of right, and punishes those Offences which any Member hath committed against the Society with such Penalites as the Law has established; whereby it is easie to discern who are, and who are not, in Political Society together. Those who are united into one Body, and have a common establish'd Law and Judicature to appeal to, with Authority to decide Controversies between them, and punish Offenders, are in Civil Society one with another; but those who have no such common Appeal, I mean on Earth, are still in the state of Nature, each being, where there is no other, Judge for himself, and

---

[3] Laslett inserts [Men] here.

[4] Locke deleted the remainder of this paragraph in the 1694 edition.

Executioner; which is, as I have before shew'd it, the perfect state of Nature.

§88. And thus the Commonwealth comes by a power to set down what punishment shall belong to the several transgressions which they think worthy of it, committed amongst the Members of that Society, (which is the power of making Laws) as well as it has the power to punish any Injury done unto any of its Members, by any one that is not of it, (which is the power of War and Peace;) and all this for the preservation of the property of all the Members of that Society, as far as is possible. But though every Man enter'd into civil Society, has quitted his power to punish Offences against the Law of Nature, in prosecution of his own private Judgment; yet with the Judgment of Offences which he has given up to the Legislative in all Cases where he can Appeal to the Magistrate, he has given up a Right to the Commonwealth to imploy his force for the Execution of the Judgments of the Commonwealth, whenever he shall be called to it, which indeed are his own Judgments, they being made by himself, or his Representative. And herein we have the original of the Legislative and Executive Power of Civil Society, which is to judge by standing Laws how far Offences are to be punished when committed within the Commonwealth; and also by occasional Judgments founded on the present Circumstances of the Fact, how far Injuries from without are to be vindicated, and in both these to imploy all the force of all the Members when there shall be need.

§89. Whereever therefore any number of Men are so united into one Society, as to quit every one his Executive Power of the Law of Nature, and to resign it to the publick, there and there only is a Political, or Civil Society. And this is done whereever any number of Men, in the State of Nature, enter into Society to make one People, one Body Politick under one Supream Government, or else when any one joyns himself to, and incorporates with any Government already made. For hereby he authorizes the Society, or which is all one, the Legislative thereof to make Laws for him as the publick good of the Sociey shall require; to the Execution whereof, his own assistance (as to his own decrees) is due. And this puts Men out of a State of Nature into that of a Commonwealth, by setting up a Judge on Earth, with Authority to determine all the Controversies, and redress the injuries, that may happen to any Member of the Commonwealth; which Judge is the Legislative, or Magistrates appointed by it. And whereever there are any number of Men, however associated, that have no such decisive power to appeal to, there they are still in the state of Nature.

§90. And hence it is evident, that Absolute Monarchy which by some Men is counted for the only Government in the World, is indeed inconsistent with Civil Society, and so can be no Form of Civil

Government at all. For the end of Civil Society, being to avoid and remedy those inconveniencies of the State of Nature which necessarily follow from every Man's being Judge in his own Case, by setting up a known Authority, to which every one of that Society may Appeal upon any injury received, or Controversie that may arise, and which every one of the Society ought to obey; whereever any persons are, who have not such an Authority to Appeal to, for the decision of any difference between them, there those persons are still in the state of Nature. And so is every Absolute Prince in respect of those who are under his *Dominion*.

§99. Whosoever therefore out of a State of Nature unite into a Community, must be understood to give up all the power necessary to the ends for which they unite into Society, to the majority of the Community, unless they expressly agreed in any number greater than the majority. And this is done by barely agreeing to unite into one Political Society, which is all the Compact that is, or needs be, between the Individuals that enter into or make up a Commonwealth. And thus that which begins and actually constitutes any Political Society, is nothing but the consent of any number of Freemen capable of a majority to unite and incorporate into such a Society. And this is that, and that only which did or could give beginning to any lawful Government in the World.

[4] The Purpose of Government

§123. If Man in the State of Nature be so free, as has been said; If he be absolute Lord of his own Person and Possessions, equal to the greatest, and subject to no Body, why will he part with his Freedom? Why will he give up this Empire, and subject himself to the Dominion and Controul of any other Power? To which 'tis obvious to Answer, that though in the state of Nature he hath such a right, yet the Enjoyment of it is very uncertain, and constantly exposed to the Invasion of others; for all being Kings as much as he, every Man his Equal, and the greater part no strict Observers of Equity and Justice, the enjoyment of the property he has in this state is very unsafe, very unsecure. This makes him willing to quit this Condition, which however free, is full of fears and continual dangers: And 'tis not without reason, that he seeks out, and is willing to joyn in Society with others who are already united, or have a mind to unite for the mutual Preservation of their Lives, Liberties, and Estates, which I call by the general Name, Property.

§124. The great and chief end therefore, of Mens uniting into Commonwealths, and putting themselves under Government, is the Preservation of their Property. To which in the state of Nature there are many things wanting.

First, There wants an establish'd, settled, known Law, received and allowed by common consent to be the Standard of Right and Wrong, and the common measure to decide all Controversies between them. For though the Law of Nature be plain and intelligible to all rational Creatures; yet Men being biassed by their Interest, as well as ignorant for want of study of it, are not apt to allow of it as a Law binding to them in the application of it to their particular Cases.

§125. *Secondly,* In the State of Nature there wants a known and indifferent Judge, with Authority to determine all differences according to the established Law. For every one in the state being both Judge and Executioner of the Law of Nature, Men being partial to themselves, Passion and Revenge is very apt to carry them too far, and with too much heat in their own Cases, as well as negligence, and unconcernedness, make them too remiss, in other Mens.

§126. *Thirdly,* In the state of Nature there often wants Power to back and support the Sentence when right, and to give it due Execution. They who by any Injustice offended, will seldom fail, where they are able, by force to make good their Injustice, such resistance many times makes the punishment dangerous, and frequently destructive, to those who attempt it.

§127. Thus Mankind, notwithstanding all the Priviledges of the state of Nature, being but in an ill condition while they remain in it, are quickly driven into Society. Hence it comes to pass, that we seldom find any number of Men live any time together in this State. The inconveniencies that they are therein exposed to, by the irregular and uncertain exercise of the Power every Man has of punishing the transgressions of others, make them take Sanctuary under the establish'd Laws of Government, and therein seek the preservation of their Property. 'Tis this makes them so willingly give up every one his single power of punishing to be exercised by such alone as shall be appointed to it amongst them; and by such Rules as the Community, or those authorised by it to them to that purpose shall agree on. And in this we have the original right and rise of both the Legislative and Executive Power, as well as of the Governments and Societies themselves.

§128. For in the State of Nature, to omit the liberty he has of innocent Delights, a Man has two Powers.

The first is to do whatsoever he thinks fit for the preservation of himself and others within the permission of the Law of Nature: by which Law common to them all, he and all the rest of Mankind are one Community, make up one Society distinct from all other Creatures, and were it not for the corruption and vitiousness of degenerate Men, there would be no need of any other, no necessity that Men should separate from this great and associate into less Combinations.

The other power a Man has in the State of Nature, is the power to punish the Crimes committed against that Law. Both these he gives up when he joyns in a private, if I may so call it, or particular Political Society, and incorporates into any Commonwealth, separate from the rest of Mankind.

§129. The first Power, *viz.* of doing whatsoever he thought fit for the preservation of himself, and the rest of Mankind, he gives up to be regulated by Laws made by the Society, so far forth as the preservation of himself, and the rest of that Society shall require; which Laws of the Society in many things confine the liberty he had by the Law of Nature.

§130. *Secondly*, the Power of punishing he wholly gives up, and engages his natural force, (which he might before imploy in the Execution of the Law of Nature, by his own single Authority, as he thought fit) to assist the Executive Power of the Society, as the Law thereof shall require. For being now in a new State, wherein he is to enjoy many Conveniencies from the labour, assistance and society of others in the same Community, as well as protection from its whole strength; he is to part also with as much of his natural liberty in providing for himself, as the good, prosperity and safety of the Society shall require; which is not only necessary but just, since the other Members of the Society do the like.

§131. But though Men when they enter into Society, give up the Equality, Liberty, and Executive Power they had in the State of Nature, into the hands of the Society, to be so far disposed of by the Legislative, as the good of the Society shall require; yet it being only with an intention in every one the better to preserve himself his Liberty and Property; (For no rational Creature can be supposed to change his condition with an intention to be worse) the power of the Society, or Legislative constituted by them, can never be suppos'd to extend farther than the common good; but is obliged to secure every ones Property by providing against those three defects above-mentioned, that made the State of Nature so unsafe and uneasie. And so whoever has the Legislative or supream Power of any Common-wealth, is bound to govern by establish'd standing Laws, promulgated and known to the People, and not by Extemporary Decrees; by indifferent and upright Judges, who are to decide Controversies by those Laws; And to imploy the force of the Community sat home, only in the Execution of such Laws, or abroad to prevent or redress Foreign Injuries, and secure the Community from Inroads and Invasion. And all this to be directed to no other end, but the Peace, Safety, and publick good of the People.

§142. These are the Bounds which the trust that is put in them by the Society, and the Law of God and Nature, have set to the Legislative Power of every Commonwealth, in all Forms of Government.

First, They are to govern by promulgated establish'd Laws, not to be varied in particular Cases, but to have one Rule for the Rich and Poor, for the Favourite at Court, and the Country Man at Plough.

Secondly, These Laws also ought to be designed for no other end ultimately but the good of the People.

Thirdly, they must not raise Taxes on the Property of the People, without the Consent of the People, given by themselves, or their Deputies. And this properly concerns only such Governments where the Legislative is always in being, or at least where the People have not reserv'd any part of the Legislative to Deputies, to be from time to time chosen by themselves.

Fourthly, The Legislative neither must nor can transfer the Power of making Laws to any Body else, or place it any where but where the People have.

[5] The Right to Revolution

§222. The Reason why Men enter into Society, is the preservation of their Property; and the end why they chuse and authorize a Legislative, is, that there may be Laws made, and Rules set as Guards and Fences to the Properties of all the Members of the Society, to limit the Power, and moderate the Dominion of every Part and Member of the Society. For since it can never be supposed to be the Will of the Society, that the Legislative should have a Power to destroy that which every one designs to secure, by entering into Society, and for which the People submitted themselves to Legislators of their own making; whenever the Legislators endeavour to take away, and destroy the Property of the People, or to reduce them to Slavery under Arbitrary Power, they put themselves into a state of War with the People, who are thereupon absolved from any farther Obedience, and are left to the common Refuge, which God hath provided for all Men, against Force and Violence. Whensoever therefore the Legislative shall transgress this fundamental Rule of Society; and either by Ambition, Fear, Folly or Corruption, endeavour to grasp themselves, or put into the hands of any other and Absolute Power over the Lives, Liberties, and Estates of the People: By this breach of Trust they forfeit the Power, the People had put into their hands for quite contrary ends, and it devolves to the People; who have a Right to resume their original Liberty, and, by the Establishment of a new Legislative (such as they shall think fit) provide for their own Safety and Security, which is the end for which they are in Society. What I have said here, concerning the Legislative in general, holds true also concerning the supreme Executor, who having a double trust put in him, both to have a part in the Legislative, and the supreme Execution of the Law, acts against both, when he goes about to set up his own Arbitrary Will, as the Law of the Society. He acts also contrary to his Trust, when he either imploys the Force, Treasure, and Offices of the Society, to corrupt the Representatives, and gain them to his purposes: When he openly pre-ingages the Electors, and prescribes to their choice, such, whom he has by Sollicitations, Threats, Promises, or otherwise won to his designs; and imploys them to bring in such, who have promised before-hand, what to Vote, and what to Enact. Thus to regulate Candidates and Electors, and new model the ways of Election what is it but to cut up the Government by the Roots, and poison the very Fountain of publick Security? For the People having reserved to themselves the Choice of Representatives, as the Fence to their Properties, could do it for no other end, but that they might always be freely chosen, and so chosen, freely act and advise, as the necessity of the Commonwealth, and the publick Good should, upon examination, and mature debate, be judged to require. This, those who give their Votes before they hear the Debate, and have weighed the Reasons on all sides, are not capable of doing. To prepare such an Assembly as this, and endeavour to set up the declared Abettors of his own Will, for the true Representatives of the People, and the Law-makers of the Society, is certainly as great a breach of trust, and as perfect a Declaration of a design to subvert the Government, as is possible to be met with. To which, if one shall add Rewards and Punishments visibly imploy'd to the same end, and all the Arts of perverted Law made use of to take off and destroy all that stand in the way of such a design, and will not comply and consent to betray the Liberties of their Country, 'twill be past doubt what is doing. What Power they ought to have in the Society, who thus imploy it contrary to the trust went along with it in its first Institution, is easie to determine; and one cannot but see, that he who has once attempted any such thing as this, cannot any longer be trusted.

§223. To this perhaps it will be said, that the People being ignorant and always discontented, to lay the Foundation of Government in the unsteady Opinion and uncertain Humour of the People, is to expose it to certain ruine: And no Government will be able long to subsist, if the People may set up a new Legislative whenever they take offence at the old one. To this I Answer quite the contrary. People are not so easily got out of their old Forms, as some are apt to suggest. They are hardly to be prevailed with to amend the acknowledg'd Faults in the Frame they have been accustom'd to. And if there be any Original defects, or adventitious ones introduced by time or corruption; 'tis not an easie thing to get them changed, even when all the World sees there is an opportunity for it. This slowness and aversion in the People to quit their old Constitutions, has in the many Revolutions which have been seen in this Kingdom, in this and former Ages, still kept us to, or after some interval of fruitless attempts, still brought us back again to our old

Legislative of King, Lords and Commons: And whatever provocations have made the Crown be taken from some of our Princes Heads, they never carried the People so far as to place it in another Line.

§224. But 'twill be said, this Hypothesis lays a ferment for frequent Rebellion. To which I Answer,

First, No more than any other Hypothesis. For when the People are made miserable, and find themselves exposed to the ill usage of Arbitrary Power; cry up their Governors as much as you will for Sons of Jupiter, let them be Sacred and Divine, descended or authoriz'd from Heaven; give them out for whom or what you please the same will happen. The People generally ill treated, and contrary to right, will be ready upon any occasion to ease themselves of a burden that sits heavy upon them. They will wish and seek for the opportunity, which in the change, weakness and accidents of humane affairs seldom delays long to offer it self. He must have lived but a little while in the World, who has not seen Examples of this in his time; and he must have read very little, who cannot produce Examples of it in all sorts of Governments in the World.

§225. Secondly, I Answer, such Revolutions happen not upon every little mismanagement in publick affairs. Great mistakes in the ruling part, many wrong and inconvenient Laws, and all the slips of humane frailty will be born by the People, without mutiny or murmur. But if a long train of Abuses, Prevarications and Artifices, all tending the same way, make the design visible to the People, and they cannot but feel what they lie under, and see whither they are going; 'tis not to be wonder'd that they should then rouze themselves, and endeavour to put the rule into such hands, which may secure to them the ends for which Government was at first erected; and without which, ancient Name, and specious Forms, are so far from being better, that they are much worse than the state of Nature, or pure Anarchy; the inconveniencies being all as great and as near, but the remedy farther off and more difficult.

§226. Thirdly, I Answer, That this Power in the People of providing for their safety a-new, by a new Legislative, when their Legislators have acted contrary to their trust, by invading their Property, is the best fence against Rebellion, and the probablest means to hinder it. For Rebellion being an Opposition, not to Persons, but Authority, which is founded only in the Constitutions and Laws of the Government; those, whoever they be, who by force break through, and by force justifie their violation of them, are truly and properly Rebels. For when Men by entering into Society and Civil Government, have excluded force, and introduced Laws for the preservation of Property Peace and Unity amongst themselves; those who set up force again in opposition to the Laws, do *Rebellare,* that is, bring back again the state of War, and are properly Rebels: Which they who are in Power, by the pretence they have to Authority, the temptation of force they have in their hands, and the Flattery of those about them being likeliest to do; the properest way to prevent the evil, is to shew them the danger and injustice of it, who are under the greatest temptation to run into it.

§227. In both the forementioned Cases, when either the Legislative is changed, or the Legislators act contrary to the end for which they were constituted; those who are guilty are guilty of Rebellion. For if any one by force takes away the establish'd Legislative of any Society, and the Laws by them made, pursuant to their trust, he thereby takes away the Umpirage which every one had consented to, for a peaceable decision of all their Controversies, and a bar to the state of War amongst them. They who remove, or change the Legislative, take away this decisive power, which no Body can have, but by the appointment and consent of the People; and so destroying the Authority which the People did, and no Body else can set up, and introducing a Power which the People hath not authoriz'd; actually introduce a state of War, which is that of Force without Authority: And thus by removing the Legislative establish'd by the Society, in whose decisions the People acquiesced and united, as to that of their own will; they unty the Knot, and expose the People a new to the state of War. And if those, who by force take away the Legislative, are Rebels, the Legislators themselves, as has been shewn, can be no less esteemed so; when they who were set up for the protection and preservation of the People, their Liberties and Properties shall by force invade and indeavour to take them away; and so they putting themselves into a state of War with those who made them the Protectors and Guardians of their Peace, are properly, and with the greatest aggravation, *Rebellantes* Rebels.

§228. But if they who say it lays a foundation for Rebellion, mean that it may occasion Civil Wars, or Intestine Broils, to tell the People they are absolved from Obedience, when illegal attempts are made upon their Liberties or Properties, and may oppose the unlawful violence of those who were their Magistrates when they invade their Properties contrary to the trust put in them; and that therefore this Doctrine is not to be allow'd, being so destructive to the Peace of the World. They may as well say upon the same ground, that honest Men may not oppose Robbers or Pirats, because this may occasion disorder or bloodshed. If any mischief come in such Cases, it is not to be charged upon him who defends his own right, but on him that invades his Neighbours. If the innocent honest Man must quietly quit all he has for Peace sake, to him who will lay violent hands upon it, I desire it may be consider'd, what a kind of Peace there will be in the World, which consists only in Violence and Rapine; and which is to be maintain'd only for the benefit of Robbers and Oppressors. Who would not think it an admirable Peace betwixt the Mighty and the Mean, when the Lamb, without resistance, yielded his Throat to be torn by the imperious Wolf? *Polyphemus's* Den gives us a perfect Pattern of such a Peace. Such a Government wherein *Ulysses* and his Companions had nothing to do, but quietly to suffer themselves to be devour'd. And no doubt, *Ulysses* who was a prudent Man, preach'd up Passive Obedience, and exhorted them to a quiet Submission, by representing to them of what concernment Peace was to Mankind; and by shewing the inconveniencies might happen, if they should offer to resist Polyphemus, who had now the power over them.

§229. The end of Government is the good of Mankind; and which is best for Mankind, that the People should be always expos'd to the boundless will of Tyranny, or that the Rulers should be sometimes liable to be oppos'd, when they grow exorbitant in the use of their Power, and imploy it for the destruction, and not the preservation of the Properties of their People?

§230. Nor let any one say, that mischief can arise from hence, as often as it shall please a busie head or turbulent spirit to desire the alteration of the Government. 'Tis true, such Men may stir whenever they please, but it will be only to their own just ruine and perdition. For till the mischief be grown general, and the ill designs of the Rulers become visible, or their attempts sensible to the greater part, the People, who are more disposed to suffer, than right themselves by Resistance, are not apt to stir. The examples of particular Injustice, or Oppression of here and there an unfortunate Man, moves them not. But if they universally have a perswasion grounded upon manifest evidence, that designs are carrying on against their Liberties, and the general course and tendency of things cannot but give them strong suspicions of the evil intention of their Governors, who is to be blamed for it? Who can help it, if they, who might avoid it, bring themselves into suspicion? Are the People to be blamed, if they have the sence of rational Creatures, and can think of things no otherwise than as they find and feel them? And is it not rather their fault who puts things in such a posture that they would not have them thought as they are? I grant, that the Pride, Ambition, and Turbulency of private Men have sometimes caused great Disorders in Commonwealths, and Factions have been fatal to States and Kingdoms. But whether the mischief hath oftner begun in the Peoples Wantonness, and a Desire to cast off the lawful Authority of their Rulers; or in the Rulers Insolence, and Endeavours to get, and exercise an Arbitrary Power over their People; whether Oppression, or Disobedience gave the first rise to the Disorder, I leave it to impartial History to determine. This I am sure, whoever, either Ruler or Subject, by force goes about to invade the Rights of either Prince or People, and lays the foundation for overturning the

Constitution and Frame of any Just Government; he is guilty of the greatest Crime, I think, a Man is capable of, being to answer for all those mischiefs of Blood, Rapine, and Desolation, which the breaking to pieces of Governments bring on a Countrey. And he who does it, is justly to be esteemed the common Enemy and Pest of Mankind; and is to be treated accordingly.

§240. Here, 'tis like, the common Question will be made, Who shall be Judge whether the Prince or Legislative act contrary to their Trust? This, perhaps, ill affected and factious Men may spread amongst the People, when the Prince only makes use of his due Prerogative. To this I reply; The People shall be Judge; for who shall be Judge whether his Trustee or Deputy acts well, and according to the Trust reposed in him, but he who deputes him, and must, by having deputed him have still a Power to discard him, when he fails in his Trust? If this be reasonable in particular Cases of private Men, why should it be otherwise in that of the greatest moment, where the Welfare of Millions is concerned, and also where the evil, if not prevented, is greater, and the Redress very difficult, dear, and dangerous?

§241. But farther, this Question, (Who shall be Judge?) cannot mean, that there is no Judge at all. For where there is no Judicature on Earth, to decide Controversies amongst Men, God in Heaven is Judge: He alone, 'tis true, is Judge of the Right. But every Man is Judge for himself, as in all other Cases, so in this, whether another hath put himself into a State of War with him, and whether he should appeal to the Supreme Judge, as *Jeptha* did.

§243. To conclude, The Power that every individual gave the Society, when he entered into it, can never revert to the Individuals again, as long as the Society lasts, but will always remain in the Community; because without this, there can be no Community, no Commonwealth, which is contrary to the original Agreement: So also when the Society hath placed the Legislative in any Assembly of Men, to continue in them and their Successors, with Direction and Authority for providing such Successors, the Legislative can never revert to the People whilst that Government lasts: Because having provided a Legislative with Power to continue for ever, they have given up their Political Power to the Legislative, and cannot resume it. But if they have set Limits to the Duration of their Legislative, and made this Supreme Power in any Person, or Assembly, only temporary: Or else when by the Miscarriages of those in Authority, it is forfeited; upon the Forfeiture of their Rulers, or at the Determination of the Time set, it reverts to the Society, and the People have a Right to act as Supreme, and continue the Legislative in themselves, or place in it a new Form, or new hands, as they think good.

XIII.

ALGERNON SIDNEY, *DISCOURSES CONCERNING GOVERNMENT,* 1698

The Discourses contain three chapters, covering ninety sections, with Chapter One often cited by the founding generation. What follows are excerpts from Chapter 1, section 5, which appeals to both nature and the Magna Carta as the foundation of liberty; and Chapter 2, section 24, which argues that popular government is less prone to sedition than monarchy. We have followed the version found in *Discourses Concerning Government*, printed and sold by the Booksellers of London and Westminster, 1698. Italics are in the original. Thomas G. West has made Sidney's *Discourses Concerning Government* available again in affordable form. See West's edition published by Liberty Classics, 1990. See also Kurland and Lerner (I: 77-82).

~

CHAPTER I
SECT. V
To depend upon the Will of a Man is Slavery.

THIS, as he thinks, is farther sweetened, by asserting, that he doth not inquire what the rights of a People are, but from whence; not considering, that whilst he denies they can proceed from the Laws of natural Liberty, or any other root than the Grace and Bounty of the Prince, he declares they can have none at all. For as Liberty solely consists in an independency upon the Will of another, and by the name of Slave we understand a man, who can neither dispose of his Person nor Goods, but enjoys all at the will of his Master; there is no such thing in nature as a Slave, if those men or Nations are not Slaves, who have no other title to what they enjoy, than the grace of the Prince, which he may revoke whensoever he pleaseth. But there is more than ordinary extravagance in his assertion, That *the greatest Liberty in the World is for a People to live under a Monarch,* when his whole Book is to prove, That this Monarch hath his right from God and Nature, is endowed with an unlimited Power of doing what he pleaseth, and can be restrained by no Law. If it be Liberty to live under such a Government, I desire to know what is Slavery. It has bin hitherto believed in the World, that the Assyrians, Medes, Arabs, Egyptians, Turks, and others like them, lived in Slavery, because their Princes were Masters of their Lives and Goods: Whereas the Grecians, Italians, Gauls, Germans, Spaniards, and Catthaginians, as long as they had any

Strength, Vertue or Courage amongst them, were esteemed free Nations, because they abhorred such a Subjection. They were, and would be governed only by Laws of their own making: *Potentiora erant Legum quam hominum Imperia.*[5] Even their Princes had the authority or credit of persuading, rather than the power of commanding. But all this was mistaken: These men were Slaves, and Asiaticks were Freemen. By the same rule the Venetians, Switsers, Grisons,[6] and Hollanders, are not free Nations: but Liberty in its perfection is enjoyed in *France,* and *Turky.* The intention of our Ancestors was, without doubt, to establish this amongst us by *Magna Charta,* and other preceding or subsequent Laws; but they ought to have added one clause, That the contents of them should be in force only so long as it should please the King. King *Alfred,* upon whose Laws *Magna Charta* was grounded, when he said the English Nation was as free as the internal thoughts of a Man, did only mean, that it should be so as long as it pleased their Master. This it seems was the end of our Law, and we who are born under it, and are descended from such as have so valiantly defended their rights against the encroachments of Kings, have followed after vain shadows, and without the expence of Sweat, Treasure, or Blood, might have secured their beloved Liberty, by casting all into the King's hands.

We owe the discovery of these Secrets to our Author, who after having so gravely declared them, thinks no offence ought to be taken at the freedom he assumes of examining things relating to the Liberty of Mankind, because he hath the right which is common to all: But he ought to have considered, that in asserting that right to himself, he allows it to all Mankind. And as the temporal good of all men consists in the preservation of it, he declares himself to be a mortal Enemy to those who endeavour to destroy it. If he were alive, this would deserve to be answered with Stones rather than Words. He that oppugns[7] the publick Liberty, overthrows his own, and is guilty of the most brutish of all Follies, whilst he arrogates to himself that which he denies to all men.

I cannot but commend his Modesty and Care *not to detract from the worth of learned men*; but it seems they were all subject to error, except himself, who is rendered infallible through Pride, Ignorance, and Impudence. But if *Hooker* and *Aristotle* were wrong in their fundamentals concerning natural Liberty, how could they be in the right

[5] "The rule of laws was more powerful than that of men." Livy, *History of Rome*, bk. 2, ch. 1. See West (1990), 17.

[6] A Grison is a canton in East Switzerland.

[7] To oppugn is to oppose.

when they built upon it? Or if they did mistake, how can they deserve to be cited? or rather, why is such care taken to pervert their sense? It seems our Author is by their errors brought to the knowledge of the Truth. *Men have heard of a Dwarf standing upon the Shoulders of a Giant, who saw farther than the Giant;* but now that the Dwarf standing on the ground sees that which the Giant did overlook, we must learn from him. If there be sense in this, the Giant must be blind, or have such eyes only as are of no use to him. He minded only the things that were far from him: These great and learned men mistook the very principle and foundation of all their Doctrine. If we will believe our Author, this misfortune befel them because they too much trusted to the Schoolmen. He names *Aristotle*, and I presume intends to comprehend *Plato, Plutarch, Thucydides, Xenophon, Polybius*, and all the antient Grecians, Italians, and others, who asserted the natural freedom of Mankind, only in imitation of the Schoolmen, to advance the power of the Pope; and would have compassed their design, if *Filmer* and his Associates had not opposed them. These men had taught us to make the unnatural distinction between *Royalist* and *Patriot*, and kept us from seeing, *That the relation between King and People is so great, that their well being is reciprocal.* If this be true, how came *Tarquin* to think it good for him to continue King at *Rome*, when the People would turn him out? or the People to think it good for them to turn him out, when he desired to continue in? Why did the Syracusians destroy the Tyranny of *Dionysius*, which he was not willing to leave, till he was pulled out by the heels? How could *Nero* think of burning *Rome*? Or why did *Caligula* wish the People had but one Neck, that he might strike it off at one blow, if their Welfare was thus reciprocal? 'Tis not enough to say, These were wicked or mad men; for other Princes may be so also, and there may be the same reason of differing from them. For if the proposition be not universally true, 'tis not to be received as true in relation to any, till it be particularly proved; and then 'tis not to be imputed to the quality of Prince, but to the personal vertue of the Man.

I do not find any great matters in the passages taken out of *Bellarmin*,[8] which our Author says, comprehend the strength of all that ever he had heard, read, or seen produced for the natural Liberty of the Subject: but he not mentioning where they are to be found, I do not think my self obliged to examin all his Works, to see whether they are rightly cited or not; however there is certainly nothing new in them: We see the same, as to the substance, in those who wrote many Ages before him, as well as in many that have lived since his time, who

---

[8]Bellamin. This is a reference to Cardinal Roberto Bellarmino a Jesuit theologian, cardinal, and Vatican librarian.

neither minded him, nor what he had written. I dare not take upon me to give an account of his Works, having read few of them; but as he seems to have laid the foundation of his Discourses in such common Notions as were assented to by all Mankind, those who follow the same method have no more regard to Jesuitism and Popery, tho he was a Jesuit and a Cardinal, than they who agree with *Faber* and other Jesuits in the principles of Geometry which no sober man did ever deny.

CHAPTER II
SECTION XXIV

Popular Governments are less Subject to Civil Disorders than Monarchies; manage them more ably, and more easily recover out of them.

It may seem strange to some that I mention Seditions, Tumults, and Wars, upon just occasions; but I can find no reason to retract the term. God intending that men should live justly with one another, dos certainly intend that he or they who do no wrong, should suffer none; and the Law that forbids Injuries, were of no use, if no Penalty might be inflicted on those that will not obey it. If Injustice therefore be evil, and Injuries forbidden, they are also to be punished; and the Law instituted for their prevention, must necessarily intend the avenging of such as cannot be prevented. The work of the Magistracy is to execute this Law; the Sword of Justice is put into their hands to restrain the fury of those within the Society who will not be a Law to themselves, and the Sword of War to protect the people against the violence of Foreigners. This is without exception, and would be in vain if it were not. But the Magistrate who is to protect the people from Injury, may, and is often known not to have done it: he sometimes renders his office useless by neglecting to do Justice; sometimes mischievous by overthrowing it. This strikes at the root of God's general Ordinance, That there should be Laws; and the particular Ordinances of all societies that appoint such as seem best to them. The Magistrate therefore is comprehended under both, and subject to both, as well as private men.

The ways of preventing or punishing Injuries, are Judicial or Extrajudicial. Judicial proceedings are of force against those who submit or may be brought to trial, but are of no effect against those who resist, and are of such power that they cannot be constrained. It were absurd to cite a man to appear before a Tribunal who can aw the Judges, or has Armies to defend him; and impious to think that he who has added treachery to his other Crimes, and usurped[9] a Power above

---

[9] The original text has "andu surped."

the Law, should be protected by the enormity of his wickedness. Legal proceedings therefore are to be used when the Delinquent submits to the Law; and all are just, when he will not be kept in order by the legal.

The word Sedition is generally applied to all numerous Assemblies, without or against the Authority of the magistrate, or of those who assume that Power. *Athaliah* and *Jezebel* were more ready to cry out Treason than *David*; and examples of that sort are so frequent, that I need not alleg them.

Tumult is from the disorderly manner of those Assemblies, where things can seldom be done regularly; and War is that *decertatio per vim*, or trial by force, to which men come when other ways are ineffectual.

If the Laws of God and Men are therefore of no effect, when the Magistracy is left at liberty to break them; and if the Lusts of those who are too strong for the Tribunals of Justice, cannot be otherwise restrained than by Sedition, Tumults, and War, those Seditions, Tumults, and Wars, are justified by the Laws of God and man.

I will not take upon me to enumerate all the cases in which this may be done, but content my self with three, which have most frequently given occasion for proceedings of this kind.

The first is, When one or more men take upon them the Power and Name of a Magistracy, to which they are not justly called.

The second, When one or more being justly called, continue in their Magistracy longer than the Laws by which they are called do prescribe.

And the third, When he or they who are rightly called, do assume a Power, tho within the time prescribed, that the Law dos not give; or turn that which the Law dos give, to an end different and contrary to that which is intended by it.

For the first, *Filmer* forbids us to examine Titles: he tells us, we must submit to the Power, whether acquired by Usurpation or otherwise; not observing the mischievous Absurdity of rewarding the most detestable Villainies with the highest Honours, and rendring the veneration due to the supreme Magistrate, as Father of the People, to one who has no other advantage above his Brethren, than what he has gained by injuriously dispossessing or murdering him that was so. *Hobbs* fearing the advantages that may be taken from such desperate nonsense, or not thinking it necessary to his end to carry the matter so far, has no regard at all to him who comes in without Title or Consent; and, denying him to be either King or Tyrant, gives him no other name than "*Hostis et Latro;*[10] "and allows all things to be lawful against him, that may be done to a public enemy or pyrate : which is as much as to say, any man may destroy him how he can. Whatever he may be guilty

[10]Enemy and pirate. Translated by West (1990), 221.

of in other respects, he dos in this follow the voice of Mankind, and the dictates of common sense: For no man can make himself a Magistrate for himself; and no man can have the right of a magistrate, who is not a Magistrate. If he be justly accounted an Enemy to all, who injures all; he above all must be the public Enemy of a Nation, who, by usurping a power over them, dos the greatest and most publick injury that a People can suffer: For which reason, by an established Law among the most virtuous Nations, every man might kill a Tyrant; and no Names are recorded in History with more honour, than of those who did it.

These are by other authors called *tyranni sine titulo.*[11] and that name is given to all those who obtain the supreme Power by illegal and unjust means. The Laws which they overthrow can give them no protection; and every man is a souldier against him who is a publick Enemy.

The same rule holds tho they are more in number, as the *Magi* who usurped the Dominion of *Persia* after the death of *Cambyses*; the thirty Tyrants at *Athens* overthrown by *Thrasibulus*; those of *Thebes* slain by *Pelopidas;* the *Decemviri* of *Rome*, and others: For tho the multitude of Offenders may sometimes procure impunity, yet that act which is wicked in one, must be so in ten or twenty; and whatever is lawful against one Usurper is so against them all.

2. If those who were rightly created continue beyond the time limited by the Law, 'tis the same thing. That which is expir'd, is as if it had never bin. He that was created Consul for a year, or Dictator for six months, was after that a private man; and if he had continued in the exercise of his Magistracy, had bin subject to the same punishment as if he had usurped it at the first. This was known to *Epaminondas*; who finding that his Enterprize against *Sparta* could not be accomplished within the time for which he was made *Bœotarches*, rather chose to trust his Countrymen with his life than to desist; and was saved merely through an admiration of his Virtue, assurance of his good Intentions, and the glory of the Action.

The *Roman Decemviri*, tho duly elected, were proceeded against as private men usurping the Magistracy, when they continued beyond their time. Other Magistrates had ceased; there was none that could regularly call the Senate or People to an Assembly: but when their ambition was manifest, and the people exasperated by the death of *Virginia*, they laid aside all ceremonies. The Senate and People met, and exercising their Authority in the same manner as if they had bin regularly called by the Magistrate appointed to that end, they abrogated the Power of the *Decemviri*, proceeded against them as enemies and tyrants, and by that means preserved themselves from utter ruin.

---

[11]Tryants without title. Translated by West (1990), 221.

3. The same course is justly used against a legal Magistrate, who takes upon him (tho within the time prescribed by the Law) to exercise a Power which the Law does not give; for in that respect he is a private man, *Quia*, as *Grotius* says, *eatenus non habet imperium;* [12] and may be restrain'd as well as any other, because he is not set up to do what he lists, but what the Law appoints for the good of the People; and as he has no other Power than what the Law allows, so the same Law limits and directs the exercise of that which he has. This Right naturally belonging to nations, is no way impair'd by the name of Supreme given to their Magistrates; for it signifies no more, than that they do act soveraignly in the matters committed to their charge. Thus are the Parliaments of *France* called *Cours Souveraines;* for they judg of Life and Death, determine Controversies concerning Estates; and there is no appeal from their Decrees: but no man ever thought, that it was therefore lawful for them to do what they pleased; or that they might not be opposed, if they should attempt to do that which they ought not. And tho the Roman Dictators and Consuls were supreme Magistrates, they were subject to the People, and might be punished as well as others if they transgressed the Law. *Thuanus* carries the word so far, that when *Barlotta, Giuistiniano,* and others who were but Colonels, were sent as Commanders in chief of three or four thousand men upon an Enterprize, he always says, *Summum Imperium ei delatum.*[13] *Grotius* explains this point, by distinguishing those who have the *Summum Imperium summo modo,* from those who have it *modo non summo.* [14] I know not where to find an Example of this Soveraign Power, enjoy'd without restriction, under a better title than Occupation; which relates not to our purpose, who seek only that which is legal and just. Therefore, laying aside that point for the present, we may follow *Grotius* in examining the Right of those who are certainly limited: *Ubi partem Imperii habet Rex, partem Senatus sive Populus;* in which case he says, *Regi in partem non suam involanti, vis justa opponi potest,* in as much as they who have a part, cannot but have a right of defending that part. *Quia data facultate, datur jus facultatem tuendi,* without which it could be of no effect.[15]

12"Since he does not so far have command." Grotius, *De jure*, bk. I, ch. 4, sec. 13. Translated by West (1990), 222.

13"Highest command is conferred on him." De Thou, *History of His Time*. Translated by West (1990), 222.

14"The supreme power in the supreme manner"..."not in the supreme manner." Grotius, De jure, bk. I, ch. 3, sec. 14. Translated by West (1990), 222.

15"When the king holds part of the supreme power, and the senate or the people holds part"..."just force can be used against a king who encroaches

The particular limits of the Rights belonging to each can only be judged by the precise Letter, or general Intention of the Law. The Dukes of *Venice* have certainly a part in the Government, and could not be called Magistrate if they had not. They are said to be supreme; all Laws and publick Acts bear their Names. The Ambassador of that State speaking to the Pope *Paul* the 5th, denied that he acknowledged any other Superior than God. Buy they are so well known to be under the Power of the Law, that divers of them have bin put to death for transgressing it; and a marble Gallows is seen at the foot of the stairs in *St. Mark's* Palace, upon which some of them, and no others, have bin executed. But if they may be duly opposed, when they commit undue acts, no man of judgment will deny, that if one of them by an outrageous Violence should endeavour to overthrow the Law, he might by violence be suppressed and chastised.

Again, some Magistrates are entrusted with a power of providing Ships, Arms, Ammunition, and Victuals for War, raising and disciplining Soldiers, appointing Officers to command in Forts and Garisons, and making Leagues with Foreign Princes and States. But if one of these should imbezle, sell, or give to an Enemy those Ships, Arms, Ammunitions, or Provisions; betray the Forts; employ only or principally, such men as will serve him in those wicked Actions, and, contrary to the trust reposed in him, make such Leagues with Foreigners, as tend to the advancement of his personal Interests, and to the detriment of the Publick, he abrogates his own Magistracy; and the Right he had, perishes (as the Lawyers say) *frustratione finis*.[16] He cannot be protected by the Law which he has overthrown, nor obtain impunity for his Crimes from the Authority that was conferred upon him, only that he might do good with it. He was *singulis major* on account of the excellence of his Office; but *universis minor,*[17] from the nature and end of his institution. The surest way of extinguishing his Prerogative, was by turning it to the hurt of those who gave it. When matters are brought to this posture, the Author of the mischief, or the Nation must perish. A Flock cannot subsist under a Shepherd that seeks its ruin, nor a People under an unfaithful Magistrate. Honour and Riches are justly heaped upon the heads of those who rightly perform their duty, because the difficulty as well as the excellency of the work is great. It requires Courage, Experience, Industry, Fidelity, and Wisdom. The Good Shepherd, says our Saviour, lays down his life for

---

upon the part which is not his own"..."since when power is given the right of protecting that power is given." Grot. de jur. bel. et pac. l. 2. See (1990), 223.

[16]Because the end (of his office) is frustrated. See West (1990), 223.

[17]Greater than the individual (citizens)...less than the whole people. See West (1990), 223.

his Sheep: The Hireling, who flies in time of danger, is represented under an ill character; but he that sets himself to destroy his Flock, is a Wolf. His Authority is incompatible with their subsistence; and whoever disapproves Tumults, Seditions, or War, by which he may be removed from it, if gentler means are ineffectual, subverts the Foundation of all Law, exalts the fury of one man to the destruction of a Nation, and giving an irresistible Power to the most abominable Iniquity, exposes all that are good to be destroy'd, and Virtue to be utterly extinguished.

* * * *

Men who delight in cavils may ask, Who shall be the Judg of these occasions? and whether I intend to give to the People the decision of their own Cause? To which I answer, that when the Contest is between the Magistrate and the People, the party to which the determination is referred, must be the Judg of his own case; and the question is only, Whether the Magistrate should depend upon the Judgment of the People, or the People on that of the Magistrate; and which is most to be suspected of injustice: That is, whether the people of *Rome* should judg *Tarquin*, or *Tarquin* judg the people? He that knew all good men abhorred him for the murder of his Wife, Brother, Father-in-law, and the best of the Senate, would certainly strike off the heads of the most eminent remaining poppies; and having incurr'd the general hatred of the people by the wickedness of his Government, he feared revenge; and endeavouring to destroy those he feared (that is the City) he might easily have accomplish'd his work, if the judgment had been referred to him. If the people judg *Tarquin*, 'tis hard to imagine how they should be brought to give an unjust Sentence: They loved their former King, and hated him only for his Villanies: They did not fancy, but know his cruelty. When the best were slain, no man that any way resembled them could think himself secure. *Brutus* did not pretend to be a Fool, till by the murder of his Brother, he found how dangerous a thing it was to be thought wise. If the people, as our Author says, be always lewd, foolish, mad, wicked, and desirous to put the Power into the hands of such men as are most like to themselves, he and his Sons were such men as they sought, and he was sure to find favourable Judges: If virtuous and good, no injustice was to be feared from them, and he could have no other reason to decline their judgment, than what was suggested by his own wickedness. *Caligula, Nero, Domitian,* and the like had probably the same considerations: But no man of common sense ever thought that the Senate and People of *Rome* did not better deserve to judg, whether such Monsters should reign over the best part of mankind to their destruction, than they to determine whether their Crimes should be punished or not.

If I mention some of these known Cases, every man's experience will suggest others of the like nature; and whosoever condemns all Seditions, Tumults, and Wars raised against such princes, must say, that none are wicked, or seek the ruin of their people, which is absurd; for *Caligula* wish'd the People had but one Neck, that he might cut it off at a blow: *Nero* set the City on fire; and we have known such as have bin worse than either of them: They must either be suffer'd to continue in the free exercise of their rage, that is, to do all the mischief they design; or must be restrain'd by a legal, judicial, or extrajudicial way; and they who disallow the extrajudicial, do as little like the judicial. They will not hear of bringing a supreme Magistrate before a Tribunal, when it may be done. *They will,* says our Author, *depose their kings.* Why should they not be deposed, if they become Enemies to their people, and set up an interest in their own persons inconsistent with publick good, for the promoting of which they were erected? If they were created by the publick consent, for the publick good, shall they not be removed when they prove to be of publick damage? If they set up themselves, may they not be thrown down? Shall it be lawful for them to usurp a power over the liberty of others, and shall it not be lawful for an injur'd People to resume their own? If injustice exalt itself, must it be for ever established? Shall great persons be rendred sacred by rapine, perjury, and murder? Shall the crimes, for which privat men do justly suffer the most grievous punishments, exempt them from all, who commit them in the highest excess, with most power, and most to the prejudice of mankind? Shall the Laws that solely aim at the prevention of Crimes be made to patronize them, and become snares to the innocent, whom they ought to protect? Has every man given up into the common store his right of avenging the Injuries he may receive, that the publick Power which ought to protect or avenge him, should be turned to the destruction of himself, his Posterity, and the society into which they enter, without any possibility of redress? Shall the Ordinance of God be rendred of no effect; or the Powers he hath appointed to be set up for the distribution of Justice, be made subservient to the lusts of one or a few men, and by impunity encourage them to commit all manner of crimes? Is the corruption of man's Nature so little known, that such as have common sense should expect Justice from those, who fear no punishment if they do Injustice; or that the modesty, integrity, and innocence, which is seldom found in one man, tho never so cautiously chosen, should be constantly found in all those who by any means attain to Greatness, and continue for ever in their Successors; or that there can be any security under their Government, if they have them not? Surely if this were the condition of men living under Government, Forests would be more safe than Cities; and 'twere better for every man to stand in his own defence, than to enter into Societies. He that lives alone might encounter such as should assault him upon equal terms, and stand or fall according to the measure of his courage and strength; but no valour can defend him, if the malice of his Enemy be upheld by a publick Power. There must therefore be a right of proceeding judicially or extrajudicially against all persons who transgress the Laws; or else those Laws, and the Societies that should subsist by them, cannot stand; and the ends for which Governments are constituted, together with the Governments themselves, must be overthrown. Extrajudicial proceedings, by Sedition, Tumult, or War, must take place, when the persons concern'd are of such power, that they cannot be brought under the Judicial. They who deny this, deny all help against an usurping Tyrant, or the perfidiousness of a lawfully created Magistrate, who adds the crimes of Ingratitude and Treachery to Usurpation. These of all men are the most dangerous Enemies to supreme Magistrates:[18] for as no man desires indemnity for such Crimes as are never committed, he that would exempt all from punishment, supposes they will be guilty of the worst; and by concluding, that the People will depose them if they have the power, acknowledg that they pursue an Interest annexed to their Persons, contrary to that of their People, which they would not bear if they could deliver themselves from it. This, shewing all those Governments to be tyrannical, lays such a burden upon those who administer them, as must necessarily weigh them down to destruction.

If it be said, that the word Sedition implies that which is evil; I answer, that it ought not then to be applied to those who seek nothing but that which is just; and tho the ways of delivering an oppressed People from the violence of a wicked Magistrate, who having armed a Crew of lewd Villains, and fatted them with the Blood and Confiscations of such as were most ready to oppose him, be extraordinary, the inward righteousness of the Act does fully justify the Authors. He that has virtue and power to save a People, can never want a right of doing it. *Valerius Asiaticus* had no hand in the death of *Caligula*; but when the furious Guards began tumultuously to enquire who had kill'd him, he appeased them with wishing he had bin the man. No wise man ever asked by what authority *Thrasibulus, Harmodius, Aristogiton, Pelopidas, Epaminondas, Dion, Timoleon, Lucius Brutus, Publicola, Horatius, Valerius, Marcus Brutus, C. Cassius,* and the like, delivered their Countries from Tyrants. Their Actions carried in themselves their own justification, and their Virtues will never be

---

[18]The original spelling is "Migistrates."

forgotten, whilst the names of *Greece* and *Rome* are remembered in the world.

If this be not enough to declare the Justice inherent in, and the Glory that ought to accompany these Works, the examples of *Moses, Aaron, Othniel, Ehud, Barac, Gideon, Samuel, Jephtha, David, Jehu, Jehoiada, the Maccabees,* and other holy men raised up by God for the deliverance of his People from their Oppressors, decide the Question. They are perpetually renowned for having led the People by extraordinary ways (which such as our Author express under the names of Sedition, Tumult, and War) to recover their Liberties, and avenge the injuries received from foreign or domestick Tyrants. The work of the Apostles was not in their time to set up or pull down any Civil State; but they so behaved themselves in relation to all the Powers of the Earth, that they gained the name of pestilent, seditious Fellows, Disturbers of the People; and left it as an inheritance to those, who in succeeding Ages, by following their steps, should deserve to be called their Successors; whereby they were exposed to the hatred of corrupt Magistrates, and brought under the necessity of perishing by them, or defending themselves against them: and he that denies them that right, dos at once condemn the most glorious Actions of the wisest, best, and holiest men that have bin in the world, together with the Laws of God and Man, upon which they were founded.

Nevertheless, there is a sort of Sedition, Tumult, and War, proceeding from Malice, which is always detestable, aiming only at the satisfaction of private Lust, without regard to the publick Good. This cannot happen in a Popular Government, unless it be amongst the Rabble; or when the Body of the People is so corrupted, that it cannot stand; but is most frequent in, and natural to absolute Monarchies.

XIV.

CATO'S *LETTERS*, 22 JULY 1721

We have reproduced Letter 38 in its entirety using the spelling and grammar found in the 1754 edition of Cato's Letters published in London for W. Wilkins, T. Woodward, J. Waltroe, and J. Peele (I: 302-312). The letters printed in this edition are unnumbered, untitled, and undated. We have followed the contemporary custom and provided a number, title, and date. For a two volume collection of the complete four-volume series of Cato's one hundred and thirty eight letters, see Ronald Hamowy's edition, *Cato's Letters: Or Essays on Liberty, Civil and Religious, And other Important Subjects,* Indianapolis, Liberty Fund, 1995 (I: 266-272). Hamowy has provided helpful annotations and a valuable introduction on the lives of Trenchard and Gordon.

Kurland and Lerner (I: 46-47) rely on David L. Jacobson's edition, *Cato's Letters,* Indianapolis, Bobbs-Merrill, 1965.

~

The World has, from Time to Time, been led into such a long Maze of Mistakes, by those who gained by deceiving, that whoever would instruct Mankind, must begin with removeing their Errors; and if they were every where honestly apprized of Truth, and restored to their Senses, there would not remain one Nation of Bigots or Slaves under the Sun: A Happiness always to be wished, but never expected.

In most Parts of the Earth, there is neither Light nor Liberty; and even in the best Parts of it they are but little encouraged, and coldly maintained, there being, in all Places, many engaged through Interest in a perpetual Conspiracy against them. They are the two greatest Civil Blessings, inseparable in their Interests, and the mutual Support of each other; and whoever would destroy one of them, must destroy both: Hence it is, that we everywhere find Tyranny and Imposture, Ignorance and Slavery joined together, and Oppressors and Deceivers mutually aiding and paying constant Court to each other. Wherever Truth is dangerous, Liberty is precarious.

Of all the Sciences that I know in the World, that of Government concerns us most, and is the easiest to be known, and yet is the least understood. Most of those who manage it would make the lower World believe that there is I know not what Difficulty and Mystery in it, far above vulgar Understandings; which Proceedings of theirs is direct Craft and Imposture: Every Ploughman knows a good Government from a bad one, from the Effects of it; he knows whether the Fruits of his Labour be his own, and whether he enjoy them in Peace and Security: And if he do not know the Principles of Government, it is for want of Thinking and Enquiry, for they lie open to common Sense; but People are generally taught not to think of them at all, or to think wrong of them.

What is Government, but a Trust committed by All, or the Most, to One or a Few, who are to attend upon the affairs of All, that every one may, with the more Security, attend upon his own? A great and honourable Trust, but too seldom honourably executed; those who possess it having it often more at Heart to encrease their Power than to make it useful, and to be terrible rather than beneficent. It is therefore a Trust, which ought to be bounded with many and strong Restraints, because Power renders Men wanton, insolent to others, and fond of themselves. Every Violation therefore of this Trust, where such Violation is considerable, ought to meet with proportionable Punishment; and the smallest Violation of it ought to meet with some, because Indulgence to the least Faults of Magistrates, may be Cruelty to a whole People.

Honesty, Diligence, and plain Sense, are the only Talents necessary for the executing of this trust; and the public Good is its only End: As to Refinements and Finesses, they are often only the false Appearances of Wisdom and Parts, and oftener tricks to hide Guilt and Emptiness; and they are generally mean and dishonest; they are the Arts of Jobbers in Politicks, who playing their own Game under the public Cover, subsist upon poor Shifts and Expedients; starv'd Politicians, who live from Hand to Mouth, from Day to Day, and following the little Views of Ambition, Avarice, and Revenge, and the like personal Passions, are ashamed to avow them, yet want Souls great enough to forsake them; small wicked Statesmen, who make a private Market of the Publick, and deceive it in order to sell it.

These are the poor Parts which great and good Governors scorn to play, and cannot play; their Designs, like their Stations, being purely publick, are open and undisguised. They do not consider their People as their Prey, nor lie in Ambush for their Subjects; nor dread, and treat and surprize them like Enemies, as all ill Magistrates do; who are not Governors but Jaylors and Spunges, who chain them and squeeze them, and yet take it very ill if they do but murmur; which is yet much less than a People so abused ought to do. There have been Times and Countries, when publick Enemies have been the same individual Men. What a melancholy Reflection is this, that the most terrible and mischievous Foes to a Nation should be its own Magistrates! And yet in every enslaved Country, which is almost every Country, this is their woful Case.

Honesty and Plainness go always together, and the Makers and Multipliers of Mysteries, in the political Way, are shrewdly to be suspected of dark designs. *Cincinnatus* was taken from the plough to save and defend the *Roman* state; an Office which he executed honestly and successfully, without the Grimace and Gains of a Statesman. Nor did he afterwards continue obstinately at the Head of Affairs, to form a Party, raise a Fortune, and settle himself in Power: As he came into it with universal Consent, he resigned it with universal Applause.

It seems that Government was not in those days become a Trade, at least not a gainful Trade—Honest *Cincinnatus* was but a Farmer: And happy had it been for the *Romans*, if, when they were enslaved, they could have taken the Administration out of the hands of the Emperors, and their refined Politicians, and committed it to such farmers, or any farmers. It is certain, that many of their Imperial Governors acted more ridicuously than a Board of Ploughmen would have done, and more barbarously than a Club of Butchers could have done.

But some have said, *It is not the Business of private Men to meddle with Government.* A bold, false, and dishonest Saying; and whoever says it, either knows not what he says, or care not, or slavishly speaks the Sense of others. It is a Cant now almost forgot in *England*, and which never prevailed but when Liberty and the Constitution were attacked, and never can prevail but upon the like Occasion.

It is a Vexation to be obliged to answer Nonsense, and confute absurdities: but since it is and has been the great design of this Paper [The *London Journal*] to maintain and explain the glorious Principles of liberty, and to expose the Arts of those who would darken or destroy them; I shall here particularly shew the Wickedness and Stupidity of the above Saying; which is fit to come from no Mouth but that of a Tyrant or a Slave, and can never be heard by any Man of and honest and free Soul, without horror and Indignation: It is, in short, a Saying, which ought to render the Man who utters it for ever incapable of Place or Credit in a free country, as it shews the malignity of his Heart, and the Baseness of his Nature, and as it is the pronouncing of a Doom upon our constitution.—A Crime, or rather a Complication of Crimes, for which a lasting Infamy ought to be but Part of the Punishment.

But to the Falsehood of the Thing: Publick Truths ought never to be kept secrets; and they who do it, are guilt of Solecism and a Contradiction: Every Man ought to know what it concerns all to know. Now, nothing upon Earth is of a more Universal Nature than Government; and every private Man upon Earth has a concern in it, because in it is concerned, and nearly and immediately concerned, his Virtue, his Property, and the security of his Person: And where all these are best preserved and advanced, the Government is best administered; and where they are not, the Government is impotent, wicked, or unfortunate; and where the Government is so; the People will be so, there being always and every where a certain Sympathy and Analogy between the Nature of the Government and the Nature of the People. This holds true in every Instance. Public men are the Patterns of private; and the Virtues and Vices of the Government become quickly the Virtues and Vices of the Governed.

Regis ad exemplum totus componitur orbis.[19]

Nor is it Example alone that does it. Ill Governments, subsisting by Vice and Rapine, are jealous of private Virtue, and Enemies of private Property. *Opes pro crimine, & ob virtutes certissimum exitium.*[20]

19"The world arranges itself after its ruler's pattern." Translated by Hamowy (1995), 269.

20"Wealth is tantamount to committing a crime and virtue brought certain destruction." Translated by Hamowy (1995), 270.

They must be wicked and mischievous to be what they are, nor are they secure as long as any Thing good or valuable is secure. Hence it is, that to drain worry, and debauch their Subjects, are the steady Maxims of their Politicks, and their favourite Arts of Reigning. In this wretched Situation, the People, to be safe, must be poor and lewd: There will be little Industry, where Property is precarious; small Honesty where Virtue is dangerous.

Profuseness or Frugality, and the like Virtues or Vices, which affect the Publick, will be practised in the City, if they are in the Court; and in the Country if they are in the City. Even *Nero* (that Royal Monster in Man's Shape) was adored by the common herd at *Rome*, as much as he was flatter'd by the Great; and both the Little and the Great admir'd, or pretended to admire his Manners, and many to imitate them. *Tacitus* tells us that those sort of People long lamented him, and rejoiced in the Choice of a Successor that resembled him, the profligate *Otho*.

Good Government does, on the contrary, produce great Virtue, much Happiness, and many People. *Greece* and *Italy*, while they continued free, were each of them, for the Number of Inhabitants, like one continued City; and for Vertue, knowledge, and great Men, they were the Standards of the World; and the Age and Country that could come nearest to them, has ever since been reckoned the happiest. Their Government, their Free Government was the root of all these Advantages, and all this Felicity and Renown; and in these great and fortunate States, the People were the Principals in the Government; and Laws were made by their Judgment and Authority, and by their Voice and Commands were Magistrates created and condemned. The city of *Rome* could conquer the World; nor could then great *Persian* monarch, the greatest then upon the Earth stand before one Greek city.

But what are *Greece* and *Italy* now? *Rome* has in it a Herd of pamper'd monks, and a few starving Lay Inhabitants; the *Campania* of *Rome*, the finest spot of Earth in *Europe*, is a Desert,. And for the modern *Greeks*, they are a few abject contemptible Slaves, kept under Ignorance, Chains, and Vileness, by the *Turkish* Monarch, who keeps a great Part of the Globe intensly miserable, that he may seem Great without being so.

Such is the Difference between one Government and another, and of such important Concernment is the Nature and Administration of Government to a People. And to say the private Men have nothing to do with Government, is to say that private Men have nothing to do with their own Happiness and Misery.

What is the Publick, but the collective Body of private Men, as every private Man is a Member of the Publick? And as the Whole ought to be concerned for the Preservation of every private Individual, it is the Duty of every Individual to be concern'd for the Whole, in which himself is included.

One Man, or a few Men, have often pretended the Publick, and meant themselves, and consulted their own personal Interest, in Instances essential to its Well-being; but the whole People, by consulting their own Interest, consult the Publick, and act for the Publick by acting for themselves; and this is particularly the Spirit of our constitution, in which the whole Nation is represented; and our Records afford Instances, where the House of Commons have declin'd entering upon a Question of Importance, till they had gone into the Country, and consulted their Principals, the People: So far were they from thinking that private Men had no Right to meddle with Government. In Truth, our whole worldly Happiness and Misery (abating for Accidents and Diseases) are owing to the Order or Mismanagement of Government; and he who says, private Men have no Concern with Government, does wisely and modestly tell us, that Men have no Concern in that which concerns them most; it is saying that People ought not to concern themselves whether they be naked or clothed, fed or starved, are deceived or instructed, and whether they be protected or destroyed: What Nonsense and Servitude in a free and wise Nation!

For myself, who have thought pretty much of these Matters, I am of Opinion, that a whole Nation are like to be as much attached to themselves, as one Man or a few Men are like to be, who may by many Means be detached from the Interest of a Nation. It is certain that one Man, and several Men, may be bribed into an Interest opposite to that of the Publick; but it is as certain that a whole Country can never find an Equivalent for itself, and consequently a whole Country can never be bribed. It is the eternal Interest of every Nation, that their Government should be good; but they who direct it frequently reason a contrary Way, and find their own Account in Plunder and Oppression; and while the publick Voice is pretended to be declared, by one or a few, for vile and private Ends, the Publick know nothing of what is done, till they feel the terrible Effects of it.

By the Bill of Rights, and the act of Settlement, at the *Revolution*, a Right is asserted to the People of applying to the King and to the Parliament by Petition and Address, for a Redress of publick Grievances and Mismanagements, when such there are, of which They are left to judge: And the Difference between free and enslaved Countries lies principally here, that in the former, their Magistrates must consult the Voice and Interest of the People; but in the latter, the private Will, Interest, and Pleasure of the Governors, are the sole End and Motives of their Administration.

Such is the Difference between *England* and *Turkey*; which Difference, they who say that private Men have no Right to concern themselves with Government, would absolutely destroy; they would convert Magistrates into Bashaws, and introduce Popery into Politicks. The late *Revolution* stands upon the very opposite Maxim; and that any Man dares to contradict it since the *Revolution*, would be amazing, did we not know that there are, in every Country, Hirelings who would betray it for a Sop.

XV.

MONTESQUIEU, *SPIRIT OF THE LAWS*, 1752

Montesquieu's *The Spirit of the Laws* was published in 1748; it went through over twenty editions prior to his death in 1755. We have reproduced those parts of the 1752 Thomas Nugent translation that represent what we shall call the "Framers's Montesquieu." We have followed the spelling and punctuation found in the second corrected and "considerably improved" edition. The footnotes are in the original. The essential arguments to which the framers referred can be found in Book III, Chapters 1-3, where the principle of democracy is identified as virtue; in Book VIII, Chapter 16, where Montesquieu warns that virtue needs the protection of "a small territory;" in Book IX, Chapter 1, where the disadvantage of being "a petty republic" is overcome by associating in an extended confederation of small republics; and in Book XI, Chapters 1-6, where Montesquieu articulates the need for a separation of the powers of government in order to secure the liberties of the citizen. See also Montesquieu, *Spirit of the Laws*, New York, Hafner Publishing Company, 1949 for a modern version of Nugent's translation with an introduction by Franz Neuman. See also Kurland and Lerner (I: 246, 624, 659).

~

BOOK III
Of the Principles of the three kinds of Government
CHAP. I
Difference between the Nature and Principle of Government.

After having examined the laws relative to the nature of each government, we must investigate those that relate to its principle.

There is this difference[21] between the nature and principle of government, that its nature is that by which it is constituted, and its

---

21This is a very important distinction, from whence I shall draw a great many consequences; for it is the key of an infinite number of laws.

principle that by which it is made to act. One is its particular structure, and the other the human passions which set it in motion.

Now laws ought to be no less relative to the principle than to the nature of each government. We must therefore inquire into this principle, which shall be the subject of this third book.

CHAP. II.

Of the Principle of different Governments.

I have already observed that it is the nature of a republican government, that either the collective body of the people, or particular families should be possessed of the sovereign power: of a monarchy, that the prince should have this sovereign power, but in the execution of it should be directed by established laws: of a despotic government, that a single person should rule according to his own will and caprice. No more do I want to enable me to discover their three principles; these are from thence naturally derived. I shall begin with a republican government, and in particular with that of democracy.

CHAP. III.

Of the Principle of Democracy.

There is no great share of probity necessary to support a monarchical or despotic government. The force of laws in one, and the prince's arm in the other, are sufficient to direct and maintain the whole. But in a popular state, one spring more is necessary, namely *virtue.*

What I have here advanced, is confirmed by the unanimous testimony of historians, and is extremely agreeable to the nature of things. For it is clear that in a monarchy, where he who commands the execution of the laws generally thinks himself above them, there is less need of virtue than in a popular government, where the person intrusted with the execution of the laws is sensible of his being subject to their authority.

Clear is it also that a monarch, who through bad council or indolence ceases to enforce the execution of the laws, may easily repair the evil; he has only to change his council; or to shake off this indolence. But when in a popular government, there is a suspension of the laws, as this can proceed only from the corruption of the republic, the state is certainly undone.

A very droll spectacle it was in the last century to behold the impotent efforts the English made for the establishment of democracy. As those who had a share in the direction of public affairs were void of all virtue, as their ambition was inflam'd by the success of the most daring of their members[22], as the spirit of a faction was su ppressed only that of a succeeding faction, the government was continually changing: the people amazed at so many revolutions, fought every where for a democracy without being able to find it. At length after a series of tumultuary motions and violent shocks, they were obliged to have recourse to the very government they had so odiously proscribed.

When Sylla wanted to restore *Rome* to its liberty, this unhappy city was incapable of receiving it. She had only some feeble remains of virtue, as this was every day diminishing, instead of being roused out of her lethargy by Cæsar, Tiberius, Caius, Claudius, Nero, and Domitian, she riveted every day her chains; the blows she struck were levelled against the tyrants, but not at the tyranny.

The politic Greeks who lived under a popular government, knew no other support but virtue. The modern inhabitants of that country are intirely taken up with manufactures, commerce, finances, riches, and luxury.

When virtue is banished, ambition invades the hearts of those who are capable of receiving it, and avarice possesses the whole community. Desires then change their objects; what they were fond of before, becomes now indifferent; they were free with laws, and they want to be free without them; every citizen is like a slave who has escaped from his master's house; what was maxim is called rigor; to rule they give the name of constraint; and of fear to attention. Frugality then, and not the thirst of gain, passes for avarice. Formerly the property of private people constituted the public treasure; but now the public treasure becomes the patrimony of private people. Then it is the members of the commonwealth riot on the public spoils, and its whole force is reduced to the power of a few, and to the licentiousness of many.

BOOK VIII.
Of the Corruption of the Principles of the three Governments.
CHAP. XVI.
Distinctive Properties of a Republic.

It is natural for a republic to have only a small territory; otherwise it cannot long subsist. In a large republic there are men of large fortunes, and consequently of less moderation; there are trusts too great to be placed in any single subject; he has interests of his own; he soon begins to think that he may be happy, great, and glorious, by oppressing his fellow citizens; and that he may raise himself to grandeur on the ruins of his country.

---

[22]Cromwell.

In an extensive republic the public good is sacrificed to a thousand private views; it is subordinate to exceptions, and depends on accidents. In a small one, the interest of the public is easier perceived, better understood, and more within the reach of every citizen; abuses have a less extent, and of course, are less protected.

The long duration of the republic of Sparta was owing to her having continued in the same extent of territory after all her wars. The sole aim of Sparta was liberty; and the sole advantage of her liberty, glory.

It was the spirit of the Greek republics to be as contented with their territories, as with their laws. Athens was first fired with ambition and gave it to Lacedæmon; but it was an ambition rather of commanding a free people than of governing slaves; rather of directing than of breaking the union. All was lost upon the starting up of monarchy, a government whose spirit is more turned to increase and advancement.

Excepting particular circumstances,[23] it is difficult for any other than a republican government to subsist longer in a single town. A prince of so petty a state would naturally endeavour to oppress his subjects, because his power would be great, while the means of enjoying it or of causing it to be respected, would be inconsiderable. The consequence is, he would trample upon his people. On the other hand, such a prince might be easily crushed by a foreign or even a domestic force; the people might every instant unite and rise up against him. Now as soon as a prince of single town is expelled, the quarrel is over; but if he has many towns, it only begins.

BOOK IX.

Of Laws In The Relation They Bear To a Defensive Force.

CHAP. I.

In what manner Republics provide for their Safety.

If a republic is small, it is destroyed by a foreign force; if it be large, it is ruined by an internal imperfection.[24]

To this twofold inconvenience both Democracies and Aristocracies are equally liable, and that whether they be good or bad. The evil is in the very thing itself; and no form can redress it.

It is therefore very probable that mankind would have been at length obligated to live constantly under the government of a single person, had they not contrived a kind of constitution that has all the internal advantages of a republican, together with the external force of a monarchical, government. I mean a confederate republic.

---

[23] As when a petty sovereign supports himself betwixt two great powers by means of their mutual jealousy; but then he has only a precarious existence.

[24] *Fato potentiœ, non fuâ vi nixae.* Tacit.

This form of government is a convention by which several small states agree to become members of a larger one which they intend to form. It is a kind of assemblage of societies, that constitute a new one, capable of increasing by means of new associations, till they arrive at such a degree of power as to be able to provide for the security of the united body.

It was these associations that contributed so long to the prosperity of Greece. By these the Romans attacked the universe, and by these alone the universe withstood them; for when Rome was arrived to her highest pitch of grandeur, it was the associations behind the Danube and the Rhine, associations formed by the terror of her arms, that enabled the Barbarians to resist her.

From hence it proceeds that Holland,[25] Germany, and the Swiss Cantons, are considered in Europe as perpetual republics.

The associations of cities were formerly more necessary than in our times. A weak, defenceless town was exposed to greater danger. By conquest it was deprived not only of the executive and legislative power, as at present, but, moreover, of all human property.[26]

A republic of this kind able to withstand an external force, may support itself without any internal corruption; the form of this society prevents all manner of inconveniences.

If a single member should attempt to usurp the supreme authority, he could not be supposed to have an equal authority and credit in all the confederate states. Were he to have too great an influence over one, this would alarm the rest; were he to subdue a part, that which would still remain free might oppose him with forces independent of those which he had usurped, and overpower him before he could be settled in his usurpation.

Should a popular insurrection happen in one of the confederate states, the others are able to quell it. Should abuses creep into one part, they are reformed by those that remain sound. The state may be destroyed on one side, and not on the other; the confederacy may be dissolved, and the confederates preserve their sovereignty.

As this government is composed of petty republics, it enjoys the internal happiness of each; and with respect to its external situation, it is possessed by means of the association, of all the advantages of large monarchies.

---

[25]It is composed of about fifty different republics. *State of the United Provinces* by M. Janisson.

[26]Civil liberty, goods, wives, children, temples, and even burying places.

BOOK XI.

Of the Laws that form political Liberty, with regard to the Constitution

CHAP. I.

A general IDEA.

I make a distinction between the laws that form political liberty with regard to the constitution, and those by which it is formed in respect to the citizen. The former shall be the subject of this book; the latter I shall examine in the next.

CHAP. II

Different significations given to the word Liberty

There is no word that has admitted of more various significations, and has made more different impressions on human minds, than that of *Liberty*. Some have taken it for a facility of deposing a person on whom they had conferred a tyrannical authority; others for the power of chusing a person whom they are obliged to obey; others for the right of bearing arms, and of being thereby enabled to use violence; others in fine for the privilege of being governed by a native of their own country or by their own laws.[27] A certain nation for a long time thought liberty consisted in the privilege of wearing a long beard.[28] Some have annexed this name to one form of government, in exclusion of others: Those who had a republican taste, applied it to this government; those who liked a monarchical state, gave it to monarchies.[29] Thus they all have applied the name of *liberty* to the government most suitable to their own customs and inclinations: and as in a republic people have not so constant and so present a view of the instruments of the evils they complain of, and likewise as the laws less, it is generally attributed to republics, and denied to monarchies. In fine as in democracies the people seem to do very near whatever they please, liberty has been placed in this sort of government, and the power of the people has been confounded with their liberty.

27I have copied, *says Cicero,* Scevola's edict, which permits the Greeks to terminate their differences among themselves according to their own laws; this makes them consider themselves as a free people. [Editors' note: Scevola is Quintus Mucius Scævola, known as Augur the Stoic. He taught the very old Cicero, and was honored by him in several dialogues.]

28The Ruffians could note bear that the Czar Peter should make them cut it off.

29The Cappadocians refused the condition of a republican state, which was offered them by the Romans.

CHAP. III.

In what Liberty consists.

It is true that in democracies the people seem to do what they please; but political liberty does not consist in an unrestrained freedom. In governments, that is, in societies directed by laws, liberty can consist only in the power of doing what we ought to will, and in not being constrained to do what we ought not to will.

We must have continually present to our minds the difference between independence and liberty. Liberty is a right of doing whatever the laws permit, and if a citizen could do what they forbid, he would no longer be possest of liberty, because all his fellow citizens would have the same power.

CHAP. IV.

The same Subject continued.

Democratic and aristocratic states are not necessarily free. Political liberty is to be met with only in moderate governments: yet even in these it is not always met with. It is there only when there is no abuse of power: but constant experience shews us that every man invested with power is apt to abuse it; he pushes on till he comes to the utmost limit. It is not strange, tho' true, to say, that virtue itself has need of limits?

To prevent this abuse, 'tis necessary that by the very disposition of things power should be a check to power. A government may be so constituted, as no man shall be compelled to do things to which the law does not oblige him, nor forced to abstain from things which the law permits.

CHAP. V.

Of the end or view of different Governments.

Tho' all governments have the same general end, which is that of preservation, yet each has another particular view. Increase of dominion was the view of Rome; war, of Sparta; religion, of the Jewish laws; commerce, that of Marseilles; public tranquillity, that of the laws of China;[30] navigation, of the laws of Rhodes; natural liberty, that of the policy of the Savages; in general the pleasures of the prince, that of despotic states; that of monarchies, the prince's and the kingdom's glory: the independence of individuals is the end aimed at by the laws of Poland, and from thence results the oppression of the whole.[31]

---

[30]The natural end of a state that has no foreign enemies , or that thinks itself secured against them by barriers.

[31]Inconveniency of the *Liberum veto.*

One nation there is also in the world, that has for the direct end of its constitution political liberty. We shall examine presently the principles on which this liberty is founded: if they are sound, liberty will appear in a mirror.

To discover political liberty in a constitution, no great labour is requisite. If we are capable of seeing it where it exists, why should we go any further in search of it?

CHAP. VI.

Of the Constitution of England.

In every government there are three sorts of power: the legislative; the executive in respect to things dependent on the law of nations; and the executive, in regard to things that depend on the civil law.

By virtue of the first, the prince or magistrate enacts temporary or perpetual laws, and amends or abrogates those that have been already [e]nacted. By the second, he makes peace or war, sends or receives embassies, establishes the public security, and provides against invasions. By the third, he punishes criminals, or determines the disputes that arise between individuals. The latter we shall call the judiciary power, and the other simply the executive power of the state.

The political liberty of the subject is a tranquillity of mind arising from the opinion each person has of his safety. In order to have this liberty, it is requisite the government be so constituted as one man need not be afraid of another.

When the legislative and executive powers are united in the same person, or in the same body of magistrates, there can be no liberty; because apprehensions may arise, lest the same monarch or senate should enact tyrannical laws, to execute them in a tyrannical manner.

Again, there is no liberty, if the power of judging be not separated from the legislative and executive powers. Were it joined with the legislative, the life and liberty of the subject would be exposed to arbitrary controul; for the judge would be then the legislator. Were it joined to the executive power, the judge might behave with all the violence of an oppressor.

There would be an end of every thing, were the same man or the same body whether of the nobles or of the people, to exercise those three powers, that of enacting laws, that of executing the public resolutions, and of judging the crimes or differences of individuals.

Most kingdoms of Europe enjoy a moderate government, because the prince who is invested with the two first powers, leaves the third to his subjects. In Turkey, where these three powers are united in the Sultan's person, the subjects groan under the weight of a most frightful oppression.

In the republics of Italy where these three powers are united, there is less liberty than in our monarchies. Hence their government is obliged to have recourse to as violent methods for its support, as even that of the Turks; witness the state inquisitors,[32] and the lion's mouth into which every informer may at all hours throw his written accusations.

What a situation must the poor subject be in under those republics! The same body of magistrates are possessed, as executors of the laws, of the whole power they have given themselves in quality of legislators. They may plunder the state by their general determinations; and as they likewise the judiciary power in their hands, every private citizen may be ruined by their particular decisions.

The whole power is here united in one body; and tho' there is no external pomp that indicates a despotic sway, yet the people feel the effects of it every moment.

Hence it is that many of the princes of Europe, whose aim has been levelled at arbitrary power, have constantly set out with uniting in their own persons, all the branches of magistracy, and all the great offices of state.

I allow indeed that the mere hereditary aristocracy of the Italian republics, does not answer exactly to the despotic power of the Eastern princes. The number of magistrates sometimes softens the power of the magistracy; the whole body of the nobles do not always concur in the same design; and different tribunals are erected, that temper each other. Thus at Venice the legislative power is in the *council,* the executive in the *pregadi,* and the judiciary in the *quarantia.* But the mischief is that these different tribunals are composed of magistrates all belonging to the same body; which constitutes almost one and the same power.

The judiciary power ought not to be given to a standing senate; it should be exercised by person taken from the body of the people[33] at certain times of the year, and pursuant to a form and manner prescribed by law, in order to erect a tribunal that should last only as long as necessity requires.

By this means the power of judging, a power so terrible to mankind, not being annexed to any particular state or profession, becomes, as it were, invisible. People have not then the judges continually present to their view; they fear the office, but not the magistrate.

In accusations of a deep or criminal nature, it is proper the person accused should have the privilege of chusing in some measure his judges in concurrence with the law; or at least he should have a right to

---

[32] At Venice.

[33] As at Athens.

except against so great a number, that the remaining part may be deemed his own choice.

The other two powers may be given rather to magistrates or permanent bodies, because they are not exercised on any private subject; one being no more than the general will of the state, and the other the execution of that general will.

But tho' the tribunals ought not to be fixt, yet the judgments ought, and to such a degree as to be always conformable to the exact letter of the law. Were they to be the private opinion of the judge, people would then live in society without knowing exactly the nature of their obligations it lays them under.

The judges ought likewise to be in the same station as the accused, or in other words, his peers, to the end that he may not imagine he is fallen into the hands of persons inclined to treat him with rigour.

If the legislature leaves the executive power in possession of a right to imprison those subjects who can give security for their good behaviour, there is an end of liberty; unless they are taken up, in order to answer without delay to a capital crime; in this case they are really free, being subject only to the power of the law.

But should the legislature think itself in danger by some secret conspiracy against the state, or by a correspondence with a foreign enemy, it might authorize the executive power, for a short and limited time, to imprison suspected persons, who in that case would lose their liberty only for a while, to preserve it for ever.

And this is the only reasonable method. that can be substituted to the tyrannical magistracy of the *Ephori,* and to the *state inquisitors* of Venice, who are also despotical.

As in a free state, every man who is supposed a free agent, ought to be his own governor; so the legislative power should reside in the whole body of the people. But since this is impossible in large states, and in small ones is subject to many inconveniences; it is fit the people should act by their representatives, what they cannot act by themselves.

The inhabitants of a particular town are much better acquainted with its wants and interests, than with those of other places; and are better judges of the capacity of their neighbours, than of that of the rest of their countrymen. The members therefore of the legislature should not be chosen from the general body of the nation; but it is proper that in every considerable place, a representative should be elected by the inhabitants.

The great advantage of representatives is their being capable of discussing affairs. For this the people collectively are extremely unfit, which is one of the chief inconveniences of a democracy.

It is not at all necessary that the representatives who have received a general instruction from their electors, should wait to be particularly instructed on every affair, as is practiced in the diets of Germany. True it is that by this way of proceeding, the speeches of the deputies might with greater propriety be called the voice of the nation: but on the other hand, this would throw them into infinite delays, would give each deputy a power of controlling the assembly; and on the most urgent and pressing occasions the springs of the nation might be stopped by a single caprice.

When the deputies, as Mr. Sidney well observes, represent a body of people as in Holland, they ought to be accountable to their constituents: but it is a different thing in England, where they are deputed by boroughs.

All the inhabitants of the several districts ought to have a right of voting at the election of a representative, except such as are in so mean a situation, as to be deemed to have no will of their own.

One great faulty there was in most of the ancient republics; that the people had a right to active resolutions, such as require some execution, a thing of which they are absolutely incapable. They ought to have no hand in the government but for the chusing of representatives, which is within their reach. For tho' few can tell the exact degree of men's capacities, yet there are none but are capable of knowing in general whether the person they chuse is better qualified than most of his neighbours.

Neither ought the representative body to be chosen for the active resolutions, for which it is not so fit; but for the enacting of laws, or to see whether the laws already enacted be duly executed, a thing they are very capable of, and which none indeed but themselves can properly perform.

In a state there are always persons distinguished by their birth, riches, or honors: but were they to be confounded with the common people, and to have only the weight of a single vote like the rest, the common liberty would be their slavery, and they would have no interest in supporting it, as most of the popular resolutions would be against them. The share they have therefore in the legislature ought to be proportioned to the other advantages in the state; which happens only when they form a body that has a right to put a stop to the enterprizes of the people, as the people have a right to oppose any incroachment of theirs.

The legislative power is therefore committed to the body of the nobles, and to the body chosen to represent the people, which have each their assemblies and deliberations apart, each their separate view and interests.

Of the three powers above-mentioned the judiciary is in some measure next to nothing. There remains therefore only two; and as these have need of a regulating power to temper them, the part of the legislative body composed of the nobility is extremely proper for this very purpose.

The body of the nobility ought to be hereditary. In the first place it is so in its own nature; and in the next there must be a considerable interest to preserve its privileges; privileges that in themselves are obnoxious to popular envy, and of course in a free state are always in danger.

But as an hereditary power might be tempted to pursue its own particular interests, and forget those of the people; it is proper that where they may reap a singular advantage from being corrupted, as in the laws relating to the supplies, they should have no other share in the legislation, than the power of rejecting, and not that of resolving.

By the *power of resolving,* I mean the right of ordaining by their own authority, or of amending what has been ordained by others. By the *power of rejecting,* I would be understood to mean the right of annulling a resolution taken by another; which was the power of the tribunes at Rome. And tho' the person possessed of the privilege of rejecting may likewise have the right of approving, yet this approbation passes for no more than a declaration, that he intends to make no use of his privilege of rejecting, and is derived from that very privilege.

The executive power ought to be in the hands of a monarch; because this branch of government, having need of expedition, is better administered by one than by many: whereas, whatever depends on the legislative power is oftentimes better regulated by many than by a single person.

But if there was no monarch, and the executive power was committed to a certain number of persons selected from the legislative body, there would be an end then of liberty; by reason the two powers would be united, as the same persons would actually sometimes have, and would moreover be always able to have, a share in both.

Were the legislative body to be a considerable time without meeting, this would likewise put an end to liberty. For of two things one would naturally follow; either that there would be no longer any legislative resolutions, and then the state would fall into anarchy; or that these resolutions would be taken by the executive power which would render it absolute.

It would be needless for the legislative body to continue always assembled. This would be troublesome to the representatives, and moreover would cut out too much work for the executive power, so as to take off its attention from executing, and oblige it to think only of defending its own prerogatives and the right it has to execute.

Again, were the legislative body to be always assembled, it might happen to be kept up only by filling the places of the deceased members with new representatives; and in that case, if the legislative body was once corrupted, the evil would be past all remedy. When different legislative bodies succeed one another, the people who have a bad opinion of that which is actually sitting, may reasonably entertain some hopes of the next: but were it to be always the same body, the people upon seeing it once corrupted, would no longer expect any good from its laws; and of course they would either become desperate or fall into a state of indolence.

The legislative body should not assemble of itself. For a body is supposed to have no will but when it is assembled; and besides were it not to assemble unanimously, it would be impossible to determine which was really the legislative body, the part assembled, or the other. And if it had a right to prorogue itself, it might happen never to be prorogued; which would be extremely dangerous in case it should ever attempt to incroach on the executive power. Besides there are seasons, some of which are more proper than others, for assembling the legislative body: it is fit therefore that the executive power should regulate the time of convening, as well as the duration of those assemblies, according to the circumstances and exigencies of state known to itself.

Were the executive power not to have a right of putting a stop to the encroachments of the legislative body, the latter would become despotic; for as it might arrogate to itself what authority it pleased, it would soon destroy all the other powers.

But it is not proper on the other hand that the legislative power should have a right to stop the executive. For as the execution has its natural limits, it is useless to confine it; besides the executive power is generally employed in momentary operations. The power therefore of the Roman tribunes was faulty, as it put a stop not only to the legislation, but likewise to the execution itself; which was attended with infinite mischiefs.

But if the legislative power in a free government has no right to stay the executive, it has a right and ought to have the means of examining in what manner its laws have been executed; an advantage which this government has over that of Crete and Sparta, where the Cosmi and the Ephori gave no account of their administration.

But whatever may be the issue of that examination, the legislative body ought not to have a power of judging the person, nor of course the conduct of him who is intrusted with the executive power. His person should be sacred, because as it is necessary for the good of the state to prevent the legislative body from rendering themselves arbitrary, the moment he is accused or tried, there is an end of liberty.

In this case the state would be no longer a monarchy, but a kind of republican, tho' not a free, government. But as the person intrusted with the executive power cannot abuse it without bad counsellors, and such as have the laws as ministers, tho' the laws favour them as subjects; these men may be examined and punished. An advantage which this government has over that of *Gnidus,* where the law allowed of no such thing as calling the *Amymones*[34] to an account, even after their administration;[35] and therefore the people could never obtain any satisfaction for the injuries done them.

Tho' in general the judiciary power ought not to be united with any part of the legislative, yet this is liable to three exceptions founded on the particular interest of the party accused.

The great are always obnoxious to popular envy; and were they to be judged by the people, they might be in danger from their judges, and would moreover be deprived of the privilege which the meanest subject is possessed of in a free state, of being tried by their peers. The nobility for this reason ought not to be cited before the ordinary courts of judicature, but before that part of the legislature which is composed of their own body.

It is possible that the law, which is clear-sighted in one sense, and blind in another, might in some cases be too severe. But as we have already observed, the national judges are no more than the mouth that pronounces the words of the law, mere passive beings incapable of moderating either its force or rigor. That part therefore of the legislative body, which we have just now observed to be a necessary tribunal on another occasion, is also a necessary tribunal in this; it belongs to its supreme authority to moderate the law in favour of the law itself, by mitigating the sentence.

It might also happen that a subject intrusted with the administration of public affairs, may infringe the rights of the people, and be guilty of crimes which the ordinary magistrates either could not, or would not punish. But, in general the legislative power cannot judge; and much less can it be a judge in this particular case, where it represents the party concerned, which is the people. It can only therefore impeach. But before what court shall it bring its impeachment? Must it go and demean itself before the ordinary tribunals, which are its inferiors, and being composed moreover of men who are chosen from the people as well as itself, will naturally be swayed by the authority of so powerful an accuser? No: in order to preserve the dignity of the people, and the security of the subject, the legislative part which represents the nobility, must bring in its charge before the legislative part which represents the nobility, who have neither the same interests nor the same passions.

---

[34]These were magistrates chosen annually by the people. See Stephen of Byzantium.

[35]It was lawful to accuse the Roman magistrates after the expiration of their several offices. See in Dionsf. Halicarn. l. 9. the affairs of *Genutius* the tribune.

Here is an advantage which this government has over most of the ancient republics, where there was this abuse, that the people were at the same time both judge and accuser.

The executive power, pursuant to what has been already said, ought to have a share in the legislature by the power of rejecting, otherwise it would soon be stripp'd of its prerogative. But should the legislative power usurp a share of the executive, the latter would be equally undone.

If the prince were to have a share in the legislature by the power of resolving, liberty would be lost. But as it is necessary he should have a share in the legislature for the support of his own prerogative, this share must consist in the power of rejecting.

The change of government at Rome was owing to this, that neither the senate who had one part of the executive power, nor the magistrates who were entrusted with the other, had the right of rejecting, which was entirely lodged in the people.

Here then is the fundamental constitution of the government we are treating of. The legislative body being composed of two parts, one checks, the other, by the mutual privilege of rejecting. They are both checked by the executive power, as the executive is by the legislative.

These three powers should naturally form a state of repose or inaction. But as there is a necessity for movement in the course of human affairs, they are forced to move, but still to move in concert.

XVI.

DAVID HUME, *OF THE ORIGINAL CONTRACT,* 1752

There are a number of recent editions of Hume's political writings. See Knud Haakonssen, editor, *David Hume: Political Essays* (Cambridge: Cambridge University Press, 1994); Stuart D. Warner and Donald W. Livingston, editors, *David Hume: Political Writings* (Indianapolis: Hackett Publishing Company, 1994); and Eugene F. Miller, editor, *Essays: Moral, Political, and Literary* (Indianapolis: Liberty Classics, 1985). One of the earliest reproductions, and available in various subsequent editions, is by T. H. Green and T. H. Grose (London: Longmans, Green, and Company, 1874). We have relied on the 1870 edition of Ward, Lock, and Tyler (London, 270-283). Reproduced below is "Of the Original Contract," Hume's thirty-fourth essay on politics. Hume's footnotes are intact, but several paragraphs toward the end of the essay concerning Roman dominions and the House of Lancaster have been cut. We begin with the fourth paragraph of his argument. See also Kurland and Lerner (I: 49-52).

~

When we consider how nearly equal all men are in their bodily force, and even in their mental powers and faculties, till cultivated by education; we must necessarily allow, that nothing but their own consent could, at first, associate them together, and subject them to any authority. The people, if we trace government to its first origin in the woods and deserts, are the source of all power and jurisdiction, and voluntarily, for the sake of peace and order, abandoned their native liberty, and received laws from their equal and companion. The conditions, upon which they were willing to submit, were either expressed, or were so clear and obvious, that it might well be esteemed superfluous to express them. If this, then, be meant by the *original contract*, it cannot be denied, that all government is, at first, founded on a contract, and that the most ancient rude combinations of mankind were formed chiefly by that principle. In vain, are we asked in what records this charter of our liberties is registered. It was not written on parchment, nor yet on leaves or barks of trees. It preceded the use of writing and all the other civilized arts of life. But we trace it plainly in the nature of man, and in the equality, or something approaching equality, which we find in all the individuals of that species. The force, which now prevails, and which is founded on fleets and armies, is plainly political, and derived from authority, the effect of established government. A man's natural force consists only in the vigour of his courage; which could never subject multitudes to the command of one. Nothing but their own consent, and their sense of the advantages resulting from peace and order, could have had that influence.

Yet even this consent was long very imperfect, and could not be the basis of a regular administration. The chieftain, who had probably acquired his influence during the continuance of war, ruled more by persuasion than command; and till he could employ force to reduce the refractory and disobedient, the society could scarcely be said to have attained a state of civil government. No compact or agreement, it is evident, was expressly formed for general submission; an idea far beyond the comprehension of savages: each exertion of authority in the chieftain must have been particular, and called forth by the present exigencies of the case: the sensible utility, resulting from his interposition, made these exertions become daily more frequent; and their frequency gradually produced an habitual, and, if you please to call it so, a voluntary, and therefore precarious, acquiescence in the people.

But philosophers, who have embraced a party, (if that be not a contradiction in terms) are not contented with these concessions. They assert, not only that government in its earliest infancy arose from consent, or rather the voluntary acquiescence of the people; but also, that, even at present, when it has attained its full maturity, it rests on no other foundation. They affirm, that all men are still born equal, and owe allegiance to no prince or government, unless bound by the obligation and sanction of a *promise*. And as no man, without some equivalent, would forego the advantages of his native liberty, and subject himself to the will of another; this promise is always understood to be conditional, and imposes on him no obligation, unless he meet with justice and protection from his sovereign. These advantages the sovereign promises him in return; and if he fail in the execution, he has broken, on his part, the articles of engagement, and has thereby freed his subject from all obligations to allegiance. Such, according to these philosophers, is the foundation of authority in every government; and such is the right of resistance, possessed by every subject.

But would these reasoners look abroad into the world, they would meet with nothing that, in the least, corresponds to their ideas, or can warrant so refined and philosophical a system. On the contrary, we find, every where, princes, who claim their subjects as their property, and assert their independent right of sovereignty, from conquest or succession. We find also, every where, subjects, who acknowledge this right in their prince, and suppose themselves born under obligations of obedience to a certain sovereign, as much as under the ties of reverence and duty to certain parents. These connections are always conceived to be equally independent of our consent, in Persia and China; in France and Spain; and even in Holland and England, wherever the doctrines above mentioned have not been carefully inculcated. Obedience or subjection becomes so familiar, that most men never make any inquiry about its origin or cause, more than about the principle of gravity, resistance, or the most universal laws of nature. Or if curiosity ever move them; as soon as they learn, that they themselves or their ancestors have, for several ages, or from time immemorial, been subject to such a form of government or such a family; they immediately acquiesce, and acknowledge their obligation to allegiance. Were you to preach, in most parts of the world, that political connections are founded altogether on voluntary consent or a mutual promise, the magistrate would soon imprison you, as seditious, for loosening the ties of obedience; if your friends did not before shut you up as delirious, for advancing such absurdities. It is strange, that an act of the mind, which every individual is supposed to have formed, and after he came to the use of reason too, otherwise it could have no authority; that this act, I say, should be so much unknown to all of them, that, over the face of the whole earth, there scarcely remain any trace or memory of it.

But the contract, on which the government is founded, is said to be the *original contract*; and consequently may be supposed too old to fall under the knowledge of the present generation. If the agreement, by which savage men first associated and conjoined their force, be here meant, this is acknowledged to be real; but being so ancient, and being obliterated by a thousand changes of government and princes, it cannot now be supposed to retain any authority. If we would say any thing to the purpose, we must assert, that every particular government, which is lawful, and which imposes any duty of allegiance on the subject, was, at first, founded on consent and a voluntary compact. But besides that this supposes the consent of the fathers to bind the children, even to the most remote generations (which republican writers will never allow), besides this, I say, it is not justified by history or experience, in any age or country of the world.

Almost all the governments, which exist at present, or of which there remains any record in story, have been founded originally, either on usurpation or conquest, or both, without any pretense of a fair consent, or voluntary subjection of the people. When an artful and bold man is placed at the head of an army or faction, it is often easy for him, by employing, sometimes violence, sometimes false pretenses, to establish his dominion over a people a hundred times more numerous than his partizans. He allows no such open communication, that his enemies can know, with certainty, their number or force. He gives them no leisure to assemble together in a body to oppose him. Even all those, who are the instruments of his usurpation, may wish his fall; but their ignorance of each other's intention keeps them in awe, and is the sole cause of his security. By such arts as these, many governments have been established; and this is all the *original contract*, which they have to boast of.

The face of the earth is continually changing, by the increase of small kingdoms into great empires, by the dissolution of great empires into smaller kingdoms, by the planting of colonies, by the migration of tribes. Is there anything discoverable in all these events, but force and violence? Where is the mutual agreement or voluntary association so much talked of?

Even the smoothest way, by which a nation may receive a foreign master, by marriage or a will, is not extremely honourable for the people; but supposes them to be disposed of, like a dowry or legacy, according to the pleasure or interest of their rulers.

But where no force interposes, and election takes place; what is this election so highly vaunted? It is either the combination of a few great men, who decide for the whole, and will allow of no opposition: or it is the fury of a multitude, that follow a seditious ringleader, who is not known, perhaps, to a dozen among them, and who owes his advancement merely to his own impudence, or to the momentary caprice of his fellows.

Are these disorderly elections, which are rare too, of such mighty authority as to be the only lawful foundation of all government and allegiance?

In reality, there is not a more terrible event, than a total dissolution of government, which gives liberty to the multitude, and makes the determination or choice of a new establishment depend upon a number, which nearly approaches to that of the body of the people: for it never comes entirely to the whole body of them. Every wise man, then, wishes to see, at the head of a powerful and obedient army, a general, who may speedily seize the prize, and give to the people a master, which they are so unfit to choose for themselves. So little correspondent is fact and reality to those philosophical notions.

Let not the establishment at the *Revolution* deceive us, or make us so much in love with a philosophical origin to government, as to imagine all others monstrous and irregular. Even that event was far from corresponding to these refined ideas. It was only the succession, and that only in the regal part of the government, which was then changed: and it was only the majority of seven hundred, who determined that change for near ten millions. I doubt not, indeed, but the bulk of those ten millions acquiesced willingly in the determination: but was the matter left, in the least, to their choice? Was it not justly supposed to be, from that moment, decided, and every man punished, who refused to submit to the new sovereign? How otherwise could the matter have ever been brought to any issue or conclusion.

The republic of Athens was, I believe, the most extensive democracy that we read of in history: yet if we make the requisite allowances for the women, the slaves, and the strangers, we shall find, that that establishment was not, at first, made, nor any law ever voted, by a tenth part of those who were bound to pay obedience to it: not to mention the islands and foreign dominions, which the Athenians claimed as theirs by rights of conquest. And as it is well known, that popular assemblies in that city were always full of licence and disorder, notwithstanding the institutions and laws by which they were checked: how much more disorderly must they prove, where they form not the established constitution, but meet tumultuously on the dissolution of the ancient government, in order to give rise to a new one? how chimercial must it be to talk of a choice in such circumstances?

The Achæans enjoyed the freest and most perfect democracy of all antiquity; yet they employed force to oblige some cities to enter into their league, as we learn from Polybius.[36]

Harry IV. and Harry VII. of England, had really no title to the throne but a parliamentary election; yet they never would acknowledge it, lest

---

[36]Lib. ii. cap 38.

they should thereby weaken their authority. Strange, if the only real foundation of all authority be consent and promise?

It is in vain to say, that all governments are or should be at first, founded on popular consent, as much as the necessity of human affairs will admit. This favours entirely my pretension. I maintain, that human affairs will never admit of this consent; seldom of the appearance of it. But that conquest or usurpation, that is, in plain terms, force, by dissolving the ancient governments, is the origin of almost all the new ones, which were ever established in the world. And that in the few cases, where consent may seem to have taken place, it was commonly so irregular, so confined, or so much intermixed either with fraud or violence, that it cannot have any great authority.

My intention here is not to exclude the consent of the people from being one just foundation of government where it has place. I only pretend, that it has very seldom had place in any degree, and never almost in its full extent. And that therefore some other foundation of government must also be admitted.

Were all men possessed of so inflexible a regard to justice, that, of themselves, they would totally abstain from the properties of others; they had for ever remained in a state of absolute liberty, without subjection to any magistrate of political society; but this is a state of perfection, of which human nature is justly deemed incapable. Again, were all men possessed of so perfect an understanding as always to know their own interests, no form of government had ever been submitted to, but what was established on consent, and was fully canvassed by every member of the society: but this state of perfection is likewise much superior to human nature. Reason, history, and experience shew us, that all political societies have had an origin much less accurate and regular: and were one to choose a period of time, when the people's consent was the least regarded in public transactions, it would be precisely on the establishment of a new government. In a settled constitution, their inclinations are often consulted; but during the fury of revolutions, conquests, and public convulsions, military force or political craft usually decides the controversy.

When a new government is established, by whatever means, the people are commonly dissatisfied with it, and pay obedience more from fear and necessity, than from any idea of allegiance or of moral obligation. The prince is watchful and jealous, and must carefully guard against every beginning or appearance of insurrection. Time, by degrees, removes all these difficulties, and accustoms the nation to regard, as their lawful or native princes, that family, which, at first, they considered as usurpers or foreign conquerors. In order to found this opinion, they have no recourse to any notion of voluntary consent or promise, which they know, never was, in this case, either expected or demanded. The original establishment was formed by violence, and submitted to from necessity. The subsequent administration is also supported by power, and acquiesced in by the people, not as a matter of choice, but of obligation. They imagine not, that their consent gives their prince a title: but they willingly consent, because they think, that from long possession, he has acquired a title, independent of their choice or inclination.

Should it be said, that, by living under the dominion of a prince, which one might leave, every individual has given a tacit consent to his authority, and promised him obedience; it may be answered, that such an implied consent can only have place, where a man imagines, that the matter depends on his choice. But where he thinks (as all mankind do who are born under established governments) that by his birth he owes allegiance to a certain prince or certain form of government; it would be absurd to infer a consent or choice, which he expressly, in this case, renounces and disclaims.

Can we seriously say, that a poor peasant or artizan has a free choice to leave his country, when he knows no foreign language or manners, and lives, from day to day, by the small wages which he acquires? We may as well assert, that man by remaining in a vessel, freely consents to the dominion of the master; though he was carried on board while asleep, and must leap into the ocean, and perish, the moment he leaves her.

What if the prince forbid his subjects to quit his dominions; as in Tiberius' time, it was regarded as a crime in a Roman knight that he had attempted to fly to the Parthians, in order to escape the tyranny of that emperor?[37] Or as the ancient Muscovites prohibited all travelling under pain of death? And did a prince observe, that many of his subjects were seized with the frenzy of migrating to foreign countries, he would doubtless, with great reason and justice, restrain them, in order to prevent the depopulation of his own kingdom. Would he forfeit the allegiance of all his subjects, by so wise and reasonable a law? Yet the freedom of their choice is surely, in that case, ravished from them.

* * * *

Did one generation of men go off the stage at once, and another succeed, as is the case with silk worms and butterflies, the new race, if they had sense enough to chuse their government, which surely is never the case with men, might voluntarily, and by general consent, establish their own form of civil polity, without any regard to the laws or

---

[37]Tacit. Ann. lib. vi. cap. 14.

precedents which prevailed among their ancestors. But as human society is in perpetual flux, one man every hour going out of the world, another coming into it, it is necessary in order to preserve stability in government, that the new brood should conform themselves to the established constitution, and nearly follow the path which their fathers, treading in the footsteps of theirs, had marked out to them. Some innovations must necessarily have place in every human institution; and it is happy where the enlightened genius of the age give these a direction to the side of reason, liberty, and justice: but violent innovations no individual is entitled to make: they are even dangerous to be attempted by the legislature: more ill than good is ever to be expected from them: and if history affords examples to the contrary, they are not to be drawn into precedent, and are only to be regarded as proofs, that the science of politics affords few rules, which will not admit of some exception, and which may not sometimes be controlled by fortune and accidents. The violent innovations in the reign of Henry VIII. proceeded from an imperious monarch, seconded by the appearance of legislative authority: those in the reign of Charles I. were derived from faction and fanaticism; and both of them have proved happy in the issues: But even the former were long the source of many disorders, and still more dangers; and if the measures of allegiance were to be taken from the latter, a total anarchy must have place in human society, and a final period at once be put to every government.

Suppose, that an usurper, after having banished his lawful prince and royal family, should establish his dominion for ten or a dozen years in any country, and should preserve so exact a discipline in his troops, and so regular a disposition in his garrisons, that no insurrection had ever been raised, or even murmur heard, against his administration: can it be asserted, that the people, who in their hearts abhor his treason, have tacitly consented to his authority, and promised him allegiance, merely because, from necessity, they live under his dominion? Suppose again their native prince restored, by means of an army, which he levies in foreign countries: they receive him with joy and exultation, and show plainly with what reluctance they had submitted to any other yoke. I may now ask, upon what foundation the prince's title stands? Not on popular consent surely: for though the people willingly acquiesce in his authority, they never imagine, that their consent made him sovereign. They consent; because they apprehend him to be already, by birth, their lawful sovereign. And as to that tacit consent, which may now be inferred from their living under his dominion, this is no more than what they formerly gave to the tyrant and usurper.

* * * *

But would we have a more regular, at least a more philosophical, refutation of this principle of an original contract, or popular consent; perhaps the following observations may suffice.

All *moral* duties may be divided into two kinds. I. Those to which men are impelled by a natural instinct or immediate propensity, which operates on them, independent of all ideas of obligation, and of all views, either to public or private utility. Of this nature are, love of children, gratitude to benefactors, pity to the unfortunate. When we reflect on the advantage which results to society from such humane instincts, we pay them the just tribute of moral approbation and esteem: but the person, actuated by them, feels their power and influence, antecedent to any such reflection.

II. The kind of moral duties are such as are not supported by any original instinct of nature, but are performed entirely from a sense of obligation, when we consider the necessities of human society, and the impossibility of supporting it, if these duties were neglected. It is thus *justice,* or a regard to the property of others, *fidelity,* or the observance of promises, become obligatory, and acquire an authority over mankind. For as it is evident that every man loves himself better than any other person, he is naturally impelled to extend his acquisitions as much as possible; and nothing can restrain him in this propensity, but reflection and experience, by which he learns the pernicious effects of that licence and the total dissolution of society which must ensue from it. His original inclination, therefore, or instinct, is here checked and restrained by a subsequent judgment or observation.

The case is precisely the same with the political or civil duty of *allegiance*, as with the natural duties of justice and fidelity. Our primary instincts lead us, either to indulge ourselves in unlimited freedom, or to seek dominion over others: and it is reflection only which engages us to sacrifice such strong passions to the interests of peace and public order. A small degree of experience and observation suffices to teach us, that society cannot possibly be maintained without the authority of magistrates, and that this authority must soon fall into contempt, where exact obedience is not paid to it. The observation of these general and obvious interests is the source of all allegiance and of that moral obligation which we attribute to it.

* * * *

We shall only observe, before we conclude, that though an appeal to general opinion may justly, in the speculative sciences of metaphysics, natural philosophy, or astronomy, be deemed unfair and inconclusive, yet in all questions with regard to morals, as well as criticism, there is really no other standard, by which any controversy can ever be decided.

And nothing is a clearer proof, that a theory of this kind is erroneous, than to find, that it leads to paradoxes repugnant to the common sentiments of mankind, and to the practice and opinion of all nations and all ages. The doctrine which founds all lawful government on an *original contract*, or consent of the people, is plainly of this kind; nor has the most noted of its partizans, in prosecution of it, scrupled to affirm, *that absolute monarchy is inconsistent with civil society, and so can be no form of civil government at all;*[38] and *that the supreme power in a state cannot take from any man, by taxes and impositions, any part of his property, without his own consent or that of his representatives.*[39] What authority any moral reasoning can have, which leads into opinions so wide of the general practice of mankind, in every place but this single kingdom, it is easy to determine.

The only passage I meet with in antiquity, where the obligation of obedience to government is ascribed to a promise, is in Plato's *Crito*: where Socrates refuses to escape from prison, because he had tacitly promised to obey the laws. Thus he builds a *Tory* consequence of passive obedience on a *Whig* foundation of the original contract.

New discoveries are not to be expected in these matters. If scarce any man, till very lately, ever imagined that government was founded on compact, it is certain, that it cannot in general, have any such foundation.

XVII.

WILLIAM BLACKSTONE, *COMMENTARIES*, 1765

William Blackstone's *Commentaries* contain a lengthy introduction and four books, the last three of which cover "the rights of things," or property law; "private wrongs," or civil law; and "public wrongs," or criminal law. The first book, and for our purposes the most interesting, is entitled "Of the Rights of Persons." Book I is divided into twenty-eight chapters. Reproduced below are substantial portions of Chapter I, "Of the Absolute Right of Individuals," Chapter II, "Of the Parliament," and Chapter VII, "Of the King's Prerogative." We have followed the spelling and grammar found in the 1765 edition by the Clarendon Press, Oxford (including Blackstone's grating use of it's for the possessive). See pages 117-141, 142-182, and 230-271 for the complete text of the three chapters. We have inserted Arabic numerals in square parenthesis to assist the reader in identifying the separate arguments. For a four-volume facsimile of Blackstone's first edition, see Stanley N. Katz, editor,

38Locke on Government, chap. vii, sect. 90.

39I[bi]d. chap. xi. sect. 138, 139, 140.

Commentaries on the Laws of England (Chicago, University of Chicago Press, 1979). See also Kurland and Lerner (I: 87-89) for a differently edited version.

~

CHAPTER I:
OF THE ABSOLUTE RIGHTS OF INDIVIDUALS

The objects of the laws of England falling into this fourfold division, the present commentaries will therefore consist of the four following parts: 1. *The rights of persons;* with the means whereby such rights may be either acquired or lost. 2. *The rights of things;* with the means also of acquiring and losing them. 3. *Private wrongs*, or civil injuries; with the means of redressing them by law. 4. *Public wrongs*, or crimes and misdemeanors; with the means of prevention and punishment.

We are now, first, to consider the *rights of persons;* with the means of acquiring and losing them.

Now the rights of persons that are commanded to be observed by the municipal laws are of two sorts; first, such as are due *from* every citizen, which are usually called civil *duties;* and, secondly, such as belong *to* him, which is the more popular acceptation of *rights* or *jura*. Both may indeed be comprized in this latter division; for, as all social duties are of a relative nature, at the same time that they are due *from* one man, or set of men, they must also be due *to* another. But I apprehend it will be more clear and easy, to consider many of them as duties required from, rather than as rights belonging to, particular persons. Thus, for instance, allegiance is usually, and therefore most easily, considered as the duty of the people, and protection as the duty of the magistrate; and yet they are, reciprocally, the rights as well as duties of each other. Allegiance is the right of the magistrate, and protection the right of the people.

Persons also are divided by the law into either natural persons, or artificial. Natural persons are such as the God of nature formed us: artificial are such as created and devised by human laws for the purposes of society and government; which are called corporations or bodies politic.

The rights of persons considered in their natural capacities are also of two sorts, absolute, and relative. Absolute, which are such as appertain and belong to particular men, merely as individuals or single persons: relative, which are incident to them as members of society, and standing in various relations to each other. The first that is, absolute rights, will be the subject of the present chapter.

By the absolute *rights* of individuals we mean those which are so in their primary and strictest sense; such as would belong to their persons merely in a state of nature, and which every man is intitled to enjoy whether out of society or in it. But with regard to the absolute *duties,* which man is bound to perform considered as a mere individual, it is not to be expected that any human municipal laws should at all explain or enforce them. For the end and intent of such laws being only to regulate the behavior of mankind, as they are members of society, and stand in various relations to each other, they have consequently no concern with any but social or relative duties. Let a man therefore be ever so abandoned in his principles, or vitious in his practice, provided he keeps his wickedness to himself, and does not offend against the rules of public decency, he is out of the reach of human laws. But if he makes his vices public, though they be such as seem principally to affect himself, (as drunkenness, or the like,) they then become, by the bad example they set, of pernicious effects to society; and therefore it is then the business of human laws to correct them. Here the circumstance of publication is what alters the nature of the case. *Public* sobriety is a relative duty, and therefore enjoined by our laws: *private* sobriety is an absolute duty, which, whether it be performed or not, human tribunals can never know; and therefore they can never enforce it by any civil sanction. But, with respect to *rights*, the case is different. Human laws define and enforce as well those rights which belong to a man considered as an individual, as those which belong to him considered as related to others.

For the principal aim of society is to protect individuals in the enjoyment of those absolute rights, which were vested in them by the immutable laws of nature; but which could not be preserved in peace without that mutual assistance and intercourse, which is gained by the institution of friendly and social communities. Hence it follows, that the first and primary end of human laws is to maintain and regulate those *absolute* rights of individuals. Such rights as are social and *relative* result from, and are posterior to, the formation of states and societies: so that to maintain and regulate these, is clearly a subsequent consideration. And therefore the principal view of human laws is, or ought always to be, to explain, protect, and enforce such rights as are absolute, which in themselves are few and simple; and, then, such rights as are relative, which arising from a variety of connexions, will be far more numerous and more complicated. These will take up a greater space in any code of laws, and hence may appear to be more attended to, though in reality they are not, than the rights of the former kind. Let us therefore proceed to examine how far all laws ought, and how far the laws of England actually do, take notice of these absolute rights, and provide for their lasting security.

The absolute rights of man, considered as a free agent, endowed with discernment to know good from evil, and with power of choosing those measures which appear to him to be most desirable, are usually summed up in one general appellation, and denominated the natural liberty of mankind. This natural liberty consists properly in a power of acting as one thinks fit, without any restraint or control, unless by the law of nature: being a right inherent in us by birth, and one of the gifts of God to man at his creation, when he endued him with the faculty of free will. But every man, when he enters into society, gives up a part of his natural liberty, as the price of so valuable a purchase; and, in consideration of receiving the advantages of mutual commerce, obliges himself to conform to those laws, which the community has thought proper to establish. And this species of legal obedience and conformity is infinitely more desirable, than that wild and savage liberty which is sacrificed to obtain it. For no man, that considers a moment, would wish to retain the absolute and uncontrolled power of doing whatever he pleases; the consequence of which is, that every other man would also have the same power; and then there would be no security to individuals in any of the enjoyments of life. Political, therefore, or civil liberty, which is that of a member of society, is no other than natural liberty so far restrained by human laws (and no farther) as is necessary and expedient for the general advantage of the publick. Hence we may collect that the law, which restrains a man from doing mischief to his fellow citizens, though it diminishes the natural, increases the civil liberty of mankind: but that every wanton and causeless restraint of the will of the subject, whether practiced by a monarch, a nobility, or a popular assembly, is a degree of tyranny. Nay, that even laws themselves, whether made with or without our consent, if they regulate and constrain our conduct in matters of mere indifference, without any good end in view, are regulations destructive of liberty: whereas if any public advantage can arise from observing such precepts, the control of our private inclinations, in one or two particular points, will conduce to preserve our general freedom in others of more importance; by supporting that state, of society, which alone can secure our independence. Thus the statute of king Edward IV, which forbad the fine gentlemen of those times (under the degree of a lord) to wear pikes upon their shoes or boots of more than two inches in length, was a law that savoured of oppression; because, however ridiculous the fashion then in use might appear, the restraining it by pecuniary penalties could serve no purpose of common utility. But the statute of king Charles II, which prescribes a thing seemingly indifferent; viz. a dress for the dead, who are ordered to be buried in woollen; is a law consistent with public liberty, for it encourages the staple trade, on which in great measure depends the universal good of the nation. So that laws, when prudently framed, are by no means subversive but rather introductive of liberty; for (as Mr. Locke has well observed) where there is no law, there is no freedom. But then, on the other hand, that constitution or frame of government, that system of laws, is alone calculated to maintain civil liberty, which leaves the subject entire master of his own conduct, except in those points wherein the public good requires some direction or restraint.

The idea and practice of this political or civil liberty flourish in their highest vigour in these kingdoms, where it fall little short of perfection, and can only be lost or destroyed by the folly or demerits of it's owner: the legislature, and of course the laws of England, being peculiarly adapted to the preservation of this inestimable blessing even in the meanest subject. Very different from the modern constitutions of other states, on the continent of Europe, and from the genius of the imperial law; which in general are calculated to vest an arbitrary and despotic power of controlling the actions of the subject, in the prince, or in a few grandees. And this spirit of liberty is so deeply implanted in our constitution, and rooted even in our very soil, that a slave or a negro, the moment he lands in England, falls under the protection of the laws, and with regard to all natural rights becomes *eo instanti* a freeman.

The absolute rights of every Englishman (which, taken in a political and extensive sense, are usually called their liberties) as they are founded on nature and reason, so they are coeval with our form of government; though subject at times to fluctuate and change: their establishment (excellent as it is) being still human. At some times we have seen them depressed by overbearing and tyrannical princes; at others so luxuriant as even to tend to anarchy, a worse state than tyranny itself, as any government is better than none at all. But the vigour of our free constitution has always delivered the nation from these embarassments, and, as soon as the convulsions consequent on the struggle have been over, the balance of our rights and liberties has settled to its proper level; and their fundamental articles have been from time to time asserted in parliament, as often as they were thought to be in danger.

First, by the great charter of liberties, which was obtained, sword in hand, from king John, and afterwards, with some alterations, confirmed in parliament by King Henry the third, his son. Which charter contained very few new grants; but, as Sir Edward Coke observes, was for the most part declaratory of the principal grounds of the fundamental laws of England. Afterwards by the statute called *confirmatio cartarum,* whereby the great charter is directed to be allowed as the common law; all judgments contrary to it are declared void; copies of it are ordered to be sent to all cathedral churches, and read twice a year to the people; and sentence of excommunication is directed to be as constantly denounced against all those that by word, deed, or counsel, act contrary thereto, or in any degree infringe it. Next by a multitude of subsequent corroborating statutes, (Sir Edward Coke, I think, reckons thirty two,) from the first Edward to Henry the fourth.

Then, after a long interval, by *the petition of right;* which was a parliamentary declaration of liberties of the people, assented to by king Charles the First in the beginning of his reign. Which was closely followed by the still more ample concessions made by that unhappy prince to his parliament, before the fatal rupture between them; and by the many salutary laws, particularly the *habeas corpus* act, passed under Charles the Second. To these succeeded *the bill of rights,* or declaration delivered by the lords and commons to the prince and princess of Orange 13 February, 1688; and afterwards enacted in parliament, when they became king and queen: which declaration concludes in these remarkable words: "and they do claim, demand, and insist upon, all and singular the premises, as their undoubted rights and liberties." And the act of parliament itself recognizes "all and singular the rights and liberties asserted and claimed in the said declaration to be the true, antient, and indubitable rights of the people of this kingdom." Lastly, these liberties were again asserted at the commencement of the present century, in the *act of settlement,* whereby the crown was limited to his present majesty's illustrious house, and some new provisions were added, at the same fortunate era, for better securing our religion, laws, and liberties; which the statute declares to be "the birthright of the people of England," according to the antient doctrine of the common law.

Thus much for the *declaration* of our rights and liberties. The rights themselves thus defined by these several statutes, consist in a number of private immunities; which will appear, from what has been premised, to be indeed no other, than either that *residuum* of natural liberty, which is not required by the laws of society to be sacrificed to public convenience; or else those civil privileges, which society hath engaged to provide, in lieu of the natural liberties so given up by individuals. These therefore were formerly, either by inheritance or purchase, the rights of all mankind; but, in most other countries of the world being now more or less debased and destroyed, they at present may be said to remain, in a peculiar and emphatical manner, the rights of the people of England. And these may be reduced to three principal or primary articles; [1] the right of personal security, [2] the right of personal liberty, and [3] the right of private property: because, as there is no other known method of compulsion or of abridging man's natural free will, but by an infringement or diminution of one or other of these important rights, the preservation of these, inviolate, may justly be said to include the preservation of our civil immunities in their largest and most extensive sense.

* * * *

CHAPTER II: OF THE PARLIAMENT

We are next to examine the laws and customs relating to parliament, thus united together, and considered as one aggregate body.

The power and jurisdiction of parliament, says Sir Edward Coke is so transcendent and absolute, that it cannot be confined, either for causes or persons, within any bounds. And of this high court, he adds, it may be truly said, *"si antiquitatem spectes, est vetustissima; si dignitatem, est honoratissima; si jurisdictionem, est capacissima."* It hath sovereign and uncontrollable authority in the making, confirming, enlarging, restraining, abrogating, repealing, reviving, and expounding of laws, concerning matters of all possible denominations, ecclesiastical or temporal, civil, military, maritime, or criminal: this being the place where that absolute despotic power which must in all governments reside somewhere, is intrusted by the constitution of these kingdoms. All mischiefs and grievances, operations and remedies, that transcend the ordinary course of the laws, are within the reach of this extraordinary tribunal. It can regulate or new model the succession to the crown; as was done in the reign of Henry VIII and William III. It can alter the established religion of the land; as was done in a variety of instances, in the reigns of King Henry VIII and his three children. It can change and create afresh even the constitution of the kingdom and of parliaments themselves; as was done by the act of union, and the several statutes for triennial and septennial elections. It can, in short, do everything that is not naturally impossible; and therefore some have not scrupled to call it's power, but a figure rather too bold, the omnipotence of parliament. True it is, that what they do, no authority upon earth can undo. So that it is a matter most essential to the liberties of this kingdom, that such members be delegated to this important trust, as are most eminent for their probity, their fortitude, and their knowledge; for it was a known apothegm of the great lord treasurer Burleigh, "that England could never be ruined but by a parliament:" and, as Sir Matthew Hale observes, "this being the highest and greatest court, over which none other can have jurisdiction in the kingdom, if by any means a misgovernment should any way fall upon it the subjects of this kingdom are left without all manner of remedy."[40] To the same purpose the president Montesquieu, though I trust too hastily, presages; that, as Rome, Sparta, and Carthage, have lost their liberty, and perished, so the constitution of England will in time lose its liberty, will perish: it will perish, whenever the legislative power shall become more corrupt than the executive.

---

[40]The 1765 Clarendon Press edition omits the quotation marks.

It must be owned that Mr. Locke, and other theoretical writers, have held, that "there remains still inherent in the people a supreme power to remove, or alter the legislative, when they find the legislative act contrary to the trust reposed in them: for when such trust is abused, it is thereby forfeited, and devolves to those who gave it." But however just this conclusion may be in theory, we cannot practically adopt it, nor take any *legal* steps for carrying it into execution, under any dispensation of government at present actually existing.[41] For this devolution of power, to the people at large, includes in it a dissolution of the whole form of government established by that people; reduces all the members to their original state of equality; and by annihilating the sovereign power, repeals all positive laws whatsoever before enacted. No human laws will therefore suppose a case, which at once must destroy all law, and compel men to build afresh upon a new foundation; nor will they make provision for so desperate an event, as must render all legal provisions ineffectual. So long therefore as the English constitution lasts, we may venture to affirm, that the power of parliament is absolute and without control.

* * * *

As to cases of ordinary public oppression, where the vitals of the constitution are not attacked, the law hath also assigned a remedy. For, as a king cannot misuse his power, without the advice of evil counsellors, and the assistance of wicked ministers, these men may be examined and punished. The constitution has therefore provided, by means of indictments, and parliamentary impeachments, that no man shall dare to assist the crown in contradiction to the laws of the land. But it is at the same time a maxim in those laws, that the king himself can do no wrong; since it would be a great weakness and absurdity in any system of positive law, to define any possible wrong, without any possible redress.

For, as to such public oppressions as tend to dissolve the constitution, and subvert the fundamentals of government, they are cases which the law will not, out of decency, suppose; being incapable of distrusting those, whom it has invested with any part of the supreme power; since such distrust would render the exercise of that power precarious and impracticable. For, wherever the law expresses it's distrust of abuse of power, it always vests a superior coercive authority in some other hand to correct it; the very notion of which destroys the

---

[41]The version in Kurland and Lerner, I: 88, reads: "But however just this conclusion may be in theory, we cannot adopt it, nor argue from it, under any dispensation of government at present actually existing."

idea of sovereignty. If therefore (for example) the two houses of parliament, or either of them, had avowedly a right to animadvert on the king, or each other, or if the king had a right to animadvert on either of the houses, that branch of the legislature, so subject to animadversion, would instantly cease to be part of the supreme power; the ballance of the constitution would be overturned; and that branch or branches, in which this jurisdiction resided, would be completely sovereign. The supposition of *law* therefore is, that neither the king nor either house of parliament (collectively taken) is capable of doing any wrong; since in such cases the law feels itself incapable of furnishing any adequate remedy. For which reason all oppressions, which may happen to spring from any branch of the sovereign power, must necessarily be out of the reach of any *stated rule,* or *express legal* provision: but, if ever they unfortunately happen, the prudence of the times must provide new remedies upon new emergencies.

Indeed, it is found by experience, that whenever the unconstitutional oppressions, even of the sovereign power, advance with gigantic strides, and threaten desolation to a state, mankind will not be reasoned out of the feelings of humanity; nor will sacrifice their liberty by a scrupulous adherence to those political maxims, which were originally established to preserve it. And therefore, though the positive laws are silent, experience will furnish us with a very remarkable case, wherein nature and reason prevailed. When king James the second invaded the fundamental constitution of the realm, the convention declared an abdication, whereby the throne was rendered vacant, which induced a new settlement of the crown. And so far as this precedent leads, and no farther, we may now be allowed to lay down the *law* of redress against public oppression. If therefore any future prince should endeavor to subvert the constitution by breaking the original contract between king and people, should violate the fundamental laws, and should withdraw himself out of the kingdom; we are now authorized to declare that this conjunction of circumstances would amount to an abdication, and the throne would be thereby vacant. But it is not for us to say, that any one, or two, of these ingredients would amount to such a situation; for there our precedent would fail us. In these therefore, or other circumstances, which a fertile imagination may furnish, since both law and history are silent, it becomes us to be silent too; leaving to future generations, whenever necessity and the safety of the whole shall require it, the exertion of those inherent (though latent) powers of society, which no climate, no time, no constitution, no contract, can ever destroy or diminish.

* * * *

After what has been premised in this chapter, I shall not (I trust) be considered as an advocate for arbitrary power, when I lay it down as a principle, that in the exertion of lawful prerogative the king is and ought to be absolute; that is, so far absolute, that there is no legal authority that can either delay or resist him. He may reject what bills, may make what treaties, may coin what money, may create what peers, may pardon what offences he pleases; unless where the constitution hath expressly, or by evident consequence, laid down some exception, or boundary; declaring, that thus far the prerogative shall go, and no farther. For otherwise the power of the crown would indeed be but a name and a shadow, insufficient for the ends of government, if, where it's jurisdiction is clearly established and allowed, any man or body of men were permitted to disobey it, in the ordinary course of law: I say, in the *ordinary* course of law; for I do not now speak of those *extraordinary* recourses to first principles, which are necessary when the contracts of society are in danger of dissolution, and the law proves too weak a defence against the violence of fraud or oppression. And yet the want of attending to this obvious distinction has occasioned these doctrines, of absolute power in the prince and of national resistance by the people, to be much misunderstood and perverted by the advocates for slavery on the one hand, and the demagogues of faction on the other. The former, observing the absolute sovereignty and transcendent dominion of the crown laid down (as it certainly is) most strongly and emphatically in our law books, as well as our homilies, have denied that any case can be excepted from so general and positive a rule; forgetting how impossible it is, in any practical system of laws, to point out beforehand those eccentrical remedies, which the sudden emergence of national distress may dictate, and which that alone can justify. On the other hand, over-zealous republicans, feeling the absurdity of unlimited passive obedience, have fancifully (or sometime factiously) gone over to the other extreme: and, because resistance is justifiable to the person of the prince when the being of the state is endangered, and the public voice proclaims such resistance necessary, they have therefore allowed to every individual the right of determining this expedience, and of employing private force to resist even private oppression. A doctrine productive of anarchy, and (in consequence) equally fatal to civil liberty as tyranny itself. For civil liberty, rightly understood, consists in protecting the rights of individuals by the united force of society: society cannot be maintained, and of course can exert no protection, without obedience to some sovereign power: and obedience is an empty name, if every individual has a right to decide how far he himself shall obey.

Chapter Three

An Expression of the American Mind

In this chapter, we show how "the American Mind" expressed both the restorative and revolutionary dimensions of the argument on behalf of a declaration of rights. Between 1764 and 1776, Americans synthesized the common law arguments of Blackstone, the novel doctrine of natural rights associated with Locke and Sidney, the teachings of Christian scripture, and the common sense position articulated by Hume and Burke.

James Otis

James Otis (1725-1783) was born into a family that had emigrated to Massachusetts from England in the early 1600s. Like many other prominent professional in the colonies--he was a graduate in law from Harvard--Otis was drawn into the great taxation debates following the Stamp Act of 1764. He acquired the reputation as a zealous and successful defender of individual rights. Like other participants, he had the ability to locate the immediate struggle over taxation within a larger theoretical context. Most importantly, Otis--following Locke and Sidney--argues that government ought not to be based on blind necessity or force: the people have the ability and the right to choose the form of government under which they shall live.

Richard Bland

Richard Bland (1710-1776) served in the colonial Virginia House of Burgesses from 1742 until 1775. He was also elected to the first

Continental Congress and to the first House of Delegates under the new state constitution. Jefferson considered Bland to be "one of the oldest, ablest and most respected" of the numerous politicians to address the crisis with Britain between 1763 and 1776. His 1766 pamphlet, *An Inquiry into the Rights of the British Colonies,* was among the earliest defenses of the colonial position on taxation. Bland's pamphlet is important because of his critical analysis of virtual representation. He set the tone for what became central to the American concept of political rights during the next decade: there should be no taxation without actual representation. Bland appeals to "the fundamental Principles of the *English* Constitution," the Saxon tradition, the "Principle of the Law of Nature," and the separate colonial charters, as authoritative sources.

Samuel Adams

Samuel Adams wrote extensively on behalf of the rights of the colonists during the critical period between 1764 and 1774. Adams joined together the separate Lockean natural right doctrine, the rights of Englishmen incorporated in the 1689 Bill of Rights, Blackstone's reliance on courts of law, and the American covenanting tradition to support the right of Bostonians to resist the importation of British law. In the final analysis, however, Adams realized that the strongest case for the colonial position was the "natural rights of the colonists as men."

John Tucker

John Tucker (1719-1792) studied theology at Harvard and graduated in 1741. Pastor Tucker's sermon, delivered in May 1771 before numerous political dignitaries is yet another example of how the revolutionary-era participants placed the particular dispute over taxation policies within a more general theoretical, even divine, framework. Of particular importance is Tucker's argument that the enlightenment principles of Locke and the Protestant Christian religion endorse the right to resist the agents of corruption and slavery: "the voice of reason...may be said to be the voice of God." Tucker also demonstrates how the American position is consistent with the constitutional heritage bequeathed by the Magna Carta.

Thomas Jefferson I: Summary View

This "Summary View" was originally prepared for "the delegates of the people of Virginia meeting in Convention." This July 1774 defense of the colonial position was signed, "a Native, and Member of the House of Burgesses," although the author of this forty-page pamphlet was Jefferson. Among other things, Jefferson articulates the fundamental compatibility between Locke's natural right doctrine and the 1689 Bill of Rights. He goes even further and suggests that they are both consistent with the common law tradition of ancient Saxon England that existed prior to the Norman invasion of 1066.

First Continental Congress

Jefferson's views were also shared with the delegates who attended the First Continental Congress in 1774, This gathering is important because it is the first official continental expression of rights, one that also envisioned the inclusion of Quebeckers. Of interest is the ease with which the Congress combines into a coherent whole the three separate claims for defending the ten rights that have been violated:

> That the inhabitants of the English colonies in North-America, by [1] the immutable laws of nature, [2] the principles of the English constitution, and [3] the several charters or compacts.

Nevertheless, the 1774 Declaration is better understood as an expression of the traditional right to petition for the redress of infractions against the common law than as a revolutionary declaration of the right to choose the form of government under which one shall live.

Edmund Burke

Edmund Burke (1729-1797) elected representative from Bristol in the English Parliament--and Parliament's appointed agent for New York--is known for his opposition to the 1789 French Revolution and his defense of law and order. Burke criticized speculative arguments that appealed to abstract notions of natural right and social contract. Thus, it seems surprising to see Burke defending the American revolutionaries in their quarrel with the British monarchy and parliament over taxation and representation. But, for Burke, the American argument was grounded in the traditional rights of Englishmen.

Thomas Jefferson II: The Declaration of Independence

The Declaration of Independence is vital to the story of the Bill of Rights in three ways.

First, it declares that the purpose of government is to secure rights, some of which are unalienable, and thus beyond the legitimate reach of those in power. At the same time, however, it places the right to operate government in the hands of the majority of the people. During the next decade, the rival claims of minority rights and majority rule change the scope of the conversation about rights.

Second, the Declaration is made on behalf of the united colonies, suggesting that there is a continental right to existence. On the other hand, the colonies are declared to be separate and independent states endowed with sovereignty over their internal affairs. The fact that

America is declared to be simultaneously a nation of people, and a nation of states, also framed the subsequent discourse over rights.

Finally, it is both restorative and revolutionary. Jefferson expressed the restorative aspects in a letter to Henry Lee:

> Neither aiming at originality of principle or sentiment, nor yet copied from any particular and previous writing, it was intended to be an expression of the American mind, and to give to that expression the proper tone and spirit called for by the occasion. All its authority rests then on the harmonizing sentiments of the day, whether expressed in conversation, in letters, printed essays, or in the elementary books of public right, as Aristotle, Cicero, Locke, Sidney, etc.

Writing to Roger Weightman, Jefferson expressed the revolutionary potential of the Declaration:

> May it be...the signal of arousing men to burst the chains under which monkish ignorance and superstition had persuaded them to bind themselves, and to assume the blessings and security of self-government. That form which we have substituted, restores the free right to the unbounded exercise of reason and freedom of opinion. All eyes are opened, or opening, to the rights of man.

Jefferson also understood the Declaration to contain a new teaching on property relations. During the first session of the newly-created Virginia assembly in the fall of 1776, representative Jefferson introduced a bill to end the "vicious" feudal practice of primogeniture. Jefferson's bill, which passed, permits a property holder "to divide the property among his children equally." Thus Jefferson envisioned that "an enlargement" of "natural right" would take place permitting the "natural aristocracy" of virtue and talent to replace the artificial aristocracy of wealth and power.

Nowhere were the novel, and transcendental, implications of the Declaration so visible than in Jefferson's attempt to include a denunciation of slavery. The Second Continental Congress received a draft of the Declaration from Jefferson that made the British rejection of the petition submitted by the First Continental Congress to end the slave trade a ground for severing ties. However, in order not to offend the sensibilities of the delegates from Georgia and South Carolina, a denunciation of slavery was omitted from the final declaration. We suggest that the inclusion of such an indictment would have had a profound impact on the continuing American conversation about rights.

XVIII.

JAMES OTIS, *THE RIGHTS OF THE BRITISH COLONIES ASSERTED AND PROVED*, 1764

The entry below is from pages 8-13 of Otis's 27-page theoretical introduction to the 80-page defense found in *The Rights of the British Colonies Asserted and Proved* (1764). The introduction is entitled, "Of the Origin of Government." We have also consulted the second edition, published in London the following year, available at The Huntington Library. Italics--and the footnotes identified by an "*"--are in the original. We have added the Arabic-numbered footnote. For a more recent rendition, see *Some Political Writings of James Otis*, with an introduction by Charles F. Mullett (Columbia: University of Missouri Press, 1929, IV: 305-357). Francis Bowen's 1844 biography of Otis is still the best available. See Jared Sparks's *The Library of American Biography*, 1844 (II: 1-199). Kurland and Lerner, (I: 52-53) also reprint parts of Otis's introduction using different spelling than found in the earliest editions.

~

Let no Man think I am about to commence advocate[ing] for *despotism*, because I affirm that government is founded on the necessity of our natures; and that an original supreme Sovereign, absolute, and uncontroulable, *earthly* power *must* exist in and preside over every society; from whose final decisions there can be no appeal but directly to Heaven. It is therefore *originally* and *ultimately* in the people. I say supreme absolute power is *originally* and *ultimately* in the people; and they never did in fact *freely*, nor can they *rightfully* make an absolute, unlimited renunciation of this divine right.* It is ever in the nature of the thing given in *trust* and on a condition, the performance of which no mortal can dispence with; namely, that the person or persons on whom the sovereignty is confered by the people, shall *incessantly* consult *their* good. Tyranny of all kinds is to be abhored, whether it be in the hands of one, or of the few, or of the many.—And though "in the last age a generation of men sprung up that would flatter Princes with an opinion that *they* have a *divine right* to absolute power;" yet "slavery is so vile and miserable an estate of man, and so directly opposite to the generous temper and courage of our nation, that it is

*The power of GOD Almighty is the only power that can properly and strictly be called supreme and absolute. In the order of nature immediately under him, comes the power of a simple *democracy,* or the power of the whole over the whole. Subordinate to both these, are all other political powers, from that of the French Monarque, to a petty constable.

hard to be conceived that an *Englishman,* much less a *gentleman,* should plead for it.**" Especially at a time when the finest writers of the most polite nations on the continent of *Europe*, are enraptured with the beauties of the civil constitution of *Great-Britain;* and envy her, no less for the *freedom* of her sons, than for her immense *wealth* and *military* glory.

But let the *origin* of government be placed where it may, the *end* of it is manifestly the good of *the whole. Salus populi supreme lex esto,* is of the law of nature, and part of that grand charter given the human race (though too many of them are afraid to assert it) by the only monarch in the universe, who has a clear and indisputable right to *absolute* power; because he is the only ONE who is *omniscient* as well as *omnipotent.*

It is evidently contrary to the first principles of reason, that supreme *unlimited* power should be in the hands of *one* man. It is the greatest "*idolatry,* begotten by *flattery,* on the body of *pride,*" that could induce one to think that a *single mortal* should be able to hold so great a power, if ever so well inclined. Hence the origin of *deifying* princes: it was from the trick of gulling the vulgar into a belief that their tyrants were *omniscient;* and that it was therefore right, that they should be considered as *omnipotent.* Hence the *Dii majorum et minorum gentium*; the great, the monarchical, the little, Provincial subordinate and subaltern gods, demi-gods, and semidemi-gods, ancient and modern. Thus deities of all kinds were multiplied and increased in *abundance*; for every devil incarnate, who could enslave a people, acquired a title to *divinity*; and thus the "rabble of the skies" was made up of locusts and caterpillars; lions, tygers and harpies; and other devourers translated from plaguing the earth!***

The *end* of government being the *good* of mankind, points out its great duties: it is above all things to provide for the security, the quiet, and happy enjoyment of life, liberty, and property. There is no one act which a government can have a *right* to make, that does not tend to the advancement of the security, tranquility and prosperity of the people. If life, liberty and property could be enjoyed in as great perfection in *solitude*, as in *society*, there would be no need of government. But the experience of ages has proved that such is the nature of man, a weak, imperfect being; that the valuable ends of live cannot be obtained, without the union and assistance of many. Hence it is clear that men

---

**Mr. Locke.

***Kingcraft and Priestcraft have fell out so often, that 'tis a wonder this grand and ancient alliance is not broken off for ever. Happy for mankind will it be, when such a separation shall take place.

cannot live apart or independent of each other: in solitude men would perish; and yet they cannot live together without contests. These contests require some arbitrator to determine them. The necessity of a common, indifferent and impartial judge, makes all men seek one; though few find him in the *sovereign power*, of their respective states or any where else in *subordination* to it.

Government is founded *immediately* on the necessities of human nature, and *ultimately* on the will of God, the author of nature; who has not left it to men in general to choose, whether they will be members of society or not, but at the hazard of their senses if not of their lives. Yet it is left to every man as he comes of age to chuse *what society* he will continue to belong to. Nay if one has a mind to turn *hermit*, and after he has been born, nursed, and brought up in the arms of society, and acquired the habits and passions of social life, is willing to run the risque of starving alone, which is generally most unavoidable in a state of hermitage, who shall hinder him? I know of no human law, founded on the law of *nature*, to restrain him from separating himself from the species, if he can find it in his heart to leave them; unless it should be said, it is against the great law of *self-preservation*: But of this every man will think himself *his own judge*.

The few *hermits* and *misanthropes* that ever that have ever existed, shew that those states are *unnatural*. If we were to take out from them, those who have made great *worldly* gain of their *godly* hermitage, and those who have been under the madness of *enthusiasm*, or *disappointed* hopes in their ambitious projects, for the detriment of mankind, perhaps there might not be left ten from *Adam* to this day.

The form of government is by *nature* and by *right* so far left to the *individuals* of each society, that they may alter it from a simple democracy or government of all over all, to any other form they please. Such alteration may and ought to be made by express compact: But how seldom this right has been asserted, history will abundantly show. For once that it has been fairly settled by compact; *fraud, force or accident* have determined it an hundred times. As the people have gained upon tyrants, these have been obliged to relax, *only* till a fairer opportunity has put it in their power to encroach again.

But if every prince since *Nimrod* had been a tyrant, it would not prove a *right* to tyranize. There can be no prescription old enough to supersede the law of nature, and the grant of God Almighty; who has given to all men a natural right to be *free*, and they have it ordinarily in their power to make themselves so, if they please.

Government having been proved to be necessary by the law of nature, it makes no difference in the thing to call it from a certain period, *civil*. This term can only relate to form, to additions to, or deviations from, the substance of government: This being founded in nature, the superstructures and the whole administration should be conformed to the law of universal reason. A supreme legislative and supreme executive power, must be placed *somewhere* in every commonwealth: Where there is no other positive provision or compact to the contrary,[1] those powers remain in the *whole body of the people*. It is also evident there can be but *one* best way of depositing those powers; but what that way is, mankind have been disputing in peace and in war more than five thousand years. If we could suppose the individuals of a community met to deliberate, whether it were best to keep those powers in *their own* hands, or dispose of them in *trust*, the following questions would occur—Whether those two great powers of *Legislation* and *Execution* should remain united? If so, whether in the hands of the many, or jointly or severally in the hands of a few, or jointly in some one individual? If both those powers are retained in the hands of the many, where nature seems to have placed them originally, the government is a simple *democracy*, or a government of all over all. This can be administered, only by establishing it as a first principle, that the votes of the majority shall be taken as the voice of the whole. If those powers are lodged in the hands of a few, the government is an *Aristocracy* or *Oligarchy*.[****] Here too the first principles of a practicable administration is, that the majority rules the whole. If those great powers are both lodged in the hands of one man, the government is a *simple Monarchy*, commonly though falsely called *absolute*, if by that term is meant a right to do as one pleases. *Sic volo, sic jubeo, stet pro ratione voluntas*, belongs not of right to any mortal man.

The same law of nature and of reason is equally obligatory on a *democracy*, an *aristocracy*, and a *monarchy*: Whenever the administrators, in any of those forms, deviate from truth, justice and equity, they verge towards tyranny, and are to be opposed; and if they prove incorrigible, they will be *deposed* by the people, if the people are not rendered too abject. Deposing the administrators of a *simple democracy* may sound oddly, but it is done every day, and in almost every vote. A, B, and C for example, make a *democracy*; today A and B are for so vile a measure as a standing army; tomorrow B and C vote it out. This is a really deposing the former administrators, as setting up and making a new king is deposing the old one. *Democracy* in the one case, and *monarchy* in the other, still remain; all that is done is to change the administration.

---

[1]Kurland and Lerner (I: 53) have "compact to the contract."

[****]For the sake of the unlettered reader it is noted, that Monarchy means the power of one great man; Aristocracy and Oligarchy that of a few; and Democracy that of all men.

The first principle and great end of government being to provide for the best good of all the people, this can be done only by a supreme legislative and executive ultimately in the people, or whole community, where God has placed it; but the inconveniencies, not to say impossibility, attending the consultations and operations of a large body of people have made it necessary to transfer the power of the whole to a *few*: This necessity gave rise to deputation, proxy or a right of representation.

XIX.

RICHARD BLAND, *AN INQUIRY INTO THE RIGHTS OF THE BRITISH COLONIES,* 1776

We have reprinted the first half of Richard Bland's *An Inquiry into the Rights of the British Colonies* on virtual representation and followed the spelling and punctuation found in the 1766 printing by Alexander Purdie in Williamsburg. We have retained Bland's footnote reference to Vattel, Locke, and Wollaston, but deleted the others. The italics are in the original. We begin at the fourth paragraph. This original version has been reproduced by Earl Gregg Swem, editor (Richmond, Appeals Press, 1922). For a contemporary version, see Hyneman and Lutz (I: 67-87).

~

The Question is whether the Colonies are represented in the *British* Parliament or not? You affirm it to be indubitable Fact that they are represented, and from thence you infer a Right in the Parliament to impose Taxes of every Kind upon them. You do not insist upon the *Power,* but upon the *Right* of Parliament to impose Taxes upon the Colonies. This is certainly a very proper Distinction, as *Right* and *Power* have very different Meanings, and convey very different Ideas: For had you told us that the Parliament of *Great Britain* have *Power,* by the Fleets and Armies of the Kingdom, to impose Taxes and to raise Contributions upon the Colonies, I should not have to presumed to dispute the Point with you; but as you insist upon the *Right* only, I must beg Leave to differ from you in Opinion, and shall give my Reasons for it.

* * * *

I cannot comprehend how Men who are excluded from voting at the Election of Members of Parliament can be represented in that

Assembly, or how those who are elected do not sit in the House as Representatives of their Constituents. These Assertions appear to me not only paradoxical, but contrary to the fundamental Principles of the *English* Constitution.

To illustrate this important Disquisition, I conceive we must recur to the civil Constitution of *England,* and from thence deduce and ascertain the Rights and Privileges of the People at the first Establishment of the Government, and discover the Alterations that have been made in them from Time to Time; and it is from the Laws of the Kingdom, founded upon the Principles of the Law of Nature, that we are to show the Obligation every Member of the State is under to pay Obedience to its Institutions. From these Principles I shall endeavor to prove that the Inhabitants of *Britain,* who have no Vote in the Election of Members of Parliament, are not represented in that Assembly, and yet that they owe Obedience to the Laws of Parliament; which, as to them, are constitutional, and not arbitrary. As to the Colonies, I shall consider them afterwards.

Now it is a Fact, as certain as History can make it, that the present civil Constitution of *England* derives its Original from those *Saxons* who, coming over to the Assistance of the *Britons* in the Time of their King *Vortiger* made themselves Masters of the Kingdom, and established a Form of Government in it similar to that they had been accustomed to live under in their native Country as similar, at least, as the Difference of their Situation and Circumstances would permit. This Government, like that from whence they came, was founded upon Principles of the most perfect Liberty: The conquered Lands were divided among the Individuals in Proportion to the Rank they held in the Nation, and every Freeman, that is, every Freeholder, was a member of their Wittinagemot, or Parliament. The other Part of the Nation, or the Non-Proprietors of Land, were of little Estimation. They, as in *Germany,* were either Slaves, mere Hewers of Wood and Drawers of Water, or Freedmen; who, being of foreign Extraction, had been manumitted by their Masters, and were excluded from the high Privilege of having a Share in the Administration of the Commonwealth, unless they became Proprietors of Land (which they might obtain by Purchase or Donation) and in that Case they has a Right to sit with the Freemen, in the Parliament or sovereign Legislature of the State.

How long this Right of being personally present in the Parliament continued, or when the Custom of sending Representatives to this great Council of the Nation, was first introduced, cannot be determined with Precision; but let the Custom of Representation be introduced when it will, it is certain that every Freeman, or, which was the same Thing in the Eye of the Constitution, every Freeholder, had a right to vote at the Election of Members of Parliament, and therefore might be said, with great Propriety, to be present in that Assembly, either in his own Person or by Representation. This Right of Election in the Freeholders is evident from the Statute 1st Hen. 5. Ch. 1st, which limits the Right of Election to those Freeholders only who are resident in the Counties the Day of the Date of the Writ of Election; but yet every resident Freeholder indiscriminately, let his Freehold be ever so small, had a Right to vote at the Election of Knights for his County so that they were actually represented. And this Right of Election continued until it was taken away by the Statute 8th Hen. 6 Ch. 7. Shillings by the year at the least.

Now this statute was deprivative of the Right of those Freeholders who came within the Description of it; but of what did it deprive them, if they were represented notwithstanding their Right of Election was taken from them? The mere Act of voting was nothing, of no Value, if they were represented as constitutionally without it as with it: But when by the fundamental Principles of the Constitution they were to be considered as Members of the Legislature, and as such had a right to be present in Person, or to send their Procurators or Attornies, and by them to give their Suffrage in the supreme Council of the Nation, this Statute deprived them of an essential Right; a Right without which by the ancient Constitution of the State, all other Liberties were but a Species of Bondage.

As these Freeholders then were deprived of their Rights to substitute Delegates to Parliament, they could not be represented, but were placed in the same Condition with the Non-Proprietors of Land, who were excluded by the original Constitution from having any Share in the Legislature, but who, notwithstanding such Exclusion, are bound to pay Obedience to the Laws of Parliament, even if they should consist of nine Tenths of the People of *Britain*; but then the Obligation of these Laws does not arise from their being virtually represented in Parliament, but from a quite different Reason.

* * * *

From hence it is evident that the Obligation of the Laws of Parliament upon the People of *Britain* who have no Right to be Electors does not arise from their being *virtually* represented, but from a quit different Principle; a Principle of the Law of Nature, true, certain, and universal, applicable to every Sort of Government, and not contrary to the common Understandings of Mankind.

If what you say is real Fact, that the nine Tenths of the People of *Britain* are deprived of the high Privilege of being Electors, it shows a great Defect in the present Constitution, which has departed so much from its original Purity; but never can prove that those People are even *virtually* represented in Parliament. And here give me Leave to observe that it would be a Work worthy of the best patriotick Spirits in the Nation to effectuate an Alteration in this putrid Part of the Constitution; and, by restoring it to its pristine Perfection, prevent any "Order or Rank of the Subjects from imposing upon or binding the rest without their Consent." But, I fear, the Gangrene has taken too deep Hold to be eradicated in these Days of Venality.

But if those People of *Britain* who are excluded from being Electors are not represented in Parliament, the Conclusion is much stronger against the People of the Colonies being represented; who are considered by the *British* Government itself, in every Instance of Parliamentary Legislation, as a distinct People.

* * * *

As then we can receive no Light from the Laws of the Kingdom, or from ancient History, to direct us in out Inquiry, we must have Recourse to the Law of Nature, and those Rights of Mankind which flow from it.

I have observed before that when Subjects are deprived of their civil Rights, or are dissatisfied with the Place they hold in the Community, they have a natural Right to quit the Society of which they are Members, and to retire into another Country. Now when Men exercise this Right, and withdraw themselves from their Country, they recover their natural Freedom and Independence: The Jurisdiction and Sovereignty of the State they have quitted ceases; and if they unite, and by common Consent take Possession of a New Country, and form themselves into a political Society, they become a sovereign State, independent of the State from which they have separated. If then the Subjects of *England* have a natural Right to relinquish their Country, and by retiring from it, and associating together, to form a new political Society and independent State, they must have a Right, by Compact with Sovereign of the Nation, to remove into a new Country, and to form a civil Establishment upon the Terms of the Compact. In such a Case, the Terms of the Compact must be obligatory and binding upon the Parties; they must be the Magna Charta, the fundamental Principles of Government, to this new Society; and every Infringement of them must be wrong, and may be opposed. It will be necessary then to examine whether any such Compact was entered into between the Sovereign and those *English* Subjects who established themselves in *America*.

XX.

SAMUEL ADAMS, *BOSTON GAZETTE* *UNTITLED*, 27 FEBRUARY, 1769 AND *RIGHTS OF THE COLONISTS*, 20 NOVEMBER, 1772

We have relied on the multi-volume 1904 edition of the writings of Samuel Adams by Harry Alonzo Cushing. Both articles were printed in the *Boston Gazette*. The first signed "E.A."--one of a number of pseudonyms adopted by Adams in newspapers during the late 1760--can be found in Cushing (I: 316-319). Adams's second commentary on the rights of the colonists, subsequently endorsed by the town of Boston in November 1772, can be found in Cushing (II: 350-359). Reproduced below is the section on "The Rights of the Colonists" that addresses their natural rights. We have retained the original spelling--for example, "John Lock", "religeon" etc.--and have included Adams's own footnotes. See also Kurland and Lerner (I: 90, and V: 60) for an edited version of the above entries.

~

[A] Adams' Untitled Article

In the days of the STUARTS, it was look'd upon by some men as a high degree of prophaness, for any subject to enquire into what was called the *mysteries* of government: *James* the first thundered his anathema against Dr. *Cowel,* for his daring presumption in treating of––those *mysteries*, and forbad his subjects to read his books, or even to keep them in their houses. In those days *passive obedience, non-resistance,* the *divine hereditary right* of kings, and their being accountable to God *alone*, were doctrines generally taught, believ'd and practiced: But behold the sudden transition of human affairs! In the very next reign the people assum'd the right of *free enquiry,* into the nature and end of government, and the conduct of those who were entrusted with it: *Laud* and Strafford were bro't to the block; and after the horrors of a civil war, in which some of the best blood of the nation was spilt as water upon the ground, they finally called to account, arraign'd, adjudg'd, condemn'd and even executed the monarch himself! and for a time held his son and heir in exile. The two sons of *Charles* the first, after the death of *Oliver Cromwell,* reigned in their turns; but by copying after their father, their administration of government was *grievous* to their subjects, and *infamous* abroad. *Charles* the second indeed reign'd till he died; but his brother *James* was oblig'd to abdicate the throne, which made room for *William* the third, and his royal consort *Mary*, the daughter of the unfortunate *James*— This was the fate of a race of Kings, bigotted to the greatest degree to the doctrines of *slavery* and regardless of the *natural, inherent, divinely hereditary* and *indefeasible* rights of their subjects.—At the revolution, the British constitution was again restor'd to its original principles, declared in the bill of rights; which was afterwards pass'd into a law, and stands as a bulwark to the natural rights of subjects. "To vindicate these rights, says Mr. *Blackstone*, when actually violated or attack'd, the subjects of England are entitled first to the regular administration and *free course of justice* in the courts of law--next to the right of *petitioning the King* and parliament for redress of grievances—and lastly, to the right of *having and using arms for self-preservation and defence*." These he calls "auxiliary subordinate rights, which serve principally as *barriers* to protect and maintain inviolate the three great and primary rights of *personal security, personal liberty* and *private property*": And that of *having arms for their defence* he tells us is "a public allowance, under due restrictions, of the *natural right of resistance and self preservation*, when the sanctions of society and laws are found *insufficient* to restrain the *violence of oppression*."—How little do those persons attend to the rights of the constitution, if they know anything about them, who find fault with a late vote of this town, calling upon the inhabitants to *provide themselves with arms for their defence* at any time; but more especially, when they had reason to fear, there would be a necessity of the means of self preservation against the *violence of oppression*.—Every one knows that the exercise of the military power is forever *dangerous* to civil rights; and we have had recent instances of *violences* that have been offer'd to *private subjects*, and the last week, even *to a magistrate in the execution of his office*!— Such violences are no more than might have been expected from *military troops*: A power, which is apt enough at all times to take a wanton lead, even when in the midst of civil society; but more especially so, when they are led to believe that *they* are become *necessary*, to awe a spirit of *rebellion*, and preserve *peace and good order*. But there are some persons, who would, if possibly they could, perswade the people *never to make use* of their *constitutional* rights or terrify them from doing it. No wonder that a resolution of this town to *keep arms* for its own defence, should be represented as having at bottom a *secret intention* to oppose the landing of the King's troops: when those very persons, who gave it this colouring, had before represented the people petitioning their Sovereign, as proceeding from a *factious* and *rebellious* spirit; and would now insinuate that there is an *impropriety* in their addressing even a plantation *Governor* upon public business—Such are the times we are fallen into!

[B] Adams' Rights of the Colonists

Ist. Natural Rights of the Colonists as Men.——

Among the Natural Rights of the Colonists are these First. a Right to *Life;* Secondly to *Liberty;* thirdly to *Property;* together with the Right to support and defend them in the best manner they can——Those are evident Branches of, rather than deductions from the Duty of Self Preservation, commonly called the first Law of Nature——

All Men have a Right to remain in a State of Nature as long as they please: And in case of intollerable Oppression, Civil or Religious, to leave the Society they belong to, and enter into another.——

When Men enter into Society, it is by voluntary consent; and they have a right to demand and insist upon the performance of such conditions, And previous limitations as form an equitable *original compact.*——

Every natural Right not expressly given up or from the nature of a Social Compact necessarily ceded remains.—

All positive and civil laws, should conform as far as possible, to the Law of natural reason and equity.——

As neither reason requires, nor religeon permits the contrary, every Man living in or out of a state of civil society, has a right peaceably and quietly to worship God according to the dictates of his conscience.——

"Just and true liberty, equal and impartial liberty" in matters spiritual and temporal, is a thing that all Men are clearly entitled to, by the eternal and immutable laws of God and nature, as well as by the law of Nations, & all well grounded municipal laws, which must have their foundation in the former.——

In regard to Religeon, mutual tolleration in the different professions thereof, is what all good and candid minds in all ages have ever practiced; and both by precept and example inculcated on mankind: And it is now generally agreed among christians that this spirit of toleration in the fullest extent consistent with the being of civil society "is the chief characteristical mark of the true church"[2] & In so much that Mr. Lock has asserted, and proved beyond the possibility of contradiction on any solid ground, that such toleration ought to be extended to all whose doctrines are not subversive of society. The only Sects which he thinks ought to be, and which by all wise laws are excluded from such toleration, are those who teach Doctrines subversive of the Civil Government under which they live. The Roman Catholicks or Papists are excluded by reason of such Doctrines as these "that Princes excommunicated may be deposed, and those they call *Hereticks* may be

[2]See Locks Letters on Toleration.

destroyed without mercy; besides their recognizing the Pope in so absolute a manner, in subversion of Government, by introducing as far as possible into the states, under whose protection they enjoy life, liberty and property, that solecism in politicks, Imperium in imperio[3] leading directly to the worst anarchy and confusion, civil discord, war and blood shed—[4]

The natural liberty of Men by entring into society is abridg'd or restrained so far only as is necessary for the Great end of Society the best gôod of the whole—

In the state of nature, every man is under God, Judge and sole Judge, of his own rights and the injuries done him: By entering into society, he agrees to an Arbiter or indifferent Judge between him and his neighbours; but he no more renounces his original right, than by taking a cause out of the ordinary course of law, and leaving the decision to referees or indifferent Arbitrations. In the last case he must pay the Referees for time and trouble; he should be also willing to pay his Just quota for the support of government, the law and constitution; the end of which is to furnish indifferent and impartial Judges in all cases that may happen, whether civil ecclesiastical, marine or military.——

"The natural liberty of man is to be free from any superior power on earth, and not to be under the will or legislative authority of man; but only to have the law of nature for his rule."——

In the state of nature men may as the *Patriarchs* did, employ hired servants for the defence of their lives, liberty and property: and they should them reasonable wages. Government was instituted for the purposed of common defence; and those who hold the reins of government have an equitable natural right to an honourable support from the same principle "that the labourer is worth of his hire: but then the same community which they serve, ought to be assessors of their pay: Governors have no right to seek what they please; by this, instead of being content with the station assigned them, that of honourable servants of the society, they would soon become Absolute masters, Despots, and Tyrants. Hence as a private man has a right to say, what wages he will give in his private affairs, so has a Community to determine what they will give and grant of their Substance, for the Administration of publick affairs. and in both cases more are ready generally to offer their Service at the proposed and stipulated price, than are able and willing to perform their duty.——

In short it is the greatest absurdity to supposed it in the power of one or any number of men at the entering into society, to renounce

---

[3]A government within a government.

[4]Editors' note: the original text does not indicate where this quote ends.

their essential natural rights, or the mans of preserving those rights when the great end of civil government from the very nature of its institution is for the support, protection and defence of those very rights: the principal of which as is before observed, are life liberty and property. If men through fear, fraud or mistake, should *in terms* renounce and give up any essential natural right, the eternal law of reason and the great end of society, would absolutely vacate such renunciation; the right of freedom being *the gift* of God Almighty, it is not in the power of Man to alienate this gift, and voluntarily become a slave——

XXI.

JOHN TUCKER, *AN ELECTION SERMON,* 1771

We have relied on the original 1771 printing by Richard Draper. Accordingly, we have retained Tucker's extensive use of italics as well as his footnote--identified with an "*"--to the "great and judicious Mr. Locke," who is also cited there as "Lock." We have numbered in square parentheses the five practical lessons to be learned. For a contemporary reproduction of Tucker's sermon, see Charles S. Hyneman and Donald S. Lutz, editors, *American Political Writings During the Founding Era* (1985) I: 158-174. We have consulted the copy at the Huntington Library.

~

I Peter II, 13, 14, 15, 16.

Submit yourselves to every ordinance of man for the Lord's sake: Whether it be to the King as supreme, or unto Governors, as unto them who are sent by him, for the punishment of evil-doers, and for the praise of them that do well.
For so is the will of God, that with well-doing ye may put to silence the ignorance of foolish men: As free, and not using your liberty for a cloak of maliciousness, but as the servants of God.

THE great and wise Author of our being, has so formed us, that the love of liberty is natural. This passion, like all other original principles of the human mind, is, in itself perfectly innocent, and designed for excellent purposes, though, like them, liable, through abuse, of becoming the cause of mischief to ourselves and others. In a civil state, the genius of whose constitution is agreeable to it, this passion, while in its full vigor, and under proper regulation, is not only the cement of the political body, but the wakeful guardian of its interests, and the great animating spring of useful and salutary operations; and then only is it unjurious to the public, or to individuals, when, thro' misapprehension of things, or by being overbalanced by self-love, it takes a wrong direction.

CIVIL and ecclesiastical societies are, in some essential points, different. Our rights, as men, and our rights, as christians, are not, in all respects, the same. It cannot, however, be reasonably supposed, but that this useful and important principle, must, in its genuine influence and operation, be friendly to both: For although our Saviour has assured us, his kingdom is not of this world; and it be manifest from the Gospel, which contains its constitution and laws, that his subjects stand in some special relation, and are under some peculiar subjection to him, distinct from their relation to, and connection with civil societies, yet we justly conclude, that as this divine polity, with its sacred maxims, proceeded from the wise and the benevolent Author of our being, none of its injunctions can be inconsistent with that love of liberty, he himself has implanted in us, nor interfere with the laws and government of human societies, whose constitution is consistent with the rights of men.

CHRIST came to set up a kingdom diverse, indeed, from the kingdoms of this world, but it was no part of his design to put down, or destroy government and rule among men. He came to procure liberty for his people, and to make them free in the most important sense, yet not to exempt them from subjection to civil powers, or to dissolve their obligations to one another, as members of political bodies.

AS to things of this nature, all ecclesiastical constitutions and laws, as coming from GOD, must leave men just as they were; because all civil societies, founded on principles of reason and equity, are, as well as the peculiar laws of Christianity, agreeable to the Deity, and certainly, intimations from the all-perfect mind cannot be contradictory.

THESE things, seem not to have been rightly apprehended, and well understood by men at all times and in all places. The Jews, some of whom were early proselyted to the christian faith, had imbibed high notions of their liberty and superiority to all others, as the peculiar people of GOD; and were loth to own subjection to the Romans, as a civil state, when they were actually under their dominion. And some converts from among the Gentiles, tho' they had not these national prejudices, yet from their subjection to Jesus Christ, as their King and Ruler, and, as 'tis probable, from mistaking the meaning of some apostolic declarations asserting their freedom as christians, disclaimed likewise all human authority over them.

MEN of this cast, gave no small trouble both to Church and State, in the early days of the Gospel. Of such, the Apostle Peter speaks where he says—*They despise government: Presumptuous are they. Self-willed, they are not afraid to speak evil of dignities.*

SUCH men as these, and their seditious, turbulent behaviour, I doubt not, this same Apostle had in view, when he delivered the instructions in my text, by which he endeavoured to guard christians against their evil practices.

BUT, as all authority, demanding submission, and all submission, due to such authority, are likely to be best understood, by having these things reduced to their first principles;——by having the foundation of such authority fairly produced, and its just boundaries, which must be the measure of submission due to it, clearly marked out: And as such submission is most likely to be duly yielded, by having the reasons and motives thereof plainly exhibited, so these are things which seem here aimed at by the Apostle: *Submit yourselves to every ordinance of man for the Lord's sake: whether it be to the King as supreme; or unto Governors, as unto them who are sent by him for the punishment of evil-doers, and for the praise of them that do well. For so is the will of God, that with well-doing ye may put to silence the ignorance of foolish men. As free, and not using your liberty for a cloke of maliciousness, but as the servants of God.*

IN these words he gives us a compendium of civil government; representing its origin and great design; that submission, or obedience which is due to it; and the true principles from which such obedience should flow.

UPON this general view of the subject, it is obvious, that if handled with any degree of propriety, it may offer useful instructions, both to Rulers, and those under their government.—A modest attempt to do this, will not, it is hoped, be disagreeable to this respectable audience, by whom I ask to be heard with patience and candor.

THE FIRST thing offered to our consideration is, the ORIGIN of civil government, from whence all authority in the state must take its rise. And this is said to be from man. *Submit yourselves to every ordinance of man,* etc. More intelligibly, perhaps, it might be rendered, "to every human institution or appointment." And this may be justly understood, as having respect to every kind of civil government, under whatever form it is administered:—It is the ordinance,—the institution or appointment of man.

THIS does not imply, however, that civil government is not from God; for thus it is sometimes represented, and is expressly said to be the *ordinance of God.* So St. Paul declares—*There is no power but of God. The powers that be, are ordained of God. Who ever therefore resisteth the power, resisteth the ordinance of God* [Romans XIII, I, 2[5]].

CIVIL government is not, indeed, so from God, as to be expressly appointed by him in his word. Much less is any particular form of it there delineated, as a standing model for the nations of the world: Nor are nay particular persons, pointed out, as having, in a lineal descent, an indefeasible right to rule over others.

BUT civil government may be said to be from God, as it is he who qualifies men for, and in his over-ruling providence, raises them to places of authority and rule; for by him *Kings reign:*—As he has given us, in his word, the character of Rulers, and pointed out both *their* duty, and the duty of those under their authority; which supposes, not only the existence of civil government, but that it is agreeable to His will: And especially and chiefly, as civil government is founded in the very nature of man, as a social being, and in the nature and constitution of things. It is manifestly for the good of society:—It is the dictate of nature:—It is the voice of reason, which may be said to be the voice of God.

IT being only thus that civil government is the ordinance of God, there is no impropriety in asserting likewise that it is the *ordinance of man*. For though it is founded in the nature of man, and in the constitution of things, which are from God, yet nothing is plainer, than that it proceeds immediately from men. It is not a matter of necessity, strictly speaking, but of choice. This is the case, as to the government in general:—This is most evidently the case, as to any particular form of government.

ALL men are naturally in a state of freedom, and have an equal claim to liberty. No one, by nature, nor by any special grant from the great Lord of all, has any authority over another. All right therefore in any to rule over others, must originate from those they rule over, and be granted by them. Hence, all government, consistent with that natural freedom, to which all have an equal claim, is founded in compact, or agreement between the parties;—between Rulers and their Subjects, and can be no otherwise. Because Rulers, receiving their authority originally and solely from the people, can be rightfully possessed of no more, than these have consented to, and conveyed to them.

AND the fundamental laws, which are the basis of government, and form the political constitution of the state;—which mark out, and fix the chief lines and boundaries between the authority of Rulers, and the liberties and privileges of the people, are, and can be no other, in a free state, than what are mutually agreed upon and consented to. Whatever

---

5 Editors' Note: We have added the biblical citation.

authority therefore the supreme power has, to make laws, to appoint officers, etc. for the regulation and government of the state, being an authority derived from the community, and granted by them, can be justly exercised, only within certain limits, and to a certain extent, according to agreement.

TO suppose otherwise, and that without a delegated power and constitutional right, Rulers may make laws, and appoint officers for their execution, and force them into effect, i.e. according to their own arbitrary will and pleasure, is to defeat the great design of civil government, and utterly to abolish it. It is to make Rulers absolutely despotic, and to subject the people to a state of slavery; because it will then be in the power of Rulers, by virtue of new laws and regulations, they shall please to make, to subvert and annihilate the present constitution, and to strip the subject of every kind of privilege.

THIS may be briefly evidenced by a single instance.

IT is essential to a free state, for without this it cannot be free, that no man shall have his property taken from him, by his own consent, given by himself or by others deputed to act for him. Let it be supposed then, that Rulers assume a power to act contrary to this fundamental principle, what must be the consequence? If by such usurped authority, they can demand and take a penny, by the same authority they may a pound, and even the whole substance of the subject, so as to make him wholly dependent on their pleasure, having nothing that he can call his own; and what is he then but a perfect slave?*

THIS, at first view, is manifestly inconsistent with all just conception of freedom; and is the very essence of arbitrary and tyrannical power.

NOW, all Rulers in a state, and all power and authority with which they are vested;—the very being, and form of government, with all its constitutional laws, being thus from the people, hence civil

---

* Men in *society having property*, they have such a right to the goods, which by the law of the community are theirs, that nobody hath a right to take their substance, or any part of it from them, without their own consent: Without this they have no property at all; for I have truly no *property* in that, which another can by right take form me when he pleases against my consent. Hence it is a mistake to think, that the supreme of legislative power of any commonwealth, can do what it will, and dispose of the estates of the subject arbitrarily, or take any part of them at pleasure.

Lock on civil Government.

government, is called, and with great propriety, the *ordinance of man,*—an human institution.

THIS is the case, as to the British government in particular, under which we have the happiness to live. Its constitutional laws are comprized in *Magna-Charta*, or the great charter of the nation. This contains, in general, the liberties and privileges of the people, and is, *virtually*, a compact between the King and them; the reigning Prince, explicitly engaging, by solemn oath, to govern according to these laws.—Beyond the extent of these then, or contrary to them, he can have no rightful authority at all.

IF the preceeding positions, and the reasonings from them are just, the following things may be noticed, as deducible therefrom, or closely connected therewith,—[1] That it is highly requisite, for the good of the state, that both Rulers and people be well acquainted with, and keep in mind the constitutional laws of government—Rulers, that they may be directed and guided thereby, and not depart from, or counteract the design of their institution, to the injury, or disquietude of the people,—And people, that knowing the bounds of submission, and the extent of their privileges, they may be guarded against transgression, and yield a ready and full obedience.

[2] EQUALLY requisite it must be likewise, for the same end, that there be no mysteries in the governing plan:—That all laws and rules of government, be as plain as possible, and easy to be understood, to prevent contentious disputes between Rulers and their subjects;—to preclude the former, from tyrannical oppression, under colour of lawful authority, and the latter from rebellious disobedience, under pretence of privilege.

FOR, it follows from what has been said, that [3] as all disobedience in subjects, to constitutional authority, is rebellion against government, and merits punishment adequate to the crime, so all assumed power in Rulers, not granted them by the constitution, is without just authority, and so far forth, can claim no submission. "As usurpation," says the great and judicious Mr. LOCKE, "is the exercise of power which another hath a right to, so Tyranny is the exercise of power beyond right, which no body can have a right to." And again, "Where-ever law ends, Tyranny begins, if the law be transgressed to another's harm. And whosoever in authority exceeds the power given him by law, and makes use of the force, he has under his command, to compass that upon the subject, which the law allows not, ceases in that to be a magistrate: And acting without authority, may be opposed as any other man, who by force invades the right of another."

AND tho' [4] it may not always be prudent and best, to resist such power, and submission may be yielded, yet that the people have a right to resist, is undeniable; otherwise the absurd and exploded doctrines of passive obedience, and non-resistance, must be admitted in their utmost extent, and their consequences patiently borne. And it must be granted [5] finally, that the people as well as their Rulers, are proper judges of the civil constitution they are under, and of their own rights and privileges; else, how shall they know when these are invaded;—when submission is due to authoritative requisitions, and when not?

XXII.
THOMAS JEFFERSON, *A SUMMARY VIEW OF THE RIGHTS OF BRITISH AMERICA, etc.*, 1774

We have followed the spelling and punctuation found in the original 1774 Williamsburg printing by Clementina Rind and reprinted in London the same year for G. Kearsly. We consulted the copy in the Huntington Library. The footnote references below have been added. For a version with a different title and different spelling see "Draft of Instructions to the Virginia Delegates in the Contintental Congress," Boyd, *Jefferson Papers* (I: 121-133), reproduced in Kurland and Lerner (I: 435-441).

~

Resolved, that it be an instruction to the said deputies when assembled in general congress with the deputies from the other states of British America, to propose to the said congress that an humble and dutiful address be presented to his majesty, begging leave to lay before him, as chief magistrate of the British empire, the united complaints of his majesty's subjects in America; complaints which are excited by many unwarrantable incroachments and usurpations, attempted to be made by the legislature of one part of the empire, upon those rights which God and the laws have given equally and independently to all. To represent to his majesty, that these his states have often individually made humble application to his imperial throne, to obtain, through its intervention, some redress of their injured rights; to none of which was ever even an answer condescended: humbly to hope that this their joint address, penned in the language of truth, and divested of those expressions of servility which would persuade his majesty that we are asking favours and not rights, shall obtain from his majesty a more respectful acceptance. And this his majesty will think we have reason to expect, when he reflects that he is no more than the chief officer of the people, appointed by the laws, and circumscribed with definite powers, to assist in working the great machine of government, erected for their use, and consequently subject to their superintendance. And in order that these our rights, as well as the invasions of them, may be laid more fully before his majesty, to take a view of them from the origin and first settlement of these countries.

To remind him, that our ancestors, before their emigration to America, were the free inhabitants of the British dominions in Europe, and possessed a right which nature has given to all men, of departing from the country in which chance, not choice, has placed them; of going in quest of new habitations, and of there establishing new societies, under such laws and regulations as to them shall seem most likely to promote public happiness. That their Saxon ancestors had, under this universal law, in like manner left their native wilds and woods in the North of Europe; had possessed themselves of the island of Britain, then less charged with inhabitants, and had established there that system of laws which has so long been the glory and protection of that country. Nor was ever any claim of superiority or dependence asserted over them by that mother country from which they had migrated; and were such a claim made, it is believed his majesty's subjects in Great Britain have too firm a feeling of the rights derived to them from their ancestors, to bow down the sovereignty of their state before such visionary pretensions. And it is thought that no circumstance has occurred to distinguish materially the British from the Saxon emigration. America was conquered, and her settlements made and firmly established, at the expence of individuals, and not of the British public. Their own blood was spilt in acquiring lands for their settlement; their own fortunes expended in making that settlement effectual; for themselves they fought, for themselves they conquered, and for themselves alone they have right to hold. Not a shilling was ever issued form the public treasures of his majesty, or his ancestors, for their assistance, till of very late times, after the colonies had become established on a firm and permanent footing. That then, indeed, having become valuable to Great Britain for her commercial purposes, his parliament was pleased to lend them assistance against an enemy, who would fain have drawn to herself the benefits of their commerce, to the great aggrandisement of herself, and danger of Great Britain. Such assistance, and is such circumstances, they had often before given to Portugal, and other allied states, with whom they carry on a commercial intercourse; yet these states never supposed, that by calling in her aid, they thereby submitted themselves to her sovereignty. Had such terms been proposed, they would have rejected them with disdain, and trusted for better to the moderation of their enemies, or to a vigorous exertion of their own force. We do not, however, mean to under-rate those aids, which to us were doubtless valuable, on whatever principles granted; but we would shew that they cannot give a title to that authority which the British parliament would arrogate over us, and that they may amply be repaid by our giving to the inhabitants of Great Britain such exclusive privileges in trade as may be advantageous to them, and at the same time not too restrictive to ourselves. That settlements having been thus effected in the wilds of America, the emigrants thought proper to adopt that system of laws under which they had hitherto lived in the mother country, and continue their union with her by submitting themselves to the same common sovereign, who was thereby made the central link connecting the several parts of the empire thus newly multiplied.

But that not long were they permitted, however far they thought themselves removed from the hand of oppression, to hold undisturbed the rights thus acquired at the hazard of their lives, and loss of their fortunes. A family of princes as then on the British throne, whose treasonable crimes against their people brought on them afterwards the exertion of those sacred and sovereign rights of punishment reserved in the hands of the people for cases of extreme necessity, and judged by the constitution unsafe to be delegated to any other judicature. While every day brought forth some new and unjustifiable exertion of power over their subjects on that side the water, it was not to be expected that those here, much less able at that time to oppose the designs of despotism, should be exempted from injury.

Accordingly that country, which had been acquired by the lives, the labours, and the fortunes of individual adventurers, was by these princes, at several times, parted out and distributed among the favourites and followers of their fortunes, and, by an assumed right of the crown alone, were erected into distinct and independent governments; a measure which it is believed his majesty's prudence and understanding would prevent him from imitating at this day, as no exercise of such a power of dividing and dismembering a country has ever occurred in his majesty's realm of England, though now of very ancient standing; nor could it be justified or acquiesced under there, or in any other part of his majesty's empire.

That the exercise of a free trade with all parts of the world, possessed by the American colonists as of natural right, and which no law of their own had taken away of abridged, was next the object of unjust encroachment. Some of the colonies having thought proper to continue the administration of their government in the name and under the authority of his majesty king Charles the first, whom, notwithstanding his late deposition by the commonwealth of England, they continued in the sovereignty of their state; the Parliament for the commonwealth took the same in high offence, and assumed upon themselves the power of prohibiting their trade with all other parts of the world except the island of Great Britain. This arbitrary act, however, they soon recalled, and by solemn treaty entered into on the 12th, day of March 1651, between the said commonwealth by their commissioners and the colony of Virginia by their house of burgesses, it was expressly stipulated by the 8th article of the said treaty, that they should have "free trade as the people of England do enjoy to all places and with all nations according to the laws of that Commonwealth." But that, upon the restoration of his majesty King Charles the Second, their rights of free commerce fell once more a victim to arbitrary power; and several acts of his reign, as well as of some of his successors, the trade of the colonies was laid under such restrictions, as shew what hopes they might form from the justice of a British parliament were its uncontrouled power admitted over these states. History has informed us that bodies of men, as well as individuals, are susceptible of the spirit of tyranny. A view of these acts of parliament for regulation, as it has been affectedly called, of the American trade, if all other evidence were removed out of the case, would undeniable evince the truth of this observation. Beside the duties they impose on our articles of export and import, they prohibit our going to any markets northward of cape Finesterre, in the kingdom of Spain, for the sale of commodities which Great Britain will not take from us, and for the purchase of others, with which she cannot supply us, and that for no other than the arbitrary purpose of purchasing for themselves, by a sacrifice of our rights and interests, certain privileges in their commerce with an allied state, who in confidence that their exclusive trade with America will be continued, while the principles of power of the British parliament be the same, have indulged themselves in every exorbitance which their avarice could dictate, or our necessities extort; have raised their commodities, called for in America, to the double and treble of what they sold for before such exclusive privileges were given them, and of what better commodities of the same kind would cost us elsewhere, and at the same time give us much less for what we carry thither, than might be had at more convenient ports. That these acts prohibit us from carrying in quest of other purchasers the surplus of our tobaccoes remaining after the consumption of Great Britain is supplied; so that we must leave them with the British merchant for whatever he will please to allow us, to be by him reshipped to foreign markets, where he will reap the benefits of making sale of them for full value. That to heighten still the idea of parliamentary justice, and to shew with what moderation they are like to exercise power, where themselves are to feel no part of its weight, we take leave to mention to his majesty certain other acts of British parliament, by which they would prohibit us from manufacturing our own use the articles we raise on our own lands with our own labor. By an act passed in the 5th year of the reign of his late majesty king George the second, an American subject is forbidden to make a hat for himself of the fur which he has taken perhaps on his own soil; an instance of despotism to which no parrallel can be produced in the most arbitrary ages of British history. By one other act, passed in the 23d year of the same reign, the iron which we make we are forbidden to manufacture, and heavy as that article is, and necessary in every branch of husbandry, besides commission and insurance, we are to pay freight for it to Great Britain, and freight for it back again, for the purpose of supporting not men, but machines, in the island of Great Britain. In the same spirit of equal and impartial legislation is to be viewed the act of parliament, passed in the 5th year of the same reign, by which American lands are made subject to the demands of British creditors, while their own lands were still continued unanswerable for their debts; from which one of these conclusions must necessarily follow, either that justice is not the same thing in America as in Britain, or else that the British parliament pay less regard to it here than there. But that we do not point out to his majesty the injustice of these acts with intent to rest on that principle the cause of their nullity; but to shew that experience confirms the propriety of those political principles which exempt us from the jurisdiction of the British parliament. The true ground on which we declare these acts void, is that the British parliament has no right to exercise authority over us.

That these exercises of usurped power have not been confined to instances alone, in which themselves were interested; but they have also intermeddled with the regulation of the internal affairs of the colonies. The act of the 9th of Anne for establishing a post-office in America seems to have had little connection with British convenience, except that of accomodating his majesty's ministers and favourites with the sale of a lucrative and easy office.

That thus have we hastened through the reigns which preceded his majesty's, during which the violation of our rights were less alarming, because repeated at more distant intervals, than that rapid and bold succession of injuries which is likely to distinguish the present from all other periods of American story. Scarcely have our minds been able to emerge from the astonishment into which one stroke of parliamentary thunder has involved us, before another more heavy, and more alarming, is fallen on us. Single acts of tyranny may be ascribed to the accidental opinion of a day; but a series of oppressions, begun at a distinguished period, and pursued unalterably through every change of ministers, too plainly prove a deliberate and systematical plan of reducing us to slavery.

* * * *

That we next proceed to consider the conduct of his majesty, as holding the executive powers of the laws of these states, and mark out his deviations from the line of duty: By the constitution of Great

Britain, as well as of the several American states, his majesty possesses the power of refusing to pass into a law any bill which has already passed the other two branches of legislature. His majesty, however, and his ancestors, conscious of the impropriety of opposing their single opinion to the united wisdom of two houses of parliament, while their proceedings were unbiassed by interested principles, for several ages past have modestly declined the exercise of this power in that part of his empire called Great Britain. But by change of circumstances, other principles than those of justice simply have obtained an influence on their determinations; the addition of new states to the British empire had produced an addition of new, and sometimes opposite interests. It is now, therefore, the great office of his majesty, to resume the exercise of his negative power, and to prevent the passage of laws by any one legislature of the empire, which might bear injuriously on the rights and interests of another. Yet this will not excuse the wanton exercise of this power which we have seen his majesty practice on the laws of the American legislatures. For the most trifling reasons, and sometimes for no conceivable reason at all, his majesty has rejected laws of the most salutary tendency. The abolition of domestic slavery is the great object of desire in those colonies where it was unhappily introduced in their infant state. But previous to the enfranchisement of the slaves we have, it is necessary to exclude all further importations from Africa; yet our repeated attempts to effect this by prohibitions, and by imposing duties which might amount to a prohibition, have been hither to defeated by his majesty's negative: thus preferring the immediate advantages of a few African corsairs[6] to the lasting interests of the American states, and to the rights of human nature deeply wounded by this infamous practice. Nay, the single interposition of an interested individual against a law was scarcely ever known to fail of success, though in the opposite scale were placed the interests of the whole country. That this is so shameful an abuse of a power trusted with his majesty for other purposes, as if not reformed, would call for some legal restrictions.

With equal inattention to the necessities of his people here, has his majesty permitted our laws to lie neglected in England for years, neither confirming them by his assent, nor annulling them by his negative; so that such of them as have no suspending clause, we hold on the most precarious of all tenures, his majesty's will; and such of them as suspend themselves till his majesty's assent be obtained, we have feared might be called into existence at some future and distant period, when time, and change of circumstances, shall have rendered them destructive

---

[6]Kurland and Lerner (I: 439) refer to "a few British corsairs."

to his people here. And to render this grievance still more oppressive, his majesty by his instructions has laid his governors under such restrictions that they can pass no law, of any moment, unless it have such suspending clause; so that, however immediate may be the call for legislative interposition, the law cannot be executed till it has twice crossed the Atlantic, by which time, the evil may have spent its whole force.

* * * *

That these are our grievances, which we have thus laid before his majesty, with that freedom of language and sentiment which becomes a free people claiming their rights, as derived from the laws of nature, and not as the gift of their chief magistrate: let those flatter who fear; it is not an American art. To give praise which is not due, might be well from the venal, but would ill beseem those who are asserting the rights of human nature. They know, and will therefore say, that kings are the servants, not the proprietors of the people. Open your breast, Sire, to liberal and expanded thought. Let not the name of George the Third be a blot in the page of history. You are surrounded by British counsellors, but remember that they are parties. You have no ministers for American affairs, because you have none taken from among us, nor amenable to the laws on which they are to give you advice. It behoves you, therefore, to think and to act for yourself and your people. The great principles of right and wrong are legible to every reader; to pursue them, requires not the aid of many counsellors. The whole art of government consists in the art of being honest. Only aim to do your duty, and mankind will give you credit where you fail. No longer persevere in sacrificing the rights of one part of the empire to the inordinate desires of another; but deal out to all equal and impartial right. Let no act be passed by any one legislature, which may infringe on the rights and liberties of another. This is the important post in which fortune has placed you, holding the balance of a great, if a well poised empire. This, Sire, is the advice of your great American council, on the observance of which, may, perhaps depend your felicity and future fame, and the preservation of that harmony, which alone can continue both to Great Britain and America, the reciprocal advantages of their connection. It is neither our wish, nor our interest, to separate from her. We are willing, on our part, to sacrifice every thing which reason can ask, to the restoration of that tranquility for which all must wish. On their part, let them be ready to establish union and a generous plan. Let them name their terms, but let them be just. Accept of every commercial preference it is in our power to give for such things as we can raise for their use, or they make for ours. But let them not think to exclude us from going to other markets to dispose of those commodities which they cannot use, nor to supply those wants which they cannot supply. Still less, let it be proposed that our properties within our own territories, shall be taxed or regulated by any power on earth but our own. The God who gave us life, gave us liberty at the same time; the hand of force may destroy, but cannot disjoin them. This, Sire, is our last, our determined resolution; and that you will be pleased to interpose with that efficacy which your earnest endeavours may ensure to procure redress of these our great grievances, to quiet the minds of your subjects in British America, against any apprehensions of future encroachment, to establish fraternal love and harmony through the whole empire, and that these may continue to the latest ages of time, is the fervent prayer of all British America!

XXIII.

FIRST CONTINENTAL CONGRESS, OCTOBER 1774

In October 1774, the First Continental Congress sent a "Declaration and Resolves" to King George III. We have followed the spelling and punctuation of the 14th October *1774 Continental Congress: Declaration and Resolves* found in Tansill (1-5). Kurland and Lerner (I: 1-3) also follow Tansill. See also Schwartz (I: 215-219), and James H. Hutson, *A Decent Respect* (52-57), for versions with slightly different punctuation. The Arabic numerals in the text are in the original.

~

Declaration and Resolves

Whereas, since the close of the last war, the British parliament, claiming a power, of right, to bind the people of America by statutes in all cases whatsoever, hath, in some acts, expressly imposed taxes on them, and in others, under various pretenses, but in fact for the purpose of raising a revenue, hath imposed rates and duties payable in these colonies, established a board of commissioners, with unconstitutional powers, and extended the jurisdiction of courts of admiralty, not only for collecting the said duties, but for the trial of causes merely arising within the body of a county.

And whereas, in consequence of other statutes, judges, who before held only estates at will in their offices, have been made dependant on the crown alone for their salaries, and standing armies kept in time of peace: And[7] whereas it has lately been resolved in parliament, that by force of a statute, made in the thirty-fifth year of the reign of King Henry the Eighth, colonists may be transported to England, and tried there upon accusations for treasons and misprisions, or concealments of treasons committed in the colonies, and by a late statute, such trials have been directed in cases therein mentioned:

And whereas, in the last session of parliament, three statutes were made; one entitled, "An act to discontinue, in such manner and for such time as are therein mentioned, the landing and discharging, lading, or shipping of goods, wares and merchandise, at the town, and within the harbour of Boston, in the province of Massachusetts-Bay in North-America;" another entitled, "An act for the better regulating the government of the province of Massachusetts-Bay in New England;" and another entitled, "An act for the impartial administration of justice, in the cases of persons questioned for any act done by them in the execution of the law, or for the suppression of riots and tumults, in the province of the Massachusetts-Bay in New England;" and another statute was then made, "for making more effectual provision for the government of the province of Quebec, etc." All which statutes are impolitic, unjust, and cruel, as well as unconstitutional, and most dangerous and destructive of American rights:

And whereas, assemblies have been frequently dissolved, contrary to the rights of the people, when they attempted to deliberate on grievances; and their dutiful, humble, loyal, and reasonable petitions to the crown for redress, have been repeatedly treated with contempt, by his Majesty's ministers of state:

The good people of the several colonies of New-Hampshire, Massachusetts-Bay, Rhode-Island and Providence Plantations, Connecticut, New-York, New-Jersey, Pennsylvania, Newcastle, Kent, and Sussex on Delaware, Maryland, Virginia, North-Carolina, and South-Carolina, justly alarmed at these arbitrary proceedings of parliament and administration, have severally elected, constituted, and appointed deputies to meet, and sit in general Congress, in the city of Philadelphia, in order to obtain such establishment, as that their religion, laws, and liberties, may not be subverted: Whereupon the deputies so appointed being now assembled, in a full and free representation of these colonies, taking into their most serious consideration, the best means of attaining the ends aforesaid, do, in the first place, as Englishmen, their ancestors in like cases have usually done, for asserting and vindicating their rights and liberties, DECLARE,

---

[7]Schwartz (I: 215), following W. C. Ford's *Journals,* does not the include the word "whereas" at this point in the text. Nor does Hutson.

That the inhabitants of the English colonies in North-America, by the immutable laws of nature, the principles of the English constitution, and the several charters or compacts, have the following RIGHTS:

Resolved, N. C. D. 1. That they are entitled to life, liberty, and property: and they have never ceded to any foreign power whatever, a right to dispose of either without their consent.

Resolved, N. C. D. 2. That our ancestors, who first settled these colonies, were at the time of their emigration from the mother country, entitled to all the rights, liberties, and immunities of free and natural-born subjects, within the realm of England.

Resolved, N. C. D. 3. That by such emigration they by no means forfeited, surrendered, or lost any of those rights, but that they were, and their descendants now are, entitled to the exercise and enjoyment of all such of them, as their local and other circumstances enable them to exercise and enjoy.

Resolved, 4. That the foundation of English liberty, and of all free government, is a right in the people to participate in their legislative council: and as the English colonists are not represented, and from their local and other circumstances, cannot properly be represented in the British parliament, they are entitled to a free and exclusive power of legislation in their several provincial legislatures, where their right of representation can alone be preserved, in all cases of taxation and internal polity, subject only to the negative of their sovereign, in such manner as has been heretofore used and accustomed: But, from the necessity of the case, and a regard to the mutual interest of both countries, we cheerfully consent to the operation of such acts of the British parliament, as are bona fide, restrained to the regulation of our external commerce, for the purpose of securing the commercial advantages of the whole empire to the mother country, and the commercial benefits of its respective members; excluding every idea of taxation internal or external, for raising a revenue on the subjects, in America, without their consent.

Resolved, N. C. D. 5. That the respective colonies are entitled to the common law of England, and more especially to the great and inestimable privilege of being tried by their peers of the vicinage, according to the course of that law.

Resolved, 6. That they are entitled to the benefit of such of the English statutes, as existed at the time of their colonization; and which they have, by experience, respectively found to be applicable to their several local and other circumstances.

Resolved, N. C. D. 7. That these, his majesty's colonies, are likewise entitled to all the immunities and privileges granted and confirmed to them by royal charters, or secured by their several codes of provincial laws.

Resolved, N. C. D. 8. That they have a right peaceably to assemble, consider of their grievances, and petition the king; and that all prosecutions, prohibitory proclamations, and commitments for the same, are illegal.

Resolved, N. C. D. 9. That the keeping a standing army in these colonies, in times of peace, without the consent of the legislature of that colony, in which such army is kept, is against law.

Resolved, N. C. D. 10. It is indispensably necessary to good government, and rendered essential by the English constitution, that the constituent branches of the legislature be independent of each other; that, therefore, the exercise of legislative power in several colonies, by a council appointed, during pleasure, by the crown, is unconstitutional, dangerous and destructive to the freedom of American legislation.

All and each of which the aforesaid deputies, in behalf of themselves, and their constituents, do claim, demand, and insist on, as their indubitable rights and liberties; which cannot be legally taken from them, altered or abridged by any power whatever, without their own consent, by their representatives in their several provincial legislatures.

In the course of our inquiry, we find many infringements and violations of the foregoing rights, which, from an ardent desire, that harmony and mutual intercourse of affection and interest may be restored, we pass over for the present, and proceed to state such acts and measures as have been adopted since the last war, which demonstrate a system formed to enslave America.

Resolved, N. C. D. That the following acts of parliament are infringements and violations of the rights of the colonists; and that the repeal of them is essentially necessary, in order to restore harmony between Great-Britain and the American colonies, viz.

The several acts of 4 Geo. III. ch. 15, and ch. 34.--5 Geo. III. ch. 25.--6 Geo. III. ch. 52.--7 Geo. III. ch. 41. and ch. 46.--8 Geo. III. ch. 22. which impose duties for the purpose of raising a revenue in America, extend the power of the admiralty courts beyond their ancient limits, deprive the American subject of trial by jury, authorise the judges certificate to indemnify the prosecutor from damages, that he might otherwise be liable to, requiring oppressive security from a claimant of ships and goods seized, before he shall be allowed to defend his property, and are subversive of American rights.

Also 12 Geo. III ch. 24. intituled, "An act for the better securing his majesty's dockyards, magazines, ships, ammunition, and stores," which declares a new offence in America, and deprives the American subject of a constitutional trial by jury of the vicinage, by authorising the trial of any person, charged with the committing any offence described in the said act, out of the realm, to be indicted and tried for the same in any shire or county within the realm.

Also the three acts passed in the last session of parliament, for stopping the port and blocking up the harbour of Boston, for altering the charter and government of Massachusetts-Bay, and that which is entituled, "An act for the better administration of justice, etc."

Also the act passed in the same session for establishing the Roman Catholic religion, in the province of Quebec, abolishing the equitable system of English laws, and erecting a tyranny there, to the great danger (from so total a dissimilarity of religion, law and government) of the neighbouring British colonies, by the assistance of whose blood and treasure the said country was conquered from France.

Also the act passed in the same session, for the better providing suitable quarters for officers and soldiers in his majesty's service, in North-America.

Also, that the keeping a standing army in several of these colonies, in time of peace, without the consent of the legislature of that colony, in which such army is kept, is against law.

To these grievous acts and measures, Americans cannot submit, but in hopes their fellow subjects in Great-Britain will, on a revision of them, restore us to that state, in which both countries found happiness and prosperity, we have for the present, only resolved to pursue the following peaceable measures: 1. To enter into a non-importation, non-consumption, and non-exportation agreement or association. 2. To prepare an address to the people of Great-Britain, and a memorial to the inhabitants of British America: and 3. To prepare a loyal address to his majesty, agreeable to resolutions already entered into.

XXIV.

EDMUND BURKE, *SPEECH ON CONCILIATION WITH THE COLONIES,* 22 MARCH 1775

We have relied on the version of Burke's speech found in the 1899 edition of *The Works of Edmund Burke* (Boston: Little, Brown and Company). Reprinted below is the heart of his explanation for pursuing reconciliation. See *Works* (II: 118-130). We have highlighted--by means of Arabic numerals in square parenthesis--Burke's six reasons for liberty that exists among the Americans. See also Kurland and Lerner (I: 3-6).

~

In this character of the Americans, a love of freedom is the predominating feature which marks and distinguishes the whole: and as an ardent is always a jealous affection, your colonies become suspicious, restive, and untractable, whenever they see the least attempt to wrest from them by force, or shuffle from them by chicane, what they think the only advantage worth living for. This fierce spirit of liberty is stronger in the English colonies, probably, than in any other people of the earth; and this from a great variety of powerful causes; which, to understand the true temper of their minds, and the direction which this spirit takes, it will not be amiss to lay open somewhat more largely.

[1] First, the people of the colonies are descendants of Englishmen. England, Sir, is a nation, which still, I hope, respects, and formerly adored, her freedom. The colonists emigrated from you when this part of your character was most predominant; and they took this bias and direction the moment they parted from your hands. They are therefore not only devoted to liberty, but to liberty according to English ideas and on English principles. Abstract liberty, like other mere abstractions, is not to be found. Liberty inheres in some sensible object; and every nation has formed itself some favorite point, which by way of eminence becomes the criterion of their happiness. It happened, you know, Sir, that the great contests for freedom in this country were from the earliest times chiefly upon the question of taxing. Most of the contests in the ancient commonwealths turned primarily on the right of election of magistrates, or on the balance among the several orders of the state. The question of money was not with them so immediate. But in England it was otherwise. On this point of taxes the ablest pens and most eloquent tongues have been exercised, the greatest spirits have acted and suffered. In order to give the fullest satisfaction concerning the importance of this point, it was not only necessary for those who in argument defended the excellence of the English Constitution to insist on this privilege of granting money as a dry point of fact, and to prove that the right had been acknowledged in ancient parchments and blind usages to reside in a certain body called a House of Commons: they went much further;: they attempted to prove, and they succeeded, that in theory it ought to be so, from the particular nature of a House of Commons, as an immediate representative of the people, whether the old records had delivered this oracle or not. They took infinite pains to inculcate, as a fundamental principle, that in all monarchies the people must in effect themselves, mediately or immediately, possess the power of granting their own money, or no shadow of liberty could subsist. The colonies draw from you, as with their life-blood, these ideas and principles. Their love of liberty, as with you, fixed and attached on this specific point of taxing. Liberty might be safe or might be endangered

in twenty other particulars without their being much pleased or alarmed. Here they felt its pulse; and as they found that beat, they thought themselves sick or sound. I do not say whether they were right or wrong in applying your general arguments to their own case. It is not easy, indeed, to make a monopoly of theorems and corollaries. The fact is, that they did thus apply those general arguments; and your mode of governing them, whether through lenity or indolence, through wisdom or mistake, confirmed them in the imagination, that they, as well as you, had an interest in these common principles.

[2] They were further confirmed in this pleasing error by the form of their provincial legislative assemblies. Their governments are popular in a high degree: some are merely popular; in all, the popular representative is the most weighty; and this share of the people in their ordinary government never fails to inspire them with lofty sentiments, and with a strong aversion from whatever tends to deprive them of their chief importance.

[3] If anything were wanting to this necessary operation of the form of government, religion would have given it a complete effect. Religion, always a principle of energy, in this new people is no way worn out or impaired; and their mode of professing it is also one main cause of this free spirit. The people are Protestants, and of that kind which is the most adverse to all implicit submission of mind and opinion. This is a persuasion not only favourable to liberty, but built upon it. I do not think, Sir, that the reason of this averseness in the dissenting churches from all that looks like absolute government is so much to be sought in their religious tenets as in their history. Every one knows that the Roman Catholic religion is at least coeval with most of the governments where it prevails, that it has generally gone hand in hand with them, and received great favor and every kind of support from authority. The Church of England, too, was formed from her cradle under the nursing care of regular government. But the dissenting interests have sprung up in direct opposition to all the ordinary powers of the world, and could justify that opposition only on a strong claim to natural liberty. Their very existence depended on the powerful and unremitted assertion of that claim. All Protestantism, even the most cold and passive, is a sort of dissent. But the religion most prevalent in our northern colonies is a refinement on the principle of resistance: it is the dissidence of dissent, and the protestantism of the Protestant religion. This religion, under a variety of denominations agreeing in nothing but in the communion of the spirit of liberty, is predominant in most of the northern provinces, where the Church of England, notwithstanding its legal rights, is in reality no more than a sort of private sect, not composing, most probably, the tenth of the people. The colonists left England when this spirit was high, and in

the emigrant was the highest of all; and even that stream of foreigners which has been constantly flowing into these colonies has, for the greatest part, been composed of dissenters from the establishments of their several countries, and have brought with them a temper and character far from alien to that of the people with whom they mixed.

[4] Sir, I can perceive, by their manner, that some gentlemen object to the latitude of this description, because in the southern colonies the Church of England forms a large body, and has a regular establishment. It is certainly true. There is, however, a circumstance attending these colonies, which, in my opinion, fully counterbalances this difference, and makes the spirit of liberty still more high and haughty than in those to the northward. It is, that in Virginia and the Carolinas they have a vast multitude of slaves. Where this is the case in any part of the world, those who are free are by far the most proud and jealous of their freedom. Freedom is to them not only an enjoyment, but a kind of rank and privilege. Not seeing there, that freedom, as in countries where it is a common blessing, and as broad and general as the air, may be united with much abject toil, with great misery, with all the exterior of servitude, liberty looks, amongst them, like something that is more noble and liberal. I do not mean, Sir, to commend the superior morality of this sentiment, which has at least as much pride as virtue in it; but I cannot alter the nature of man. The fact is so; and these people of the southern colonies are much more strongly, and with a higher and more stubborn spirit, attached to liberty, than those to the northward. Such were all the ancient commonwealths; such were our Gothic ancestors; such in our days were the Poles; and such will be all the masters of slaves, who are not slaves themselves. In such a people, the haughtiness of domination combines with the spirit of freedom, fortifies it, and renders it invincible.

[5] Permit me, Sir, to add another circumstance in our colonies, which contributes no mean part towards the growth and effect of this untractable spirit: I mean their education. In no country, perhaps, in the world is the law so general a study. The profession itself is numerous and powerful, and in most provinces it takes the lead. The greater number of the deputies sent to the Congress were lawyers. But all who read, and most do read, endeavor to obtain some smattering in that science. I have been told by an eminent bookseller, that in no branch of his business, after tracts of popular devotion, were so many books as those on the law exported to the plantations. The colonists have now fallen into the way of printing them for their own use. I hear that they have sold nearly as many of Blackstone's "Commentaries" in America as in England. General Gage marks out this disposition very particularly in a letter on your table. He states, that all the people in his government are lawyers, or smatterers in law,—and that in Boston

they have been enabled, by successful chicane, wholly to evade many parts on one of your capital penal constitutions. The smartness of debate will say, that this knowledge ought to teach them more clearly the rights of legislature, their obligations to obedience, and the penalties of rebellion. All this is mighty well. But my honorable and learned friend on the floor, who condescends to mark what I say for animadversion, will disdain that ground. He has heard, as well as I, that, when great honors and great emoluments do not win over this knowledge to the service of the state, it is a formidable adversary to government. If the spirit be not tamed and broken by these happy methods, it is stubborn and litigious. *Abeunt studia in mores.* This study renders men acute, inquisitive, dexterous, prompt in attack, ready in defence, full of resources. In other countries, the people, more simple, and of a less mercurial cast, judge of an ill principle in government only by an actual grievance; here they anticipate the evil, and judge of the pressure of the grievance by the badness of the principle. They augur misgovernment at a distance, and snuff the approach of tyranny in every tainted breeze.

[6] The last cause of this disobedient spirit in the colonies is hardly less powerful than the rest, as it is not merely moral, but laid deep in the natural constitution of things. Three thousand miles of ocean lie between you and them. No contrivance can prevent the effect of this distance in weakening government. Seas roll, and months pass, between the order and the execution; and the want of a speedy explanation of a single point is enough to defeat an whole system. You have, indeed, winged ministers of vengeance, who carry your bolts in their pounces to the remotest verge of the sea: but there a power steps in, that limits the arrogance of raging passions and furious elements, and says, "So far shalt thou go, and no farther." Who are you, that should fret and rage, and bite the chains of Nature? Nothing worse happens to you than does to all nations who have extensive empire; and it happens in all the forms into which empire can be thrown. In large bodies, the circulation of power must be less vigorous at the extremities. Nature has said it. The Turk cannot govern Egypt, and Arabia, and Kurdistan, as he governs Thrace; nor has he the same dominion in Crimea and Algiers which he has at Brusa and Smyrna. Despotism itself is obliged to truck and huckster. The Sultan gets such obedience as he can. He governs with a loose rein, that he may govern at all; and the whole of the force and vigor of his authority in his centre is derived from a prudent relaxation in all his borders. Spain, in her provinces, is perhaps not so well obeyed as you are in yours. She complies, too; she submits; she watches times. This is the immutable condition, the eternal law, of extensive and detached empire.

Then, Sir, from these six capital sources, of descent, of form of government, of religion in the northern provinces, of manners in the southern, of education, of the remoteness of situation from the first mover of government,—from all these causes a fierce spirit of liberty has grown up. It has grown with the growth of the people in your colonies, and increased with the increase of their wealth: a spirit, that, unhappily meeting with an exercise of power in England, which, however lawful, is not reconcilable to any ideas of liberty, much less with theirs, has kindled this flame that is ready to consume us.

XXV.

THOMAS JEFFERSON, LATER REFLECTIONS ON THE DECLARATION OF INDEPENDENCE, 1820s

We have relied on H. A. Washington, editor, *The Writings of Thomas Jefferson* (New York: John C. Riker, 1853). This nine-volume edition was authorized in 1853 by Congress. Our first two entries are from Jefferson's autobiography. *Writings* (I: 1-110) reprints the entire autobiography. We have added the footnote references. See also Kurland and Lerner (I: 522-524, 525). Our third and fourth entries are letters written by Jefferson in the last years of his life. See *Writings* (VII: 407, and 450-451).

~

[A] Notes on Debates in Congress, July 2-4, 1776

Congress proceeded the same day to consider the Declaration of Independance, which had been reported and lain[8] on the table the Friday preceding, and on Monday referred to a committee of the whole. The pusillanimous idea that we had friends in England worth keeping terms with, still haunted the minds of many. For this reason, those passages which conveyed censures on the people of England were struck out, lest they should give them offence. The clause too, reprobating the enslaving the inhabitants of Africa, was struck out in complaisance to South Carolina and Georgia, who had never attempted to restrain the importation of slaves, and who, on the contrary, still wished to continue it. Our northern brethren also, I believe, felt a little tender under those censures; for though their people have very few slaves themselves, yet they had been pretty considerable carriers of them to others. The debates, having taken up the greater parts of the 2d, 3d, and 4th days of July, were, in the evening of the last, closed; the

---

[8]Kurland and Lerner (I: 522), have "laid" on the table.

Declaration was reported by the committee, agreed to by the House, and signed by every member present, except Mr. Dickinson. As the sentiments of men are known not only by what they receive, but what they reject also, I will state the form of the Declaration as originally reported. The parts struck out by Congress shall be distinguished by a black line drawn under them; and those inserted by them shall be placed in the margin or in a concurrent column(s).[9]

A Declaration by the Representatives of the United States of America, in *General* Congress assembled

When, in the course of human events, it becomes necessary for one people to dissolve the political bands which have connected them with another, and to assume among the powers of the earth the separate and equal station to which the laws of nature and of nature's God entitle them, a decent respect to the opinions of mankind requires that they should declare the causes which impel them to the separation.

We hold these truths to be self evident: that all men are created equal; that they are endowed by their creator with *(certain)* inherent and inalienable rights; that among these are life, liberty and the pursuit of happiness; that to secure these rights, governments are instituted among men, deriving their just powers from the consent of the governed; that whenever any form of government becomes destructive of these ends, it is the right of the people to alter or to abolish it, and to institute new government, laying its foundation on such principles, and organizing its powers in such form, as to them shall seem most likely to effect their safety and happiness. Prudence, indeed, will dictate that governments long established should not be changed for light and transient causes; and accordingly all experience hath shewn that mankind are more disposed to suffer while evils are sufferable, than to right themselves by abolishing the forms to which they are accustomed. But when a long train of abuses and usurpations, begun at a distinguished period and pursuing invariably the same object, evinces a design to reduce them under absolute despotism, it is their right, it is their duty to throw off such government, and to provide new guards for their future security. Such has been the patient sufferance of these colonies; and such is now the necessity which constrains them to *(alter)* expunge their former systems of government. The history of the present king of Great Britain is a history of *(repeated)* unremitting injuries and usurpations, among which appears no solitary fact to contradict the uniform tenor of the rest but all have *(all having)* in direct

[9]We have followed Jefferson and underlined the parts deleted by Congress. The parts inserted by Congress are italicized within parentheses in the body of the text.

object the establishment of an absolute tyranny over these states. To prove this let facts be submitted to a candid world for the truth of which we pledge a faith yet unsullied by falsehood.

He has refused his assent to laws the most wholsome and necessary for the public good.

He has forbidden his governors to pass laws of immediate and pressing importance, unless suspended in their operation till his assent should be obtained; and, when so suspended, he has utterly neglected to attend to them.

He has refused to pass other laws for the accomodation of large districts of people, unless those people would relinquish the right of representation in the legislature, a right inestimable to them and formidable to tyrants only.

He has called together legislative bodies at places unusual, uncomfortable, and distant from the depository of their public records, for the sole purpose of fatiguing them into compliance with his measures.

He has dissolved representative houses repeatedly and continually for opposing with manly firmness his invasions on the rights of the people.

He has refused for a long time after such dissolutions to cause others to be elected, whereby the legislative powers, incapable of annihilation, have returned to the people at large for their exercise, the state remaining, in the meantime, exposed to all the dangers of invasion from without and convulsions within.

He has endeavored to prevent the population of these states; for that purpose obstructing the laws for naturalization of foreigners, refusing to pass others to encourage their migrations hither, and raising the conditions of new appropriations of lands.

He has *(obstructed)* suffered the administration of justice totally to cease in some of these states *(by)* refusing his assent to laws for establishing judiciary powers.

He has made our judges dependant on his will alone for the tenure of their offices, and the amount and paiment of their salaries.

He has erected a multitude of new offices by a self assumed power and sent hither swarms of new officers to harrass our people and eat our their substance.

He has kept among us in times of peace standing armies and ships of war without the consent of our legislatures.

He has affected to render the military independent of, and superior to, the civil power.

He has combined with others to subject us to a jurisdictions foreign to our constitutions and unacknowleged by our laws, giving his assent to their acts of pretended legislation for quartering large bodies of armed troops among us; for protecting them by a mocktrial from punishment for any murders which they should commit on the inhabitants of these states; for cutting off our trade with all parts of the world; for imposing taxes on us without our consent; for depriving us *(in many cases)* of the benefits of trial by jury; for transporting us beyond seas to be tried for pretended offences; for abolishing the free system of English laws in a neighboring province, establishing therein an arbitrary government, and enlarging its boundaries, so as to render it at once an example and fit instrument for introducing the same absolute rule into these (*colonies*) states; for taking away our charters, abolishing our most valuable laws, and altering fundamentally the forms of our governments; for suspending our own legislatures, and declaring themselves invested with power to legislate for us in all cases whatsoever.

He has abdicated government here *(by declaring us out of his protection and waging war against us.)* withdrawing his governors, and declaring us our of his allegiance and protection

He has plundered our seas, ravaged our coasts, burnt our towns, and destroyed the lives of our people.

He is at this time transporting large armies of foreign mercenaries to complete the works of death, desolation and tyranny already begun with circumstances of cruelty and perfidy *(scarcely paralleled in the most barbarous ages, and totally)* unworthy the head of a civilized nation.

He has constrained our fellow citizens taken captive on the high seas, to bear arms against their country, to become the executioners of their friends and brethren, or to fall themselves by their hands.

He has *(excited domestic insurrections among us, and has)* endeavored to bring on the inhabitants of our frontiers the merciless Indian savages, whose known rule of warfare is an undistinguished destruction of all ages, sexes, and conditions of existence.

He has incited treasonable insurrections of our fellow citizens, with the allurements of forfeiture and confiscation of our property.

He has waged cruel war against human nature itself, violating its most sacred rights of life and liberty in the persons of a distant people who never offended him, captivating and carrying them into slavery in another hemisphere or to incur miserable death in their transportation thither. This piratical warfare, the opprobrium of INFIDEL powers, is the warfare of the *CHRISTIAN* king of Great Britain. Determined to keep open a market where MEN should be bought and sold, he has prostituted his negative for suppressing every legislative attempt to prohibit or to restrain this execrable commerce. And that this assemblage of horrors might want no fact of distinguished die, he is now exciting those very people to rise in arms among us, and to purchase that liberty of which he has deprived them, by murdering the people on whom he also obtruded them: thus paying off former crimes committed against the LIBERTIES of one people, with crimes which he urges them to commit against the LIVES of another.

In every stage of these oppressions we have petitioned for redress in the most humble terms: our repeated petitions have been answered only by repeated injuries. A prince whose character is thus marked by every act which may define a tyrant is unfit to be the ruler of a *(free)* people who mean to be free. Future ages will scarcely believe that the hardiness of one man adventured, within the short compass of twelve years only, to lay a foundation so broad and so undisguised for tyranny over a people fostered and fixed in principle of freedom.

Nor have we been wanting in attentions to our British brethren. We have warned them from time to time of attempts by their legislature to extend *(an unwarrantable)* a jurisdiction over *(us)* these our states. We have reminded them of the circumstances of our emigration and settlement here, no one of which could warrant so strange a pretension: that these were effected at the expence of our own blood and treasure, unassisted by the wealth or the strength of Great Britain: that in constituting indeed our several forms of government, we had adopted one common king, thereby laying a foundation for perpetual league and amity with them: but that submission to their parliament was no part of our constitution, nor ever in idea, if history may be credited: and, we *(have)* appealed to their native justice and magnanimity and *(we have conjured them by)* as well as to the ties of our common kindred to disavow these usurpations which *(would inevitably)* were likely to interrupt our connection and correspondence. They too have been deaf to the voice of justice and of consanguinity, and when occasions have been given them, by the regular course of their laws, of removing from their councils the disturbers of our harmony, they have, by their free election, re-established them in power. At this very time too, they are permitting their chief magistrate to send over not only soldiers of our common blood, but Scotch and foreign mercenaries to invade and destroy us. These facts have given the last stab to agonizing affection, and manly spirit bids us to renounce for ever these unfeeling brethren. We must endeavor to forget our former love for them, and to hold them as we hold the rest of mankind, enemies in war, in peace friends. We might have been a free and a great people together; but a communication of grandeur and of freedom, it seems, is below their dignity. Be it so, since they will have it. The road to happiness and to glory is open to us too. We will tread it apart from them, and (*we must therefore*) acquiesce in the necessity which denounces our eternal separation (*and hold them as we hold the rest of mankind, enemies in war, in peace friends)!*[10]

[Left hand column]

We, therefore, the representatives of the United States of America in General Congress assembled, do in the name, and by the authority of the good people of these states reject and renounce all allegiance and subjection to the kings of Great Britain and all others who may hereafter claim by, through or under them; we utterly dissolve all political connection which may heretofore have subsisted between us and the people or parliament of Great Britain: and finally we do assert and declare these colonies to be free and independent states, and that as free and independent states, they have full power to levy war, conclude peace, contract alliances, establish commerce, and to do all other acts and things which independant states may of right do.

And for the support of this declaration, we mutually pledge to each other our lives, our fortunes, and our sacred honour.

[Right hand Column]

We, therefore, the representatives of the United States of America in General Congress assembled, appealing to the supreme judge of the world for the rectitude of our intentions, do in the name, and by the authority of the good people of these colonies, solemnly publish and declare, that these united colonies are, and of right ought to be free and independant states; that they are absolved from all allegiance to the British crown, and that all political connection between them and the state of Great Britain is, and ought to be, totally dissolved; and that as free and independent states, they have full power to levy war, conclude peace, contract alliances, establish commerce and to do all other acts and things which independant states may of right do.

And for the support of this declaration, with a firm reliance on the protection of divine providence, we mutually pledge to each other our lives, our fortunes, and our sacred honour.

[B] Bill for Abolition of Entails, 11-12 August 1776

On the 12th, I obtained leave to bring in a bill declaring tenants in tail to hold their lands in fee simple. In the earlier times of the colony, when lands were to be obtained for little or nothing, some provident individuals procured large grants; and, desirous of founding great

---

[10]The final four paragraphs were placed next to each other in the Washington edition: the first and second appeared in a left hand column, and the third and fourth were placed in a right hand column.

families for themselves, settled them on their descendants in fee tail. The transmission of this property from generation to generation, in the same name, raised up a distinct set of families, who, being privileged by law in the perpetuation of their wealth, were thus formed into a Patrician order, distinguished by the splendor and luxury of their establishments. From this order, too, the king habitually selected his counsellors of State; the hope of which distinction devoted the whole corps to the interests and will of the crown. To annul this privilege, and instead of an aristocracy of wealth, of more harm and danger, than benefit, to society, to make an opening for the aristocracy of virtue and talent, which nature has wisely provided for the direction of the interests of society, and scattered with equal hand through all its conditions, was deemed essential to a well-ordered republic.—To effect it, no violence was necessary, no deprivation of natural right, but rather an enlargement of it by a repeal of the law. For this would authorize the present holder to divide the property among his children equally, as his affections were divided; and would place them, by natural generation, on the level of their fellow citizens. But this repeal was strongly opposed by Mr. Pendleton, who was zealously attached to ancient establishments; and who, taken all in all, was the ablest man in debate I have ever met with. He had not indeed the poetical fancy of Mr. Henry, his sublime imagination, his lofty and overwhelming diction; but he was cool, smooth and persuasive; his language flowing, chaste and embellished; his conceptions quick, acute and full of resource; never vanquished: for if he lost the main battle, he returned upon you, and regained so much of it as to make it a drawn one, by dexterous manoeuvres, skirmishes in detail, and the recovery of small advantages which, little singly, were important all together. You never knew when you were clear of him, but were harassed by his perseverance, until the patience was worn down of all who had less of it than himself. Add to this, that he was one of the most virtuous and benevolent of men, the kindest friend, the most amiable and pleasant of companions, which ensured a favorable reception to whatever came from him. Finding that the general principles of entails could not be maintained, he took his stand on an amendment which he proposed, instead of an absolute abolition, to permit the tenant in tail to convey in fee simple, if he chose it; and he was within a few votes of saving so much of the old law. But the bill passed finally for entire abolition.

[C] Jefferson to Henry Lee, 8 May 1825

But with respect to our rights, and the acts of the British government contravening those rights, there was but one opinion on this side of the water. All American whigs thought alike on these subjects. When forced, therefore, to resort to arms for redress, an appeal to the tribunal of the world was deemed proper for our justification. This was the object of the Declaration of Independence. Not to find out new principles, or new arguments, never before thought of, not merely to say things which had never been said before; but to place before mankind the common sense of the subject, in terms so plain and firm as to command their assent, and to justify ourselves in the independent stand we are compelled to take. Neither aiming at originality of principle or sentiment, nor yet copied from any particular and previous writing, it was intended to be an expression of the American mind, and to give to that expression the proper tone and spirit called for by the occasion. All its authority rests then on the harmonizing sentiments of the day, whether expressed in conversation, in letters, printed essays, or in the elementary books of public right, as Aristotle, Cicero, Locke, Sidney, etc. The historical documents which you mention as in your possession, ought all to be found, and I am persuaded you will find, to be corroborative of the facts and principles advanced in that Declaration. Be pleased to accept assurances of my great esteem and respect.

[D] Jefferson to Roger C. Weightman, 24 June 1826

May it [The Declaration of Independence] be to the world, what I believe it will be, (to some parts sooner, to others later, but finally to all,) the signal of arousing men to burst the chains under which monkish ignorance and superstition had persuaded them to bind themselves, and to assume the blessings and security of self-government. That form which we have substituted, restores the free right to the unbounded exercise of reason and freedom of opinion. All eyes are opened, or opening, to the rights of man. The general spread of the light of science has already laid open to every view the palpable truth, that the mass of mankind has not been born with saddles on their backs, nor a favored few booted and spurred, ready to ride them legitimately, by the grace of God. These are grounds of hope for others. For ourselves, let the annual return of this day forever refresh our recollections of these rights, and an undiminished devotion to them.

Chapter Four

A New and More Noble Course

On May 15, 1776, the Second Continental Congress issued a "Resolve" to the thirteen colonial assemblies: "adopt such a government as shall, in the opinion of the representatives of the people, best conduce to the happiness and safety of their constituents in particular, and America in general." Between 1776 and 1780, elected representatives met in deliberative bodies--as founders--and chose republican governments. Connecticut and Rhode Island retained their colonial charters, but the other eleven reaffirmed the American covenanting tradition and created governments dedicated to securing rights. What transpired was the most extensive documentation of the rights of the people the world had ever witnessed.

We have reproduced three state constitutions: Virginia, the first to be written and adopted one week prior to the Declaration of Independence; New Jersey, adopted on 2 July 1776, and the first to exclude a prefatory bill of rights; and Pennsylvania, the third constitution adopted and considered the most radical. Together, they capture the diversity and uniformity of the revolutionary conversation over bicameralism, separation of powers, length of service, and how rights were to be secured by a republican frame of government. They express the American covenanting tradition--reinforced by the enlightenment doctrine of natural rights--that it is the right of the people to choose their form of government. These constitutions are practical expressions of the ideal that government ought to be founded on deliberation and consent rather than accident and force.

Seven states attached a prefatory declaration of rights to the frame of government: Virginia (June 1776), Delaware (September 1776), Pennsylvania (September 1776), Maryland (November 1776), North Carolina (December 1776), Massachusetts (March 1780), and New Hampshire (June 1784). These declarations were, in effect, a preamble stating the purposes for which the people have chosen the particular form of government. There is a remarkable uniformity among the seven states with regard to the kinds of civil and criminal rights that were to be secured. The Virginia, Delaware, Pennsylvania, and Massachusetts Declarations capture both the similarity, and the subtle differences, given to "the free exercise of religion," "the establishment of religion," the freedom of press, the right to petition, the right to bear arms, the quartering of troops, the protection from unreasonable searches and seizures, the centrality of trial by jury, the right to confrontation of witnesses and the right to counsel, the importance of "due process of law," and the protection against excessive fines and cruel and unusual punishment.

Four of the states decided not to "prefix" a bill of rights to their newly founded republican constitutions: New Jersey (July 1776), Georgia (February 1777), New York (April 1777), and South Carolina (March 1778). Nevertheless, each had prefaces confirming the authority of the covenanting tradition and also incorporated individual protections into the body of their constitutions.

Virginia

The Virginia Bill of Rights was adopted by the House of Burgesses in June, 1776. Among the delegates were George Mason, the most important contributor, and twenty-five-year-old James Madison who drafted the section on the "free exercise of religion." The "rights" listed in the first five sections might strike the contemporary reader as odd; it is important to remember, however, that among the most fundamental rights articulated by the revolutionary generation was the right of the people to choose their form of government. Sections six through fourteen cover familiar ground. Most of the civil rights and criminal procedures listed were part of the Americanized version of the "rights of Englishmen" tradition. Section fifteen reflects the traditional republican argument that free government could survive only if the people were virtuous. Because colonial America turned to religion to perform this important political function, there was a presumption that religion had an "established" status. In 1776, the Anglican church was the established church of Virginia, and there is nothing in the Virginia Bill of Rights that challenges this establishment. On the other hand, Madison's natural right argument, incorporated in section sixteen, challenged the public dimension of religion on the ground that the exercise of religion should be "free" of "force or violence."

The same Convention also framed and adopted the Virginia Constitution. The first, and longest, section anticipates the Declaration of Independence: Twenty-one separate indictments are listed against King George. Section two provides the authorization for establishing a new foundation. Sections three through thirteen pertain to the bicameral legislature; and the remainder focus on the election of executive officers. Section twenty-one lays the foundation for the Northwest and Southwest Territories.

New Jersey

The 1776 New Jersey Constitution, framed by a convention that met from May 26 through July 3, was the second to be adopted and the first to omit a prefatory Bill of Rights. Nevertheless, the constitution appeals to "the nature of things" and the American covenanting tradition. Moreover, civil rights and criminal procedures are addressed in four of the thirty-nine articles. Article XVI provides that "all criminals shall be admitted to the same privileges of witness and counsel, as their prosecutors doe or shall be entitled to," and Article XXII confirms the common law tradition with the trial by jury being given permanent protection. Two articles address the issue of religious rights. Article XVIII guarantees to all "the inestimable privilege of worshipping Almighty God in a manner agreeable to the dictates of his own conscience," and proclaims that no one shall ever be obliged to support financially any ministry "contrary to what he believes to be right, or has deliberately or voluntarily engaged himself to perform." Article XVIX states that there "shall be no establishment of any one religious sect in this Province, in preference to another," and that all persons of "any Protestant sect...shall fully and freely enjoy every privilege and immunity, enjoyed by others their fellow subjects." New Jersey was the first state to prohibit the establishment of a specific sect as the official religion.

Pennsylvania

The Pennsylvania Constitution, prefaced by a Preamble and Declaration of Rights, was framed by a specially-elected convention that met from mid-July to the end of September 1776. Although the document was not submitted to the people for ratification, it expresses the radical dimension of the conversation over what frame of government would best secure the rights of the people: Pennsylvania was the only state to choose a unicameral rather than a bicameral legislature. Although the legislature was very powerful, the constitution calls for an "open" assembly with policy making taking place under the full scrutiny of an informed electorate. In section forty-seven, the framers created an elected Council of Censors to provide periodic review of the operation of the laws and institutions "in order that the freedom of the commonwealth may be preserved inviolate for ever." This model was subsequently praised by Jefferson in his *Notes on Virginia* and criticized by Madison in *Federalist* 47-51.

John Adams's 1779 judgment that the Pennsylvania Bill of Rights "is taken almost verbatim from that of Virginia" is correct as far as it concerns the common law tradition. Nevertheless, all sixteen deserve to be reproduced in their entirety in order to appreciate the remarkable uniformity and subtle differences among the states. It is particularly important to note that Pennsylvania repeats the claim that "a firm adherence to justice, moderation, temperance, industry, and frugality are absolutely necessary to preserve the blessings of liberty," and that only Christians are eligible to hold office. Also noteworthy are the sections dealing with searches and seizures, freedom of speech, the right to bear arms, "the natural inherent right to emigrate," and the right to assemble.

Delaware

The Delaware Declaration of Rights followed Pennsylvania and appealed to natural rights and the common law tradition. Of particular interest is the concern for the *political* rights of the people: the right to hold officials accountable, the right to participate in government and to petition for redress of grievances, and the right to no *ex post facto* laws.

Massachusetts

The Massachusetts Declaration of Rights and Constitution, drafted over a six-month period, was adopted in Spring 1780. It was the first to be ratified by the people rather than by the people's representatives. Actually, the 1780 Constitution was a revised version of the 1778 Constitution rejected in large part because of the absence of a Bill of Rights. The town of Boston declared "that all Forms of Government should be prefaced by a Bill of Rights; in this we find no Mention of any." Eleven towns also objected to the denial of the right of suffrage to free "negroes, Indians, and mulattoes" in Article V. The Essex Result--the combined judgment of the twelve towns of Essex County reached at a county convention--also expressed concern that the foundation was illegitimate because the people were excluded from the adoption process.

The Massachusetts Preamble confirmed the "right of the people to set up what government they believe will secure their safety, prosperity, and happiness." The provisions in "Part the First" dealing with search and seizure, self-incrimination, confrontation of witnesses, self-incrimination, cruel and unusual punishments, freedom of press, the right to petition, and that no one shall be deprived of "life, liberty, or estate, but by the judgment of his peers, or the law of the land," were common among all the states that adopted a Bill of Rights. Massachusetts, also included specific political rights of the people: the right to no *ex post facto* laws, frequent elections, an independent judiciary, and the right to a strict separation of governmental powers "to the end that it may be a government of laws and not of men." As was the case in Virginia and Pennsylvania, the need for "piety, justice, moderation, temperance, industry, and frugality" was listed in the Bill of Rights. What is distinctive about Massachusetts is that the virtue of the people was to be secured by established religion. The third "right" was that of the citizens to support, financially, the establishment of Protestantism as the public religion. To be sure, no one particular sect would be given preference over another; all were "equally under the protection of the law" and the "free exercise" of religion was protected.

Madison and Jefferson

Virginia entered unfamiliar territory with the disestablishment of the Anglican church in 1779. Nevertheless, there were two competing models to which legislators could turn. The Massachusetts model endorsed the establishment of the Christian Protestant religion and, to that end, the legislature was constitutionally mandated to tax inhabitants for the support of public religious instruction. The taxpayer, nevertheless, was free to name the specific religion that was to receive the assessment. On the other hand, the Pennsylvania model warned that such taxation threatened the right of an individual to the free exercise of religion. In December 1784, the Virginia Assembly considered an Assessment Bill, consistent with the Massachusetts model, that would financially support the propagation of Christianity as the state religion. James Madison, the principle author of this protest addressed to the Virginia Assembly, urged the legislators to reject the proposed legislation. In the process, Madison pushed the national conversation even further in the direction of individual free exercise of religion and away from community endorsed religion. The practical manifestation of Madison's efforts was the Assembly adoption in 1785 of Jefferson's Statute of Religious Liberty introduced in 1779. The Virginia Senate passed the statute in January 1786.

XXVI.

VIRGINIA DECLARATION OF RIGHTS AND CONSTITUTION, 12 AND 29 JUNE 1776

The Arabic numerals identifying the separate sections of the Declaration of Rights are in the original. We have followed W.W. Hening (IX: 109-119) and added section numbers to the Constitution. These sections are identified by Roman numerals. Footnotes have been added. See also Thorpe (VII: 3812-3819). For a version that differs in spelling and punctuation, see Kurland and Lerner (I: 6-9), and Schwartz (II: 234-235.)

~

CHAP. I.

A **DECLARATION OF RIGHTS** *made by the representatives of the good people of* Virginia, *assembled in full and free Convention; which rights do pertain to them and their posterity, as the basis and foundation of government.*

1. THAT all men are by nature equally free and independent, and have certain inherent rights, of which, when they enter into a state of society, they cannot, by any compact, deprive or divest their posterity; namely, the enjoyment of life and liberty, with the means of acquiring and possessing property, and pursuing and obtaining happiness and safety.

2. That all power is vested in, and consequently derived from, the people; that magistrates are their trustees and servants, and at all times amenable to them.

3. That government is, or ought to be, instituted for the common benefit, protection, and security of the people, nation, or community; of all the various modes and forms of government, that is best, which is capable of producing the greatest degree of happiness and safety, and is most effectually secured against the danger of mal-administration; and that whenever any government shall be found inadequate or contrary to these purposes, a majority of the community hath an indubitable, unalienable, and indefeasible right, to reform, alter, or abolish it, in such manner as shall be judged most conducive to the public weal.

4. That no man, or set of men, are entitled to exclusive or separate emoluments and privileges from the community, but in consideration of publick services; which, not being descendible, neither ought the offices of magistrate, legislator, or judge to be hereditary.

5. That the legislative and executive powers of the State should be separate and distinct from the judiciary;[1] and that the members of the two first may be restrained from oppression, by feeling and participating the burthens of the people, they should, at fixed periods, be reduced to a private station, return into that body from which they were originally taken, and the vacancies be supplied by frequent, certain, and regular elections, in which all, or any part of the former members, to be again eligible, or ineligible, as the laws shall direct.
6. That elections of members to serve as representatives of the people, in assembly, ought to be free; and that all men, having sufficient evidence of permanent common interest with, and attachment to, the community, have the right of suffrage, and cannot be taxed or deprived of their property for publick uses without their own consent, or that of their representative so elected, nor bound by any law to which they have not, in like manner, assented,[2] for the publick good.
7. That all power of suspending laws, or the execution of laws, by any authority, without consent of the representatives of the people, is injurious to their rights, and ought not to be exercised.
8. That in all capital or criminal prosecutions a man hath a right to demand the cause and nature of his accusation, to be confronted with the accusers and witnesses, to call for evidence in his favor, and to a speedy trial by an impartial jury of twelve men of his vicinage,[3] without whose unanimous consent he cannot be found guilty, nor can he be compelled to give evidence against himself; that no man be deprived of his liberty, except by the law of the land or the judgment of his peers.
9. That excessive bail ought not to be required, nor excessive fines imposed, nor cruel and unusual punishments inflicted.
10. That general warrants, whereby any officer or messenger may be commanded to search suspected places without evidence of a fact committed, or to seize any person or persons not named, or whose offence is not particularly described and supported by evidence, are grievous and oppressive, and ought not to be granted.
11. That in controversies respecting property, and in suits between man and man, the ancient trial by jury is preferable to any other, and ought to be held sacred.

---

[1]Kurland and Lerner (I: 6), and Schwartz (II: 235), state that the legislative and executive powers should be distinct from the "Judicative."

[2]Thorpe--incorrectly--uses the word "assembled."

[3]Thorpe specifies "an impartial jury of twelve men." (VII: 3813.)

12. That the freedom of the press is one of the great[4] bulwarks of liberty, and can never be restrained but by despotick governments.
13. That a well regulated militia, composed of the body of the people, trained to arms, is the proper, natural, and safe defence of a free state; that standing armies, in time of peace, should be avoided, as dangerous to liberty; and that, in all cases, the military should be under strict subordination to, and governed by, the civil power.
14. That the people have a right to uniform government; and therefore, that no government separate from, or independent of, the government of *Virginia,* ought to be erected or established within the limits thereof.
15. That no free government, or the blessing of liberty, can be preserved to any people, but by a firm adherence to justice, moderation, temperance, frugality, and virtue, and by frequent recurrence to fundamental principles.
16. That religion, or the duty which we owe to our CREATOR, and the manner of discharging it, can be directed only by reason and conviction, not by force or violence, and therefore all men are equally entitled to the free exercise of religion, according to the dictates of conscience; and that it is the mutual duty of all to practise Christian forbearance, love, and charity, towards each other.

CHAP. II.

The **CONSTITUTION** *or* **FORM** *of* **GOVERNMENT**, *agreed to and resolved upon by the Delegates and Representatives of the several counties and corporations of Virginia.*

I. WHEREAS *George* the third, King of *Great Britain* and *Ireland,* and elector of *Hanover,* heretofore intrusted with the exercise of the kingly office in this government, hath endeavoured to pervert[5] the same into a detestable and insupportable tyranny, by putting his negative on laws the most wholesome and necessary for the publick good:
By denying his governours permission to pass laws of immediate and pressing importance, unless suspended in their operation for his assent, and, when so suspended, neglecting to attend to them for many years:
By refusing to pass certain other laws, unless the persons to be benefitted by them would relinquish the inestimable right of representation in the legislature:

---

[4]Kurland and Lerner refer to the freedom of the press as one of the "greatest" bulwarks. See also Schwartz (II: 235).

[5]Thorpe (VII: 3814) uses instead the word "prevent."

By dissolving legislative Assemblies repeatedly and continually, for opposing with manly firmness his invasions of the rights of the people:
When dissolved, by refusing to call others for a long space of time, thereby leaving the political system without any legislative head:
By endeavouring to prevent the population of our country, and, for that purpose, obstructing the laws for the naturalization of foreigners:
By keeping among us, in times of peace, standing armies and ships of war:
By affecting to render the military independent of, and superiour to, the civil power:
By combining with others to subject us to a foreign jurisdiction, giving his assent to their pretended acts of legislation:
For quartering large bodies of armed troops among us:
For cutting off our trade with all parts of the world:
For imposing taxes on us, without our consent:
For depriving us of the benefits of trial by jury:
For transporting us beyond seas, to be tried for pretended offences:
For suspending our own legislatures, and declaring themselves invested with power to legislate for us in all cases whatsoever:
By plundering our seas, ravaging our coasts, burning our towns, and destroying the lives of our people:
By inciting insurrections of our fellow subjects, with the allurements of forfeiture and confiscation:
By prompting our negroes to rise in arms among us, those very negroes whom, by an inhuman use of his negative, he hath refused us permission to exclude by law:
By endeavoring to bring on the inhabitants of our frontiers the merciless *Indian* savages, whose known rule of warfare is an undistinguished destruction of all ages, sexes, and conditions of existence:
By transporting, at this time, a large army of foreign mercenaries, to complete the works of death, desolation, and tyranny, already begun with circumstances of cruelty and perfidy unworthy the head of a civilized nation:
By answering our repeated petitions for redress with a repetition of injuries:
And finally, by abandoning the helm of government, and declaring us out of his allegiance and protection.
By which several acts of misrule, the government of this country, as formerly exercised under the crown of *Great Britain*, is **TOTALLY DISSOLVED**.
II. We therefore, the delegates and representatives of the good people of *Virginia*, having maturely considered the premises, and viewing with

great concern the deplorable condition to which this once happy country must be reduced, unless some regular, adequate mode of civil polity is speedily adopted, and in compliance with a recommendation of the General Congress, do ordain and declare the future form of government of *Virginia* to be as followeth:

III. The legislative, executive, and judiciary departments, shall be separate and distinct, so that neither exercise the powers properly belonging to the other; nor shall any person exercise the powers of more than one of them at the same time, except that the justices of the county courts shall be eligible to either House of Assembly.

IV. The legislative shall be formed of two distinct branches, who, together, shall be a complete legislature. They shall meet once, or oftener, every year, and shall be called the GENERAL ASSEMBLY OF VIRGINIA.

V. One of these shall be called the HOUSE OF DELEGATES, and consist of two representatives to be chosen for each county, and for the District of *West-Augusta,* annually, of such men as actually reside in, and are freeholders of the same, or duly qualified according to law, and also of one delegate or representative to be chosen annually for the city of Williamsburgh, and one for the borough of Norfolk, and a representative for each of such other cities and boroughs as may hereafter be allowed particular representation by the legislature; but when any city or borough shall so decrease as that the number of persons having right of suffrage therein shall have been for the space of seven years successively less than half the number of voters in some one county in *Virginia,* such city or borough thenceforward shall cease to send a delegate or representative to the Assembly.

VI. The other shall be called the SENATE, and consist of twenty four members, of whom thirteen shall constitute a House to proceed on business, for whose election the different counties shall be divided into twenty four districts, and each county of the respective district, at the time of the election of its delegates, shall vote for one Senator, who is actually a resident and freeholder within the district, or duly qualified according to law, and is upwards of twenty five years of age; and the sheriffs of each county within five days at farthest after the last county election in the district, shall meet at some convenient place, and from the poll so taken in their respective counties return as a Senator the man who shall have the greatest number of votes in the whole district. To keep up this Assembly by rotation, the districts shall be equally divided into four classes, and numbered by lot. At the end of one year after the general election, the six members elected by the first division shall be displaced, and the vacancies thereby occasioned supplied from such class or division, by new election, in the manner aforesaid. This rotation shall be applied to each division, according to its number, and continued in due order annually.

VII. The right of suffrage in the election of members for both Houses shall remain as exercised at present, and each House shall choose its own speaker, appoint its own officers, settle its own rules of proceeding, and direct writs of election for supplying intermediate vacancies.

VIII. All laws shall originate in the House of Delegates, to be approved or rejected by the Senate, or to be amended with the consent of the House of Delegates; except money bills, which in no instance shall be altered by the Senate, but wholly approved or rejected.

IX. A Governour, or chief magistrate, shall be chosen annually, by joint ballot of both Houses, to be taken in each House respectively, deposited in the conference room, the boxes examined jointly by a committee of each house, and the numbers severally reported to them, that the appointments may be entered (which shall be the mode of taking the joint ballot of both Houses in all cases) who shall not continue in that office longer than three years successively, nor be eligible until the expiration of four years after he shall have been out of that office. An adequate, but moderate salary, shall be settled on him during his continuance in office; and he shall, with the advice of a Council of State, exercise the executive powers of government according to the laws of this commonwealth; and shall not, under any pretence, exercise any power or prerogative by virtue of any law, statute, or custom, of *England:* But he shall, with the advice of the Council of State, have the power of granting reprieves or pardons, except where the prosecution shall have been carried on by the House of Delegates, or the law shall otherwise particularly direct; in which cases, no reprieve or pardon shall be granted, but by resolve of the House of Delegates.

X. Either House of the General Assembly may adjourn themselves respectively. The Governour shall not prorogue or adjourn the Assembly during their sitting, nor dissolve them at any time; but he shall, if necessary, either by advice of the Council of State, or on application of a majority of the House of Delegates, call them before the time to which they shall stand prorogued or adjourned.

XI. A Privy Council, or Council of State, consisting of eight members, shall be chosen by joint ballot of both Houses of Assembly, either from their own members or the people at large, to assist in the administration of government. They shall annually choose out of their own members a president, who, in case of the death, inability, or necessary[6] absence of the Governor from the government, shall act as Lieutenant Governor. Four members shall be sufficient to act, and their advice and proceedings shall be entered on record; and signed by the members present (to any part whereof any member may enter his dissent) to be laid before the General Assembly, when called for by them. This Council may appoint their own clerk, who shall have a salary settled by law, and take an oath of secrecy in such matters as he shall be directed by the board to conceal. A sum of money appropriated to that purpose shall be divided annually among the members, in proportion to their attendance; and they shall be incapable, during their continuance in office, of sitting in either House of Assembly. Two members shall be removed by joint ballot of both Houses of Assembly at the end of every three years, and be ineligible for the three next years. These vacancies, as well as those occasioned by death or incapacity, shall be supplied by new elections, in the same manner.

XII. The delegates for *Virginia* to the Continental Congress shall be chosen annually, or superseded in the mean time by joint ballot of both Houses of Assembly.

XIII. The present militia officers shall be continued, and vacancies supplied by appointment of the Governour, with the advice of the Privy Council, or recommendations from the respective county courts; but the Governour and Council shall have a power of suspending any officer, and ordering a court-martial on complaint for misbehaviour or inability, or to supply vacancies of officers happening when in actual service. The Governour may embody the militia, with the advice of the Privy Council; and, when embodied, shall alone have the direction of the militia under the laws of the country.

XIV. The two Houses of Assembly shall, by joint ballot, appoint Judges of the Supreme Court of Appeals, and General Court, Judges in Chancery, Judges of Admiralty, Secretary, and the Attorney-General, to be commissioned by the Governour, and continue in office during good behaviour. In case of death, incapacity, or resignation, the Governour, with the Advice of the Privy Council, shall appoint persons to succeed in office, to be approved or displaced by both Houses. These officers shall have fixed and adequate salaries, and, together with all others holding lucrative offices, and all ministers of the Gospel of every denomination, be incapable of being elected members of either House of assembly, or the Privy Council.

XV. The Governour, with the advice of the Privy Council, shall appoint Justices of the Peace for the counties; and in case of vacancies,

---

[6]Kurland and Lerner (I: 8) add "if necessary" at this point, whereas Thorpe (VII: 3817) deletes entirely the word "necessary."

or a necessity of increasing the number hereafter, such appointments to be made upon the recommendation of the respective county courts. The present acting Secretary in *Virginia,* and Clerks of all the County Courts, shall continue in office. In case of vacancies, either by death, incapacity, or resignation, a Secretary shall be appointed as before directed, and the Clerks by the respective courts. The present and future Clerks shall hold their offices during good behaviour, to be judged of and determined in the General Court. The Sheriffs and Coroners shall be nominated by the respective courts, approved by the Governour, with the advice of the Privy Council, and commissioned by the Governour. The Justices shall appoint Constables, and all fees of the aforesaid officers be regulated by law.

XVI. The Governour, when he is out of office, and others offending against the state, either by mal-administration, corruption, or other means by which the safety of the state may be endangered, shall be impeachable by the House of Delegates. Such impeachment to be prosecuted by the Attorney-General, or such other person or persons as the House may appoint in the General Court, according to the laws of the land. If found guilty, he or they shall be either for ever disabled to hold any office under government, or removed from such Office *pro tempore,* or subjected to such pains or penalties as the laws shall direct.

XVII. If all, or any of the Judges of the General Court, shall, on good grounds (to be judged of by the House of Delegates) be accused of any of the crimes or offences before-mentioned, such House of Delegates may, in like manner, impeach the Judge or Judges so accused, to be prosecuted in the Court of Appeals; and he or they, if found guilty, shall be punished in the same manner as is prescribed in the preceding clause.

XVIII. Commissions and grants shall run, *In the name of the* COMMONWEALTH *of* VIRGINIA, and bear test by the Governour with the seal of the commonwealth annexed. Writs shall run in the same manner, and bear test by the clerks of the several courts. Indictments shall conclude, *Against the peace and dignity of the commonwealth.*

XIX. A treasurer shall be appointed annually, by joint ballot of both Houses.

XX. All escheats, penalties, and forfeitures, heretofore going to the king, shall go to the commonwealth, save only such as the legislature may abolish, or otherwise provide for.

XXI. The territories contained within the charters erecting the colonies of *Maryland, Pennsylvania, North* and *South Carolina,* are hereby ceded, released, and for ever confirmed to the people of those colonies respectively, with all the rights of property, jurisdiction, and government, and all other rights whatsoever which might at any time heretofore have been claimed by *Virginia*, except the free navigation and use of the rivers *Potowmack* and *Pohomoke*,[7] with the property of the *Virginia* shores or strands bordering on either of the said rivers, and all improvements which have been or shall be made thereon. The western and northern extent of *Virginia* shall in all other respects stand as fixed by the Charter of King *James* the first, in the year one thousand six hundred and nine, and by the publick treaty of peace between the courts of *Great Britain* and *France* in the year one thousand seven hundred and sixty three; unless by act of legislature, one or more territories shall hereafter be laid off, and governments established westward of the *Allegheny* mountains. And no purchase of land shall be made of the *Indian* natives but on behalf of the publick, by authority of the General Assembly.

XXII. In order to introduce this government, the representatives of the people met in Convention shall choose a Governour and Privy Council, also such other officers directed to be chosen by both Houses as may be judged necessary to be immediately appointed. The Senate to be first chosen by the people, to continue until the last day of *March* next, and the other officers until the end of the succeeding session of Assembly. In case of vacancies, the speaker of either House shall issue writs for new elections.[8]

XXVII.

CONSTITUTION OF NEW JERSEY, 3 JULY 1776

New Jersey was the first state to incorporate a declaration of rights within the body of the Constitution itself. We have followed Thorpe (V: 2594-2598). See also Schwartz (II: 256-261). Kurland and Lerner (V: 71. 353) reproduce Articles XVIII (free exercise of religion), and XIX (religious establishment), and XXII (trial by jury). The Roman numerals are in the original.

~

WHEREAS all the constitutional authority ever possessed by the kings of Great Britain over these colonies, or their other dominions, was, by compact, derived from the people, and held of them, for the common

---

[7]Thorpe (VII: 3818) spells these rivers "Patomaque" and "Pokomoke."

[8]Hening notes (119) that "*Patrick Henry, esq.* was elected Governor, and the members of the Privy Council were chosen the same day on which the Constitution was adopted."

interest of the whole society; allegiance and protection are, in the nature of things, reciprocal ties, each equally depending upon the other, and liable to be dissolved by the others being refused or withdrawn. And whereas George the Third, king of Great Britain, has refused protection to the good people of these colonies; and, by assenting to sundry acts of the British parliament, attempted to subject them to the absolute dominion of that body; and has also made war upon them, in the most cruel and unnatural manner, for no other cause, than asserting their just rights—all civil authority under him is necessarily at an end, and a dissolution of government in each colony has consequently taken place. And whereas, in the present deplorable situation of these colonies, exposed to the fury of a cruel and relentless enemy, some form of government is absolutely necessary, not only for the preservation of good order, but also the more effectually to unite the people, and enable them to exert their whole force in their own necessary defence: and as the honorable the continental congress, the supreme council of the American colonies, has advised such of the colonies as have not yet gone into measures, to adopt for themselves, respectively, such government as shall best conduce to their own happiness and safety, and the well-being of America in general:—We, the representatives of the colony of New Jersey, having been elected by all the counties, in the freest manner, and in congress assembled, have, after mature deliberations, agreed upon a set of charter rights and the form of a Constitution, in manner following, viz.

I. That the government of this Province shall be vested in a Governor, Legislative Council, and General Assembly.

II. That the Legislative Council, and General Assembly, shall be chosen, for the first time, on the second Tuesday in August next; the members whereof shall be the same in number and qualifications as are herein after mentioned; and shall be and remain vested with all the powers and authority to be held by any future Legislative Council and Assembly of this Colony, until the second Tuesday in October, which shall be in the year of our Lord one thousand seven hundred and seventy-seven.

III. That on the second Tuesday in October yearly, and every year forever (with the privilege of adjourning from day to day as occasion may require) the counties shall severally choose one person, to be a member of the Legislative Council of this Colony, who shall be, and have been, for one whole year next before the election, an inhabitant and freeholder in the county in which he is chosen, and worth at least one thousand pounds proclamation money, of real and personal estate, within the same county; that, at the same time, each county shall also choose three members of Assembly; provided that no person shall be entitled to a seat in the said Assembly unless he be, and have been, for one whole year next before the election, an inhabitant of the county he is to represent, and worth five hundred pounds proclamation money, in real and personal estate, in the same county: that on the second Tuesday next after the day of election, the Council and Assembly shall separately meet; and that the consent of both Houses shall be necessary to every law; provided, that seven shall be a quorum of the Council, for doing business, and that no law shall pass, unless there be a majority of all the Representatives of each body personally present, and agreeing thereto. Provided always, that if a majority of the representatives of this Province, in Council and General Assembly convened, shall, at any time or times hereafter, judge it equitable and proper, to add to or diminish the number or proportion of the members of Assembly for any county or counties in this Colony, then, and in such case, the same may, on the principles of more equal representation, be lawfully done; anything in this Charter to the contrary notwithstanding: so that the whole number of Representatives in Assembly shall not, at any time, be less than thirty-nine.

IV. That all inhabitants of this colony, of full age, who are worth fifty pounds proclamation money, clear estate in the same, and have resided within the county in which they claim a vote for twelve months immediately preceding the election, shall be entitled to vote for Representatives in council and Assembly; and also for all other public officers, that shall be elected by the people of the county at large.

V. That the Assembly, when met, shall have power to choose a Speaker, and other their officers; to be judges of the qualifications and elections of their own members; sit upon their own adjournments; prepare bills, to be passed into laws; and to empower their Speaker to convene them, whenever any extraordinary occurrence shall render is necessary.

VI. That the Council shall also have power to prepare bills to pass into laws, and have other like powers as the Assembly, and in all respects be a free and independent branch of the Legislature of this Colony; save only, that they shall not prepare or alter any money bill--which shall be the privilege of the Assembly; that the Council shall, from time to time, be convened by the Governor or Vice-President, but must be convened, at all times, when the Assembly sits; for which purpose the Speaker of the House of Assembly shall always, immediately after an adjournment, give notice to the Governor, or Vice-President, of the time and place to which the House is adjourned.

VII. That the Council and Assembly jointly, at their first meeting after each annual election, shall, by a majority of votes, elect some fit person within the Colony, to be Governor for one year, who shall be constant President of the Council, and have a casting vote in their proceedings; and that the council themselves shall choose a Vice-President who shall act as such in the absence of the Governor.

VIII. That the Governor, or, in his absence, the Vice-President of the Council, shall have the supreme executive power, be Chancellor of the Colony, and act as captain-general and commander in chief of all the militia, and other military force in this Colony; and that any three or more of the Council shall, at all times, be a privy-council, to consult them; and that the Governor be ordinary or surrogate-general.

IX. That the Governor and Council, (seven whereof shall be a quorum) be the Court of Appeals, in the last resort, in all clauses of law, as heretofore; and that they possess the power of granting pardons to criminals, after condemnation, in all cases of treason, felony, or other offences.

X. That captains, and all other inferior officers of the militia, shall be chosen by the companies, in the respective counties; but field and general officers, by the council and Assembly.

XI. That the Council and Assembly shall have power to make the Great Seal of this Colony, which shall be kept by the Governor, or, in his absence, by the Vice-President of the Council, to be used by them ass occasion may require: and it shall be called, *The Great Seal of the Colony of New-Jersey*

XII. That the Judges of the Supreme Court shall continue in office for seven years: the judges of the Inferior Court of Common Pleas in the several counties, Justices of the Peace, Clerks of the Supreme Court, Clerks of the Inferior Court of Common Pleas and Quarter Sessions, the Attorney-General, and Provincial Secretary, shall continue in office for five years: and the Provincial Treasurer shall continue in office for one year; and that they shall be severally appointed by the Council and Assembly, in manner aforesaid, and commissioned by the Governor, or, in his absence, the Vice-President of the Council. Provided always, that the said officers, severally, shall be capable of being re-appointed, at the end of the terms severally before limited; and that any of the said officers shall be liable to be dismissed, when adjudged guilty of misbehaviour, by the Council, on an impeachment of the Assembly.

XIII. That the inhabitants of each county, qualified to vote as aforesaid, shall at the time and place of electing their Representatives, annually elect one Sheriff, and one or more Coroners; and that they may re-elect the same person to such offices, until he shall have served three years, but no longer; after which, three years must elapse before the same person is capable of being elected again. When the election is certified to the Governor, or Vice-President, under the hands of six freeholders of the county for which they were elected, they shall be immediately commissioned to serve in their respective offices.

XIV. That the townships, at their annual town meetings for electing other officers, shall choose constables for the districts respectively; and also three or more judicious freeholders of good character, to hear and finally determine all appeals, relative to unjust assessments, in cases of public taxation; which comissioners of appeal shall, for that purpose, sit at some suitable time or times, to be by them appointed, and made known to the people by advertisements.

XV. That the laws of the Colony shall begin in the following style, viz. "Be it enacted by the Council and General Assembly of this Colony, and it is hereby enacted by authority of the same:" that all commissions, granted by the Governor or Vice-President, shall run thus—"The Colony of New-Jersey to A. B. &c. greeting:" and that all writs shall likewise run in the name of the Colony: and that all indictments shall conclude in the following manner, viz. "Against the peace of this Colony, the government and dignity of the same."

XVI. That all criminals shall be admitted to the same privileges of witnesses and counsel, as their prosecutors are or shall be entitled to.

XVII. That the estates of such persons as shall destroy their own lives, shall not, for that offence, be forfeited; but shall descend in the same manner, as they would have done, had such persons died in the natural way; nor shall any article, which may occasion accidentally the death of any one, be henceforth deemed a deodand, or in anywise forfeited, on account of such misfortune.

XVIII. That no person shall ever, within this Colony, be deprived of the inestimable privilege of worshipping Almighty God in a manner agreeable to the dictates of his own conscience; nor, under any pretence whatever, be compelled to attend any place of worship, contrary to his own faith and judgment; nor shall any person, within this Colony, ever be obliged to pay tithes, taxes, or any other rates, for the purpose of building or repairing any other church or churches, place or places of worship, or for the maintenance of any minister or ministry, contrary to what he believes to be right, or has deliberately or voluntarily engaged himself to perform.

XIX. That there shall be no establishment of any one religious sect in this Province, in preference to another; and that no Protestant inhabitant of this Colony shall be denied the enjoyment of any civil right, merely on account of his religious principles; but that all persons, profession a belief in the faith of any Protestant sect, who shall demean themselves peaceably under the government, as hereby established, shall be capable of being elected into any office of profit or trust, or being a member of either branch of the Legislature, and shall fully and freely enjoy every privilege and immunity, enjoyed by others their fellow subjects.

XX. That the legislative department of this government may, as much as possible, be preserved from all suspicion of corruption, none of the

Judges of the supreme or other Courts, Sheriffs, or any other person or persons possessed of any post of profit under the government, other than Justices of the Peace, shall be entitled to a seat in the Assembly: but that, on his being elected, and taking his seat, his office or post shall be considered as vacant.

XXI. That all the laws of this Province, contained in the edition lately published by Mr. Allinson, shall be and remain in full force, until altered by the Legislature of this Colony (such only excepted, as are incompatible with this Charter) and shall be, according as heretofore, regarded in all respects, by all civil officers, and others, the good people of this Province.

XXII. That the common law of England, as well as so much of the statute law, as have been heretofore practised in this Colony, shall still remain in force, until they shall be altered by a future law of the Legislature; such parts only excepted, as are repugnant to the rights and privileges contained in this Charter; and that the inestimable right of trial by jury shall remain confirmed as a part of the laws of this Colony, without repeal, forever.

XXIII. That every person, who shall be elected as aforesaid to be a member of the Legislative Council, or House of Assembly, shall, previous to this taking his seat in Council or Assembly, take the following oath or affirmation, viz:

"I, *A. B.*, do solemnly declare, that, as a member of the Legislative Council, [*or Assembly, as the case may be,*] of the Colony of New-Jersey, I will not assent to any law, vote or proceeding, which shall appear to me injurious to the public welfare of said Colony, nor that shall annul or repeal that part of the third section in the Charter of this Colony, which establishes, that the elections of members of the Legislative Council and Assembly shall be annual; nor that part of the twenty-second section in said Charter, respecting the trial by jury, nor that shall annul, repeal, or alter any part or parts of the eighteenth or nineteenth sections of the same."

And any person or persons, who shall be elected as aforesaid, is hereby empowered to administer to the said members the said oath or affirmation.

Provided always, and it is the true intent and meaning of this Congress, that if a reconciliation between Great-Britain and these Colonies should take place, and the latter be taken again under the protection and government of the crown of Britain, this Charter shall be null and void––otherwise to remain firm and inviolable.

In Provincial Congress, New Jersey,
Burlington, July 2, 1776.
By order of Congress. SAMUEL TUCKER, *Pres.*
WILLIAM PATTERSON, *Secretary*

XXVIII.

PENNSYLVANIA DECLARATION OF RIGHTS AND CONSTITUTION, 28 SEPTEMBER 1776

For organizational purposes, we have divided the text into three parts. Part 1 contains a preamble. Part 2 lists sixteen "rights." The Roman numerals are in the original text. Part 3 reproduces the forty-seven sections of the plan of government. The Arabic numerals are in the original text. We have followed the spelling, abbreviations, and punctuation found in Thorpe's version. See Thorpe (V: 3081-3092), and also Schwartz (II: 262-275).

~

[Part 1: Preamble]

WHEREAS all government ought to be instituted and supported for the security and protection of the community as such, and to enable the individuals who compose it to enjoy their natural rights, and the other blessings which the Author of existence has bestowed upon man; and whenever these great ends of government are not obtained, the people have a right, by common consent to change it, and take such measures as to them may appear necessary to promote their safety and happiness. AND WHEREAS the inhabitants of this commonwealth have in consideration of protection only, heretofore acknowledged allegiance to the king of Great Britain; and the said king has not only withdrawn that protection, but commenced, and still continues to carry on, with unabated vengeance, a most cruel and unjust war against them, employing therein, not only the troops of Great Britain, but foreign mercenaries, savages and slaves, for the avowed purpose of reducing them to a total and abject submission to the despotic domination of the British parliament, with many other acts of tyranny, (more fully set forth in the declaration of Congress) whereby all allegiance and fealty to the said king and his successors, are dissolved and at an end, and all power and authority derived from him ceased in these colonies. AND WHEREAS it is absolutely necessary for the welfare and safety of the inhabitants of said colonies, that they be henceforth free and independent States, and that just, permanent, and proper forms of government exist in every part of them, derived from and founded on the authority of the people only, agreeable to the directions of the honourable American Congress. We, the representatives of the freemen of Pennsylvania, in general convention met, for the express purpose of framing such a government, confessing the goodness of the great Governor of the universe (who alone knows to what degree of earthly happiness mankind may attain, by perfecting the arts of government) in permitting the people of this State, by common consent, and without violence, deliberately to form for themselves such just rules as they shall think best, for governing their future society; and being fully convinced, that it is our indispensable duty to establish such original principles of government, as will best promote the general happiness of the people of this State, and their posterity, and provide for future improvements, without partiality for, or prejudice against any particular class, sect, or denomination of men whatever, do, by virtue of the authority vested in use by our constituents, ordain, declare, and establish, the following *Declaration of Rights* and *Frame of Government*, to be the CONSTITUTION of this commonwealth, and to remain in force therein for ever, unaltered, except in such articles as shall hereafter on experience be found to require improvement, and which shall by the same authority of the people, fairly delegated as this frame of government directs, be amended or improved for the more effectual obtaining and securing the great end and design of all government, herein before mentioned.

[Part 2: Bill of Rights]
A DECLARATION OF THE RIGHTS OF THE INHABITANTS OF THE COMMONWEALTH, OR STATE OF PENNSYLVANIA

I. That all men are born equally free and independent, and have certain natural, inherent and inalienable rights, amongst which are, the enjoying and defending life and liberty, acquiring, possessing and protecting property, and pursuing and obtaining happiness and safety.

II. That all men have a natural and unalienable right to worship Almighty God according to the dictates of their own consciences and understanding: And that no man ought or of right can be compelled to attend any religious worship, or erect or support any place of worship, or maintain any ministry, contrary to, or against, his own free will and consent: Nor can any man, who acknowledges the being of a God, be justly deprived or abridged of any civil right as a citizen, on account of his religious sentiments or peculiar mode of religious worship: And that no authority can or ought to be vested in, or assumed by any power whatever, that shall in any case interfere with, or in any manner controul, the right of conscience in the free exercise of religious worship.

III. That the people of this State have the sole, exclusive and inherent right of governing and regulating the internal police of the same.

IV. That all power being originally inherent in, and consequently derived from, the people; therefore all officers of government, whether legislative or executive, are their trustees and servants, and at all time accountable to them.

V. That government is, or ought to be, instituted for the common benefit, protection and security of the people, nation or community; and not for the particular emolument or advantage of any single man, family, or sett of men, who are a part only of that community; And that the community hath an indubitable, unalienable and indefeasible right to reform, alter, or abolish government in such manner as shall be by that community judged most conducive to the public weal.

VI. That those who are employed in the legislative and executive business of the State, may be restrained from oppression, the people have a right, at such periods as they may think proper, to reduce their public officers to a private station, and supply the vacancies by certain and regular elections.

VII. That all elections ought to be free; and that all free men having a sufficient evident common interest with, and attachment to the community, have a right to elect officers, or to be elected into office.

VIII. That every member of society hath a right to be protected in the enjoyment of life, liberty and property, and therefore is bound to contribute his proportion towards the expence of that protection, and yield his personal service when necessary, or an equivalent thereto: But no part of a man's property can be justly taken from him, or applied to public uses, without his own consent, or that of his legal representatives: Nor can any man who is conscientiously scrupulous of bearing arms, be justly compelled thereto, if he will pay such equivalent, nor are the people bound by any laws, but such as they have in like manner assented to, for their common good.

IX. That in all prosecutions for criminal offences, a man hath a right to be heard by himself and his council, to demand the cause and nature of his accusation, to be confronted with the witnesses, to call for evidence in his favour, and a speedy public trial, by an impartial jury of the country, without the unanimous consent of which jury he cannot be found guilty; nor can he be compelled to give evidence against himself; nor can any man be justly deprived of his liberty except by the laws of the land, or the judgment of his peers.

X. That the people have a right to hold themselves, their houses, papers, and possessions free from search and seizure, and therefore warrants without oaths or affirmations first made, affording a sufficient foundation for them, and whereby any officer or messenger may be commanded or required to search suspected places, or to seize any person or persons, his or their property, not particularly described, are contrary to that right, and ought not to be granted.

XI. That in controversies respecting property, and in suits between man and man, the parties have a right to trial by jury, which ought to be held sacred.

XII. That the people have a right to freedom of speech, and of writing, and publishing their sentiments; therefore the freedom of the press ought not to be restrained.

XIII. That the people have a right to bear arms for the defence of themselves and the state; and as standing armies in the time of peace are dangerous to liberty, they ought not to be kept up; And that the military should be kept under strict subordination to, and governed by, the civil power.

XIV. That a frequent recurrence to fundamental principles, and a firm adherence to justice, moderation, temperance, industry, and frugality are absolutely necessary to preserve the blessings of liberty, and keep a government free: The people ought therefore to pay particular attention to these points in the choice of officers and representatives, and have a right to exact a due and constant regard to them, from their legislatures and magistrates, in the making and executing such laws as are necessary for the good government of the state.

XV. That all men have a natural inherent right to emigrate from one state to another that will receive them, or to form a new state in vacant countries, or in such countries as they can purchase, whenever they think that thereby they may promote their own happiness.

XVI. That the people have a right to assemble together, to consult for their common good, to instruct their representatives, and to apply to the legislature for redress of grievances, by address, petition, or remonstrance.

[Part 3: Frame of Government]

PLAN OR FRAME OF GOVERNMENT FOR COMMONWEALTH OR STATE OF PENNSYLVANIA

SECTION 1. The commonwealth or state of Pennsylvania shall be governed hereafter by an assembly of the representatives of the freemen of the same, and a president and council, in manner and form following—

SECT. 2. The supreme legislative power shall be vested in a house of representatives of the freemen of the commonwealth or state of Pennsylvania.

SECT. 3. The supreme executive power shall be vested in a president and council.

SECT. 4. Courts of justice shall be established in the city of Philadelphia, and in every county of this state.

SECT. 5. The freemen of this commonwealth and their sons shall be trained and armed for its defence under such regulations, restrictions, and exceptions as the general assembly shall by law direct, preserving always to the people the right of choosing their colonels and all commissioned officers under that rank, in such manner and as often as by the said laws shall be directed.

SECT. 6. Every freemen of the full age of twenty-one years, having resided in this state for the space of one whole year next before the day of election for representatives, and paid public taxes during that time, shall enjoy the right of an elector: Provided always that sons of freeholders of the age of twenty-one years shall be intitled to vote although they have not paid taxes.

SECT. 7. The house of representatives of the freemen of this commonwealth shall consist of persons most noted for wisdom and virtue, to be chosen by the freemen of every city and county of this commonwealth respectively. And no person shall be elected unless he has resided in the city or county for which he shall be chosen two years immediately before the said election; nor shall any member, while he continues such, hold any other office, except in the militia.

SECT. 8. No person shall be capable of being elected a member to serve in the house of representatives of the freemen of this commonwealth more than four years in seven.

SECT. 9. The members of the house of representatives shall be chosen annually by ballot, by the freemen of the commonwealth, on the second Tuesday in October forever, (except this present year,) and shall meet on the fourth Monday of the same month, and shall be stiled, *The general assembly of the representatives of the freemen of Pennsylvania*, and shall have power to choose their speaker, the treasurer of the state, and their other officers; sit on their own adjournments; prepare bills and enact them into laws; judge of the elections and qualifications of their own members; they may expel a member, but not a second time for the same cause; they may administer oaths or affirmations on examination of witnesses; redress grievances; impeach state criminals; grant charters of incorporation; constitute towns, boroughs, cities, and counties; and shall have all other powers necessary for the legislature of a free state or commonwealth: But they shall have no power to add to, alter, abolish, or infringe any part of this constitution.

SECT. 10. A quorum of the house of representatives shall consist of two-thirds of the whole number of members elected; and having met and chosen their speaker, shall each of them before they proceed to business take and subscribe, as well the oath or affirmation of fidelity and allegiance hereinafter directed, as the following oath or affirmation, viz:

I _____ do swear (or affirm) that as a member of this assembly, I will not propose or assent to any bill, vote, or resolution, which shall appear to me injurious to the people; nor do or consent to any act or thing whatever, that shall have a tendency to lessen or abridge their rights and privileges, as declared in the constitution of this state; but will in all things conduct myself as a faithful honest representative and guardian of the people, according to the best of my judgment and abilities.

And each member, before he takes his seat, shall make and subscribe the following declaration, viz:

I do believe in one God, the creator and governor of the universe, the rewarder of the good and the punisher of the wicked. And I do acknowledge the Scriptures of the Old and New Testament to be given by Divine Inspiration.

And no further or other religious test shall ever hereafter be required of any civil officer or magistrate in this State.

SECT. 11. Delegates to represent this state in congress shall be chosen by ballot by the future general assembly at their first meeting, and annually forever afterwards, as long as such representation shall be necessary. Any delegate may be superseded at any time, by the general assembly appointing another in his stead. No man shall sit in congress longer than two years successively, nor be capable of re-election for three years afterwards: and no person who holds any office in the gift of the congress shall hereafter be elected to represent this commonwealth in congress.

SECT. 12. If any city or cities, county or counties shall neglect or refuse to elect and send representatives to the general assembly, two-thirds of the members from the cities or counties that do elect and send representatives, provided they be a majority of the cities and counties of the whole state, when met, shall have all the powers of the general assembly, as fully and amply as if the whole were present.

SECT. 13. The doors of the house in which the representatives of the freemen of this state shall sit in general assembly, shall be and remain open for the admission of all persons who behave decently, except only when the welfare of this state may require the doors to be shut.

SECT. 14. The votes and proceedings of the general assembly shall be printed weekly during their sitting, with the yeas and nays, on any question, vote or resolution, where any two members require it, except when the vote is taken by ballot; and when the yeas and nays are so taken every member shall have a right to insert the reasons of his vote upon the minutes, if he desires it.

SECT. 15. To the end that laws before they are enacted may be more maturely considered, and the inconvenience of hasty determinations as much as possible prevented, all bills of public nature shall be printed for the consideration of the people, before they are read in general assembly the last time for debate and amendment; and, except on occasions of sudden necessity, shall not be passed into laws until the next session of assembly; and for the more perfect satisfaction of the public, the reasons and motives of making such laws shall be fully and clearly expressed in the preambles.

SECT. 16. The stile of the laws of this commonwealth shall be, "Be it enacted, and it is hereby enacted by the representatives of the freemen of the commonwealth of Pennsylvania in general assembly met, and by the authority of the same." And the general assembly shall affix their seal to every bill, as soon as it is enacted into a law, which seal shall be kept by the assembly, and shall be called, *The seal of the laws of Pennsylvania*, and shall not be used for any other purpose.

SECT. 17. The city of Philadelphia and each county of this commonwealth respectively, shall on the first Tuesday of November in this present year, and on the second Tuesday of October annually for the two next succeeding years, *viz.* the year one thousand seven hundred and seventy-seven, and the year one thousand seven hundred and seventy-eight, choose six persons to represent them in general assembly. But as representation in proportion to the number of taxable inhabitants is the only principle which can at all times secure liberty, and make the voice of a majority of the people the law of the land; therefore the general assembly shall cause complete lists of the taxable inhabitants in the city and each county in the commonwealth respectively, to be taken and returned to them, on or before the last meeting of the assembly elected in the year one thousand seven hundred and seventy-eight, who shall appoint a representation to each, in proportion to the number of taxables in such returns; which representation shall continue for the next seven years afterwards at the end of which, a new return of the taxable inhabitants shall be made, and a representation agreeable thereto appointed by the said assembly, and so on septennially forever. The wages of the representatives in general assembly, and all other state charges shall be paid out of the state treasury.

SECT. 18. In order that the freemen of this commonwealth may enjoy the benefit of election as equally as may be until the representation shall commence, as directed in the foregoing section, each county at its own choice may be divided into districts, hold elections therein, and elect their representatives in the county, and their other elective officers, as shall be hereafter regulated by the general assembly of this state. And no inhabitant of this state shall have more than one annual vote at the general election for representatives in assembly.

SECT. 19. For the present the supreme executive council of this state shall consist of twelve persons chosen in the following manner: The freemen of the city of Philadelphia, and of the counties of Philadelphia, Chester, and Bucks, respectively, shall choose by ballot one person for the city, and one for each county aforesaid, to serve for three years and no longer, at the time and place for electing representatives in general assembly. The freemen of the counties of Lancaster, York,

Cumberland, and Berks, shall, in like manner elect one person for each county respectively, to serve as counsellors for two years and no longer. And the counties of Northampton, Bedford, Northumberland and Westmoreland, respectively, shall, in like manner, elect one person for each county, to serve as counsellors for one year, and no longer. And at the expiration of the time for which each counsellor was chosen to serve, the freemen of the city of Philadelphia, and of the several counties in this state, respectively, shall elect one person to serve as counsellor for three years and no longer; and so on every third year forever. By this mode of election and continual rotation, more men will be trained to public business, there will in every subsequent year be found in the council a number of persons acquainted with the proceedings of the foregoing years, whereby the business will be more consistently conducted, and moreover, the danger of establishing an inconvenient aristocracy will be effectually prevented. All vacancies in the council that may happen by death, resignation, or otherwise, shall be filled at the next general election for representatives in general assembly, unless a particular election for that purpose shall be sooner appointed by the president and council. No member of the general assembly or delegate in congress, shall be chosen a member of the council. The president and vice-president shall be chosen annually by the joint ballot of the general assembly and council, of the members[9] of the council. Any person having served as a counsellor for three successive years, shall be incapable of holding that office for four years afterwards. Every member of the council shall be a justice of the peace for the whole commonwealth, by virtue of his office.

In case new additional counties shall hereafter be erected in this state, such county or counties shall elect a counsellor, and such county or counties shall be annexed to the next neighbouring counties, and shall take rotation with such counties.

The council shall meet annually, at the same time and place with the general assembly.

The treasurer of the state, trustees of the loan office, naval officers, collectors of customs or excise, judge of the admiralty, attornies general, sheriffs, and prothonotaries,[10] shall not be capable of a seat in the general assembly, executive council, or continental congress.

---

[9]In Schwartz (II: 270), the passage reads "of the member of the council." The plural, "members," is in the original and makes more sense than the singular "member." The intent would have been clearer had the Pennsylvania framers written "from the members of the council."

[10]In certain law courts, the chief clerk is known as a prothonotary.

SECT. 20. The president, and in his absence the vice-president, with the council, five of whom shall be a quorum, shall have power to appoint and commissionate judges, naval officers, judge of the admiralty, attorney general and all other officers, civil and military, except such as are chosen by the general assembly or the people, agreeable to this frame of government, and the laws that may be made hereafter; and shall supply every vacancy in any office, occasioned by death, resignation, removal or disqualification, until the office can be filled in the time and manner directed by law or this constitution. They are to correspond with other states, and transact business with the officers of government, civil and military; and to prepare such business as may appear to them necessary to lay before the general assembly. They shall sit as judges, to hear and determine on impeachments, taking to their assistance for advice only, the justices of the supreme court. And shall have power to grant pardons, and remit fines, in all cases whatsoever, except in cases of impeachment; and in cases of treason and murder, shall have power to grant reprieves, but not to pardon, until the end of the next sessions of assembly; but there shall be no remission or mitigation of punishments on impeachments, except by act of the legislature; they are also to take care that the laws be faithfully executed; they are to expedite the execution of such measures as may be resolved upon by the general assembly; and they may draw upon the treasury for such sums as shall be appropriated by the house: They may also lay embargoes, or prohibit the exportation of any commodity, for any time, not exceeding thirty days, in the recess of the house only. They may grant such licences, as shall be directed by law, and shall have power to call together the general assembly when necessary before the day to which they shall stand adjourned. The president shall be commander in chief of the forces of the state, but shall not command in person, except advised thereto by the council, and then only so long as they shall approve thereof. The president and council shall have a secretary, and keep fair books of their proceedings, wherein any counsellor may enter his dissent, with his reasons in support of it.

SECT. 21. All commissions shall be in the name, and by the authority of the freemen of the commonwealth of Pennsylvania, sealed with the state seal, signed by the president or vice-president, and attested by the secretary; which seal shall be kept by the council.

SECT. 22. Every officer of state, whether judicial or executive, shall be liable to be impeached by the general assembly, either when in office, or after his resignation or removal for mal-administration:[11] All

---

[11]Schwartz's version (II: 271) has "mal-administrations."

impeachments shall be before the president or vice-president and council, who shall hear and determine the same.

SECT. 23. The judges of the supreme court of judicature shall have fixed salaries, be commissioned for seven years only, though capable of re-appointment at the end of that term, but removable for misbehaviour at any time by the general assembly; they shall not be allowed to sit as members in the continental congress, executive council, or general assembly, nor to hold any other office civil or military, nor to take or receive fees or perquisites of any kind.

SECT. 24. The supreme court, and the several courts of common pleas of this commonwealth, shall, besides the powers usually exercised by such courts, have the powers of a court of chancery, so far as relates to the perpetuating testimony, obtaining evidence from places not within this state, and the care of the persons and estates of those who are *non compotes mentis,* and such other powers as may be found necessary by future general assemblies, not inconsistent with this constitution.

SECT. 25. Trials shall be by jury as heretofore: And it is recommended in the legislature of this state, to provide by law against every corruption or partiality in the choice, return, or appointment of juries.

SECT. 26. Courts of sessions, common pleas, and orphans courts shall be held quarterly in each city and county; and the legislature shall have power to establish all such other courts as they may judge for the good of the inhabitants of the state. All courts shall be open, and justice shall be impartially administered without corruption or unnecessary delay: All their officers shall be paid an adequate but moderate compensation for their services: And if any officer shall take greater or other fees than the law allows him, either directly or indirectly, it shall ever after disqualify him from holding any office in this state.

SECT. 27. All prosecutions shall commence in the name and by the authority of the freemen of the commonwealth of Pennsylvania; and all indictments shall conclude with these words, "*Against the peace and dignity of the same.*" The style of all process hereafter in this state shall be, *The commonwealth of Pennsylvania.*

SECT. 28. The person of a debtor, where there is not a strong presumption of fraud, shall not be continued in prison, after delivering up, *bona fide*, all his estate real and personal, for the use of his creditors, in such manner as shall be hereafter regulated by law. All prisoners shall be bailable by sufficient sureties, unless for capital offences, when the proof is evident, or presumption great.

SECT. 29. Excessive bail shall not be exacted for bailable offences: And all fines shall be moderate.

SECT. 30. Justices of the peace shall be elected by the freeholders of each city and county respectively, that is to say, two or more persons may be chosen for each ward, township, or district, as the law shall hereafter direct: And their names shall be returned to the president in council, who shall commissionate one or more of them for each ward, township, or district so returning, for seven years, removable for misconduct by the general assembly. But if any city or county, ward, township, or district in this commonwealth, shall hereafter incline to change the manner of appointing their justices of the peace as settled in this article, the general assembly may make laws to regulate the same, agreeable to the desire of a majority of the freeholders of the city or county, ward, township, or district so applying. No justice of the peace shall sit in the general assembly unless he first resigns his commission; nor shall he be allowed to take any fees, nor any salary or allowance, except such as the future legislature may grant.

SECT. 31. Sheriffs and coroners shall be elected annually in each city and county, by the freemen; that is to say, two persons for each office, one of whom for each, is to be commissioned by the president in council. No person shall continue in the office of sheriff more than three successive years, or be capable of being again elected during four years afterwards. The election shall be held at the same time and place appointed for the election of representatives: And the commissioners and assessors, and other officers chosen by the people, shall also be then and there elected, as has been usual heretofore, until altered or otherwise regulated by the future legislature of this state.

SECT. 32. All elections, whether by the people or in general assembly, shall be by ballot, free and voluntary: And any elector, who shall receive any gift or reward for his vote, in meat, drink, monies, or otherwise, shall forfeit his right to elect for that time, and suffer such other penalties as future laws shall direct. And any person who shall directly or indirectly give, promise, or bestow any such rewards to be elected, shall be thereby rendered incapable to serve for the ensuing year.

SECT. 33. All fees, licence money, fines and forfeitures heretofore granted, or paid to the governor, or his deputies for the support of government, shall hereafter be paid into the public treasury, unless altered or abolished by the future legislature.

SECT. 34. A register's office for the probate of wills and granting letters of administration, and an office for the recording of deeds, shall be kept in each city and county: The officers to be appointed by the general assembly, removable at their pleasure, and to be commissioned by the president in council.

SECT. 35. The printing presses shall be free to every person who undertakes to examine the proceedings of the legislature, or any part of government.

SECT. 36. As every freeman to preserve his independence, (if without a sufficient estate) ought to have some profession, calling, trade or farm, whereby he may honestly subsist, there can be no necessity for, nor use in establishing offices of profit, the usual effects of which are dependence and servility unbecoming freemen, in the possessors and expectants; faction, contention, corruption, and disorder among the people. But if any man is called into public service, to the prejudice of his private affairs, he has a right to a reasonable compensation: And whenever an office, through increase of fees or otherwise, becomes so profitable as to occasion many to apply for it, the profits ought to be lessened by the legislature.

SECT. 37. The future legislature of this state, shall regulate intails in such a manner as to prevent perpetuities.

SECT. 38. The penal laws as heretofore used shall be reformed by the legislature of this state, as soon as may be, and punishments made in some cases less sanguinary, and in general more proportionate to the crimes.

SECT. 39. To deter more effectually from the commission of crimes, by continued visible punishments of long duration, and to make sanguinary punishments less necessary, houses ought to be provided for punishing by hard labour, those who shall be convicted of crimes not capital; wherein the criminals shall be imployed for the benefit of the public, or for reparation of injuries done to private persons: And all persons at proper times shall be admitted to see the prisoners at their labour.

SECT. 40. Every officer, whether judicial, executive or military, in authority under this commonwealth, shall take the following oath or affirmation of allegiance, and general oath of office before he enters on the execution of his office.

THE OATH OR AFFIRMATION OF ALLEGIANCE

I _______ do swear (or affirm) that I will be true and faithful to the commonwealth of Pennsylvania: And that I will not directly or indirectly do any act or thing prejudicial or injurious to the constitution or government thereof, as established by the convention.

THE OATH OR AFFIRMATION OF OFFICE

I _______ do swear (or affirm) that I will faithfully execute the office of _______ for the ______ of ______ and will do equal right and justice to all men, to the best of my judgment and abilities, according to law.

SECT. 41. No public tax, custom or contribution shall be imposed upon, or paid by the people of this state, except by a law for that purpose: And before any law be made for raising it, the purpose for which any tax is to be raised ought to appear clearly to the legislature to be of more service to the community than the money would be, if not collected; which being well observed, taxes can never be burthens.

SECT. 42 Every foreigner of good character who comes to settle in this state, having first taken an oath or affirmation of allegiance to the same, may purchase, or by other just means acquire, hold, and transfer land or other real estate; and after one year's residence, shall be deemed a free denizen thereof, and entitled to all the rights of a natural born subject of this state, except that he shall not be capable of being elected a representative until after two years residence.

SECT. 43. The inhabitants of this state shall have liberty to fowl and hunt in seasonable times on the lands they hold, and on all other lands therein not inclosed; and in like manner to fish in all boatable waters, and others not private property.

SECT. 44. A school or schools shall be established in each county by the legislature, for the convenient instruction of youth, with such salaries to the masters paid by the public, as may enable them to instruct youth at low prices: And all useful learning shall be duly encouraged and promoted in one or more universities.

SECT. 45. Laws for the encouragement of virtue and prevention of vice and immorality, shall be made and constantly kept in force, and provision shall be made for their due execution: And all religious societies or bodies of men heretofore united or incorporated for the advancement of religion or learning, or for other pious and charitable purposes, shall be encouraged and protected in the enjoyment of the privileges, immunities and estates which they were accustomed to enjoy, or could of right have enjoyed, under the laws and former constitution of this state.

SECT. 46. The declaration of rights is hereby declared to be a part of the constitution of this commonwealth, and ought never to be violated on any pretence whatever.

SECT. 47. In order that the freedom of the commonwealth may be preserved inviolate forever, there shall be chosen by ballot by the freemen in each city and county respectively, on the second Tuesday in October, in the year one thousand seven hundred and eighty-three, and on the second Tuesday in October, in every seventh year thereafter, two persons in each city and county of this state, to be called the COUNCIL OF CENSORS; who shall meet together on the second Monday of November next ensuing their election; the majority of whom shall be a quorum in every case, except as to calling a convention, in which two-thirds of the whole number elected shall agree: And whose duty it shall be to enquire whether the constitution has been preserved inviolate in every part; and whether the legislative and executive branches of government have performed their duty as guardians of the people, or assumed to themselves, or exercised other or greater powers than they are intitled to by the constitution: They are also to enquire whether the public taxes have been justly laid and collected in all parts of this commonwealth, in what manner the public monies have been disposed of, and whether the laws have been duly executed. For these purposes they shall have power to send for persons, papers, and records; they shall have authority to pass public censures, to order impeachments, and to recommend to the legislature the repealing such laws as appear to them to have been enacted contrary to the principles of the constitution. These powers they shall continue to have, for and during the space of one year from the day of their election and no longer: The said council of censors shall also have power to call a convention, to meet within two years after their sitting, if there appear to them an absolute necessity of amending any article of the constitution which may be defective, explaining such as may be thought not clearly expressed, and of adding such as are necessary for the preservation of the rights and happiness of the people: But the articles to be amended, and the amendments proposed, and such articles as are proposed to be added or abolished, shall be promulgated at least six months before the day appointed for the election of such convention, for the previous consideration of the people, that they may have an opportunity of instructing their delegates on the subject.

Passed in Convention the 28th day of September, 1776, and signed by their order.

BENJ. FRANKLIN, *Prest.*

XXIX.

DELAWARE DECLARATION OF RIGHTS, 11 SEPTEMBER 1776

We have relied on the *Delaware Code Annotated* edited by W. M. Willson, *et.al.*, (Charlottesville, VA: The Michie Company, 1975). The identification of twenty-three sections by Arabic numerals is in the original. See also Kurland and Lerner (V: 5-6) and Schwartz (II: 276-278) who rely on the *Laws of Delaware*. Thorpe does not include the Delaware Declaration of Rights in his coverage of colonial and state charters. See also Claudia L. Bushman, Harold B. Hancock, and Elizabeth Moyne Homsey, editors, *Proceedings of the Assembly of the Lower Counties on Delaware 1770-1776, of the Constitutional Convention of 1776, and of the House of Assembly of the Delaware State 1776-1781* (Newark: University of Delaware Press, 1986: 212-214).

~

A Declaration of Rights and Fundamental Rules of the Delaware State, formerly stiled, The Government of the counties of New-Castle, Kent and Sussex, upon Delaware

SECTION 1. That all government of right originates from the people, is founded in compact only, and instituted solely for the good of the whole.

SECT. 2. That all men have a natural and unalienable right to worship Almighty God according to the dictates of their own consciences and understandings; and that no man ought or of right can be compelled to attend any religious worship or maintain any ministry contrary to or against his own free will and consent, and that no authority can or ought to be vested in, or assumed by any power whatever that shall in any case interfere with, or in any manner controul the right of conscience in the free exercise of religious worship.

SECT. 3. That all persons professing the Christian religion ought forever to enjoy equal rights and privileges in this state, unless, under colour of religion, any man disturb the peace, the happiness or safety of society.

SECT 4. That people of this state have the sole exclusive and inherent right of governing and regulating the internal police of the same.

SECT. 5. That persons intrusted with the Legislative and Executive Powers are the Trustees and Servants of the public, and as such accountable for their conduct; wherefore whenever the ends of government are perverted, and public liberty manifestly endangered by the Legislative singly, or a treacherous combination of both, the people may, and of right ought to establish a new, or reform the old government.

SECT. 6. That the right in the people to participate in the Legislature, is the foundation of liberty and of all free government, and for this end all elections ought to be free and frequent, and every freeman, having sufficient evidence of a permanent common interest with, and attachment to the community, hath a right of suffrage.

SECT. 7. That no power of suspending laws, or the execution of laws, ought to be exercised unless by the Legislature.

SECT. 8. That for redress of grievances, and for amending and strengthening of the laws, the Legislature ought to be frequently convened.

SECT. 9. That every man hath a right to petition the Legislature for the redress of grievances in a peaceable and orderly manner.

SECT. 10. That every member of society hath a right to be protected in the enjoyment of life, liberty and property, and therefore is bound to contribute his proportion towards the expense of that protection, and yield his personal service when necessary, or an equivalent thereto; but no part of a man's property can be justly taken from him or applied to public uses without his own consent or that of his legal Representatives: Nor can any man that is conscientiously scrupulous of bearing arms in any case be justly compelled thereto if he will pay such equivalent.

SECT. 11. That retrospective laws, punishing offences committed before the existence of such laws, are oppressive and unjust, and ought not to be made.

SECT. 12. That every freeman for every injury done him in his goods, lands or person, by any other person, ought to have remedy by the course of the law of the land, and ought to have justice and right for the injury done to him freely without sale, fully without any denial, and speedily without delay, according to the law of the land.

SECT. 13. That trial by jury of facts where they arise is one of the greatest securities of the lives, liberties and estates of the people.

SECT. 14. That in all prosecutions for criminal offences, every man hath a right to be informed of the accusation against him, to be allowed counsel, to be confronted with the accusers or witnesses, to examine evidence on oath in his favour, and to a speedy trial by an impartial jury, without whose unanimous consent he ought not to be found guilty.

SECT. 15. That no man in the courts of Common Law ought to be compelled to give evidence against himself.

SECT. 16. That excessive bail ought not to be required, nor excessive fines imposed, nor cruel or unusual punishments inflicted.

SECT. 17. That all warrants without oath to search suspected places, or to seize any person or his property, are grievous and oppressive; and all general warrants to search suspected, or to apprehend all persons suspected, without naming or describing the place or any person in special, are illegal and ought not to be granted.

SECT. 18. That a well regulated militia is the proper, natural and safe defence of a free government.

SECT. 19. That standing armies are dangerous to liberty, and ought not to be raised or kept up without the consent of the Legislature.

SECT. 20. That in all cases and at all times the military ought to be under strict subordination to and governed by the civil power.

SECT. 21. That no soldier ought to be quartered in any house in time of peace without the consent of the owner; and in time of war in such manner only as the Legislature shall direct.

SECT. 22. That the independency and uprightness of judges are essential to the impartial administration of justice, and a great security to the rights and liberties of the people.

SECT. 23. That the liberty of the press ought to be inviolably preserved.

XXX.

MASSACHUSETTS DECLARATION OF RIGHTS, 2 MARCH 1780

We have reproduced the Preamble and Declaration of Rights of the Massachusetts Constitution, authorized by the Massachusetts House of Representatives in 1822. See *The Constitution of the State of Massachusetts, adopted 1780 With Amendments Annexed* (Boston: Russell and Gardner). The Roman numerals in the text are in the original. For a reproduction which relies on extensive use of the lower case, see Thorpe (III: 1888-1911). Kurland and Lerner (I: 11-23) rely on Oscar and Mary Handlin, editors, *The Popular Sources of Political Authority: Documents on the Massachusetts Constitution of 1780* (Boston: Harvard University Press, 1966: 441-172).

~

A CONSTITUTION OR FORM OF GOVERNMENT FOR THE COMMONWEALTH OF MASSACHUSETTS

PREAMBLE.

THE end of the institution, maintenance, and administration of government, is to secure the existence of the body politic, to protect it, and to furnish the individuals, who compose it, with the power of enjoying, in safety and tranquility, their natural rights, and the blessings of life: and whenever these great objects are not obtained, the people have a right to alter the government, and to take measures, necessary for their safety, prosperity, and happiness. The body politic is formed by a voluntary association of individuals. It is a social compact, by which the whole people covenants with each citizen, and each citizen with the whole people, that all shall be governed by certain laws for the common good. It is the duty of the people, therefore, in framing a Constitution of Government, to provide for an equitable mode of making laws, as well as for an impartial interpretation, and a faithful execution of them; that every man may, at all times, find his security in them. We, therefore, the people of Massachusetts, acknowledging, with grateful hearts, the goodness of the Great Legislator of the Universe, in affording us, in the course of his providence, an opportunity, deliberately and peaceably, without fraud, violence or surprize, of entering into an original, explicit, and solemn compact with each other; and of forming a new Constitution of Civil Government, for ourselves and posterity; and devoutly imploring His direction in so interesting a design, do agree upon, ordain, and establish, the following Declaration of Rights, and Frame of Government, as the Constitution of the Commonwealth of Massachusetts.

A
DECLARATION OF THE RIGHTS
OF THE
INHABITANTS
OF THE
COMMONWEALTH OF MASSACHUSETTS.

ARTICLE I.

ALL men are born free and equal, and have certain natural, essential, and unalienable rights; among which may be reckoned the right of enjoying and defending their lives and liberties; that of acquiring, possessing, and protecting property; in fine, that of seeking and obtaining their safety and happiness.

II.

It is the right, as well as the duty of all men in society, publicly, and at stated seasons, to worship the Supreme Being, the great Creator and Preserver of the Universe. And no subject shall be hurt, molested, or restrained, in his person, liberty, or estate, for worshipping God, in the manner and season, most agreeable to the dictates of his own conscience; or for his religious profession or sentiments; provided he doth not disturb the public peace, or obstruct others in their religious worship.

III.

As the happiness of a people, and the good order and preservation of civil government, essentially depend upon piety, religion, and morality; and as these cannot be generally diffused through a community, but by the institution of the public worship of God, and of public instructions in piety, religion, and morality:--Therefore, to promote their happiness, and to secure the good order and preservation of their government, the people of this Commonwealth have a right to invest their Legislature with power to authorize and require, and the Legislature shall, from time to time, authorize and require, the several towns, parishes, precincts, and other bodies politic, or religious societies, to make suitable provision at their own expense, for the institution of the public worship of God, and for the support and maintenance of public protestant teachers of piety, religion, and morality, in all cases, where such provision shall not be made voluntarily. And the people of this Commonwealth have also a right to, and do, invest their Legislature with authority, to enjoin, upon all the subjects, an attendance upon the instructions of the public teachers aforesaid, at stated times and seasons, if there be any, on whose instructions they can conscientiously, and conveniently attend: Provided, notwithstanding, that the several towns, parishes, precincts, and other bodies politic, or religious societies, shall, at all times, have the exclusive right of electing their public teachers, and of contracting with them, for their support and maintenance. And all monies, paid by the subject to the support of public worship, and of the public teachers aforesaid, shall, if he require it, be uniformly applied to the support of the public teacher or teachers, of his own religious sect or denomination, provided there be any, on whose instructions he attends: otherwise it may be paid towards the support of the teacher or teachers, of the parish, or precinct, in which the said monies are raised. And every denomination of christians, demeaning themselves peaceably, and as good subjects of the Commonwealth, shall be equally under the protection of the law: and no subordination of any one sect or denomination, to another, shall ever be established by law.

IV.

The people of this Commonwealth have the sole and exclusive right of governing themselves, as a Free, Sovereign, and Independent State; and do, and forever hereafter shall, exercise and enjoy every power, jurisdiction, and right, which is not, or may not hereafter be, by them expressly delegated to the United States of America, in Congress assembled.

V.

All power residing originally in the people, and being derived from them, the several magistrates, and officers of government, vested with authority, whether legislative, executive, or judicial, are their substitutes and agents, and are at all times accountable to them.

VI.

No man, or corporation, or association of men, have any other title, to obtain advantages, or particular and exclusive privileges, distinct from those of the community, than what arises from the consideration of services, rendered to the public. And this title being in nature, neither hereditary, nor transmissible to children, or descendants, or relations by blood, the idea of a man born a magistrate, lawgiver, or judge, is absurd and unnatural.

VII.

Government is instituted for the common good; for the protection, safety, prosperity, and happiness of the people; and not for the profit, honor, or private interest of any one man, family, or class of men. Therefore, the people alone have an incontestible, unalienable, and indefeasible right, to institute government; and to reform, alter, or totally change the same, when their protection, safety, prosperity and happiness, require it.

VIII.

In order to prevent those, who are vested with authority, from becoming oppressors, the people have a right, at such periods, and in such manner, as they shall establish by their frame of government, to cause their public officers to return to private life; and to fill up vacant places by certain and regular elections and appointments.

IX.

All elections ought to be free; and all the inhabitants of this Commonwealth, having such qualifications, as they shall establish by their frame of government, have an equal right to elect officers, and to be elected, for public employments.

X.

Each individual of the society has a right to be protected by it, in the enjoyment of his life, liberty, and property, according to standing laws. He is obliged, consequently, to contribute his share to the expense of this protection; to give his personal service, or an equivalent, when necessary. But no part of the property of any individual can, with justice, be taken from him, or applied to public uses, without his own consent, or that of the representative body of the people. In fine, the people of this Commonwealth are not controllable by any other laws, than those to which their constitutional representative body have given their consent. And whenever the public exigencies require, that the property of any individual should be appropriated to public uses, he shall receive a reasonable compensation therefor.

XI.

Every subject of the Commonwealth ought to find a certain remedy, by having recourse to the laws, for all injuries or wrongs, which he may receive, in his person, property, or character. He ought to obtain right and justice freely, and without being obliged to purchase it; completely, and without any denial; promptly, and without delay; conformably to the laws.

XII.

No subject shall be held to answer for any crimes or offence, until the same is fully and plainly, substantially and formally, described to him; or be compelled to accuse, or furnish evidence against himself. And every subject shall have a right to produce all proofs that may be favorable to him; to meet the witnesses against him, face to face; and to be fully heard in his defence, by himself, or his council, at his election. And no subject shall be arrested, imprisoned, despoiled, or deprived of his property, immunities, or privileges, put out of the protection of the law, exiled, or deprived of his life, liberty, or estate, but by the judgment of his peers, or the law of the land. And the legislature shall not make any law, that shall subject any person to a capital or infamous punishment, excepting for the government of the army and navy, without trial by jury.

XIII.

In criminal prosecutions, the verification of facts, in the vicinity where they happen, is one of the greatest securities of the life, liberty and property of the citizen.

XIV.

Every subject has a right to be secure from all unreasonable searches, and seizures, of his person, his houses, his papers, and all his possessions. All warrants, therefore, are contrary to this right, if the cause or foundation of them be not previously supported by oath or affirmation; and if the order, in the warrant, to a civil officer, to make search in suspected places, or to arrest one or more suspected persons, or to seize their property, be not accompanied with a special designation of the persons or objects of search, arrest, or seizure: And no warrant ought to be issued, but in cases, and with the formalities, prescribed by the laws.

XV.

In all controversies concerning property, and in all suits between two or more persons, except in cases in which it has heretofore been otherwise used and practised, the parties have a right to a trial by jury; and this method of procedure shall be held sacred, unless, in causes arising on the high seas, and such as relate to mariners' wages, the Legislature shall hereafter find it necessary to alter it.

XVI.

The liberty of the press is essential to the security of freedom in a State; it ought not, therefore, to be restrained in this Commonwealth.

XVII.

The people have a right to keep and to bear arms for the common defence. And as in time of peace, armies are dangerous to liberty, they ought not to be maintained, without the consent of the Legislature; and the military power shall always be held in an exact subordination to the civil authority, and be governed by it.

XVIII.

A frequent recurrence to the fundamental principles of the Constitution, and a constant adherence to those of piety, justice, moderation, temperance, industry, and frugality, are absolutely necessary, to preserve the advantages of liberty, and to maintain a free government. The people ought, consequently, to have a particular attention to all those principles, in the choice of their officers and representatives; and they have a right to require of their law-givers and magistrates, an exact and constant observance of them, in the formation and execution of the laws, necessary for the good administration of the Commonwealth.

XIX.

The people have a right, in an orderly and peaceable manner, to assemble to consult upon the common good; give instructions to their representatives; and to request of the legislative body, by the way of addresses, petitions, or remonstrances, redress of the wrongs done them, and of the grievances they suffer.

XX.

The power of suspending the laws, or the execution of the laws, ought never to be exercised, but by the Legislature; or, by authority derived from it, to be exercised in such particular cases only, as the Legislature shall expressly provide for.

XXI.

The freedom of deliberation, speech, and debate, in either House of the Legislature, is so essential to the rights of the people, that it cannot be the foundation of any accusation, or prosecution, action, or complaint, in any other court or place whatsoever.

XXII.

The Legislature ought frequently to assemble, for the redress of grievances, for correcting, strengthening, and confirming the laws, and for making new laws, as the common good may require.

XXIII.

No subsidy, charge, tax, impost, or duties, ought to be established, fixed, laid, or levied, under any pretext whatsoever, without the consent of the people, or their representatives in the Legislature.

XXIV.

Laws made to punish for actions done before the existence of such laws, and which have not been declared crimes by preceding laws, are unjust, oppressive, and inconsistent with the fundamental principles of a free government.

XXV.

No subject ought, in any case, or in any time, to be declared guilty of treason or felony by the Legislature.

XXVI.

No magistrate, or court of law, shall demand excessive bail, or sureties, impose excessive fines, or inflict cruel or unusual punishments.

XXVII.

In time of peace, no soldier ought to be quartered in any house, without the consent of the owner; and in time of war, such quarters ought not to be made, but by the civil magistrate, in a manner ordained by the Legislature.

XXVIII.

No person can, in any case, be subjected to law martial, or to any penalties or pains, by virtue of that law, except those employed in the army or navy, and except the militia, in actual service, but by authority of the Legislature.

XXIX.

It is essential to the preservation of the rights of every individual, his life, liberty, property, and character, that there be an impartial interpretation of the laws, and administration of justice. It is the right of every citizen, to be tried by judges, as free, impartial, and independent, as the lot of humanity will admit. It is, therefore, not only the best policy, but for the security of the rights of the people, and of every citizen, that the Judges of the Supreme Judicial Court should hold their offices as long as they behave themselves well; and that they should have honorable salaries, ascertained and established by standing laws.

XXX.

In the government of this Commonwealth, the legislative department shall never exercise the executive and judicial powers, or either of them; the executive shall never exercise the legislative and judicial powers, or either of them; the judicial shall never exercise the legislative and executive powers, or either of them; to the end, it may be a government of laws, and not of men.

XXXI.

JAMES MADISON'S MEMORIAL AND REMONSTRANCE, 20 JUNE 1785 AND THOMAS JEFFERSON'S STATUTE OF RELIGIOUS LIBERTY, 31 OCTOBER 1785

We have followed the format of Madison's *Memorial and Remonstrance* found in *The Letters and Other Writings of James Madison* (II: 162-169). For slightly different versions, see Madison's *Papers* (VIII: 298-304), Hunt's Madison's *Writings of James Madison* (II: 183-191), and Banning's, *Jefferson and Madison* (118-124). The Arabic numerals and the footnote references are in the original. See also Kurland and Lerner (V: 82-84). There are several versions of Jefferson's *Statute of Religious Liberty*. Kurland and Lerner (I: 77) reproduce the 1779 bill, as does Banning (116-118). The version below is the bill passed by the Assembly in 1785, and follows W.W. Hening, *Statutes at Large* (XII: 84-86). We have added footnotes showing those parts of Jefferson's 1779 version that were subsequently excised. The Roman numerals are in the original text.

~

[A] Madison's Memorial and Remonstrance

To the Honorable the General Assembly of the Commonwealth of Virginia:

We, the subscribers, citizens of the said Commonwealth, having taken into serious consideration a Bill printed by order of the last session of General Assembly, entitled "A Bill establishing a provision for Teachers of the Christian Religion," and conceiving that the same, if finally armed with the sanctions of a law, will be a dangerous abuse of power, are bound as faithful members of a free State to remonstrate against it, and to declare the reasons by which we are determined. We remonstrate against the said Bill—

1. Because we hold it for a fundamental and undeniable truth, "that Religion, or the duty which we owe to our Creator, and the manner of discharging it, can be directed only by reason and conviction, not by force or violence."[12] The Religion, then, of every man must be left to the conviction and conscience of every man; and it is the right of every man to exercise it, as these may dictate. This right is in its nature an unalienable right. It is unalienable, because the opinions of men, depending only on the evidence contemplated by their own minds, cannot follow the dictates of other men. It is unalienable, also, because what is here a right towards men is a duty towards the Creator. It is the duty of every man to render to the Creator such homage, and such only, as he believes to be acceptable to him. This duty is precedent, both in order of time and in degree of obligation, to the claims of Civil Society. Before any man can be considered as a member of Civil society, he must be considered as a subject of the Governor of the Universe, and if a member of Civil Society who enters into any subordinate Association must always do it with a reservation of his duty to the General Authority, much more must every man who becomes a member of any particular Civil Society do it with a saving of his allegiance to the Universal Sovereign. We maintain, therefore, that in matters of Religion, no man's right is abridged by the institution of Civil Society, and that Religion is wholly exempt from its cognizance. True it is, that no other rule exists by which any question which may divide a Society can be ultimately determined than the will of the majority; but it is also true that the majority may trespass on the rights of the minority.

2. Because, if Religion be exempt from the authority of the Society at large, still less can it be subject to that of the Legislative Body. The latter are but the creatures and vicegerents[13] of the former. Their

---

[12]Declaration of Rights, Article 16.

[13][Editors' note: a vicegerent is a king-appointed substitute.]

jurisdiction is both derivative and limited. It is limited with regard to the co-ordinate departments; more necessarily is it limited with regard to the constituents. The preservation of a free Government requires, not merely that the metes and bounds which separate each department of power be invariably maintained, but more especially that neither of them be suffered to overleap the great Barrier which defends the rights of the people. The Rulers who are guilty of such an encroachment exceed the commission from which they derive their authority, and are Tyrants. The people who submit to it are governed by laws made neither by themselves nor by an authority derived from them, and are slaves.

3. Because it is proper to take alarm at the first experiment on our liberties. We hold this prudent jealousy to be the first duty of citizens, and one of the noblest characteristics of the late Revolution. The freemen of America did not wait till usurped power had strengthened itself by exercise, and entangled the question in precedents. They saw all the consequences in the principle, and they avoided the consequences by denying the principle. We revere this lesson too much soon to forget it. Who does not see that the same authority which can establish Christianity, in exclusion of all other Religions, may establish, with the same ease, any particular sect of Christians, in exclusion of all other sects? that the same authority which can force a citizen to contribute three pence only of his property for the support of any one establishment, may force him to conform to any other establishment in all cases whatsoever?

4. Because the Bill violates that equality which ought to be the basis of every law, and which is more indispensible, in proportion as the validity or expediency of any law is more liable to be impeached. "If all men are by nature equally free and independent,"[14] all men are to be considered as entering into Society on equal conditions; as relinquishing no more, and therefore retaining no less, one than another, of their natural rights. Above all are they to be considered as retaining an "*equal* title to the free exercise of Religion according to the dictates of Conscience."[15] Whilst we assert for ourselves a freedom to embrace, to profess, and to observe, the Religion which we believe to be of divine origin, we cannot deny an equal freedom to them whose minds have not yet yielded to the evidence which has convinced us. If this freedom be abused, it is an offence against God, not against man. To God, therefore, not to man, must an account of it be rendered. As the bill violates equality by subjecting some to peculiar burdens, so it violates the same principle by granting to others peculiar exemptions. Are the

---

[14]Declaration of Rights, Article I.

[15]Article 16.

Quakers and Menonists the only Sects who think a compulsive support of their Religions unnecessary and unwarrantable? Can their piety alone be entrusted with the care of public worship? Ought their Religions to be endowed above all others with extraordinary privileges, by which proselytes may be enticed from all others? We think too favorably of the justice and good sense of these denominations to believe that they either covet pre-eminences over their fellow-citizens, or that they will be seduced by them from the common opposition to the measure.

5. Because the Bill implies, either that the Civil Magistrate is a competent Judge of Religious truths, or that he may employ Religion as an engine of civil policy. The first is an arrogant pretension, falsified by the contradictory opinions of Rulers in all ages, and throughout the world; the second, an unhallowed perversion of the means of salvation.

6. Because the establishment proposed by the Bill is not requisite for the support of the Christian Religion. To say that it is, is a contradiction to the Christian Religion itself, for every page of it disavows a dependence on the powers of this world. It is a contradiction to fact, for it is known that this Religion both existed and flourished, not only without the support of human laws, but in spite of every opposition from them; and not only during the period of miraculous aid, but long after it had been left to its own evidence and the ordinary care of providence. Nay, it is a contradiction in terms; for a Religion not invented by human policy must have pre-existed and been supported, before it was established by human policy. It is, moreover, to weaken in those who profess this Religion a pious confidence in its innate excellence and the patronage of its Author; and to foster in those who still reject it a suspicion that its friends are too conscious of its fallacies to trust it to its own merits.

7. Because experience witnesseth that ecclesiastical establishments, instead of maintaining the purity and efficacy of Religion, have had a contrary operation. During almost fifteen Centuries has the legal establishment of Christianity been on trial. What have been its fruits? More or less, in all places, pride and indolence in the Clergy; ignorance and servility in the laity; in both, superstition, bigotry, and persecution. Enquire of the Teachers of Christianity for the ages in which it appeared in its greatest lustre; those of every Sect point to the ages prior to its incorporation with civil policy. Propose a restoration of this primitive state, in which its Teachers depended on the voluntary rewards of their flocks; many of them predict its downfall. On which side ought their testimony to have greatest weight; when for or when against their interest?

8. Because the establishment in question is not necessary for the support of Civil Government. If it be urged as necessary for the support of Civil Government only as it is a means of supporting Religion, and it be not necessary for the latter purpose, it cannot be necessary for the former. If Religion be not within the cognizance of Civil Government, how can its legal establishment be necessary to Civil Government? What influence, in fact, have ecclesiastical establishments had on Civil Society? In some instances they have been seen to erect a spiritual tyranny on the ruins of the civil authority; in many instances they have been seen upholding the thrones of political tyranny; in no instance have they been seen the guardians of the liberties of the people. Rulers who wished to subvert the public liberty may have found an established Clergy convenient auxiliaries. A just Government, instituted to secure and perpetuate it, needs them not. Such a Government will be best supported by protecting every citizen in the enjoyment of his Religion with the same equal hand which protects his person and his property; by neither invading the equal rights of any sect, nor suffering any Sect to invade those of another.

Because the proposed establishment is a departure from that generous policy which, offering an Asylum to the persecuted and oppressed of every Nation and Religion, promised a lustre to our country, and an accession to the number of its citizens. What a melancholy mark is the Bill of sudden degeneracy! Instead of holding forth an Asylum to the persecuted, it is itself a signal of persecution. It degrades from the equal rank of Citizens all those whose opinions in Religion do not bend to those of the Legislative authority. Distant as it may be in its present form from the Inquisition, it differs from it only in degree. The one is the first step, the other the last, in the career of intolerance. The magnanimous sufferer under this cruel scourge in foreign Regions must view the Bill as a Beacon on our Coast warning him to seek some other haven, where liberty and philanthropy, in their due extent, may offer a more certain repose from his Troubles.

Because it will have a like tendency to banish our citizens. The allurements presented by other situations are every day thinning their number. To superadd a fresh motive to emigration by revoking the liberty which they now enjoy would be the same species of folly which has dishonoured and depopulated flourishing kingdoms.

Because it will destroy that moderation and harmony which the forbearance of our laws to intermeddle with Religion has produced among its several Sects. Torrents of blood have been spilt in the old world by vain attempts of the secular arm to extinguish Religious discord by proscribing all difference in Religious opinion. Time has at length revealed the true remedy. Every relaxation of narrow and rigorous policy, wherever it has been tried, has been found to assuage the disease. The American theatre has exhibited proofs that equal and complete liberty, if it does not wholly eradicate it, sufficiently destroys its malignant influence on the health and prosperity of the State. If, with the salutary effects of this system under our own eyes, we begin to contract the bounds of Religious freedom, we know no name that will too severely reproach our folly. At least, let warning be taken at the first fruits of the threatened innovation. The very appearance of the Bill has transformed "that christian forbearance, love and charity,"[16] which of late mutually prevailed, into animosities and jealousies, which may not soon be appeased. What mischiefs may not be dreaded, should this enemy to the public quiet be armed with the force of a law?

Because the policy of the Bill is adverse to the diffusion of the light of Christianity. The first wish of those who enjoy this precious gift ought to be, that it may be imparted to the whole race of mankind. Compare the number of those who have as yet received it with the number still remaining under the dominion of false Religions, and how small is the former! Does the policy of the Bill tend to lessen the disproportion? No; it at once discourages those who are strangers to the light of revelation from coming into the Region of it, and countenances by example the nations who continue in darkness in shutting out those who might convey it to them. Instead of Levelling as far as possible, every obstacle to the victorious progress of truth, the Bill, with an ignoble and unchristian timidity, would circumscribe it with a wall of defence against the encroachments of error.

Because attempts to enforce, by legal sanctions, acts obnoxious to so great a proportion of citizens, tend to enervate the laws in general, and to slacken the bands of Society. If it be difficult to execute any law which is not generally deemed necessary or salutary, what must be the case where it is deemed invalid and dangerous? And what may be the effect of so striking an example of impotency in the Government on it general authority?

Because a measure of such singular magnitude and delicacy ought not to be imposed without the clearest evidence that it is called for by a majority of citizens; and no satisfactory method is yet proposed by which the voice of the majority in this case may be determined, or its influence secured. "The people of the respective Counties are, indeed, requested to signify their opinion respecting the adoption of the Bill to the next Session of Assembly." But the representation must be made equal before the voice either of the Representatives or of the Counties will be that of the people. Our hope is, that neither of the former will, after due consideration, espouse the dangerous principle of the Bill.

---

[16]Declaration of Rights, Article 16.

Should the event disappoint us, it will still leave us in full confidence that a fair appeal to the latter will reverse the sentence against our liberties.

Because, finally, "the equal right of every Citizen to the free exercise of his Religion, according to the dictates of conscience," is held by the same tenure with all our other rights. If we recur to its origin, it is equally the gift of nature; if we weigh its importance, it cannot be less dear to us; if we consult the Declaration of those rights "which pertain to the good people of Virginia as the basis and foundation of Government,"[17] it is enumerated with equal solemnity, or rather studied emphasis. Either, then, we must say, that the will of the Legislature is the only measure of their authority, and that in the plenitude of that authority they may sweep away all our fundamental rights, or, that they are bound to leave this particular right untouched and sacred. Either we must say, that they may controul the freedom of the press, may abolish the trial by jury, may swallow up the Executive and Judiciary powers of the State; nay, that they may despoil us of our very right of suffrage, and erect themselves into an independent and hereditary Assembly; or we must say, that they have no authority to enact into law the Bill under consideration.

We, the Subscribers, say that the General Assembly of this Commonwealth have no such authority: And in order that no effort may be omitted on our part against so dangerous an usurpation, we oppose to it this remonstrance; earnestly praying, as we are in duty bound, that the Supreme Lawgiver of the Universe, by illuminating those to whom it is addressed, may, on the one hand, turn their councils from every act which would affront his holy prerogative, or violate the trust committed to them; and on the other, guide them into every measure which may be worthy of his blessing, redound to their own praise, and establish more firmly the liberties, the prosperity, and the happiness of the Commonwealth.

[B] Jefferson's Statute of Religious Liberty

An act for establishing religious freedom

I. WHEREAS[18] Almighty God hath created the mind free;[19] that all attempts to influence it by temporal punishments or burthens, or by

---

[17]Declaration of Rights, title.

[18]Excised from the 1779 edition was the following passage: "Well aware that the opinions and belief of men depend not on their own will, but follow involuntarily the evidence proposed to their minds, that."

[19]Excised passage: "and manifested his Supreme will that free it shall remain, by making it altogether insusceptible of restraint".

civil incapacitations, tend only to beget habits of hypocrisy and meanness, and are a departure from the plan of the Holy author of our religion, who being Lord both of body and mind, yet chose not to propagate it by coercions on either, as was in his Almighty power to do;[20] that the impious presumption of legislators and rulers, civil as well as ecclesiastical, who being themselves but fallible and uninspired men, have assumed dominion over the faith of others, setting up their own opinions and modes of thinking as the only true and infallible, and as such endeavouring to impose them on others, hath established and maintained false religions over the greatest part of the world, and through all time; that to compel a man to furnish contributions of money for the propagation of opinions which he disbelieves, is sinful and tyrannical; that even the forcing him to support this or that teacher of his own religious persuasion, is depriving him of the comfortable liberty of giving his contributions to the particular pastor, whose morals he would make his pattern, and whose powers he feels most persuasive to righteousness, and is withdrawing from the ministry those temporary rewards, which proceeding from an approbation of their personal conduct, are an additional incitement to earnest and unremitting labours for the instruction of mankind; that our civil rights have no dependance on our religious opinions, any more than on our opinions in physics or geometry; that therefore the proscribing any citizen as unworthy the public confidence by laying upon him an incapacity of being called to offices of trust and emolument, unless he profess or renounce this or that religious opinion, is depriving him injuriously of those privileges and advantages to which in common with his fellow citizens he has a natural right; that it tends only[21] to corrupt the principles of that very religion it is meant to encourage, by bribing with a monopoly of worldly honours and emoluments, those who will externally profess and conform to it; that though indeed these are criminal who do not withstand such temptation, yet neither are those innocent who lay the bait in their way;[22] that to suffer the civil magistrate to intrude his powers into the field of opinion, and to restrain the profession or propagation of principles on supposition of their ill tendency, is a dangerous fallacy, which at once destroys all religious liberty, because he being of course judge of that tendency will make his own opinions the rule of judgment, and approve or condemn

---

[20]Excised passage: "but to extend it by its influence on reason alone".

[21]Hening, *Statutes* (XII: 85) has the word, "only," instead of "also." Kurland and Lerner (I: 77) and Banning (117) use "also."

[22]Excised passage: "that the opinions of men are not the object of civil government, nor under its jurisdiction:"

the sentiments of others only as they shall square with or differ from his own; that it is time enough for the rightful purposes of civil government, for its officers to interfere when principles break out into overt acts against peace and good order; and finally, that truth is great and will prevail if left to herself, that she is the proper and sufficient antagonist to error, and has nothing to fear from the conflict, unless by human interposition disarmed of her natural weapons, free argument and debate, errors ceasing to be dangerous when it is permitted freely to contradict[23] them:

II. *Be it enacted by the General Assembly,* That no man shall be compelled to frequent or support any religious worship, place, or ministry whatsoever, nor shall be enforced, restrained, molested, or burthened in his body or goods, nor shall otherwise suffer on account of his religious opinions or belief; but that all men shall be free to profess, and by argument to maintain, their opinions in matters of religion, and that the same shall in no wise diminish, enlarge, or affect their civil capacities.

III. And though we well know that this assembly elected by the people for the ordinary purposes of legislation only, have no power to restrain the acts of succeeding assemblies, constituted with powers equal to our own, and that therefore to declare this act to be irrevocable would be of no effect in law; yet we are free to declare, and do declare, that the rights hereby asserted are of the natural rights of mankind, and that if any act shall be hereafter passed to repeal the present, or to narrow its operation, such act will be an infringement of natural right.

---

[23]Kurland and Lerner (I: 77) use the word, "contract," rather than "contradict." Banning (117) uses "contradict."

Chapter Five

We Have Errors to Correct

By the mid 1780s, it became clear to George Washington that "we have errors to correct." The state governments regularly refused compliance with requisitions, they violated the treaty of peace with Great Britain, and the union was unable to regulate interstate commerce. Several attempts to grant additional powers to Congress failed because of the inability to secure the required unanimity among the states. Writing to John Jay, in August 1786, Washington declared "that our affairs are drawing rapidly to a crisis." He knew the remedy: "I do not conceive we can exist long as a nation without having lodged somewhere a power, which will pervade the whole Union in as energetic a manner, as the authority of the State Governments extends over the several States." Washington concluded: "What a triumph for the advocates of despotism to find that we are incapable of governing ourselves, and that systems founded on the basis of equal liberty are merely ideal and fallacious!" This chapter covers the continental attempt to correct the errors of the 1780s.

Articles of Confederation

The Second Continental Congress not only issued a directive to the colonial legislatures to create new state constitutions; they also initiated the adoption of the first governmental system for the United States. Representatives John Dickinson, Samuel Adams, Roger Sherman, and, Richard Henry Lee helped draft the Articles of Confederation. The requirement that adoption be unanimous, however, delayed implementation of the Articles until March 1781: Maryland insisted that Congress, rather than Virginia, control the land in the Northwest and Southwest territories.

The Articles of Confederation play a crucial role in the American story of the Bill of Rights. On the one hand, because the Articles confirm the pre-eminence of the states, the relationship between rulers and ruled that undergirds the debate became anchored at the state level rather than at the continental level. On the other hand, the Articles introduce the possibility of an extended conversation because each state must protect "all privileges and immunities of free citizens in the several States."

A fundamental ambiguity lay at the heart of the Articles. Article III stated that this was to be "a firm league of friendship," and Article XIII declared that "the union shall be perpetual." Yet according to Article II, each state retains every power that is not "expressly delegated" to the Congress. Not granted to Congress were the powers to tax and to regulate interstate commerce; between 1781 and 1786 attempts to pass amendments that would bestow these powers on Congress failed to secure the required unanimous consent of the state legislatures.

Americans turned to the covenanting tradition of specially called deliberative conventions to address these continental-wide problems. The commissioners attending the Anapolis Convention, in September 1786, invited the states to send delegates to a Grand Convention. Henceforth, the conversation over the Bill of Rights would be conducted within a larger political framework.

Between November 1786 and February 1787, Virginia, New Jersey, Pennsylvania, North Carolina, Delaware, and Georgia chose delegates to attend the convention in Philadelphia. Other state legislatures, for example, New York, Massachusetts, and Connecticut, were reluctant to endorse the Annapolis recommendation for a "proposed convention on the second Monday in May next at the city of Philadelphia" absent 1) a formal authorization by the Confederation Congress and 2) ground rules limiting the scope of the convention. The Confederation Congress considered the report of the Annapolis commissioners in February, 1787. On February 21, the delegates* agreed to make Congress, rather than the Annapolis Convention, the authorizing agent, and limited the scope of the convention to "revising" the Articles.

---

*In attendance were Rufus King, William Johnson, James Madison, William Blount, George Few, and William Pierce. Three months later, they were delegates to the Grand Convention in Philadelphia.

James Madison's Vices of the Political System

Washington wrote to Madison expressing his wish that "the Convention may adopt no temporising expedient, but probe the defects of the Constitution to the bottom, and provide radical cures, whether they are agreed to or not." Madison's *Vices* is, in effect, the first draft of his famous defense of the extended republic in *Federalist* 10. Madison criticized the Articles because they lacked "the great vital principles of a Political Constitution," namely, "sanction," and "coercion." The "evil" that alarmed him the most was that individual rights were being violated by unjust majorities in the state legislatures. Madison shifted the ground of the conversation over rights away from securing the rights of the people against the unrestrained conduct of monarchs and aristocrats to the then unfamiliar ground of securing the rights of minorities from omnipotent majorities. In the process, he questioned the efficacy of such traditional republican solutions as "a prudent regard" for the common good, "respect for character," and the restraints provided by religion. Madison's argument was that rights would not be secure until the constitutional protection the Articles gave to the state legislatures was removed. "A modification of the Sovereignty" was needed. The solution, said Madison, was to create an extended republic in which a multiplicity of opinions, passions, and interests "check each other."

The Northwest Ordinance

The much-maligned Confederation Congress, based in New York, had difficulty meeting to discuss continental issues in 1787 because of an inability to secure the quorum requirement. Yet a quorum was found from time to time and the business of the country was conducted. One of the greatest achievements of the Confederation Congress came during the 1787 session; they passed the Northwest Ordinance at the very moment the Constitutional Convention was on the verge of collapse.

Four clauses deserve attention: Article I protects the free exercise of religion; Article II contains a list of the civil rights and criminal procedures that were deeply rooted in the colonial experience and common throughout the states; Article III calls for the encouragement of "religion, morality, and knowledge;" and Article VI, secures the abolition of slavery in exchange for a fugitive slave clause.

Conventional History of the Constitution

To be sure, neither of the two main plans that shaped the discussion in Philadelphia during the summer of 1787--The Virginia Plan and The New Jersey Plan--addressed directly the issues of civil rights and criminal procedures that were present in the state constitutions. Nevertheless, it would be erroneous to conclude that the issue of rights was not on the minds of the framers and, therefore, we can skip directly to the ratification controversy without losing an essential part of the story.

The Virginia Plan reflects the modification of sovereignty recommended by Madison in his *Vices*. It strips the states *qua* states of the structural pre-eminence which they occupied under the Articles of Confederation. In particular, the states no longer had the right to either equal representation in the federal structure or the right to elect representatives to the Congress. The Plan introduced bicameralism and the separation of powers to the federal structure; here too the states lost their structural identity. The states fared no better in the area of powers: Congress was granted the right "to legislate in all cases to which the separate States were incompetent...[and]...to negative all laws passed by the several States, contravening in the opinion of the national legislature the articles of Union." Madison himself provided the theoretical defense of the principle of popular representation underlying the Virginia Plan on June 6th: it provided "more effectively for the security of private rights, and the steady dispensation of Justice. Interferences with these were evils which had more perhaps than any thing else, produced this convention."

By contrast, the New Jersey Plan retained the structural features of the Articles of Confederation and focused instead on enhancing the power of a unicameral Congress in which each state was equally represented. The Plan acknowledged the defects in the Articles, but these "vices" were due solely to the want of power. It would authorize Congress "to pass acts for raising a revenue...[and]...for the regulation of trade & commerce as well with foreign nations as with each other."

On July 16th the delegates adopted, by a narrow margin, the "Connecticut Compromise" which gave equal representation to the people in the House and equal representation to each State in the Senate. Thus, the Bill of Rights story was destined to be complicated by the constitutionalization of two competing principles: the rights of the people and the rights of the states. A more immediate consequence of the structural compromise was that the framers turned their attention to the question of powers.

The Committee of Detail Report was presented to the Convention on August 6th. Among other things, the Report reflected the decision to abandon a feature of the Virginia Plan that Madison deemed essential: Congress was no longer authorized to "legislate in all cases to which the separate States are incompetent." Instead, the powers of Congress were enumerated. On August 16th, the delegates began discussing the list of eighteen different powers of the legislature contained in Article VII.

The Committee received twelve propositions from Pinckney on Monday, August 20th. Four placed specific restraints on the legislative power: the writ of habeas corpus shall be suspended only "upon the most urgent and pressing occasions," and then only for a limited time; "the liberty of the Press shall be inviolably preserved;" standing armies in peace time shall require the consent of the legislature; and "no soldier shall be quartered in any House in time of peace without the consent of the owner." A fifth proposition stated that "No religious test or qualification shall ever be annexed to any oath of office under the authority of the U. S." The delegates did not stop to consider Pinckney's proposed "Bill of Rights;" instead, they resumed their discussion of the Report.

On September 12, the Convention received the Committee of Style Report. This final draft of the Constitution included a preamble and seven articles. The preamble reaffirmed the covenanting tradition and the enlightenment claim that the people have the right to choose their form of government. Of particular importance, is the way in which the Report conceptually presents the relationship between powers and rights. The old Article VII, Section 1, became Article 1, Section 8, where the powers of Congress were listed. This was followed by Section 9, that introduced restraints on the national legislature, and Section 10 that expanded the restraints on the state legislatures. Article III retained the right to trial by jury in criminal cases, and extended the judicial power to include all cases "arising under this constitution." Finally, Pinckney's no-religious-test provision was incorporated in the oath supporting the supremacy clause in Article VI. But there was no mention of liberty of the press, standing armies in time of peace, the quartering of troops, or other rights that had become part of the American landscape.

George Mason expressed the wish that "the plan had been prefaced with a Bill of Rights." Such a preface, Mason continued, "would give great quiet to the people; and with the aid of the State declarations, a bill might be prepared in a few hours." Elbridge Gerry supported Mason in the unsuccessful effort to create a drafting committee. On September 14th, Mason, supported by Randolph, attempted to include a warning against "standing armies in time of peace." Only Virginia and Georgia voted in favor. Mason also attempted to insert into Article 1, section 9, a clause declaring "that the liberty of the press should be inviolably observed." Sherman responded: "It is unnecessary. The power of Congress does not extend to the Press." Only Massachusetts, Virginia, Maryland, and South Carolina voted in favor.

XXXII.

ARTICLES OF CONFEDERATION, 1781

We have followed the spelling and punctuation used by James D. Richardson, *Messages and Papers* (I: 9-18) who relies on the *Journals of the Continental Congress.* Tansill, *Documents* (27-37) also follows the Journals, but presents a different format for the signing of the document. Kurland and Lerner (I: 23-26) reprint Tansill, but with changes in the original use of the upper-case. For another authentic version see Merrill Jensen, *Documentary History* (I: 78-137). The Roman numerals identifying each of the thirteen articles are in the original.

~

To all to whom these Presents shall come, we the under signed Delegates of the States affixed to our Names send greeting. Whereas the Delegates of the United States of America in Congress assembled did on the fifteenth day of November in the Year of Our Lord One thousand Seven Hundred and Seventy seven, and in the Second Year of the Independence of America agree to certain articles of Confederation and perpetual Union between the States of Newhampshire, Massachusetts-bay, Rhodeisland and Providence Plantations, Connecticut, New York, New Jersey, Pennsylvania, Delaware, Maryland, Virginia, North-Carolina, South-Carolina and Georgia in the Words following, viz. "Articles of Confederation and perpetual Union between the states of Newhampshire, Massachusetts-bay, Rhodeisland and Providence Plantations, Connecticut, New-York, New-Jersey, Pennsylvania, Delaware, Maryland, Virginia, North-Carolina, South-Carolina and Georgia.

Article I. The Stile of this confederacy shall be "The United States of America."

Article II. Each state retains its sovereignty, freedom and independence, and every Power, Jurisdiction and right, which is not by this confederation expressly delegated to the United States, in Congress assembled.

Article III. The said states hereby severally enter into a firm league of friendship with each other, for their common defence, the security of their Liberties, and their mutual and general welfare, binding themselves to assist each other, against all force offered to, or attacks made upon them, or any of them, on account of religion, sovereignty, trade, or any other pretence whatever.[1]

---

[1] Richardson (I: 9) has incorrectly transcribed "whatever" as "whatseever."

Article IV. The better to secure and perpetuate mutual friendship and intercourse among the people of the different states in this union, the free inhabitants of each of these states, paupers, vagabonds and fugitives from Justice excepted, shall be entitled to all privileges and immunities of free citizens in the several states; and the people of each state shall have free ingress and regress to and from any other state, and shall enjoy therein all the privileges of trade and commerce, subject to the same duties, impositions and restrictions as the inhabitants thereof respectively, provided that such restriction shall not extend so far as to prevent the removal of property imported into any state, to any other state of which the Owner is an inhabitant; provided also that no imposition, duties or restriction shall be laid by any state, on the property of the united states, or either of them.

If any Person guilty of, or charged with treason, felony, or other high misdemeanor in any state, shall flee from Justice, and be found in any of the united states, he shall upon demand of the Governor or executive power, of the state from which he fled, be delivered up and removed to the state having jurisdiction of his offence.

Full faith and credit shall be given in each of these states to the records, acts and judicial proceedings of the courts and magistrates of every other state.

Article V. For the more convenient management of the general interests of the united states, delegates shall be annually appointed in such manner as the legislature of each state shall direct, to meet in Congress on the first Monday in November, in every year, with a power reserved to each state, to recal its delegates, or any of them, at any time within the year, and to send others in their stead, for the remainder of the Year.

No state shall be represented in Congress by less than two, nor by more than seven Members; and no person shall be capable of being a delegate for more than three years in any term of six years; nor shall any person, being a delegate, be capable of holding any office under the united states, for which he, or another for his benefit receives any salary, fees or emolument of any kind.

Each state shall maintain its own delegates in a meeting of the states, and while they act as members of the committee of the states.

In determining questions in the united states, in Congress assembled, each state shall have one vote.

Freedom of speech and debate in Congress shall not be impeached or questioned in any Court, or place out of Congress, and the members of congress shall be protected in their persons from arrests and imprisonments, during the time of their going to and from, and attendance on congress, except for treason, felony, or breach of the peace.

Article VI. No state, without the Consent of the united states in congress assembled, shall send any embassy to, or receive any embassy from, or enter into any conference, agreement, alliance or treaty with any King prince or state; nor shall any person holding any office of profit or trust under the united states, or any of them, accept of any present, emolument, office or title of any kind whatever from any king, prince or foreign state; nor shall the united states in congress assembled, or any of them, grant any title of nobility.

No two or more states shall enter into any treaty, confederation or alliance whatever between them, without the consent of the united states in congress assembled, specifying accurately the purposes for which the same is to be entered into, and how long it shall continue.

No state shall lay any imposts or duties, which may interfere with any stipulations in treaties, entered into by the united states in congress assembled, with any king, prince or state, in pursuance of any treaties already proposed by congress, to the courts of France and Spain.

No vessels of war shall be kept up in time of peace by any state, except such number only, as shall be deemed necessary by the united states in congress assembled, for the defence of such state, or its trade; nor shall any body of forces be kept up by any state, in time of peace, except such number only, as in the judgment of the united states, in congress assembled, shall be deemed requisite to garrison the forts necessary for the defence of such state; but every state shall always keep up a well regulated and disciplined militia, sufficiently armed and accoutred, and shall provide and constantly have ready for use, in public stores, a due number of field pieces and tents, and a proper quantity of arms, ammunition and camp equipage.

No state shall engage in any war without the consent of the united states in congress assembled, unless such state be actually invaded by enemies, or shall have received certain advice of a resolution being formed by some nation of Indians to invade such state, and the danger is so imminent as not to admit of a delay, till the united states in congress assembled can be consulted: nor shall any state grant commissions to any ships or vessels of war, nor letters of marque or reprisal, except it be after a declaration of war by the united states in congress assembled, and then only against the kingdom or state and the subjects thereof, against which war has been so declared, and under such regulations as shall be established by the united states in congress assembled, unless such state be infested by pirates, in which case vessels of war may be fitted out for that occasion, and kept so long as the danger shall continue, or until the united states in congress assembled shall determine otherwise.

Article VII. When land-forces are raised by any state for the common defence, all officers of or under the rank of colonel, shall be appointed by the legislature of each state respectively by whom such forces shall be raised, or in such manner as such state shall direct, and all vacancies shall be filled up by the State which first made the appointment.

Article VIII. All charges of war, and all other expences that shall be incurred for the common defence or general welfare, and allowed by the united states in congress assembled, shall be defrayed out of a common treasury, which shall be supplied by the several states, in proportion to the value of all land within each state, granted to or surveyed for any Person, as such land and the buildings and improvements thereon shall be estimated according to such mode as the united states in congress assembled, shall from time to time direct and appoint. The taxes for paying that proportion shall be laid and levied by the authority and direction of the legislatures of the several states within the time agreed upon by the united states in congress assembled.

Article IX. The united states in congress assembled, shall have the sole and exclusive right and power of determining on peace and war, except in the cases mentioned in the sixth article—of sending and receiving ambassadors—entering into treaties and alliances, provided that no treaty of commerce shall be made whereby the legislative power of the respective states shall be restrained from imposing such imposts and duties on foreigners, as their own people are subjected to, or from prohibiting the exportation or importation of any species of goods or commodities, whatsoever—of establishing rules for deciding in all cases, what captures on land or water shall be legal, and in what manner prizes taken by land or naval forces in the service of the united states shall be divided or appropriated.—of granting letters of marque and reprisal in times of peace—appointing courts for the trial of piracies and felonies committed on the high seas and establishing courts for receiving and determining finally appeals in all cases of captures, provided that no member of congress shall be appointed a judge of any of the said courts.

The united states in congress assembled shall also be the last resort on appeal in all disputes and differences now subsisting or that hereafter may arise between two or more states concerning boundary, jurisdiction or any other cause whatever; which authority shall always be exercised in the manner following.

* * * *

The united states in congress assembled shall also have the sole and exclusive right and power of regulating the alloy and value of coin struck by their own authority, or by that of the respective states—fixing the standard of weights and measures throughout the united states.—regulating the trade and managing all affairs with the Indians, not members of any of the states, provided that the legislative right of any state within its own limits be not infringed or violated—establishing or regulating post-offices from one state to another, throughout all the united states, and exacting such postage on the papers passing thro' the same as may be requisite to defray the expences of the said office—appointing all officers of the land forces, in the service of the united states, excepting regimental officers.—appointing all the officers of the naval forces, and commissioning all officers whatever in the service of the united states—making rules for the government and regulation of the said land and naval forces, and directing their operations.

The united states in congress assembled shall have authority to appoint a committee, to sit in the recess of congress, to be denominated "A Committee of the States," and to consist of one delegate from each state; and to appoint such other committees and civil officers as may be necessary for managing the general affairs of the united states under their direction—to appoint one of their number to preside, provided that no person be allowed to serve in the office of president more than one year in any term of three years; to ascertain the necessary sums of Money to be raised for the service of the united states, and to appropriate and apply the same for defraying the public expences—to borrow money, or emit bills on the credit of the united states, transmitting every half year to the respective states an account of the sums of Money so borrowed or emitted,—to build and equip a navy—to agree upon the number of land forces, and to make requisitions from each state for its quota, in proportion to the number of white inhabitants in such state; which requisition shall be binding, and thereupon the legislature of each state shall appoint the regimental officers, raise the men and cloath, arm and equip them in a soldier like manner, at the expence of the united states, and the officers and men so cloathed, armed and equipped shall march to the place appointed, and within the time agreed on by the united states in congress assembled: But if the united states in congress assembled shall, on consideration of circumstances judge proper that any state should not raise men, or should raise a smaller number than its quota, and that any other state should raise a greater number of men than the quota thereof, such extra number shall be raised, officered, cloathed, armed and equipped in the same manner as the quota of such state, unless the legislature of such state shall judge that such extra number cannot be safely spared out of the same, in which case they shall raise officer, cloath, arm and equip as many of such extra number as they judge can be safely spared. And the officers and men so cloathed, armed and equipped, shall march to the place appointed, and within the time agreed on by the united states in congress assembled.

The united states in congress assembled shall never engage in a war, nor grant letters of marque and reprisal in time of peace, nor enter into any treaties or alliances, nor coin money, nor regulate the value thereof, nor ascertain the sums and expences necessary for the defence and welfare of the united states, or any of them, nor emit bills, nor borrow money on the credit of the united states, nor appropriate money, nor agree upon the number of vessels of war, to be built or purchased, or the number of land or sea forces to be raised, nor appoint a commander in chief of the army or navy, unless nine states assent to the same: nor shall a question on any other point, except for adjourning from day to day be determined, unless by the votes of a majority of the united states in congress assembled.

The congress of the united states shall have power to adjourn to any time within the year, and to any place within the united states, so that no period of adjournment be for a longer duration than the space of six Months, and shall publish the Journal of their proceedings monthly, except such parts thereof relating to treaties, alliances or military operations, as in their judgment require secresy; and the yeas and nays of the delegates of each state on any question shall be entered on the Journal, when it is desired by any delegate; and the delegates of a state, or any of them, at his or their request shall be furnished with a transcript of the said Journal, except such parts as are above excepted, to lay before the legislatures of the several states.

Article X. The committee of the states, or any nine of them, shall be authorized to execute, in the recess of congress, such of the powers of congress as the united states in congress assembled, by the consent of nine states, shall from time to time think expedient to vest them with; provided that no power be delegated to the said committee, for the exercise of which, by the articles of confederation, the voice of nine states in the congress of the united states assembled is requisite.

Article XI. Canada acceding to this confederation, and joining in the measures of the united states, shall be admitted into, and entitled to all the advantages of this union: but no other colony shall be admitted into the same, unless such admission be agreed to by nine states.

Article XII. All bills of credit emitted, monies borrowed and debts contracted by, or under the authority of congress, before the assembling of the united states, in pursuance of the present confederation, shall be deemed and considered as a charge against the united states, for payment and satisfaction whereof the said united states, and the public faith are hereby solemnly pledged.

Article XIII. Every state shall abide by the determinations of the united states in congress assembled, on all questions which by this confederation are submitted to them. And the Articles of this confederation shall be inviolably observed by every state, and the union shall be perpetual; nor shall any alteration at any time hereafter be made in any of them; unless such alteration be agreed to in a congress of the united states, and be afterwards confirmed by the legislatures of every state.

And Whereas it hath pleased the Great Governor of the World to incline the hearts of the legislatures we respectively represent in congress, to approve of, and to authorize us to ratify the said articles of confederation and perpetual union. Know Ye that we the under-signed delegates, by virtue of the power and authority to us given for that purpose, do by these presents, in the name and in behalf of our respective constituents, fully and entirely ratify and confirm each and every of the said articles of confederation and perpetual union, and all and singular the matters and things therein contained: And we do further solemnly plight and engage the faith of our respective constituents, that they shall abide by the determinations of the united states in congress assembled, on all questions, which by the said confederation are submitted to them. And that the articles thereof shall be inviolably observed by the states we respectively represent, and that the union shall be perpetual. In Witness whereof we have hereunto set our hands in Congress. Done at Philadelphia in the state of Pennsylvania the ninth day of July in the Year of our Lord one Thousand seven Hundred and Seventy-eight, and in the third year of the independence of America.[2]

---

[2]We follow Richardson and reproduce the names of the signers in upper-case. The more common practice is to list the names in the lower-case format. In this regard, see Jensen (I: 93-94) and Kurland and Lerner (I: 26). The latter, however, unlike Jensen, but following Tansill and Elliot, have also standardized the format through a consistent use of commas, periods, and the upper-case. In the Richardson version of the original document, confirmed by Jensen, only Van Dyke, Delaware, has a comma after his name. On the other hand, William Duer, New York, Richard Hutson, South Carolina, and Edward Langworthy, Georgia, are the only signers to have a period after their name. There was a similar lack of consistency in the original representation of the state announcements. Some states upper-cased "on the part and behalf of" and two states used "&" as an abbreviation. New Jersey was the only state to have either a period or a slash at the end of its declaration.

JOSIAH BARTLETT
JOHN WENTWORTH Junr
August 8th 1778

On the part & behalf of the State of NewHampshire

JOHN HANCOCK
SAMUEL ADAMS
ELBRIDGE GERRY
FRANCIS DANA
JAMES LOVELL
SAMUEL HOLTEN

On the part and behalf of The State of Massachusetts Bay

WILLIAM ELLERY
HENRY MARCHANT
JOHN COLLINS

On the part and behalf of the State of Rhode-Island and Providence Plantations

ROGER SHERMAN
SAMUEL HUNTINGTON
OLIVER WOLCOTT
TITUS HOSMER
ANDREW ADAMS

On the part and behalf of the State of Connecticut

JA^{S} DUANE
FRA^{S} LEWIS
W^{M} DUER
GOUV MORRIS

On the part and behalf of the State of New York

JNO WITHERSPOON
NATH^{L} SCUDDER

On the Part and in Behalf of the State of New Jersey. Novr 26th, 1778.—

ROB^{T} MORRIS
DANIEL ROBERDEAU
JON^{A} BAYARD SMITH.
WILLIAM CLINGAN[3]
JOSEPH REED 22d July 1778[4]

On the part and behalf of the State of Pennsylvania

---

[3]Kurland and Lerner (I: 26), following Tansill (36), have reproduced this person's name as "William Clingar," rather than "William Clingan." Elliot (I: 85) lists "Clingan" from Pennsylvania as a signer.

[4]Jensen (I: 94) questions the accuracy of the date.

THO M: KEAN Feby 22d 1779
JOHN DICKINSON May 5th 1779 On the part & behalf of the
NICHOLAS VAN DYKE, State ofDelaware

JOHN HANSON March 1 1781
DANIEL CARROLL d[itt]o On the part and behalf of the State of Maryland

RICHARD HENRY LEE
JOHN BANISTER On the Part and Behalf of the State
THOMAS ADAMS of Virginia
JNO HARVIE
FRANCIS LIGHTFOOT LEE

JOHN PENN July 21st 1778
CORNS HARNETT On the part and Behalf of the State
JNO WILLIAMS of No Carolina

HENRY LAURENS.
WILLIAM HENRY DRAYTON On the part and on behalf of the
JNO MATHEWS State of South-Carolina
RICHD HUTSON.
THOS HEYWARD Junr

JNO WALTON 24th July 1778
EDWD TELFAIR On the part & behalf of the State of
EDWD LANGWORTHY. Georgia

XXXIII.

JAMES MADISON, *VICES OF THE POLITICAL SYSTEM OF THE UNITED STATES*, APRIL 1787

We have relied on *Writings* and retained Madison's abbreviations, punctuation, and spelling; the Arabic numerals are also in the original text. For the complete original version, including the location of Madison's "fistnotes," and inserts, see Madison's *Writings* (I: 319-328). We have followed Kurland and Lerner (I: 166-169), and placed Madison's section headings in the main body of the text rather than in the margin. We have, however, put the headings in upper-case in order to distinguish them clearly from Madison's commentary.

~

1. FAILURE OF THE STATES TO COMPLY WITH THE CONSTITUTIONAL REQUISITIONS.

This evil has been so fully experienced both during the war and since the peace, results so naturally from the number and independent authority of the States, and has been so uniformly examplified in every similar Confederacy, that it may be considered as not less radically and permanently inherent in, than it is fatal to the object of, the present System.

2. ENCROACHMENTS BY THE STATES ON THE FEDERAL AUTHORITY.

Examples of this are numerous and repetitions may be foreseen in almost every case where any favorite object of a State shall present a temptation. Among these examples are the wars and Treaties of Georgia with the Indians, the unlicensed compacts between Virginia and Maryland, and between Pennsylvania and New Jersey, the troops raised and to be kept up by Massachusetts.

3. VIOLATIONS OF THE LAW OF NATIONS AND OF TREATIES.

From the number of Legislatures, the sphere of life from which most of their members are taken, and the circumstances under which their legislative business is carried on, irregularities of this kind must frequently happen. Accordingly, not a year has passed without instances of them in some one or other of the States. The Treaty of peace, the treaty with France, the treaty with Holland, have each been violated. The causes of these irregularities must necessarily produce frequent violations of the law of nations in other respects.

As yet foreign powers have not been rigorous in animadverting on us. This moderation, however, cannot be mistaken for a permanent partiality to our faults, or a permanent security against those disputes with other nations, which, being among the greatest of public calamities, it ought to be least in the power of any part of the community to bring on the whole.

4. TRESPASSES OF THE STATES ON THE RIGHTS OF EACH OTHER.

These are alarming symptoms, and may be daily apprehended, as we are admonished by daily experience. See the law of Virginia restricting foreign vessels to certain ports; of Maryland in favor of vessels belonging to her *own citizens;* of New York in favor of the same.

Paper money, instalments of debts, occlusion of courts, making property a legal tender, may likewise be deemed aggressions on the rights of other States. As the citizens of every State, aggregately taken, stand more or less in the relation of creditors or debtors to the citizens of every other State, acts of the debtor State in favor of debtors affect the creditor State in the same manner, as they do its own citizens, who are, relatively, creditors towards other citizens. This remark may be extended to foreign nations. If the exclusive regulation of the value and alloy of coin was properly delegated to the federal authority, the policy of it equally requires a controul on the States in the cases above mentioned. It must have been meant—1. To preserve uniformity in the circulating medium throughout the nation. 2. To prevent those frauds on the citizens of other States, and the subjects of foreign powers, which might disturb the tranquillity at home, or involve the Union in foreign contests.

The practice of many States in restricting the commercial intercourse with other States, and putting their productions and manufactures on the same footing with those of foreign nations, though not contrary to the federal articles, is certainly adverse to the spirit of the Union, and tends to beget retaliating regulations, not less expensive and vexatious in themselves than they are destructive of the general harmony.

5. WANT OF CONCERT IN MATTERS WHERE COMMON INTEREST REQUIRES IT.

This defect is strongly illustrated in the state of our commercial affairs. How much has the national dignity, interest, and revenue, suffered from this cause? Instances of inferior moments are the want of uniformity in the laws concerning naturalization and literary property; of provision for national seminaries; for grants of incorporation for national purposes, for canals and other works of general utility; which may at present be defeated by the perverseness of particular States whose concurrence is necessary.

6. WANT OF GUARANTY TO THE STATES OF THEIR CONSTITUTIONS AND LAWS AGAINST INTERNAL VIOLENCE.

The Confederation is silent on this point, and therefore by the second article the hands of the federal authority are tied. According to Republican Theory, Right and power being both vested in the majority, are held to be synonymous. According to fact and experience, a minority may, in an appeal to force, be an overmatch for the majority. 1. If the minority happen to include all such as possess the skill and habits of military life, and such as possess the great pecuniary resources, one third only may conquer the remaining two-thirds. 2. One-third of those who participate in the choice of the rulers, may be rendered a majority by the accession of those whose poverty excludes them from a right of suffrage, and who for obvious reasons will be more likely to join the standard of sedition than that of the established Government.

3. Where slavery exists, the republican Theory becomes still more fallacious.

7. WANT OF SANCTION TO THE LAWS, AND OF COERCION IN THE GOVERNMENT OF THE CONFEDERACY.

A sanction is essential to the idea of law, as coercion is to that of Government. The federal system being destitute of both, wants the great vital principles of a Political Constitution. Under the form of such a Constitution, it is in fact nothing more than a treaty of amity, of commerce, and of alliance, between independent and Sovereign States. From what cause could so fatal an omission have happened in the articles of Confederation? From a mistaken confidence that the justice, the good faith, the honor, the sound policy of the several legislative assemblies would render superfluous any appeal to the ordinary motives by which the laws secure the obedience of individuals; a confidence which does honor to the enthusiastic virtue of the compilers, as much as the inexperience of the crisis apologizes for their errors. The time which has since elapsed has had the double effect of increasing the light and tempering the warmth with which the arduous work may be revised. It is no longer doubted that a unanimous and punctual obedience of 13 independent bodies to the acts of the federal Government ought not to be calculated on. Even during the war, when external danger supplied in some degree the defect of legal and coercive sanctions, how imperfectly did the States fulfil their obligations to the Union? In time of peace we see already what is to be expected. How, indeed, could it be otherwise? In the first place, every general act of the Union must necessarily bear unequally hard on some particular member or members of it; secondly, the partiality of the members to their own interests and rights, a partiality which will be fostered by the courtiers of popularity, will naturally exaggerate the inequality where it exists, and even suspect it where it has no existence; thirdly, a distrust of the voluntary compliance of each other may prevent the compliance of any, although it should be the latent disposition of all. Here are causes and pretexts which will never fail to render federal measures abortive. If the laws of the States were merely recommendatory to their citizens, or if they were to be rejudged by county authorities, what security, what probability would exist that they would be carried into execution? Is the security or probability greater in favor of the acts of Congress, which, depending for their execution on the will of the State legislatures, which are tho' nominally authoritative, in fact recommendatory only?

8. WANT OF RATIFICATION BY THE PEOPLE OF THE ARTICLES OF CONFEDERATION.

In some of the States the Confederation is recognized by and forms a part of the Constitution. In others, however, it has received no other sanction than that of the Legislative authority. From this defect two evils result: 1. Whenever a law of a State happens to be repugnant to an act of Congress, particularly when the latter is of posterior date to the former, it will be at least questionable whether the latter must not prevail; and as the question must be decided by the Tribunals of the State, they will be most likely to lean on the side of the State.

2. As far as the Union of the States is to be regarded as a league of sovereign powers, and not as a political Constitution, by virtue of which they are become one sovereign power, so far it seems to follow from the doctrine of compacts, that a breach of any of the articles of the confederation by any of the parties to it absolves the other parties from their respective obligations, and gives them a right if they choose to exert it, of dissolving the Union altogether.

9. MULTIPLICITY OF LAWS IN THE SEVERAL STATES.

In developing the evils which viciate the political system of the United States, it is proper to include those which are found within the States individually, as well as those which directly affect the States collectively, since the former class have an indirect influence on the general malady, and must not be overlooked in forming a compleat remedy. Among the evils, then, of our situation, may well be ranked the multiplicity of laws, from which no State is exempt. As far as laws are necessary to mark with precision the duties of those who are to obey them, and to take from those who are to administer them a discretion which might be abused, their number is the price of liberty. As far as the laws exceed this limit they are a nuisance; a nuisance of the most pestilent kind. Try the Codes of the several States by this test, and what a luxuriancy of legislation do they present. The short period of independency has filled as many pages as the century which preceded it. Every year, almost every session, adds a new volume. This may be the effect in part, but it can only be in part, of the situation in which the revolution has placed us. A review of the several Codes will shew that every necessary and useful part of the least voluminous of them might be compressed into one tenth of the compass, and at the same time be rendered tenfold as perspicuous.

10. MUTABILITY OF THE LAWS OF THE STATES.

This evil is intimately connected with the former, yet deserves a distinct notice, as it emphatically denotes a vicious legislation. We daily see laws repealed or superseded before any trial can have been made of their merits ,and even before a knowledge of them can have reached the remoter districts within which they were to operate. In the regulations of trade this instability becomes a snare not only to our citizens but to foreigners also.

11. INJUSTICE OF THE LAWS OF STATES.

If the multiplicity and mutability of laws prove a want of wisdom, their injustice betrays a defect still more alarming; more alarming, not merely because it is a greater evil in itself, but because it brings more into question the fundamental principle of republican Government, that the majority who rule in such Governments are the safest guardians both of public good and of private rights. To what causes is this evil to be ascribed?

These causes lie —1. in the Representative bodies. 2. In the people themselves.

1. Representative appointments are sought from 3 motives: 1. Ambition 2. Personal interest. 3. Public good. Unhappily, the two first are proved by experience to be most prevalent. Hence, the candidates who feel them, particularly, the second, are most industrious, and most successful in pursuing their object; and forming often a majority in the legislative Councils, with interested views, contrary to the interest and views of their constituents, join in a perfidious sacrifice of the latter to the former. A succeeding election, it might be supposed, would displace the offenders, and repair the mischief. But how easily are base and selfish measures masked by pretexts of public good and apparent expediency? How frequently will a repetition of the same arts and industry which succeeded in the first instance again prevail on the unwary to misplace their confidence?

How frequently, too, will the honest but unenlightened representative be the dupe of a favorite leader, veiling his selfish views under the professions of public good, and varnishing his sophistical arguments with the glowing colours of popular eloquence?

2. A still more fatal, if not more frequent cause, lies among the people themselves. All civilized societies are divided into different interests and factions, as they happen to be creditors or debtors, rich or poor, husbandmen, merchants, or manufacturers, members of different religious sects, followers of different political leaders, inhabitants of different districts, owners of different kinds of property and &., &c. In republican Government, the majority, however composed, ultimately give the law. Whenever, therefore, an apparent interest or common

passion unites a majority, what is to restrain them from unjust violations of the rights and interests of the minority, or of individuals? Three motives only: 1. A prudent regard to their own good, as involved in the general and permanent good of the community. This consideration, although of decisive weight in itself, is found by experience to be too often unheeded. It is too often forgotten, by nations as well as by individuals, that honesty is the best policy. 2dly. Respect for character. However strong this motive may be in individuals, it is considered as very insufficient to restrain them from injustice. In a multitude its efficacy is diminished in proportion to the number which is to share the praise or the blame. Besides, as it has reference to public opinion, which within a particular society, is the opinion of the majority, the standard is fixed by those whose conduct is to be measured by it. The public opinion without the society will be little respected by the people at large of any Country. Individuals of extended views and of national pride may bring the public proceedings to this standard, but the example will never be followed by the multitude. Is it to be imagined that an ordinary citizen or even an Assembly-man of R. Island, in estimating the policy of paper money, ever considered or cared in what light the measure would be viewed in France or Holland; or even in Massachusetts or Connecticut? It was a sufficient temptation to both that it was for their interest; it was a sufficient sanction to the latter that it was popular in the State; to the former that it was so in the neighbourhood. 3dly. Will Religion, the only remaining motive be a sufficient restraint? It is not pretended to be such, on men individually considered. Will its effect be greater on them considered in an aggregate view? Quite the reverse. The conduct of every popular assembly acting on oath, the strongest of religious ties, proves that individuals join without remorse in acts against which their consciences would revolt if proposed to them under the like sanction, separately, in their closets. When, indeed, Religion is kindled into enthusiasm, its force, like that of other passions, is increased by the sympathy of a multitude. But enthusiasm is only a temporary state of religion, and, while it lasts, will hardly be seen with pleasure at the helm of Government. Besides, as religion in its coolest state, is not infallible, it may become a motive to oppression as well as a restraint from injustice. Place three individuals in a situation wherein the interest of each depends on the voice of the others, and give to two of them an interest opposed to the rights of the third? Will the latter be secure? The prudence of every man would shun the danger. The rules and forms of justice suppose and guard against it. Will two thousand in a like situation be less likely to encroach on the rights of one thousand? The contrary is witnessed by the notorious factions and oppressions which take place in corporate towns, limited as the opportunities are, and in little republics, when uncontrouled by apprehensions of external danger. If an enlargement of the sphere is found to lessen the insecurity of private rights, it is not because the impulse of a common interest or passion is less predominant in this case with the majority; but because a common interest or passion is less apt to be felt, and the requisite combinations less easy to be formed, by a great than by a small number. The society becomes broken into a greater variety of interests and pursuits of passions, which check each other, whilst those who may feel a common sentiment have less opportunity of communication and concert. It may be inferred that the inconveniences of popular States contrary to the prevailing Theory, are in proportion not to the extent, but to the narrowness of their limits.

The great desideratum in Government is such a modification of the sovereignty as will render it sufficiently neutral between the different interests and factions to controul one part of the Society from invading the rights of another, and, at the same time, sufficiently controuled itself from setting up an interest adverse to that of the whole society. In absolute Monarchies the prince is sufficiently neutral towards his subjects, but frequently sacrifices their happiness to his ambition or his avarice. In small Republics, the sovereign will is sufficiently controuled from such a Sacrifice of the entire Society, but is not sufficiently neutral towards the parts composing it. As a limited monarchy tempers the evils of an absolute one; so an extensive Republic meliorates the administration of a small Republic.

An auxiliary desideratum for the melioration of the Republican form is such a process of elections as will most certainly extract from the mass of the society the purest and noblest characters which it contains; such as will at once feel most strongly the proper motives to pursue the end or their appointment, and be most capable to devise the proper means of attaining it.

XXXIV.

NORTHWEST ORDINANCE, 13 JULY 1787

We have followed the twentieth-century practice of MacDonald, *Documentary Source Book* (209-216), Tansill, *Documents* (47-54), and Kurland and Lerner (I: 27-29), and organized the Northwest Ordinance into sections. Thorpe's *Federal and State Constitutions* (II: 957-962), and Jensen's *Documentary History* (I: 168-174), present slightly different versions of the Northwest Ordinance. See W. C. Ford, editor, *Journals of the Continental Congress*, 1904 (XXII: 281-343) for an original version of the text and the debates. Schwartz (II: 385-402) reprints an edited version of Ford's coverage. We have followed Tansill and made it easier for the reader to identify where the six articles of the Northwest Ordinance begin and end. We have also followed Tansill's spelling and punctuation.

~

ARTICLE I

No person, demeaning himself in a peaceful and orderly manner, shall ever be molested on account of his mode of worship, or religious sentiments, in the said territory.

ARTICLE II

The inhabitants of the said territory shall always be entitled to the benefits of the writs of *habeas corpus*,[5] and of the trial by jury; of a proportionate representation of the people in the legislature, and of judicial proceedings according to the course of the common law. All persons shall be bailable, unless for capital offences, where the proof shall be evident, or the presumption great. All fines shall be moderate; and no cruel or unusual punishment shall be inflicted. No man shall be deprived of his liberty or property, but by the judgment of his peers, or the law of the land, and should the public exigencies make it necessary, for the common preservation, to take any person's property, or to demand his particular services, full compensation shall be made for the same. And, in the just preservation of rights and property, it is understood and declared, that no law ought ever to be made or have force in the said territory, that shall, in any manner whatever, interfere with or affect private contracts, or engagements, *bona fide*, and without fraud previously formed.

ARTICLE III

Religion, morality, and knowledge being necessary to good government and the happiness of mankind, schools and the means of education shall forever be encouraged. The utmost good faith shall always be observed towards the Indians; their lands and property shall never be taken from them without their consent; and in their property, rights, and liberty they never shall be invaded or disturbed unless in just and lawful wars authorized by Congress; but laws founded in justice and

---

[5] Jensen (I: 172) and Schwartz (II: 400) have "writ" rather than "writs."

humanity shall, from time to time, be made, for preventing wrongs being done to them, and for preserving peace and friendship with them.

ARTICLE IV

The said territory, and the States which may be formed therein, shall forever remain a part of this confederacy of the United States of America, subject to the articles of Confederation, and to such alterations therein as shall be constitutionally made; and to all the acts and ordinances of the United States in Congress assembled, conformable thereto. The inhabitants and settlers in the said territory shall be subject to pay a part of the Federal debts, contracted, or to be contracted, and a proportional part of the expenses of government to be apportioned on them by Congress, according to the same common rule and measure by which apportionments thereof shall be made on the other States; and the taxes for paying their proportion shall be laid and levied by the authority and direction of the legislatures of the district, or districts, or new States, as in the original States, within the time agreed upon by the United States in Congress assembled. The legislatures of those districts, or new States, shall never interfere with the primary disposal of the soil by the United States in Congress assembled, nor with any regulations Congress may find necessary for securing the title in such soil to the *bona -fide* purchasers. No tax shall be imposed on lands the property of the United States; and in no case shall non-resident proprietors be taxed higher then residents. The navigable waters leading into the Mississippi and Saint Lawrence, and the carrying places between the same, shall be common highways, and forever free, as well to the inhabitants of the said territory as to the citizens of the United States, and those of any other States that may be admitted into the confederacy, without any tax, impost, or duty therefor.

ARTICLE V

There shall be formed in the said territory not less than three nor more than five States; and the boundaries of the States, as soon as Virginia shall alter her act of cession and consent to the same, shall become fixed and established as follows, to wit: The western State, in the said territory, shall be bounded by the Mississippi, the Ohio, and the Wabash Rivers; a direct line drawn from the Wabash and Post Vincents, due north, to the territorial line between the United States and Canada; and by the said territorial line to the Lake of the Woods and Mississippi. The middle State shall be bounded by the said direct line, the Wabash from Post Vincents to the Ohio, by the Ohio, by a direct line drawn due north from the mouth of the Great Miami to the said territorial line, and by the said territorial line. The eastern State shall be bounded by the last-mentioned direct line, the Ohio, Pennsylvania, and the said territorial line: *Provided, however,* And it is further understood and declared, that the boundaries of these three States shall be subject so far to be altered, that, if Congress shall hereafter find it expedient, they shall have authority to form one or two States in that part of the said territory which lies north of an east and west line drawn through the southerly bend or extreme of Lake Michigan. And whenever any of the said States shall have sixty thousand free inhabitants therein, such State shall be admitted by its delegates, into the Congress of the United States, on an equal footing with the original States, in all respects whatever; and shall be at liberty to form a permanent constitution and State government: *Provided*, the constitution and government, so to be formed, shall be republican, and in conformity to the principles contained in these articles; and, so far as it can be consistent with the general interest of the confederacy, such admission shall be allowed at an earlier period, and when there may be a less number of free inhabitants in the State than sixty thousand.

ARTICLE VI

There shall be neither slavery nor involuntary servitude in the said territory, otherwise than in the punishment of crimes, whereof the party shall have been duly convicted: *Provided, always,* That any person escaping into the same, from whom labor or service is lawfully claimed in any one of the original States, such fugitive may be lawfully reclaimed, and conveyed to the person claiming his or her labor or service as aforesaid.

Be it ordained by the authority aforesaid, That the resolutions of the 23d of April, 1784, relative to the subject of this ordinance, be, and the same are hereby, repealed, and declared null and void.

Done by the United States, in Congress assembled, the 13th day of July, in the year of our Lord 1787, and of their sovereignty and independence the twelfth.

XXXV.

CONVENTIONAL HISTORY OF THE CONSTITUTION, SUMMER 1787

Since each of the delegates had copies of the documents under discussion, there are more than forty potentially authentic copies of the Virginia Resolutions, introduced by Edmund Randolph, and the New Jersey

Plan defended by William Patterson. See Robert A. Rutland, editor, *The Papers of James Madison* (X: 12-15) for a discussion of the authenticity of the extant copies of the Virginia Plan. We follow the practice of twentieth-century scholarship and utilize the copies included in Madison's *Notes*.

Tansill's official version of the *Notes* remained true to Madison's original. We have reprinted Tansill (116-119 and 204-207), and retained Madison's inconsistent use of "Resolved," "Resd.," "Resolvd," and "Resold" in the Virginia Plan, his consistent use of "Resd." in the New Jersey Plan, as well as the absence of a period at the end of Virginia Resolutions 11 and 14. The Arabic numerals are in the original. Farrand (I: 20-22), Jensen (I: 243-245), and Rutland (X: 15-18) each reprint Madison's copy of the Virginia Plan; similarly Farrand (I: 242-45) and Jensen (I: 250-253) reprint the New Jersey Plan. See also Elliot, *Debates* (V: 127-128, and 191-193).

We have also followed Tansill (571-572, 706-707, and 716) for our coverage of the debates at the Convention. We have, however, excluded his footnote references, added Arabic numerals in parenthesis to indicate Pinckney's twelve propositions, and the eighteen powers of Congress. We have also italicized the four rights included in Article I, Sections 9 and 10 of the Committee of Style Report. Lastly, we have included a copy of the final draft of the Constitution. See Tansill (989-1001) for the Constitution.

~

[A] The Virginia Plan, May 29, 1787

1. Resolved that the Articles of Confederation ought to be so corrected & enlarged as to accomplish the objects proposed by their institution; namely, "common defence, security of liberty and general welfare."

2. Res[d] therefore that the rights of suffrage in the National Legislature ought to be proportioned to the Quotas of contribution, or to the number of free inhabitants, as the one or the other rule may seem best in different cases.

3. Res[d] that the National Legislature ought to consist of two branches.

4. Res[d] that the members of the first branch of the National Legislature ought to be elected by the people of the several States every.....for the term of ; to be of the age of years at least, to receive liberal stipends by which they may be compensated for the devotion of their time to public service; to be ineligible to any office established by a particular State, or under the authority of the United States, except those peculiarly belonging to the functions of the first branch, during the term of service, and for the space of after its expiration; to be incapable of reelection for the space of after the expiration of their term of service, and to be subject to recall.

5. Resol[d] that the members of the second branch of the National Legislature ought to be elected by those of the first, out of a proper number of persons nominated by the individual Legislatures, to be of the age of years at least; to hold their offices for a term sufficient to ensure their independency, to receive liberal stipends, by which they may be compensated for the devotion of their time to public service; and to be ineligible to any office established by a particular State, or under the authority of the United States, except those peculiarly belonging to the functions of the second branch, during the term of service, and for the space of after the expiration thereof.

6. Resolved that each branch ought to possess the right of originating Acts; that the National Legislature ought to be impowered to enjoy the Legislative Rights vested in Congress by the Confederation & moreover to legislate in all cases to which the separate States are incompetent, or in which the harmony of the United States may be interrupted by the exercise of individual Legislation; to negative all laws passed by the several States, contravening in the opinion of the National Legislature the articles of Union; and to call forth the force of the Union ag[st] any member of the Union failing to fulfill its duty under the articles thereof.

7. Res[d] that a National Executive be instituted; to be chosen by the National Legislature for the term of years, to receive punctually at stated times, a fixed compensation for the services rendered, in which no increase or diminution shall be made so as to affect the Magistracy, existing at the time of increase or diminution, and to be ineligible a second time; and that besides a general authority to execute the National laws, it ought to enjoy the Executive rights vested in Congress by the Confederation.

8. Res[d] that the Executive and a convenient number of the National Judiciary, ought to compose a Council of revision with authority to examine every act of the National Legislature before it shall operate, & every act of a particular Legislature before a Negative thereon shall be final; and that the dissent of the said Council shall amount to a rejection, unless the Act of the National Legislature be again passed, or that of a particular Legislature be again negatived by of the members of each branch.

9. Res[d] that a National Judiciary be established to consist of one or more supreme tribunals, and of inferior tribunals to be chosen by the National Legislature, to hold their offices during good behaviour; and to receive punctually at stated times fixed compensation for their services, in which no increase or diminution shall be made so as to affect the persons actually in office at the time of such increase or diminution. that the jurisdiction of the inferior tribunals shall be to hear &

determine in the first instance, and of the supreme tribunals to hear and determine in the dernier resort, all piracies & felonies on the high seas, captures from an enemy; cases in which foreigners or citizens of other States applying to such jurisdictions may be interested, or which respect the collection of the National revenue; impeachments of any National officers, and questions which may involve the national peace and harmony.

10. Resolv[d] that provision ought to be made for the admission of States lawfully arising within the limits of the United States, whether from a voluntary junction of Government & Territory or otherwise, with the consent of a number of voices in the National legislature less than the whole.

11. Res[d] that a Republican Government & the territory of each State, except in the instance of a voluntary junction of Government & territory, ought to be guarantied by the United States to each State

12. Res[d] that provision ought to be made for the continuance of Congress and their authorities and privileges, until a given day after the reform of the articles of Union shall be adopted, and for the completion of all their engagements.

13. Res[d] that provision ought to be made for the amendment of the Articles of Union whensoever it shall seem necessary, and that the assent of the National Legislature ought not to be required thereto.

14. Res[d] that the Legislative Executive & Judiciary powers within the several States ought to be bound by oath to support the articles of Union

15. Res[d] that the amendments which shall be offered to the Confederation, by the Convention ought at a proper time, or times, after the approbation of Congress to be submitted to an assembly or assemblies of Representatives, recommended by the several Legislatures to be expressly chosen by the people, to consider & decide thereon.

[B] The New Jersey Plan, Friday, 15 June 1787

1. Res[d] that the articles of Confederation ought to be so revised, corrected & enlarged, as to render the federal Constitution adequate to the exigences of Government, & the preservation of the Union.

2. Res[d] that in addition to the powers vested in the U. States in Congress, by the present existing articles of Confederation, they be authorized to pass acts for raising a revenue, by levying a duty or duties on all goods or merchandizes of foreign growth or manufacture, imported into any part of the U. States, by Stamps on paper, vellum or parchment, and by a postage on all letters or packages passing through the general post-office, to be applied to such federal purposes as they

shall deem proper & expedient; to make rules & regulations for the collection thereof; and the same from time to time, to alter & amend in such manner as they shall think proper: to pass Acts for the regulation of trade & commerce as well with foreign nations as with each other: provided that all punishments, fines, forfeitures & penalties to be incurred for contravening such acts rules and regulations shall be adjudged by the Common law Judiciaries of the State in which any offence contrary to the true intent & meaning of such Acts rules & regulations shall have been committed or perpetrated, with liberty of commencing in the first instance all suites & prosecutions for that purpose in the superior common law Judiciary in such State, subject nevertheless, for the correction of all errors, both in law & fact in rendering Judgment, to an appeal to the Judiciary of the U. States.

3. Res[d] that whenever requisitions shall be necessary, instead of the rule for making requisitions mentioned in the articles of Confederation, the United States in Cong[s] be authorized to make such requisitions in proportion to the whole number of white & other free citizens & inhabitants of every age sex and condition including those bound to servitude for a term of years & three fifths of all other persons not comprehended in the foregoing description, except Indians not paying taxes; that if such requisitions be not complied with, in the time specified therein, to direct the collection thereof in the non complying States & for that purpose to devise and pass acts directing & authorizing the same; provided that none of the powers hereby vested in the U. States in Cong[s] shall be exercised without the consent of at least States, and in that proportion if the number of Confederated States should hereafter be increased or diminished.

4. Res[d] that the U. States in Cong[s] be authorized to elect a federal Executive to consist of persons, to continue in office for the term of.....years, to receive punctually at stated times a fixed compensation for their services, in which no increase or diminution shall be made so as to affect the persons composing the Executive at the time of such increase or diminution, to be paid out of the federal treasury; to be incapable of holding any other office or appointment during their time of service and for years thereafter; to be ineligible a second time, & removeable by Cong[s] on application by a majority of the Executives of the several States; that the Executives besides their general authority to execute the federal acts ought to appoint all federal officers not otherwise provided for, & to direct all military operations; provided that none of the persons composing the federal Executive shall on any occasion take command of any troops, so as personally to conduct any enterprise as General or in other capacity.

5. Res^{d} that a federal Judiciary be established to consist of a supreme Tribunal the Judges of which to be appointed by the Executive, & to hold their offices during good behaviour, to receive punctually at stated times a fixed compensation for their services in which no increase or diminution shall be made, so as to affect the persons actually in office at the time of such increases or diminution; that the Judiciary so established shall have authority to hear & determine in the first instance on all impeachments of federal officers, & by way of appeal in the dernier resort in all cases touching the rights of Ambassadors, in all cases of captures from an enemy, in all cases of piracies & felonies on the high seas, in all cases in which foreigners may be interested, in the construction of any treaty or treaties, or which may arise on any of the Acts for regulation of trade, or the collection of the federal Revenue: that none of the Judiciary shall during the time they remain in Office be capable of receiving or holding any other office or appointment during their time of service, or for.....thereafter.

6. Res^{d} that all Acts of the U. States in Cong^{s} made by virtue & in pursuance of the powers hereby & by the articles of Confederation vested in them, and all Treaties made & ratified under the authority of the U. States shall be the supreme law of the respective States so far forth as those Acts or Treaties shall relate to the said States or their Citizens, and that the Judiciary of the several States shall be bound thereby in their decisions, any thing in the respective laws of the Individual States to the contrary notwithstanding; and that if any State, or any body of men in any State shall oppose or prevent ye[6] carrying into execution such acts or treaties, the federal Executive shall be authorized to call forth ye power of the Confederated States, or so much thereof as may be necessary to enforce and compel an obedience to such Acts, or an observance of such Treaties.

7. Res^{d} that provision be made for the admission of new States into the Union.

8. Res^{d} the rule for naturalization ought to be the same in every State.

9. Res^{d} that a Citizen of one State committing an offense in another State of the Union, shall be deemed guilty of the same offense as if it had been committed by a Citizen of the State in which the offense was committed.

---

[6]Tansill, incorrectly, uses the abbreviation, "yd.," instead of "ye."

[C] Propositions introduced by Charles Pinckney, 20 August 1787

Mr. PINKNEY[7] submitted to the House, in order to be referred to the Committee of detail, the following propositions—

[1] "Each House shall be the Judge of its own privileges, and shall have authority to punish by imprisonment every person violating the same; or who, in the place where the Legislature may be sitting and during the time of its Session, shall threaten any of its members for anything said or done in the House—or who shall assault any of them therefor—or who shall assault or arrest any witness or other person ordered to attend either of the Houses in his way going or returning; or who shall rescue any person arrested by their order."

[2] "Each branch of the Legislature, as well as the Supreme Executive shall have authority to require the opinions of the supreme Judicial Court upon important questions of law, and upon solemn occasions"

"The privileges and benefit of the Writ of Habeas corpus shall be enjoyed in this Government in the most expeditious and ample manner; and shall not be suspended by the Legislature except upon the most urgent and pressing occasions, and for a limited time not exceeding.....months."

[3] "The liberty of the Press shall be inviolably preserved"

[4] "No troops shall be kept up in time of peace, but by consent of the Legislature"

[5] "The military shall always be subordinate to the Civil power, and no grants of money shall be made by the Legislature for supporting military Land forces, for more than one year at a time"

[6] "No soldier shall be quartered in any House in time of peace whiteout consent of the owner."

[7] "No person holding the office of President of the U.S., a Judge of the Supreme Court, Secretary for the department of Foreign Affairs, of Finance, of Marine, of War, or of , shall be capable of holding at the same time any other office of Trust or Emolument under the U.S. or an individual State"

[8] "No religious test or qualification shall ever be annexed to any oath of office under the authority of the U.S."

[9] "The U.S. shall be for ever considered as one Body corporate and politic in law, and entitled to all the rights privileges, and immunities, which to Bodies corporate do or ought to appertain"

[10] "The Legislature of the U.S. shall have the power of making the great Seal which shall be kept by the President of the U. S. or in

---

[7]Madison regularly mispelled Pinckney's name.

his absence by the President of the Senate, to be used by them as the occasion may require.—It shall be called the great Seal of the U. S. and shall be affixed to all laws."

[11] "All Commissions and writs shall run in the name of the U.S."

[12] "The Jurisdiction of the supreme Court shall be extended to all controversies between the U.S. and an individual State, or the U. S. and the Citizens of an individual State"

These propositions were referred to the Committee of detail without debate or consideration of them, by the House.

[D] Committee of Style Report, Article I, Section 8 and Article 1 Sections 9 and 10, 12 September 1787

Sect. 8. The Congress may by joint ballot appoint a treasurer.

They shall have power

[1] To lay and collect taxes, duties, imposts and excises; to pay the debts and provide for the common defence and general welfare of the United States.

[2] To borrow money on the credit of the United States.

[3] To regulate commerce with foreign nations, and among the several States, and with the Indian tribes.

[4] To establish an uniform rule of naturalization, and uniform laws on the subject of bankruptcies throughout the United States.

[5] To coin money, regulate the value thereof, and of foreign coin, and fix the standard of weights and measures.

[6] To provide for the punishment of counterfeiting the securities and current coin of the United States.

[7] To establish post offices and post roads.

[8] To promote the progress of science and useful arts, by securing for limited times to authors and inventors the exclusive right to their respective writings and discoveries.

[9] To constitute tribunals inferior to the supreme court.

[10] To define and punish piracies and felonies committed on the high seas, and (punish) offences against the law of nations.

[11] To declare war, grant letters of marque and reprisal, and make rules concerning captures on land and water.

[12] To raise and support armies: but no appropriation of monies to that use shall be for a longer term than two years.

[13] To provide and maintain a navy.

[14] To make rules for the government and regulation of the land and naval forces.

[15] To provide for calling forth the militia to execute the laws of the union, suppress insurrections and repel invasions.

[16] To provide for organizing, arming and disciplining the militia, and for governing such part of them as may be employed in the service of the United States, reserving to the States respectively, the appointment of the officers, and the authority of training the militia according to the discipline prescribed by Congress.

[17] To exercise exclusive legislation in all cases whatsoever, over such district (not exceeding ten Miles square) as may, by cession of particular States, and the acceptance of Congress, become the seat of the government of the United States, and to exercise like authority over all places purchased by the consent of the legislature of the State in which the same shall be, for the erection of forts, magazines, arsenals, dock-yards, and other needful buildings

—And

[18] To make all laws which shall be necessary and proper for carrying into execution the foregoing powers, and all other powers vested by this constitution in the government of the United States, or in any department or officer thereof.

Sect. 9. The migration or importation of such persons as any of the States now existing shall think proper to admit, shall not be prohibited by the Congress prior to the year one thousand eight hundred and eight, but a tax or duty may be imposed on such importation, not exceeding ten dollars for each person.

The privilege of the writ of habeas corpus shall not be suspended, unless when in cases of rebellion or invasion the public safety may require it.

No bill of attainder shall be passed, nor any ex post facto law.

No capitation tax shall be laid, unless in proportion to the census herein before directed to be taken.

No tax or duty shall be laid on articles exported from any state.

No money shall be drawn from the treasury, but in consequence of appropriations made by law.

No title of nobility shall be granted by the United States: And no person holding any office of profit or trust under them, shall, without the consent of the Congress, accept of any present, emolument, office, or title, of any kind whatever, from any king, prince, or foreign state.

Sect. 10. No state shall coin money, nor emit bills of credit, nor make any thing but gold and silver coin a tender in payment of debts, nor *pass any bill of attainder, nor ex post facto laws, nor laws altering or impairing the obligation of contracts*; nor grant letters of marque or reprisal, nor enter into any treaty, alliance, or confederation, nor *grant any title of nobility.*

No state shall, without the consent of the Congress, lay any imposts or duties on imports or exports, nor with such consent, but t o the use of the treasury of the United States. Nor keep troops, nor ships of war in time of peace, nor enter into any agreement or compact with another state, nor with any foreign power. Nor engage in any war, unless actually invaded, or the danger of invasion so imminent, as not to admit of delay until the Congress can be consulted.

[E] Gerry and Mason propose a Committee to draft a Bill of Rights, 12 September 1787

M[r] WILLIAMSON, observed to the House that no provision was yet made for juries in Civil cases and suggested the necessity of it.

M[r] GORHAM. It is not possible to discriminate equity cases from those in which juries are proper. The Representatives of the people may be safely trusted in this matter.

M[r] GERRY urged the necessity of Juries to guard ag[st] corrupt Judges. He proposed that the Committee last appointed should be directed to provide a clause for securing the trial by Juries.

Col: MASON perceived the difficulty mentioned by M[r] Gorham. The jury cases can not be specified. A general principle laid down on this and some other points would be sufficient. He wished the plan had been prefaced with a Bill of Rights, & would second a Motion if made for the purpose. It would give great quiet to the people; and with the aid of the State declarations, a bill might be prepared in a few hours.

M[r] GERRY concurred in the idea & moved for a Committee to prepare a Bill of Rights. Col: MASON 2[ded] the motion.

M[r] SHERMAN, was for securing the rights of the people where requisite. The State Declarations of Rights are not repealed by this Constitution; and being in force are sufficient. There are many cases where juries are proper which cannot be discriminated. The Legislature may be safely trusted.

Col: MASON. The Laws of the U. S. are to be paramount to State Bills of Rights.

On the question for a Com[e] to prepare a Bill of Rights

N.H. no. Mas. abs[t] C[t]. no. N. J. no. P[a]. no. Del no. M[d] no. V[a] no. N.C. no. S. C. no. Geo. no.

[F] The Constitution of the United States of America, 17 September 1787

We the people of the United States, in Order to form a more perfect Union, establish Justice, insure domestic Tranquility, provide for the common defence, promote the general Welfare, and secure the Blessings of Liberty to ourselves and our Posterity, do ordain and establish this Constitution for the United States of America.

Article. I.

Section. 1. All legislative Powers herein granted shall be vested in a Congress of the United States, which shall consist of a Senate and House of Representatives.

Section. 2. The House of Representatives shall be composed of Members chosen every second Year by the People of the several States, and the Electors in each State shall have the Qualifications requisite for Electors of the most numerous Branch of the State Legislature.

No Person shall be a Representative who shall not have attained to the Age of twenty five Years, and been seven Years a citizen of the United States, and who shall not, when elected, be an Inhabitant of that State in which he shall be chosen.

Representatives and direct Taxes shall be apportioned among the several States which may be included within this Union, according to their respective Numbers, which shall be determined by adding to the whole Number of free Persons, including those bound to Service for a Term of Years, and excluding Indians not taxed, three fifths of all other Persons. The actual Enumeration shall be made within three Years after the first Meeting of the Congress of the United States, and within every subsequent Term of ten Years, in such Manner as they shall by Law direct. The Number of Representatives shall not exceed one for every thirty Thousand, but each State shall have at Least one Representative; and until such enumeration shall be made, the State of New Hampshire shall be entitled to chuse three, Massachusetts eight, Rhode-Island and Providence Plantations one, Connecticut five, New York six, New Jersey four, Pennsylvania eight, Delaware one, Maryland six, Virginia ten, North Carolina five, South Carolina five, and Georgia three.

When vacancies happen in the Representation from any State, the Executive Authority thereof shall issue Writs of Election to fill such Vacancies.

The House of Representatives shall chuse their Speaker and other Officers; and shall have the sole Power of Impeachment.

Section. 3. The Senate of the United States shall be composed of two Senators from each State, chosen by the legislature thereof, for six Years; and each Senator shall have one Vote.

Immediately after they shall be assembled in Consequence of the first Election, they shall be divided as equally as may be into three Classes. The Seats of the Senators of the first Class shall be vacated at the expiration of the second Year, of the second Class at the expiration of the fourth Year, and of the third Class at the expiration of the sixth Year, so that one third may be chosen every second Year; and if Vacancies happen by Resignation, or otherwise, during the Recess of the Legislature of any State, the Executive thereof may make temporary

Appointments until the next Meeting of the Legislature, which shall then fill such Vacancies.

No person shall be a Senator who shall not have attained to the Age of thirty Years, and been nine Years a Citizen of the United States, and who shall not, when elected, be an Inhabitant of that State for which he shall be chosen.

The Vice-President of the United States shall be President of the Senate, but shall have no Vote, unless they be equally divided.

The Senate shall chuse their other Officers, and also a President pro tempore, in the Absence of the Vice-President, or when he shall exercise the Office of President of the United States.

The Senate shall have the sole Power to try all Impeachments. When sitting for that Purpose, they shall be on Oath or Affirmation. When the President of the United States is tried, the Chief Justice shall preside: And no Person shall be convicted without the Concurrence of two thirds of the Members present.

Judgment in cases of Impeachment shall not extend further than to removal from Office, and disqualification to hold and enjoy any Office of honor, Trust or Profit under the United States: but the Party convicted shall nevertheless be liable and subject to Indictment, Trial, Judgment and Punishment, according to Law.

Section. 4. The Times, Places and Manner of holding Elections for Senators and Representatives, shall be prescribed in each State by the Legislature thereof; but the Congress may at any time by Law make or alter such Regulations, except as to the Places of chusing Senators.

The Congress shall assemble at least once in every Year, and such Meeting shall be on the first Monday in December, unless they shall by Law appoint a different Day.

Section. 5. Each House shall be the Judge of the Elections, Returns and Qualifications of its own Members, and a Majority of each shall constitute a Quorum to do Business; but a smaller Number may adjourn from day to day, and may be authorized to compel the Attendance of absent Members, in such Manner, and under such Penalties as each House may provide.

Each House may determine the Rules of its Proceedings, punish its Members for disorderly Behavior, and, with the Concurrence of two thirds, expel a Member.

Each House shall keep a Journal of its Proceedings, and from time to time publish the same, excepting such Parts as may in their Judgment require Secrecy; and the Yeas and Nays of the Members of either House on any question shall, at the Desire of one fifth of those Present, be entered on the Journal.

Neither House, during the Session of Congress, shall, without the Consent of the other, adjourn for more than three days, nor to any other Place than that in which the two Houses shall be sitting.

Section. 6. The Senators and Representatives shall receive a Compensation for their Services, to be ascertained by Law, and paid out of the Treasury of the United States. They shall in all Cases, except Treason, Felony and Breach of the Peace, be privileged from Arrest during their Attendance at the Session of their respective Houses, and in going to and returning from the same; and for any Speech or Debate in either House, they shall not be questioned in any other Place.

No Senator or Representative shall, during the Time for which he was elected, be appointed to any civil Office under the Authority of the United States, which shall have been created, or the Emoluments whereof shall have been increased during such time; and no Person holding any Office under the United States, shall be a Member of either House during his Continuance in Office.

Section. 7. All Bills for raising Revenue shall originate in the House of Representatives; but the Senate may propose or concur with Amendments as on other Bills.

Every Bill which shall have passed the House of Representatives and the Senate, shall, before it become a Law, be presented to the President of the United States; If he approve he shall sign it, but if not he shall return it, with his Objections to that House in which it shall have originated, who shall enter the Objections at large on their Journal, and proceed to reconsider it. If after such Reconsideration two thirds of that house shall agree to pass the Bill, it shall be sent, together with the Objections, to the other House, by which it shall likewise be reconsidered, and if approved by two thirds of that House, it shall become a Law. But in all such Cases the Votes of both Houses shall be determined by yeas and Nays, and the Names of the Persons voting for and against the Bill shall be entered on the Journal of each House respectively. If any Bill shall not be returned by the President within ten Days (Sundays excepted) after it shall have been presented to him, the Same shall be a Law, in like Manner as if he had signed it, unless the Congress by their Adjournment prevent its Return in which case it shall not be a Law.

Every Order, Resolution, or Vote to which the Concurrence of the Senate and House of Representatives may be necessary (except on a question of Adjournment) shall be presented to the President of the United States; and before the Same shall take Effect, shall be approved by him, or being disapproved by him, shall be repassed by two thirds of the Senate and House of Representatives, according to the Rules and Limitations prescribed in the Case of a Bill.

Section. 8. The Congress shall have Power To lay and collect Taxes, Duties, Imposts and Excises, to pay the Debts and provide for the common Defence and general Welfare of the United States; but all Duties, Imposts and Excises shall be uniform throughout the United States;

To borrow Money on the credit of the United States;

To regulate Commerce with foreign Nations, and among the several States, and with the Indian Tribes;

To establish an uniform Rule of Naturalization, and uniform Laws on the subject of Bankruptcies throughout the United States;

To coin Money, regulate the Value thereof, and of foreign Coin, and fix the Standard of Weights and Measures;

To provide for the Punishment of counterfeiting the Securities and current Coin of the United States;

To establish Post Offices and Post Roads;

To promote the Progress of Science and useful Arts, by securing for limited Times to Authors and Inventors the exclusive Right to their respective Writings and Discoveries;

To constitute Tribunals inferior to the supreme Court;

To define and punish Piracies and Felonies committed on the high Seas, and Offenses against the Law of Nations;

To declare War, grant Letters of Marque and Reprisal, and make Rules concerning Captures on Land and Water;

To raise and support Armies, but no Appropriation of Money to that Use shall be for a longer Term than two Years;

To provide and maintain a Navy;

To make Rules for the Government and Regulation of the land and naval Forces;

To provide for calling forth the Militia to execute the Laws of the Union, suppress Insurrections and repel Invasions;

To provide for organizing, arming, and disciplining, the Militia, and for governing such Part of them as may be employed in the Service of the United States, reserving to the States respectively, the Appointment of the Officers, and the Authority of training the Militia according to the discipline prescribed by Congress;

To exercise exclusive Legislation in all Cases whatsoever, over such District (not exceeding ten Miles square) as may, by Cession of particular States, and the Acceptance of Congress, become the Seat of the Government of the United States, and to exercise like Authority over all Places purchased by the Consent of the Legislature of the State in which the Same shall be, for the Erection of Forts, Magazines, Arsenals, dock-Yards, and other needful Buildings;—And

To make all Laws which shall be necessary and proper for carrying into Execution the foregoing Powers, and all other Powers vested by this Constitution in the Government of the United States, or in any Department or Officer thereof.

Section. 9. The Migration or Importation of such Persons as any of the States now existing shall think proper to admit, shall not be prohibited by the Congress prior to the Year one thousand eight hundred and eight, but a Tax or duty may be imposed on such Importation, not exceeding ten dollars for each Person.

The Privilege of the Writ of Habeas Corpus shall not be suspended, unless when in Cases of Rebellion or Invasion the public Safety may require it.

No Bill of Attainder or ex post facto Law shall be passed.

No Capitation, or other direct, Tax shall be laid, unless in Proportion to the Census or Enumeration herein before directed to be taken.

No Tax or Duty shall be laid on Articles exported from any State.

No Preference shall be given by any Regulation of Commerce or Revenue to the Ports of one State over those of another: nor shall Vessels bound to, or from, one State, be obliged to enter, clear, or pay Duties in another.

No Money shall be drawn from the Treasury, but in Consequence of Appropriations made by Law; and a regular Statement and Account of the Receipts and Expenditures of all public Money shall be published from time to time.

No Title of Nobility shall be granted by the United States: And no Person holding any Office of Profit or Trust under them, shall, without the Consent of the Congress, accept of any present, Emolument, Office, or Title, of any kind whatever, from any King, Prince, or foreign State.

Section. 10. No State shall enter into any Treaty, Alliance, or Confederation; grant Letters of Marque and Reprisal; coin Money; emit Bills of Credit; make any Thing but gold and silver Coin a Tender in Payment of Debts; pass any Bill of Attainder, ex post facto Law, or Law impairing the Obligation of Contracts, or grant any Title of Nobility.

No State shall, without the Consent of the Congress, lay any Imposts or Duties on Imports or Exports, except what may be absolutely necessary for executing it's [sic] inspection Laws: and the net Produce of all Duties and Imposts, laid by any State on Imports or Exports, shall be for the Use of the Treasury of the United States; and all such Laws shall be subject to the Revision and Controul of the Congress.

No State shall, without the Consent of Congress, lay any Duty of Tonnage, keep Troops, or Ships of War in time of Peace, enter into any Agreement or Compact with another State, or with a foreign Power, or engage in War, unless actually invaded, or in such imminent Danger as will not admit of delay.

Article. II.

Section. 1. The executive Power shall be vested in a President of the United States of America. He shall hold his Office during the Term of four Years, and, together with the Vice President, chosen for the same Term, be elected, as follows

Each State shall appoint, in such Manner as the Legislature thereof may direct, a Number of Electors, equal to the whole Number of Senators and Representatives to which the State may be entitled in the Congress: but no Senator or Representative, or Person holding an Office of Trust or Profit under the United States, shall be appointed an Elector.

The Electors shall meet in their respective States, and vote by Ballot for two Persons, of whom one at least shall not be an Inhabitant of the same State with themselves. And they shall make a List of all the Persons voted for, and of the Number of Votes for each; which List they shall sign and certify, and transmit sealed to the Seat of the Government of the United States, directed to the President of the Senate. The President of the Senate shall, in the Presence of the Senate and House of Representatives, open all the Certificates, and the Votes shall then be counted. The Person having the greatest Number of Votes shall be the President, if such Number be a Majority of the whole Number of Electors appointed; and if there be more than one who have such Majority, and have an equal Number of votes, then the House of Representatives shall immediately chuse by Ballot one of them for President; and if no Person have a Majority, then from the five highest on the List the said House shall in like Manner chuse the President. But in chusing the President, the Votes shall be taken by States, the Representation from each State having one Vote; A quorum for this Purpose shall consist of a Member or Members from two thirds of the States, and a Majority of all the States shall be necessary to a Choice. In every Case, after the Choice of the President, the Person having the greatest Number of Votes of the Electors shall be the Vice President. But if there should remain two or more who have equal Votes, the Senate shall chuse from them by Ballot the Vice President.

The Congress may determine the Time of chusing the Electors, and the Day on which they shall give their Votes; which Day shall be the same throughout the United States.

No Person except a natural born Citizen, or a Citizen of the United States, at the time of the Adoption of this Constitution, shall be eligible to the Office of President; neither shall any Person be eligible to that Office who shall not have attained to the Age of thirty five Years, and been fourteen Years a Resident within the United States.

In Case of the Removal of the President from Office, or of his Death, Resignation, or Inability to discharge the Powers and Duties of the said Office, the Same shall devolve on the Vice President, and the Congress may by Law provide for the Case of Removal, Death, Resignation or Inability, both of the President and Vice President, declaring what Officer shall then act as President, and such Officer shall act accordingly, until the Disability be removed, or a President shall be elected.

The President shall, at stated Times, receive for his Services, a Compensation, which shall neither be encreased nor diminished during the Period for which he shall have been elected, and he shall not receive within that Period any other Emolument from the United States, or any of them.

Before he enter on the Execution of his Office, he shall take the following Oath or Affirmation:—"I do solemnly swear (or affirm) that I will faithfully execute the Office of President of the United States, and will to the best of my Ability, preserve, protect and defend the Constitution of the United States."

Section. 2. The President shall be Commander in Chief of the Army and Navy of the United States, and of the Militia of the several States, when called into the actual Service of the United States; he may require the Opinion, in writing, of the principal Officer in each of the executive Departments, upon any Subject relating to the Duties of their respective Offices, and he shall have Power to grant Reprieves and Pardons for Offenses against the United States, except in Cases of Impeachment.

He shall have Power, by and with the Advice and Consent of the Senate, to make Treaties, provided two thirds of the Senators present concur; and he shall nominate, and by and with the Advice and Consent of the Senate, shall appoint Ambassadors, other public Ministers and Consuls, Judges of the supreme Court, and all other Officers of the United States, whose Appointments are not herein otherwise provided for, and which shall be established by Law: but the Congress may by Law vest the Appointment of such inferior Officers, as they think proper, in the President alone, in the Courts of Law, or in the Heads of Departments.

The President shall have Power to fill up all Vacancies that may happen during the Recess of the Senate, by granting Commissions which shall expire at the End of their next Session.

Section. 3. He shall from time to time give to the Congress Information of the State of the Union, and recommend to their Consideration such Measures as he shall judge necessary and expedient;

he may, on extraordinary Occasions, convene both Houses, or either of them, and in Case of Disagreement between them, with Respect to the Time of Adjournment, he may adjourn them to such Time as he shall think proper; he shall receive Ambassadors and other public Ministers; he shall take Care that the Laws be faithfully executed, and shall Commission all the Officers of the United States.

Section. 4. The President, Vice President and all civil Officers of the United States, shall be removed from Office on Impeachment for, and Conviction of, Treason, Bribery, or other high Crimes and Misdemeanors.

Article III.

Section. 1. The judicial Power of the United States, shall be vested in one supreme Court, and in such inferior Courts as the Congress may from time to time ordain and establish. The Judges, both of the supreme and inferior Courts, shall hold their Offices during good Behaviour, and shall, at stated Times, receive for their Services, a Compensation, which shall not be diminished during their Continuance in Office.

Section. 2. The judicial Power shall extend to all Cases, in Law and Equity, arising under this Constitution, the Laws of the United States, and Treaties made, or which shall be made, under their Authority;—to all Cases affecting Ambassadors, other public Ministers and Consuls;—to all Cases of admiralty and maritime Jurisdiction;—to Controversies to which the United States shall be a Party;—to Controversies between two or more States;—between a State and Citizens of another State;—between Citizens of different States; —between Citizens of the same State claiming Lands under Grants of different States, and between a State, or the Citizens thereof, and foreign States, Citizens or Subjects.

In all cases affecting Ambassadors, other public Ministers and Consuls, and those in which a State shall be Party, the supreme Court shall have original Jurisdiction. In all the other Cases before mentioned, the supreme Court shall have appellate Jurisdiction, both as to Law and Fact, with such Exceptions, and under such Regulations as the Congress shall make.

The Trial of all Crimes, except in Cases of Impeachment, shall be by Jury; and such Trial shall be held in the State where the said Crimes shall have been committed; but when not committed within any State, the Trial shall be at such Place or Places as the Congress may by Law have directed.

Section. 3. Treason against the United States, shall consist only in levying War against them, or in adhering to their Enemies, giving them Aid and Comfort. No Person shall be convicted of Treason unless on the Testimony of two Witnesses to the same overt Act, or on Confession in open Court.

The Congress shall have power to declare the Punishment of Treason, but no Attainder of Treason shall work Corruption of Blood, or Forfeiture except during the Life of the Person attainted.

Article. IV.

Section. 1. Full Faith and Credit shall be given in each State to the public Acts, Records, and judicial Proceedings of every other State. And the Congress may by general Laws prescribe the Manner in which such Acts, Records, and Proceedings shall be proved, and the Effect thereof.

Section. 2. The Citizens of each State shall be entitled to all Privileges and Immunities of Citizens in the several States.

A Person charged in any State with Treason, Felony, or other Crime, who shall flee from Justice, and be found in another State, shall on Demand of the executive Authority of the State from which he fled, be delivered up, to be removed to the State having Jurisdiction of the Crime.

No person held to Service or Labor in one State, under the Laws thereof, escaping into another, shall, in Consequence of any Law or Regulation therein, be discharged from such Service or Labour, but shall be delivered up on Claim of the Party to whom such Service or Labour may be due.

Section. 3. New States may be admitted by the Congress into this Union; but no new State shall be formed or erected within the Jurisdiction of any other State; nor any State be formed by the Junction of two or more States, or Parts of States, without the Consent of the Legislatures of the States concerned as well as of the Congress.

The Congress shall have Power to dispose of and make all needful Rules and Regulations respecting the Territory or other Property belonging to the United States; and nothing in this Constitution shall be so construed as to Prejudice any Claims of the United States, or of any particular State.

Section. 4. The United States shall guarantee to every State in this Union a Republican Form of Government, and shall protect each of them against Invasion; and on Application of the Legislature, or of the Executive (when the Legislature cannot be convened) against domestic Violence.

Article. V.

The Congress, whenever two thirds of both Houses shall deem it necessary, shall propose Amendments to this Constitution, or, on the Application of the Legislatures of two thirds of the several States, shall call a Convention for proposing Amendments, which, in either Case, shall be valid to all Intents and Purposes, as Part of this Constitution, when ratified by the Legislatures of three fourths of the several States, or by Conventions in three fourths thereof, as the one or the other Mode of Ratification may be proposed by the Congress; Provided that no Amendment which may be made prior to the Year one thousand eight hundred and eight shall in any Manner affect the first and fourth Clauses in the Ninth Section of the first Article; and that no State, without its Consent, shall be deprived of it's [sic] equal Suffrage in the Senate.

Article. VI.

All Debts contracted and Engagements entered into, before the Adoption of this Constitution, shall be as valid against the United States under this Constitution, as under the Confederation.

This Constitution, and the Laws of the United States which shall be made in Pursuance thereof; and all Treaties made, or which shall be made, under the Authority of the United States, shall be the supreme Law of the Land; and the Judges in every State shall be bound thereby, any Thing in the Constitution or Laws of any State to the Contrary notwithstanding.

The Senators and Representatives before mentioned, and the Members of the several State Legislatures, and all executive and judicial Officers, both of the United States and of the several States, shall be bound by Oath or Affirmation, to support this Constitution; but no religious Test shall ever be required as a Qualification to any Office or public Trust under the United States

Article. VII.

The Ratification of the Conventions of nine States, shall be sufficient for the Establishment of this Constitution between the States so ratifying the Same.

Done in Convention by the Unanimous Consent of the States present the Seventeenth Day of September in the Year of our Lord one thousand seven hundred and Eighty seven and of the Independence of the United States of America the Twelfth In Witness whereof We have hereunto subscribed our Names,

G° WASHINGTON--
Presid[t] and deputy from Virginia

New Hampshire JOHN LANGDON
NICHOLAS GILMAN

Massachusetts	NATHANIEL GORHAM	
	RUFUS KING	
Connecticut	W^{M} SAM^{L} JOHNSON	
	ROGER SHERMAN	
New York	ALEXANDER HAMILTON	
New Jersey	WIL: LIVINGSTON	W^{M} PATERSON.
	DAVID BREARLY.	JONA: DAYTON
Pennsylvania	B FRANKLIN	ROB^{T} MORRIS
	THOMAS MIFFLIN	GEO. CLYMER
	THO^{S} FITZSIMONS	JAMES WILSON
	JARED INGERSOLL	GOUV MORRIS
Delaware	GEO: READ	JACO: BROOM
	GUNNING BEDFORD jun	
	JOHN DICKINSON	
	RICHARD BASSETT	
Maryland	JAMES MCHENRY	
	DAN OF S^{T} THO^{S} JENIFER	
	DAN^{L} CARROLL	
Virginia	JOHN BLAIR—	
	JAMES MADISON Jr.	
North Carolina	W^{M} BLOUNT	
	RICH^{D} DOBBS SPAIGHT.	
	HU WILLIAMSON	
South Carolina	J. RUTLEDGE	
	CHARLES COTESWORTH PINCKNEY	
	CHARLES PINCKNEY	
	PIERCE BUTLER	
Georgia	WILLIAM FEW	
	ABR BALDWIN	

Attest: William Jackson, Secretary

Chapter Six

The General Voice Calls for a Bill of Rights

In *Federalist* 1, Alexander Hamilton captured the gravity of the historical moment at which the world had arrived: the American people were "to decide the important question, whether societies of men are really capable or not of establishing good government from reflection and choice, or whether they are forever destined to depend for their political constitutions on accident and force." It was as if the experience of the American covenanting tradition, the hope of such enlightenment thinkers as Locke, Sydney, and Cato, and the skepticism of Blackstone, Hume, and Burke were being put to the test. The Federalists argued that the proposed Constitution was consistent with the Declaration of Independence and secured the principles of the revolution from imminent collapse. The most articulate members of the Antifederalist opposition concurred with Hamilton's assessment that the "fortune of mankind" was at stake. They argued that the new understanding of federalism and republicanism, undergirding the proposed Constitution, placed the rights won by the revolution in danger. They pointed to the absence of a bill of rights as evidence that rights were insecure under the proposed Constitution. And despite Federalist efforts to dismiss a bill of rights as unnecessary and dangerous, the Antifederalists made sure its absence remained central to the ratification conversation.

It is useful to view the Antifederalist opposition in terms of two separate, and not necessarily compatible, political persuasions. On the one hand, there were Antifederalists who opposed the new structure and the additional powers granted to the general government. Accordingly, they sought amendments that would, if effect, undo the work of the framers of 1787. On the other hand, a significant number of Antifederalists accepted the new framework but were concerned that inadequate attention had been given to securing individual rights. Once the Constitution had been ratified, James Madison attempted to alleviate these concerns by prodding the First Congress to support amendments that would attach a declaration of rights and to reject amendments that would alter the fundamental nature of the new government.

Federalist Defense

Throughout the nine-month ratification campaign, proponents of the Constitution defended the absence of a bill of rights. James Wilson's State House speech, delivered in Philadelphia three weeks after the Constitutional Convention adjourned, articulated the Federalist position: a bill of rights is unnecessary and dangerous. Wilson argued that at the *state* level, a bill of rights is necessary and salutary because "everything which is not reserved, is given," but "superfluous and absurd" at the federal level because "everything which is not given, is reserved." Wilson's theory of "distinction" was invoked by both supporters and opponents. Another distinction to which Federalists appealed was the difference between a monarchy and a republic. Hamilton, for example, remarked that "bills of rights are, in their origin, stipulations between kings and their subjects, abridgments of prerogative in favor of privilege, reservations of rights not surrendered to the prince." A third, and ingenious, argument was that the Constitution actually contains protection for the most essential rights in Article I, sections 9 and 10. Later, Madison offered a fourth, and more compelling, defense: individual rights are better secured through a well-structured government than by "parchment barriers."

Antifederalist Criticisms

The first of George Mason's ten objections to the Constitution begins: "There is no declaration of rights." In particular, "there is no declaration of any kind for preserving liberty of the press, the trial by jury in civil cases, nor against the danger of standing armies in times of peace." Mason's position is that a federal bill of rights is both imperative and valuable. He was concerned that Congress may abuse the supremacy clause and the necessary and proper clause. The supremacy clause makes federal laws "paramount to the laws and constitutions of the several states." Thus, "the declaration of rights, in the separate states, are of no security." The necessary and proper clause enables Congress to "grant monopolies in trade and commerce, constitute new crimes, inflict unusual and severe punishments, and extend their power as far as they should think proper."

Richard Henry Lee, presumed author of the influential Federal Farmer essays, and the prominent New York Antifederalist Brutus reiterate Mason's claim that a bill of rights is necessary and proper. Each articulate the traditional argument that a bill of rights is needed to protect the people from the tyranny of the few. There was no doubt in their minds that the new plan of government--separation of powers, bicameralism, and federalism to the contrary notwithstanding--concentrated power in the hands of the few. There is also a remarkable uniformity to the specific individual rights that need protection: rights of conscience, freedom of the press, freedom of association, no unreasonable searches and seizures, trial by jury in civil cases, no cruel and unusual punishment, are frequently listed.

State Ratifying Conventions

The "out-of-doors" argument reproduced in pamphlets, essays, newspapers, and correspondence over the absence of a bill of rights was duplicated in the official debates that took place at the specially-called state ratifying conventions. The exchange between Wilson and Antifederalists John Smilie and Robert Whitehill, in Pennsylvania, captures the essential character of the debates from north to south. Wilson reiterated his "principle of federal delegation" to support his contention that a bill of rights is unnecessary and dangerous. In addition, he argued that bills of rights make sense only within the British context. In response, Smilie and Whitehill argued that the new Constitution envisages a complete government rather than a confederal alliance. Thus, a bill of rights is neither an "unnecessary" nor "imprudent" precaution against the abuse of power by politicians.

By early January, 1788, Delaware (30-0), Pennsylvania (46-23), New Jersey (38-0), Georgia (26-0), and Connecticut (128-40) had ratified the Constitution. No one changed their minds in these five conventions. Nevertheless, the Report issued by the twenty-three Pennsylvania opponents had a considerable impact on the subsequent campaign. The Report proposed two different kinds of amendments. On the one hand, the minority called for amendments that would re-establish the principles of the Articles of Confederation. These were unfriendly to the Constitution. On the other hand, they proposed that a declaration of rights be annexed to the Constitution. What became the first, fourth, fifth, sixth, seventh, and eighth amendments to the Constitution were included in their list.

The fate of the Constitution, and the Bill of Rights, were determined in the Massachusetts, New Hampshire, Virginia, and New York ratifying conventions. A compromise--"ratify now, amend later"--was needed in each of these four states to secure ratification. In Massachusetts, ten delegates switched their votes and the Constitution was ratified by a 187-168 majority. A switch of five votes ensured ratification in New Hampshire (57-47), and Virginia (89-79). In New York, the Antifederalists outnumbered the Federalists by a margin of 46-19 going into the convention. In the end, the Constitution was ratified by a vote of 30-27. In all four states, a list of amendments was proposed with the understanding that they would be submitted to the First Congress for consideration. There were two different kinds of recommendations: some called for an alteration in the structure and powers of the federal government, others sought to protect the rights of individuals with respect to the federal government. All nine of Massachusetts's recommendations are of the first kind. New Hampshire was the first to add a brief declaration of the rights of citizens to the list of amendments. In Virginia, and New York, the two kinds of amendments are explicitly separated: the declaration of rights in Virginia (twenty) and New York (twenty-four) precede the actual list of recommended amendments.

The Jefferson-Madison Correspondence

The correspondence between Madison in the United States and Jefferson in Paris is a critical part of the story of the adoption of the Bill of Rights. In a 24 October 1788 letter, Madison summarized the political problem that was to be solved by the Constitution: "To prevent instability and injustice in the legislation of the States." What Madison was able to achieve, he explained to Jefferson, was the creation of an extended republic that would secure the civil and religious rights of individuals from the danger of majority faction. Jefferson responded favorably two months later. He was troubled, however, by Wilson's argument that a bill of rights was unnecessary. He reminded Madison that "a bill of rights is what the people are entitled to against every government on earth, general or particular; and what no just government should refuse, or rest on inference." He listed six essential rights that should be declared: "freedom of religion, freedom of the press, protection against standing armies, restriction of monopolies, the eternal and unremitting force of the habeas corpus laws, and trials by jury in all matters." He reiterated his list of six rights upon being informed by Madison that the Constitution had been adopted:

> I sincerely rejoice at the acceptance of our new constitution by nine States. It is a good canvas, on which some strokes only want retouching. What these are, I think are sufficiently manifested by the general voice from north to south, which calls for a bill of rights.

With the ratification of the Constitution, Madison promoted the adoption of a bill of rights and the rejection of amendments that would radically alter the new government's structure and power. He did so for both theoretical and prudential reasons. Madison distanced himself from the argument that a bill of rights may be dangerous as well as unnecessary. The danger of listing rights was overcome by declaring that the enumeration "of certain rights, shall not be construed to deny or disparage others retained by the people." The prudential reasons included conciliating "honorable and patriotic" opponents who wanted to "revise" the Constitution by including a bill of rights and defeating the call for a second convention that would "abolish" the Constitution. He saw the First Congress as the "proper mode" to accomplish the objective of revision.

Jefferson also altered his position as a result of the exchange. He admitted that majority tyranny rather than minority tyranny was the main source of faction, that parchment barriers are often inefficacious, and that a declaration of rights should be added in a "way which will not endanger the whole frame of the government, or any essential part of it." Besides, he had discovered that these parchment rights could be protected by an independent judiciary.

Madison Argues for Amendments

On June 8, 1789, Madison had difficulty persuading the Federalist majority in the House of Representatives to take seriously the issue of amending the Constitution. Some representatives doubted that amendments were needed while others argued that consideration be postponed. Madison insisted that Congress attend to the wishes of "a respectable number of our constituents," that the representatives "incorporate such amendments in the Constitution as will secure those rights, which they consider as not sufficiently guarded." Of Madison's nine amendment proposals, none aimed at altering the structure or powers of the general government. Madison's plan was to open up the Constitution and insert specific changes where appropriate. For example, he would have attached the theoretical premises of the Declaration of Independence to the Preamble. The longest and most important proposal is the fourth; it actually adds ten additional exceptions to the powers of Congress in Article I, section 9. The list contains seven of the ten amendments adopted subsequently.

Madison defended these "moderate" and "proper" revisions. Madison, in effect, revisits the exchange he had with Jefferson; this time Jefferson's arguments blend with Madison's own to form a "conclusive" new defense that is neither wholly Madisonian nor wholly Jeffersonian, but a mixture of both. The new plan envisages "independent tribunals of justice" guarding the declared rights from factious legislative majorities. No longer are bills of rights conceived simply in terms of protecting the people from the abuse of power by the few. The blending is clearest in the fifth proposition. There Madison mixed Jefferson's notion that "a bill of rights is what the people are entitled to against every government on earth," with his own concern that the greatest danger to liberty is at the state level. The result is a proposition declaring that "no State shall violate the equal right of the conscience, freedom of the press, or trial by jury in criminal cases; because it is proper that every Government should be disarmed of powers which trench upon those particular rights."

Congressional History of the Bill of Rights

The Congressional debate on Madison's propositions is not without irony. Roger Sherman, arguably Madison's leading and most persuasive opponent during the structural phase of the 1787 Philadelphia Convention, objected to his attempt to incorporate the revisions "neatly" within the body of the Constitution. If the revisions are added as "supplements," said Madison, "they will create unfavorable comparison" with the original Constitution. Sherman, however, prevailed. The original work of the framers, he argued, should remain intact. Moreover, Sherman urged his colleagues to reject incorporating the Declaration of Independence into the Preamble: "the words 'We the people,' in the original Constitution, are as copious and expressive as possible; any addition will only drag out the sentence without illuminating it." On the other hand, Sherman proved to be an important ally in defeating the attempts of the South Carolina delegation to introduce amendments that would "change the principles of the Government." A final irony occurs with the decision of the House to add the bill of rights as a "supplement" to the Constitution: Madison's fourth proposition that protects three essential rights against the tyrannical conduct of state government emerged as the fourteenth of the seventeen amendments submitted to the Senate for their approval! The Senate rejected this proposal. In the end, Congress submitted twelve amendments to the States for approval. Ten were ratified.

XXXVI.

FEDERALISTS DEFEND THE ABSENCE OF A BILL OF RIGHTS, FALL 1787-SPRING 1788

James Wilson's "State House" Speech, delivered on 6 October 1787, was the first official defense of the Constitution and responds directly to the objections George Mason had expressed during the last month of the convention. It was published in the *Pennsylvania Herald* and widely distributed as "an authoritative explanation" of the Constitution. We have relied on the version found in Ford *Pamphlets* (155-161). See also Jensen, *Documentary History* (II: 167-172). Wilson's argument is repeated by Edmund Randolph at the Virginia Ratifying Convention in June 1788 and as late as 12 August 1788 in *Federalist* 84, the last essay published in *The New York Packet* but the first to deal directly with the Bill of Rights controversy. We have followed the version of *Federalist* 84 found in the 1788 "McLean edition;" the footnotes are in the original.

~

[A] James Wilson's State House Speech, 6 October 1787

SUBSTANCE OF AN ADDRESS
TO A
MEETING OF THE CITIZENS OF PHILADELPHIA,
DELIVERED, 6 OCTOBER 1787,
BY THE HONORABLE
JAMES WILSON, ESQUIRE,
ONE OF THE DELEGATES FROM THE STATE OF
PENNSYLVANIA TO THE LATE CONTINENTAL CONGRESS

Mr. Chairman and Fellow Citizens,

Having received the honour of an appointment to represent you in the late convention, it is, perhaps, my duty to comply with the request of many gentlemen, whose characters and judgments I sincerely respect, and who have urged that this would be a proper occasion to lay before you any information, which will serve to elucidate and explain the principles and arrangements of the constitution that has been submitted to the consideration of the United States. I confess that I am unprepared for so extensive and so important a disquisition: but the insidious attempts, which are clandestinely and industriously made to pervert and destroy the new plan, induce me the more readily to engage in its defence: and the impressions of four months constant attendance to the subject, have not been so easily effaced, as to leave me without an answer to the objections which have been raised.

It will be proper, however, before I enter into the refutation of the charges that are alleged, to mark the leading discrimination between the state constitutions, and the constitution of the United States. When the people established the powers of legislation under their separate governments, they invested their representatives with every right and authority which they did not in explicit terms reserve: and therefore upon every question, respecting the jurisdiction of the house of assembly, if the frame of government is silent, the jurisdiction is efficient and complete. But in delegating fœderal powers, another criterion was necessarily introduced: and the congressional authority is to be collected, not from tacit implication, but from the positive grant, expressed in the instrument of the union. Hence, it is evident, that in the former case, everything which is not reserved, is given: but in the latter, the reverse of the proposition prevails, and everything which is not given, is reserved. This distinction being recognized, will furnish and answer to those who think the omission of a bill of rights, a defect in the proposed constitution: for it would have been superfluous and absurd, to have stipulated with a fœderal body of our own creation, that we should enjoy those privileges, of which we are not divested either by the intention of that act that has brought that body into existence. For instance, the liberty of the press, which has been a copious subject of declamation and opposition: what controul can proceed from the fœderal government, to shackle or destroy that sacred palladium of national freedom? If, indeed, a power similar to that which has been granted for the regulation of commerce, had been granted to regulate literary publications it would have been as necessary to stipulate that the liberty of the press should be preserved inviolate, as that the impost should be general in its operation. With respect, likewise, to the particular district of ten miles, which is to be the seat of government, it will undoubtedly be proper to observe this salutary precaution, as there the legislative power will be vested in the president, senate, and house of representatives of the United States. But this could not be an object with the convention: for it must naturally depend upon a future compact; to which the citizens immediately interested, will, and ought to be parties: and there is no reason to suspect, that so popular a privilege will in that case be neglected. In truth, then, the proposed system possesses no influence whatever upon the press; and it would have been merely nugatory, to have introduced a formal declaration upon the subject; nay, that very declaration might have been construed to imply that some degree of power was given, since we undertook to define its extent.

Another objection that has been fabricated against the new constitution, is expressed in this disingenuous form—"the trial by jury is abolished in civil cases." I must be excused, my fellow citizens, if, upon this point, I take advantage of my professional experience, to detect the futility of the assertion. Let it be remembered, then, that the business of the fœderal constitution was not local, but general—not limited to the views and establishments of a single state, but co-extensive with the continent, and comprehending the views and establishments of thirteen independent sovereignties. When, therefore, this subject was in discussion, we were involved in difficulties, which pressed on all sides, and no precedent could be discovered to direct our course. The cases open to a jury, differed in the different states; it was therefore impracticable, on that ground, to have made a general rule. The want of uniformity would have rendered any reference to the practice of the states idle and useless: and it could not, with any propriety, be said, that "the trial by jury shall be as heretofore:" since there has never existed any fœderal system of jurisprudence, to which the declaration could relate. Besides, it is not in all cases that the trial by jury is adopted in civil questions: for causes depending in courts of admiralty, such as relate to maritime captures, and such as are agitated in the courts of equity, do not require the intervention of that tribunal. How, then, was the line of discrimination to be drawn? The convention found the task too difficult for them: and they left the business as it stands—in the fullest confidence, that no danger could possibly ensue, since the proceedings of the supreme court are to be regulated by the congress, which is a faithful representation of the people: and the oppression of government is effectually barred, by declaring that in all criminal cases, the trial by jury shall be preserved.

* * * *

After all, my fellow-citizens, it is neither extraordinary nor unexpected, that the constitution offered to your consideration, should meet with opposition. It is the nature of man to pursue his own interest, in preference to the public good; and I do not mean to make any personal reflection, when I add, that it is the interest of a very numerous, powerful, and respectable body, to counteract and destroy the excellent work produced by the late convention. All the officers of government, and all the appointments for the administration of justice and the collection of the public revenue, which are transferred from the individual to the aggregate sovereignty of the states, will necessarily turn the stream of influence and emolument into a new channel. Every person, therefore, who either enjoys, or expects to enjoy a place of profit under the present establishment, will object to the proposed innovation? not, in truth, because it is injurious to the liberties of his country, but because it effects his schemes of wealth and consequence. I will confess, indeed, that I am not a blind admirer of this plan of government, and that there are some parts of it, which, if my wish had prevailed, would certainly have been altered. But, when I reflect how widely men differ in their opinions, and that every man (and the observation applies likewise to every state) has an equal pretension to assert his own, I am satisfied that anything nearer to perfection could not have been accomplished. If there are errors, it should be remembered, that the seeds of reformation are sown in the work itself, and the concurrence of two thirds of the congress may at any time introduce alterations and amendments. Regarding it, then, in every point of view, with a candid and disinterested mind, I am bold to assert, that it is the BEST FORM OF GOVERNMENT WHICH HAS EVER BEEN OFFERED TO THE WORLD.

FINIS.

[B] *Federalist* No. 84, 28 May 1788

In the course of the foregoing review of the Constitution, I have taken notice of, and endeavored to answer most of the objections which have appeared against it. There however remain a few which either did not fall naturally under any particular head or were forgotten in their proper places. These shall now be discussed; but as the subject has been drawn into great length, I shall so far consult brevity as to comprise all my observations on these miscellaneous points in a single paper.

The most considerable of these remaining objections is that the plan of the convention contains no bill of rights. Among other answers given to this, it has been upon different occasions remarked that the constitutions of several of the States are in a similar predicament. I add that New York is of this number. And yet the opposers of the new system, in this State, who profess an unlimited admiration for its constitution, are among the most intemperate partisans of a bill of rights. To justify their zeal in this matter they allege two things: one is that, though the constitution of New York has no bill or rights prefixed to it, yet it contains, in the body of it, various provisions in favor of particular privileges and rights which, in substance, amount to the same thing; the other is that the Constitution adopts, in their full extent, the common and statute law of Great Britain, by which many other rights not expressed in it are equally secured.

To the first I answer that the Constitution proposed by the convention contains, as well as the constitution of this State, a number of such provisions.

Independent of those which relate to the structure of the government, we find the following: Article 1, section 3, clause 7—"Judgment in cases of impeachment shall not extend further than to removal from office and disqualification to hold and enjoy any office of honor, trust, or profit under the United States; but the party convicted shall, nevertheless, be liable and subject to indictment, trial, judgment, and punishment according to law." Section 9, of the same article, clause 2–—"The privilege of the writ of *habeas corpus* shall not be suspended, unless when in cases of rebellion or invasion the public safety may require it." Clause 3—"No bill of attainder or *ex post facto* law shall be passed." Clause 7—"No title of nobility shall be granted by the United States; and no person holding any office of profit or trust under them shall, without the consent of the Congress, accept of any present, emolument, office, or title of any kind whatever, from any king, prince, or foreign state." Article 3, section 2, clause 3—"The trial of all crimes, except in cases of impeachment, shall be by jury; and such trial shall be held in the State where the said crimes shall have been committed; but when not committed within any State, the trial shall be at such place or places as the Congress may by law have directed." Section 3, of the same article—"Treason against the United States shall consist only in levying war against them, or in adhering to their enemies, giving them aid and comfort. No person shall be convicted of treason, unless on the testimony of two witnesses to the same overt act, or on confession in open court." And clause 3, of the same section—"The Congress shall have power to declare the punishment of treason; but no attainder of treason shall work corruption of blood, or forfeiture, except during the life of the person attainted."

It may well be a question whether these are not, upon the whole, of equal importance with any which are to be found in the constitution of this State. The establishment of the writ of *habeas corpus*, the prohibition of *ex post facto* laws, and of TITLES OF NOBILITY, *to which we have no corresponding provision in our Constitution*, are perhaps greater securities to liberty and republicanism than any it contains. The creation of crimes after the commission of the fact, or, in other words, the subjecting of men to punishment for things which, when they were done, were breaches of no law, and the practice of arbitrary imprisonments, have been, in all ages, the favorite and most formidable instruments of tyranny. The observations of the judicious Blackstone,* in reference to the latter, are well worthy of recital: "To bereave a man of life [says he] or by violence to confiscate his estate, without accusation or trial, would be so gross and notorious an act of

**Vide* Blackstone's *Commentaries,* Vol. 1, Page 136.

despotism as must at once convey the alarm of tyranny throughout the whole nation; but confinement of the person, by secretly hurrying him to jail, where his sufferings are unknown or forgotten, is a less public, a less striking, and therefore a *more dangerous engine* of arbitrary government." And as a remedy for this fatal evil he is everywhere peculiarly emphatical in his encomiums on the *habeas corpus* act, which in one place he calls "the BULWARK of the British Constitution."†

Nothing need be said to illustrate the importance of the prohibition of titles of nobility. This may truly be denominated the cornerstone of republican government; for so long as they are excluded there can never be serious danger that the government will be any other than that of the people.

To the second, that is, to the pretended establishment of the common and statute law by the Constitution, I answer that they are expressly made subject "to such alterations and provisions as the legislature shall from time to time make concerning the same." They are therefore at any moment liable to repeal by the ordinary legislative power, and of course have no constitutional sanction. The only use of the declaration was to recognize the ancient law and to remove doubts which might have been occasioned by the Revolution. This consequently can be considered as no part of a declaration of rights, which under our constitutions must be intended as limitations of the power of the government itself.

It has been several times truly remarked that bills of rights are, in their origin, stipulations between kings and their subjects, abridgments of prerogative in favor of privilege, reservations of rights not surrendered to the prince. Such was MAGNA CHARTA, obtained by the barons, sword in hand, from King John. Such were the subsequent confirmations of that charter by subsequent princes. Such was the *Petition of Rights* assented to by Charles the First in the beginning of his reign. Such, also, was the Declaration of Right presented by the Lords and Commons to the Prince of Orange in 1688, and afterwards thrown into the form of an act of Parliament called the Bill of Rights. It is evident, therefore, that, according to their primitive signification, they have no application to constitutions, professedly founded upon the power of the people and executed by their immediate representatives and servants. Here, in strictness, the people surrender nothing; and as they retain everything they have no need of particular reservations, "WE, THE PEOPLE of the United States, to secure the blessings of liberty to ourselves and our posterity, do *ordain* and *establish* this Constitution

†Idem, Vol. 4, page 438.

for the United States of America." Here is a better recognition of popular rights than volumes of those aphorisms which make the principal figure in several of our State bills of rights and which would sound much better in a treatise of ethics than in a constitution of government.

But a minute detail of particular rights is certainly far less applicable to a Constitution like that under consideration, which is merely intended to regulate the general political interests of the nation, than to a constitution which has the regulation of every species of personal and private concerns. If, therefore, the loud clamors against the plan of the convention, on this score, are well founded, no epithets of reprobation will be too strong for the constitution of this State. But the truth is that both of them contain all which, in relation to their objects, is reasonably to be desired.

I go further and affirm that bills of rights, in the sense and to the extent in which they are contended for, are not only unnecessary in the proposed Constitution but would even be dangerous. They would contain various exceptions to powers which are not granted; and, on this very account, would afford a colorable pretext to claim more than were granted. For why declare that things shall not be done which there is no power to do? Why, for instance, should it be said that the liberty of the press shall not be restrained, when no power is given by which restrictions may be imposed? I will not contend that such a provision would confer a regulating power; but it is evident that it would furnish, to men disposed to usurp, a plausible pretense for claiming that power. They might urge with a semblance of reason that the Constitution ought not to be charged with the absurdity of providing against the abuse of an authority which was not given, and that the provision against restraining the liberty of the press afforded a clear implication that a power to prescribe proper regulations concerning it was intended to be vested in the national government. This may serve as a specimen of the numerous handles which would be given to the doctrine of constructive powers, by the indulgence of an injudicious zeal for bills of rights.

On the subject of the liberty of the press, as much as has been said, I cannot forbear adding a remark or two: in the first place, I observe, that there is not a syllable concerning it in the constitution of this State; in the next, I contend that whatever has been said about it in that of any other State amounts to nothing. What signifies a declaration that "the liberty of the press shall be inviolably preserved"? What is the liberty of the press? Who can give it any definition which would not leave the utmost latitude for evasion? I hold it to be impracticable; and from this I infer that its security, whatever fine declarations may be inserted in any constitution respecting it, must altogether depend on public opinion, and on the general spirit of the people and of the government.* And here, after all, as is intimated upon another occasion, must we seek for the only solid basis of all our rights.

There remains but one other view of this matter to conclude the point. The truth is, after all the declamations we have heard, that the Constitution is itself, in every rational sense, and to every useful purpose, A BILL OF RIGHTS. The several bills of rights in Great Britain form its Constitution, and conversely the constitution of each State is its bill of rights. And the proposed Constitution, if adopted, will be the bill of rights of the Union. Is it one object of a bill of rights to declare and specify the political privileges of the citizens in the structure and administration of the government? This is done in the most ample and precise manner in the plan of the convention; comprehending various precautions for the public security which are not to be found in any of the State constitutions. Is another object of a bill of rights to define certain immunities and modes of proceeding, which are relative to personal and private concerns? This we have seen has also been attended to in a variety of cases in the same plan. Adverting therefore to the substantial meaning of a bill of rights, it is absurd to allege that it is not to be found in the work of the convention. It may be said that it does not go far enough though it will not be easy to make this appear; but it can with no propriety be contended that there is no such thing. It certainly must be immaterial what mode is observed

---

*To show that there is a power in the Constitution by which the liberty of the press may be affected, recourse has been had to the power of taxation. It is said that duties may be laid upon the publications so high as to amount to a prohibition. I know not by what logic it could be maintained that the declarations in the State constitutions, in favor of the freedom of the press, would be a constitutional impediment to the imposition of duties upon publications by the State legislatures. It cannot certainly be pretended that any degree of duties, however low, would be an abridgment of the liberty of the press. We know that newspapers are taxed in Great Britain, and yet it is notorious that the press nowhere enjoys greater liberty than in that country. And if duties of any kind may be laid without a violation of that liberty, it is evident that the extent must depend on legislative discretion, regulated by public opinion; so that, after all, general declarations respecting the liberty of the press will give it no greater security than it will have without them. The same invasions of it may be effected under the State constitutions which contain those declarations through the means of taxation, as under the proposed Constitution, which has nothing of the kind. It would be quite as significant to declare that government ought to be free, that taxes ought not to be excessive, etc., as that the liberty of the press ought not to be restrained.

as to the order of declaring the rights of the citizens if they are to be found in any part of the instrument which establishes the government. And hence it must be apparent that much of what has been said on this subject rests merely on verbal and nominal distinctions, entirely foreign from the substance of the thing.

XXXVII.

ANTIFEDERALIST CRITICISMS, FALL 1787

We have included three Antifederalist criticisms of the Constitution. On 13 September 1787, Mason wrote his objections on his copy of the Committee of Style Report. This original version, with an added footnote by Mason, can be found in Farrand (II: 637-640). See also Storing, *The Complete Anti-Federalist* (II: 9-14), W.B. Allen and Gordon Lloyd, editors *The Essential Antifederalist* (11-13), and Schwartz (III: 443-447). We rely on Ford *Pamphlets* (New York: Da Capo Press, 1968, 327-332). We have identified the ten objections by Arabic numerals placed in square parentheses. Secondly, we have reproduced a letter from Richard Henry Lee to Edmund Randolph containing a list of proposed amendments. Lee originally presented them in one continuous paragraph; to assist the reader, we have broken the paragraph down into fourteen thematic divisions. We have relied on the spelling and punctuation found in Allen and Lloyd (22-27). See Kaminski (VII, [1]: 59-67) for a complete account of Lee's amendment proposals. Our third entry is Brutus Essay II, published in the *New York Journal*. He wrote sixteen essays between October 1787 and April 1788. See also Storing (II: 372-377), and Kurland and Lerner (I: 452-453).

~

[A] Mason's Objections to the Constitution, September 1787

[1] There is no declaration of rights: and the laws of the general government being paramount to the laws and constitutions of the several states, the declarations of rights, in the separate states, are no security. Nor are the people secured even in the enjoyment of the benefit of the common law, which stands here upon no other foundation than its having been adopted by the respective acts forming the constitutions of the several states.

[2] In the House of Representatives there is not the substance, but the shadow only of representation; which can never produce proper information in the legislature, or inspire confidence in the people.—The laws will, therefore, be generally made by men little concerned in, and unacquainted with, their effects and consequences.

[3] The Senate have the power of altering all money-bills, and of originating appropriations of money, and the salaries of the officers of their own appointment, in conjunction with the President of the United States—Although they are not the representatives of the people, or amenable to them. These, with their other great powers, (viz. their powers in the appointment of ambassadors, and all public officers, in making treaties, and in trying all impeachments) their influence upon, and connection with, the supreme executive from these causes, their duration of office, and their being a constant existing body, almost continually sitting, joined with their being one complete branch of the legislature, will destroy any balance in the government, and enable them to accomplish what usurpations they please upon the rights and liberties of the people.

[4] The judiciary of the United States is so constructed and extended, as to absorb and destroy the judiciaries of the several states; thereby rendering laws as tedious, intricate, and expensive, and justice as unattainable by a great part of the community, as in England; and enabling the rich to oppress and ruin the poor.

[5] The President of the United States has no constitutional council (a thing unknown in any safe and regular government.) he will therefore be unsupported by proper information and advice; and will generally be directed by minions and favorites—or he will become a tool to the Senate—or a council of state will grow out of the principal officers of the great departments—the worst and most dangerous of all ingredients for such a council, in a free country; for they may be induced to join in any dangerous or oppressive measures, to shelter themselves, and prevent an inquiry into their own misconduct in office. Whereas, had a constitutional council been formed (as was proposed) of six members, viz., two from the eastern, two from the middle, and two from the southern states, to be appointed by vote of the states in the House of Representatives, with the same duration and rotation of office as the Senate, the executive would always have had safe and proper information and advice; the president of such a council might have acted as Vice-President of the United States, *pro tempore,* upon any vacancy or disability of the chief magistrate, and long continued sessions of the Senate, would in a great measure have been prevented. From this fatal defect of a constitutional council, has arisen the improper power of the Senate, in the appointment of the public officers, and the alarming dependence and connexion between that branch of the legislature and the supreme executive. Hence, also, sprung that unnecessary officer, the Vice-President, who, for want of other employment, is made President of the Senate, thereby dangerously blending the executive and

legislative powers; besides always giving to some one of the states an unnecessary and unjust pre-eminence over the others.

[6] The President of the United States has the unrestrained power of granting pardon for treason; which may be sometimes exercised to screen from punishment those whom he had secretly instigated to commit the crime, and thereby prevent a discovery of his own guilt. By declaring all treaties supreme laws of the land, the executive and the Senate have, in many cases, an exclusive power of legislation, which might have been avoided, by proper distinctions with respect to treaties, and requiring the assent of the House of Representatives, where it could be done with safety.

[7] By requiring only a majority to make all commercial and navigation laws, the five southern states (whose produce and circumstances are totally different from those of the eight northern and eastern States) will be ruined: for such rigid and premature regulations may be made, as will enable the merchants of the northern and eastern states not only to demand an exorbitant freight, but to monopolize the purchase of the commodities, at their own price, for many years, to the great injury of the landed interest, and the impoverishment of the people: and the danger is the greater, as the gain on one side will be in proportion to the loss on the other. Whereas, requiring two-thirds of the members present in both houses, would have produced mutual moderation, promoted the general interest, and removed an insuperable objection to the adoption of the government.

[8] Under their own construction of the general clause at the end of the enumerated powers, the Congress may grant monopolies in trade and commerce, constitute new crimes, inflict unusual and severe punishments, and extend their power as far as they shall think proper; so that the state legislatures have no security for the powers now presumed to remain to them, or the people for their rights. There is no declaration of any kind for preserving the liberty of the press, the trial by jury in civil cases, nor against the danger of standing armies in time of peace.

[9] The state legislatures are restrained from laying export duties on their own produce—the general legislature is restrained from prohibiting the further importation of slaves for twenty odd years, though such importations render the United States weaker, more vulnerable, and less capable of defence. Both the general legislature, and the state legislatures are expressly prohibited making *ex post facto* laws, though there never was, nor can be, a legislature but must and will make such laws, when necessity and the public safety require them, which will hereafter be a breach of all the constitutions in the union, and afford precedents for other innovations.

[10] This government will commence in a moderate aristocracy; it is at present impossible to foresee whether it will, in its operation, produce a monarchy, or a corrupt oppressive aristocracy; it will most probably vibrate some years between the two, and then terminate in the one or the other.

[B] Lee's Amendment Proposals, 16 October 1787

It having been found from universal experience, that the most expressed declarations and reservations are necessary to protect the just rights and liberty of mankind from the silent powerful and ever active conspiracy of those who govern; and it appearing to be the sense of the good people of America, by the various bills or declarations of rights whereon the government of the greater number of states are founded: that such precautions are necessary to restrain and regulate the exercise of the great powers given to the rulers. In conformity with these principles, and from respect for the public sentiment on this subject, it is submitted, that the new constitution proposed for the government of the United States be bottomed upon a declaration or bill of rights, clearly and precisely stating the principles upon which this social compact is founded, to wit: (1) that the rights of conscience in matters of religion ought not to be violated, (2) that the freedom of the press shall be secured, (3) that the trial by jury in criminal and civil cases, and the modes prescribed by the common law for the safety of life in criminal prosecutions shall be held sacred, (4) that standing armies in times of peace are dangerous to liberty, and ought not to be permitted unless assented to by two-thirds of the members composing each house of the legislature under the new constitution, (5) that the elections should be free and frequent, (6) that the right administration of justice should be secured by the independence of the judges, (7) that excessive bail, excessive fines, or cruel and unusual punishments should not be demanded or inflicted, (8) that the right of the people to assemble peaceably for the purpose of petitioning the legislature shall not be prevented, (9) that the citizens shall not be exposed to unreasonable searches, seizure of their persons, houses, papers or property; (10) and it is necessary for the good of society, that the administration of government be conducted with all possible maturity of judgment, for which reason it has been the practice of civilized nations and so determined by every state in the Union, that a council of state or privy council should be appointed to advise and assist in the arduous business assigned to the executive power. Therefore let the new constitution be so amended as to admit the appointment of a privy council to consist of eleven members chosen by the president, but responsible for the advice they may give. For which purpose the advice given shall be entered in a council book, and signed by the giver in all affairs of great moment, and that the counselors act under an oath of office. In order to prevent the dangerous blending of the legislative and executive powers, and to secure responsibility, the privy, and not the senate, shall be joined with the president in the appointment of all officers civil and military under the new constitution, that the constitution be so altered as not to admit the creation of a vice president, when duties as assigned may be discharged by the privy council, except in the instance of proceedings in the senate, which may be supplied by a speaker chosen from the body of senators by themselves as usual, that so may be avoided the establishment of a great officer of state, who is sometimes to be joined with the legislature, and sometimes administer the government, rendering responsibility difficult, besides giving unjust and needless pre-eminence to that state from whence this officer may have come, [11] that such parts of the new constitution be amended as provide imperfectly for the trial of criminals by a jury of the vicinage, and so supply the omission of a jury trial in civil causes or disputes about property between individuals, whereby the common law is directed, and as generally it is secured by the several state constitutions. (12) That such parts of the new constitution be amended as permit the vexatious and oppressive callings of citizens from their own country, and all controversies between citizens of different states and between citizens and foreigners, to be tried in a far distant court, and as it may be without a jury, whereby in a multitude of cases, the circumstances of distance and expense, may compel numbers to submit to the most unjust and ill founded demand. (13) That in order to secure the rights of the people more effectually from violation, the power and respectability of the house of representatives be increased, by increasing the number of delegates to that house where the popular interest must chiefly depend for protection, (14) that the constitution be so amended as to increase the number of votes necessary to determine questions in cases where a bare majority may be seduced by strong motives of interest to injure and oppress the minority of the community as in commercial regulations, where advantage may be taken of circumstances to ordain rigid and premature laws that will in effect amount to monopolies, to the great impoverishment of those states whose peculiar situation expose them to such injuries.

[C] Brutus II, 1 November 1787

When a building is to be erected which is intended to stand for ages, the foundation should be firmly laid. The constitution proposed to your acceptance, is designed not for yourselves alone, but for generations yet unborn. The principles, therefore, upon which the social compact is founded, ought to have been clearly and precisely stated, and the most express and full declaration of rights to have been made—But on this subject there is almost an entire silence.

If we may collect the sentiments of the people of America, from their own most solemn declarations, they hold this truth as self evident, that all men are by nature free. No one man, therefore, or any class of men, have a right, by the law of nature, or of God, to assume or exercise authority over their fellows. The origin of society then is to be sought, not in any natural right which one man has to exercise authority over another, but in the united consent of those who associate. The mutual wants of men, at first dictated the propriety of forming societies; and when they were established, protection and defence pointed out the necessity of instituting government. In a state of nature every individual pursues his own interest; in this pursuit it frequently happened, that the possessions or enjoyments of one were sacrificed to the views and designs of another; thus the weak were a prey to the strong, the simple and unwary were subject to impositions from those who were more crafty and designing. In this state of things, every individual was insecure; common interest therefore directed, that government should be established, in which the force of the whole community should be collected, and under such directions, as to protect and defend every one who composed it. The common good, therefore, is the end of civil government, and common consent, the foundation on which it is established. To effect this end, it was necessary that a certain portion of natural liberty should be surrendered, in order, that what remained should be preserved: how great a proportion of natural freedom is necessary to be yielded by individuals, when they submit to government, I shall not now enquire. So much, however, must be given up, as will be sufficient to enable those, to whom the administration of the government is committed, to establish laws for the promoting the happiness of the community, and to carry those laws into effect. But it is not necessary, for this purpose, that individuals should relinquish all their natural rights. Some are of such a nature that they cannot be surrendered. Of this kind are the rights of conscience, the right of enjoying and defending life, etc. Others are not necessary to be resigned, in order to attain the end for which government is instituted, these therefore ought not to be given up. To surrender them, would counteract the very end of government, to wit, the common good. From these observations it appears, that in forming a government on its true principles, the foundation should be laid in the manner I before stated, by expressly reserving to the people such of their essential natural rights, as are not necessary to be parted with. The same reasons which at first induced mankind to associate and institute government, will operate to influence them to observe this precaution. If they had been disposed to conform themselves to the rule of immutable righteousness, government would not have been requisite. It was because one part exercised fraud, oppression, and violence on the other, that men came together, and agreed that certain rules should be formed, to regulate the conduct of all, and the power of the whole community lodged in the hands of rulers to enforce an obedience to them. But rulers have the same propensities as other men; they are as likely to use the power with which they are vested for private purposes, and to the injury and oppression of those over whom they are placed, as individuals in a state of nature are to injure and oppress one another. It is therefore as proper that bounds should be set to their authority, as that government should have at first been instituted to restrain private injuries.

This principle, which seems so evidently founded in the reason and nature of things, is confirmed by universal experience. Those who have governed, have been found in all ages ever active to enlarge their powers and abridge the public liberty. This has induced the people in all countries, where any sense of freedom remained, to fix barriers against the encroachments of their rulers. The country from which we have derived our origin, is an eminent example of this. Their magna charta and bill of rights have long been the boast, as well as the security, of that nation. I need say no more, I presume, to an American, than, that this principle is a fundamental one, in all the constitutions of our own states; there is not one of them but what is either founded on a declaration or bill of rights, or has certain express reservation of rights interwoven in the body of them. From this it appears, that at a time when the pulse of liberty beat high and when an appeal was made to the people to form constitutions for the government of themselves, it was their universal sense, that such declarations should make a part of their frames of government. It is therefore the more astonishing, that this grand security, to the rights of the people, is not to be found in this constitution.

It has been said, in answer to this objection, that such declaration of rights, however requisite they might be in the constitutions of the states, are not necessary in the general constitution, because, "in the former case, every thing which is not reserved is given, but in the latter the reverse of the proposition prevails, and every thing which is not given is reserved."[1] It requires but little attention to discover, that this mode of reasoning is rather specious than solid. The powers, rights, and authority, granted to the general government by this constitution,

[1]Brutus quotes from James Wilson's State House Speech.

are as complete, with respect to every object to which they extend, as that of any state government—It reaches to every thing which concerns human happiness—Life, liberty, and property, are under its controul. There is the same reason, therefore, that the exercise of power, in this case, should be restrained within proper limits, as in that of the state governments. To set this matter in a clear light, permit me to instance some of the articles of the bills of rights of the individuals states, and apply them to the case in question.

For the security of life, in criminal prosecutions, the bills of rights of most of the states have declared, that no man shall be held to answer for a crime until he is made fully acquainted with the charge brought against him; he shall not be compelled to accuse, or furnish evidence against himself—The witnesses against him shall be brought face to face, and he shall be fully heard by himself or counsel. That it is essential to the security of life and liberty, that trial of facts be in the vicinity where they happen. Are not provisions of this kind as necessary in the general government, as in that of a particular state? The powers vested in the new Congress extend in many cases to life; they are authorised to provide for the punishment of a variety of capital crimes, and no restraint is laid upon them in its exercise, save only, that "the trial of all crimes, except in cases of impeachment, shall be by jury; and such trial shall be in the state where the said crimes shall have been committed." No man is secure of a trial in the county where he is charged to have committed a crime; he may be brought from Niagara to New-York, or carried from Kentucky to Richmond for trial for an offence, supposed to be committed. What security is there, that a man shall be furnished with a full and plain description of the charges against him? That he shall be allowed to produce all proof he can in his favor? That he shall see the witnesses against him face to face, or that he shall be fully heard in his own defence by himself or counsel?

For the security of liberty it has been declared, "that excessive bail should not be required, nor excessive fines imposed, nor cruel or unusual punishments inflicted—That all warrants, without oath or affirmation to search suspected places, or seize any person, his papers or property, are grievous and oppressive."[2]

These provisions are as necessary under the general government as under that of the individual states; for the power of the former is as complete to the purpose of requiring bail, imposing fines, inflicting punishments, granting search warrants, and seizing persons, papers, or property, in certain cases, as the other.

---

[2]See Virginia, Pennsylvania, and Massachusetts.

For the purpose of securing the property of the citizens, it is declared by all the states, "that in all controversies at law, respecting property, the ancient mode of trial by jury is one of the best securities of the rights of the people, and ought to remain sacred and inviolable."

Does not the same necessity exist of reserving this right, under this national compact, as in that of these states? Yet nothing is said respecting it. In the bills of rights of the states it is declared, that a well regulated militia is the proper and natural defence of a free government—That as standing armies in time of peace are dangerous, they are not to be kept up, and that the military should be kept under strict subordination to, and controuled by the civil power.

The same security is as necessary in this constitution, and much more so; for the general government will have the sole power to raise and to pay armies, and are under no controul in the exercise of it; yet nothing of this is to be found in this new system.

I might proceed to instance a number of other rights, which were as necessary to be reserved, such as, that elections should be free, that the liberty of the press should be held sacred; but the instances adduced, are sufficient to prove, that this argument is without foundation.—Besides, it is evident, that the reason here assigned was not the true one, why the framers of this constitution omitted a bill of rights; if it had been, they would not have made certain reservations, while they totally omitted others of more importance. We find they have, in the 9th section of the lst article, declared, that the writ of habeas corpus shall not be suspended, unless in cases of rebellion—that no bill of attainder, or expost facto law, shall be passed—that no title of nobility shall be granted by the United States, &c. If every thing which is not given is reserved, what propriety is there in these exceptions? Does this constitution any where grant the power of suspending the habeas corpus, to make expost facto laws, pass bills of attainder, or grant titles of nobility? It certainly does not in express terms. The only answer that can be given is, that these are implied in the general powers granted. With equal truth it may be said, that all the powers, which the bills of right, guard against the abuse of, are contained or implied in the general ones granted by this constitution.

So far it is from being true, that a bill of rights is less necessary in the general constitution than in those of the states, the contrary is evidently the fact.—This system, if it is possible for the people of America to accede to it, will be an original compact, and being the last, will, in the nature of things vacate every former agreement inconsistent with it. For it being a plan of government received and ratified by the whole people, all other forms, which are in existence at the time of its adoption, must yield to it. This is expressed in positive and unequivocal terms, in the 6th article, "That this constitution and the laws of the United States, which shall be made in pursuance thereof, and all treaties made, or which shall be made, under the authority of the United States, shall be the supreme law of the land; and the judges in every state shall be bound thereby, any thing in the *constitution*, or laws of any state, *to the contrary* notwithstanding.

"The senators and representatives before mentioned, and the members of the several state legislatures, and all executive and judicial officers both of the United States, and of the several states shall be bound, by oath or affirmation, to support this constitution."

It is therefore not only necessarily implied thereby, but positively expressed, that the different state constitutions are repealed and entirely done away, so far as they are inconsistent with this, with the laws which shall be made in pursuance thereof, or with treaties made, or which shall be made, under the authority of the United States; of what avail will the constitutions of the respective states be to preserve the rights of its citizens? should they be plead, the answer would be, the constitution of the United States, and the laws made in pursuance thereof, is the supreme law, and all legislatures and judicial officers, whether of the general or state governments are bound by oath to support it. No priviledge, reserved by the bills of rights, or secured by the state government, can limit the power granted by this, or restrain any laws made in pursuance of it. It stands therefore on its own bottom, and must receive a construction by itself without any reference to any other—And hence it was of the highest importance, that the most precise and express declarations and reservations of rights should have been made.

This will appear the more necessary, when it is considered, that not only the constitution and laws made in pursuance thereof, but all treaties made, or which shall be made, under the authority of the United States, are the supreme law of the land, and supersede the constitutions of all the states. The power to make treaties, is vested in the president, by and with the advice and consent of two thirds of the senate. I do not find any limitation, or restriction, to the exercise of this power. The most important article in any constitution may therefore be repealed, even without a legislative act. Ought not a government, vested with such extensive and indefinite authority, to have been restricted by a declaration of rights? It certainly ought.

So clear a point is this, that I cannot help suspecting, that persons who attempt to persuade people, that such reservations were less necessary under this constitution than under those of the states, are wilfully endeavouring to deceive, and to lead you into an absolute state of vassalage.

XXXVIII.

PENNSYLVANIA RATIFYING CONVENTION, OCTOBER-DECEMBER 1787

We have reproduced three entries that capture the debate which took place in Pennsylvania over the exclusion of a bill of rights from the proposed Constitution. First, the excerpts from James Wilson's speeches represent the Federalist position that a bill of rights is "unnecessary" and "imprudent." See Elliot's *Debates* (II: 434-437, 453-454). See also Kurland and Lerner (I: 453-454). Second, we have included selections from two Antifederalists--John Smilie and Robert Whitehill--who argued against Wilson's position. Their comments are not included in Elliot's *Debates*. See John B. McMaster and Frederick Stone, editors, *Pennsylvania and the Federal Constitution: 1787-1788* (Lancaster, PA: The Historical Society of Pennsylvania, 1888), for the Antifederalist arguments (249-251, 254-256, and 261). See also Kurland and Lerner (I: 455-456). The third entry is from the "Pennsylvania Minority Report" signed by the twenty-three delegates who voted against the adoption of the Constitution. The report first appeared in the 18 December 1787 issue of the *Pennsylvania Packet and Daily Advertiser.* See Chapter VI in McMaster and Stone for the complete report. We have relied on Allen and Lloyd (53-70).

~

[A] The Remarks of James Wilson, 28 October, 4 December 1787

This will be a proper time for making an observation or two on what may be called the preamble to this Constitution. I had occasion, on a former day, to mention that the leading principle in the politics, and that which pervades the American constitutions, is, that the supreme power resides in the people. This Constitution, Mr. President, opens with a solemn and practical recognition of that principle:—"We, *the people of the United States,* in order to form a more perfect union, establish justice, &c., *do* ordain and establish this Constitution for the United States of America." It is announced in *their* name—it receives its political existence from *their* authority: they ordain and establish. What is the necessary consequence? Those who ordain and establish have the power, if they think proper, to repeal and annul. A proper attention to this principle may, perhaps, give ease to the minds of some who have heard much concerning the necessity of a bill of rights.

Its establishment, I apprehend, has more force than a volume written on the subject. It renders this truth evident—that the people have a right to do what they please with regard to the government. I confess I feel a kind of pride in considering the striking difference between the foundation on which the liberties of this country are declared to stand in this Constitution, and the footing on which the liberties of England are said to be placed. The Magna Charta of England is an instrument of high value to the people of that country. But, Mr. President, from what source does that instrument derive the liberties of the inhabitants of that kingdom? Let it speak for itself. The king says, "*We* have *given* and *granted* to all archbishops, bishops, abbots, priors, earls, barons, and to all the freemen of this our realm, these liberties following, to be kept in our kingdom of England forever." When this was assumed as the leading principle of that government, it was no wonder that the people were anxious to obtain bills of rights, and to take every opportunity of enlarging and securing their liberties. But here, sir, the fee-simple remains in the people at large, and by this Constitution they do not part with it.

I am called upon to give a reason why the Convention omitted to add a bill of rights to the work before you. I confess, sir, I did think that, in point of propriety, the honorable gentleman ought first to have furnished some reasons to show such an addition to be necessary; it is natural to prove the affirmative of a proposition; and, if he had established the propriety of this addition, he might then have asked why it was not made.

I cannot say, Mr. President, what were the reasons of every member of that convention for not adding a bill of rights. I believe the truth is, that such an idea never entered the mind of many of them. I do not recollect to have heard the subject mentioned till within about three days of the time of our rising; and even then, there was no direct motion offered for any thing of the kind. I may be mistaken in this; but as far as my memory serves me, I believe it was the case. A proposition to adopt a measure that would have supposed that we were throwing into the general government every power not expressly reserved by the people, would have been spurned at, in that house, with the greatest indignation. Even in a single government, if the powers of the people rest on the same establishment as is expressed in this Constitution, a bill of rights is by no means a necessary measure. In a government possessed of enumerated powers, such a measure would be not only unnecessary, but preposterous and dangerous. Whence comes this notion, that in the United States there is no security without a bill of rights? Have the citizens of South Carolina not security for their liberties? They have no bill of rights. Are the citizens on the eastern side of the Delaware less free, or less secured in their liberties, than those on the western side? The state of New Jersey has no bill of rights. The state of New York has no bill of rights. The states of Connecticut and Rhode Island have no bill of rights. I know not whether I have exactly enumerated the states who have not thought it necessary to add *a bill of rights* to their constitutions; but this enumeration, sir, will serve to show by experience, as well as principle, that even in single governments, a bill of rights is not an essential or necessary measure. But in a government consisting of enumerated powers such as is proposed for the United States, a bill of rights would not only be unnecessary, but in my humble judgment, highly imprudent. In all societies, there are many powers and rights which cannot be particularly enumerated. A bill of rights annexed to a constitution is *an enumeration of the powers* reserved. If we attempt an enumeration, every thing that is not enumerated is presumed to be given. The consequence is, that an imperfect enumeration would throw all implied power into the scale of the government, and the rights of the people would be rendered incomplete. On the other hand, an imperfect enumeration of the powers of government reserves all implied power to the people; and by that means the constitution becomes incomplete. But of the two, it is much safer to run the risk on the side of the constitution; for an omission in the enumeration of the powers of government is neither so dangerous nor important as an omission in the enumeration of the rights of the people.

* * * *

A good deal has already been said concerning a *bill of rights*. I have stated, according to the best of my recollection, all that passed in Convention relating to that business. Since that time, I have spoken with a gentleman, who has not only his memory, but full notes that he had taken in that body, and he assures me that, upon this subject, no direct motion was ever made at all; and certainly, before we heard this so violently supported out of doors, some pains ought to have been taken to have tried its fate within; but the truth is, a bill of rights would, as I have mentioned already, have been not only unnecessary, but improper. In some governments, it may come within the gentleman's idea, when he says it can do no harm; but even in these governments, you find bills of rights do not uniformly obtain; and do those states complain who have them not? Is it a maxim in forming governments, that not only all the powers which are given, but also that all those which are reserved, should be enumerated? I apprehend that the powers given and reserved form the whole rights of the people, as men and as citizens. I consider that there are very few who understand the whole of these rights. All the political writers, from *Grotius* and *Puffendorf* down to *Vattel*, have treated on this subject; but in no one of those books, nor in the aggregate of them all, can you find a complete enumeration of rights appertaining to the people as men and as citizens.

There are two kinds of government—that where general power is intended to be given to the legislature, and that where the powers are particularly enumerated. In the last case, the implied result is, that nothing more is intended to be given than what is so enumerated, unless it results from the nature the government itself. On the other hand, when general legislative powers are given, then the people part with their authority, and, on the gentleman's principle of government, retain nothing. But in a government like the proposed one, there can be no necessity for a bill of rights, for, on my principle, the people never part with their power. Enumerate all the rights of men! I am sure, sir, that no gentleman in the late Convention would have attempted such a thing. I believe the honorable speakers in opposition of this floor were members of the assembly which appointed delegates to that Convention; if it had been thought proper to have sent them into that body, how luminous would the dark conclave have been!—so the gentleman has been pleased to denominate that body. Aristocrats as they were, they pretended not to define the rights of those who sent them there We ask, repeatedly, What harm could the addition of a bill of rights do? If it can do no good, I think that a sufficient reason to refuse having any thing to do with it. But to whom are we to report this bill of rights, if we should adopt it? Have we authority from those who sent us here to make one?

[B] The Remarks of John Smilie and Robert Whitehill, 28 November 1787

Mr. Smilie. I expected, Mr. President, that the honorable gentleman would have proceeded to a full and explicit investigation of the proposed system, and that he would have made some attempts to prove that it was calculated to promote the happiness, power and general interest of the United States. I am sorry that I have been mistaken in this expectation, for surely the gentleman's talents and opportunities would have enabled him to furnish considerable information upon this important subject; but I shall proceed to make a few remarks upon those words in the preamble of this plan, which he has considered of so super-excellent a quality. Compare them, Sir, with the language used in forming the state constitution, and however superior they may be to the terms of the great charter of England; still, in common candor, they must yield to the more sterling expressions employed in this act. Let these speak for themselves:

"That all men are born equally free and independent, and have certain natural, inherent and unalienable rights, among which are the enjoying and defending life and liberty, acquiring possessing and protecting property, and pursuing and obtaining happiness and safety.

"That the people of this state have the sole, exclusive and inherent right of governing and regulating the internal police of the same.

"That all power being originally inherent in, and consequently derived from the people; therefore all officers of government, whether legislative or executive, are their trustees and servants, and at all times accountable to them

"That government is, or ought to be, instituted for the common benefit, protection and security of the people, nation or community; and not for the particular emolument or advantage of any single man, family, or set of men, who are a part only of that community. And that the community hath an indubitable, unalienable, and indefeazible right to reform, alter or abolish government in such manner as shall be by that community judged most conducive to the public weal."

But the gentleman takes pride in the superiority of this short preamble when compared with Magna Charta—why, sir, I hope the rights of men are better understood at this day than at the framing of that deed, and we must be convinced that civil liberty is capable of still greater improvement and extension, than is known even in its present cultivated state. True, sir, the supreme authority naturally rests in the people, but does it follow, that therefore a declaration of right would be superfluous? Because the people have a right to alter and abolish government, can it therefore be inferred that every step taken to secure that right would be superfluous and nugatory? The truth is, that unless some criterion is established by which it could be easily and constitutionally ascertained how far our governors may proceed, and by which it might appear when they transgress their jurisdiction, this idea of altering and abolishing government is a mere sound without substance. Let us recur to the memorable declaration of the 4th of July, 1776. Here it is said:

"When in the course of human events, it becomes necessary for one people to dissolve the political bands which have connected them with another, and to assume among the powers of the earth the separate and equal station to which the laws[3] of nature's God entitle them, a decent respect to the opinions of mankind requires that they should declare the causes which impel them to the separation.

"We hold these truths to be self-evident; that all men are created equal; that they are endowed by their Creator with certain unalienable rights; that among these are life, liberty, and the pursuit of happiness. That to secure these rights, governments are instituted among men,

---

[3]Kurland and Lerner (I: 455) insert [of nature and] in the text.

deriving their just powers from the consent of the governed; that when any form of government becomes destructive of these ends, it is the right of the people to alter or to abolish it, and to institute a new government, laying its foundation on such principles, and organizing its powers in such form, as to them shall seem most likely to effect their safety and happiness."

Now, Sir, if in the proposed plan, the gentleman can show any similar security for the civil rights of the people, I shall certainly be relieved from a weight of objection to its adoption, and I sincerely hope, that as he has gone so far, he will proceed to communicate some of the reasons (and undoubtedly they must have been powerful ones) which induced the late federal convention to omit a bill of rights, so essential in the opinion of many citizens to a perfect form of government.

* * * *

The arguments which have been urged, Mr. President, have not, in my opinion, satisfactorily shown that a bill of rights would have been an improper, nay, that it is not a necessary appendage to the proposed system. As it has been denied that Virginia possesses a bill of rights, I shall on that subject only observe that Mr. Mason, a gentleman certainly of great information and integrity has assured me that such a thing does exist, and I am persuaded I shall be able at a future period to lay it before the convention. But, Sir, the state of Delaware has a bill of rights and I believe one of the honorable members (Mr. M'Kean) who now contests the necessity and propriety of that instrument, took a very conspicuous part in the formation of the Delaware government. It seems, however that the members of the federal convention were themselves convinced, in some degree, of the expediency and propriety of a bill of rights, for we find them expressly declaring that the writ of habeas corpus and the trial by jury in criminal cases shall not be suspended or infringed. How does this indeed agree with the maxim that whatever is not given is reserved? Does it not rather appear from the reservation of these two articles that everything else, which is not specified, is included in the powers delegated to the government? This, Sir, must prove the necessity of a full and explicit declaration of rights; and when we further consider the extensive, and undefined powers vested in the administrators of this system, when we consider the system itself as a great political compact between the governors and the governed, a plain, strong, and accurate criterion by which the people might at once determine when, and in what instance their rights were violated, is a preliminary, without which, this plan ought not to be adopted. So loosely, so inaccurately are the powers which are enumerated in this constitution defined, that it will be impossible, without a test of that kind, to ascertain the limits of authority, and to declare when government has degenerated into oppression. In that event the contest will arise between the people and the rulers: "You have exceeded the powers of your office, you have oppressed us," will be the language of the suffering citizen. The answer of the government will be short—"We have not exceeded our power; you have no test by which you can prove it." Hence, Sir, it will be impracticable to stop the progress of tyranny, for there will be no check but the people and their exertions must be futile and uncertain; since it will be difficult, indeed, to communicate to them the violation that has been committed, and their proceedings will be neither systematical nor unanimous. It is said, however, that the difficulty of framing a bill of rights was insurmountable; but, Mr. President, I cannot agree in this opinion. Our experience, and the numerous precedents before us, would have furnished a very sufficient guide. At present there is no security even for the rights of conscience, and under the sweeping force of the sixth article, every principle of a bill of rights, every stipulation for the most sacred and invaluable privileges of man, are left at the mercy of government.

Mr. Whitehill. I differ, Sir, from the honorable member from the city, as to the impropriety or necessity of a bill of rights. If, indeed, the constitution itself so well defined the powers of the government that no mistake could arise, and we were well assured that our governors would always act right, then we might be satisfied without an explicit reservation of those rights with which the people ought not, and mean not to part. But, Sir, we know that it is the nature of power to seek its own augmentation, and thus the loss of liberty is the necessary consequence of a loose or extravagant delegation of authority. National freedom has been, and will be the sacrifice of ambition and power, and it is our duty to employ the present opportunity in stipulating such restrictions as are best calculated to protect us from oppression and slavery. Let us then, Mr. President, if other countries cannot supply an adequate example, let us proceed upon our own principles, and with the great end of government in view, the happiness of the people, it will be strange if we err. Government, we have been told, Sir, is yet in its infancy: we ought not therefore to submit to the shackles of foreign schools and opinions. In entering into the social compact, men ought not to leave their rulers at large, but erect a permanent landmark by which they may learn the extent of their authority, and the people be able to discover the first encroachments on their liberties.

* * * *

A bill of rights, Mr. President, it has been said, would not only be unnecessary, but it would be dangerous, and for this special reason, that because it is not practicable to enumerate all the rights of the people, therefore it would be hazardous to secure such of the rights as we can enumerate! Truly, Sir, I will agree that a bill of rights may be a dangerous instrument, but it is to the views and projects of the aspiring ruler, and not the liberties of the citizen. Grant but this explicit criterion, and our governors will not venture to encroach; refuse it, and the people cannot venture to complain. From the formal language of magna charta we are next taught to consider a declaration of rights as superfluous; but, Sir, will the situation and conduct of Great Britain furnish a case parallel to that of America? It surely will not be contended that we are about to receive our liberties as a grant or concession from any power upon earth; so that if we learn anything from the English charter, it is this: that the people having negligently lost or submissively resigned their rights into the hands of the crown, they were glad to recover them upon any terms; their anxiety to secure the grant by the strongest evidence will be an argument to prove, at least, the expediency of the measure, and the result of the whole is a lesson instructing us to do by an easy precaution, what will hereafter be an arduous and perhaps insurmountable task.

[C] Dissent of the Minority, 18 December 1787

The convention met, and the same disposition was soon manifested in considering the proposed constitution that had been exhibited in every other stage of business. We were prohibited by an express vote of the convention from taking any question on the separate articles of the plan, and reduced to the necessity of adopting or rejecting *in toto*. It is true the majority permitted us to debate on each article, but restrained us from proposing amendments. They also determined not to permit us to enter on the minutes our reasons of dissent against any of the articles, nor even on the final question our reasons of dissent against the whole. Thus situated we entered on the examination of the proposed system of government, and found it to be such as we could not adopt without, as we conceived, surrendering up your dearest rights. We offered our objections to the convention, and opposed those parts of the plan, which, in our opinion, would be injurious to you, in the best manner we were able; and close our arguments by offering the following propositions to the convention.

1. The right of conscience shall be held inviolable, and neither the legislative, executive nor judicial powers of the United States shall have authority to alter, abrogate, or infringe any part of the constitution of

the several states which provide for the preservation of liberty in matters of religion.

2. That in controversies respecting property, and in suits between man and man, trial by jury shall remain as heretofore, as well in the federal courts, as in those of the several states.

3. That in all capital and criminal prosecutions, a man has a right to demand the cause and nature of his accusation, as well in the federal courts, as in those of the several states; to be heard by himself and his counsel; to be confronted with the accusers and witnesses; to call for evidence in his favor, and a speedy trial by an impartial jury of his vicinage, without whose unanimous consent, he cannot be found guilty, nor can he be compelled to give evidence against himself; and that no man be deprived of his liberty, except by the law of the land or the judgment of his peers.

4. That excessive bail ought not to be required nor excessive fines imposed, nor cruel nor unusual punishments inflicted.

5. That warrants unsupported by evidence, whereby any officer or messenger may be commanded or required to search suspected places, or to seize any person or persons, his or their property, not particularly described, are grievous and oppressive, and shall not be granted either by the magistrates of the federal government or others.

6. That the people have a right to the freedom of speech, of writing and publishing their sentiments. Therefore, the freedom of the press shall not be restrained by any law of the United States.

7. That the people have a right to bear arms for the defense of themselves and their own state, or the United States, or for the purpose of killing game; and no law shall be passed for disarming the people or any of them, unless for crimes committed, or real danger of public injury from individuals; and as standing armies in the time of peace are dangerous to liberty, they ought not to be kept up; and that the military shall be kept under strict subordination to and be governed by the civil powers.

8. The inhabitants of the several states shall have liberty to fowl and hunt in seasonable time, on the lands they hold, and on all other lands in the United States not enclosed, and in like manner to fish in all navigable waters, and others not private property, without being restrained therein by any laws to be passed by the legislature of the United States.

9. That no law shall be passed to restrain the legislatures of the several states from enacting laws for imposing taxes, except imposts and duties on goods imported or exported, and that no taxes, except imposts and duties upon goods imported and exported, and postage on letters shall be levied by the authority of Congress.

10. That the house of representatives be properly increased in number; that elections shall remain free; that the several states shall have power to regulate the elections for senators and representatives, without being controlled either directly or indirectly by any interference on the part of the Congress; and that elections of representatives be annual.

11. That the power of organizing arming, and disciplining the militia (the manner of disciplining the militia to be prescribed by Congress) remain with the individual states, and that Congress shall not have authority to call or march any of the militia out of their own state, without the consent of such state, and for such length of time only as such state shall agree.

That the sovereignty, freedom and independency of the several states shall be retained, and every power, jurisdiction and right which is not by this constitution expressly delegated to the United States in Congress assembled.

12. That the legislative, executive, and judicial powers be kept separate; and to this end that a constitutional council be appointed, to advise and assist the president, who shall be responsible for the advice they give, thereby the senators would be relieved from almost constant attendance; and also that the judges be made completely independent.

13. That no treaty which shall be directly opposed to the existing laws of the United States in Congress assembled, shall be valid until such laws shall be repealed, or made conformable to such treaty; neither shall any treaties be valid which are in contradiction to the constitution of the United States, or the constitutions of the several states.

14. That the judiciary power of the United States shall be confined to cases affecting ambassadors, other public ministers and consuls; to cases of admiralty and maritime jurisdiction; to controversies to which the United States shall be a party; to controversies between two or more states; between a state and citizens of different states; between citizens claiming lands under grants of different states; and between a state or the citizen thereof and foreign states, and in criminal cases, to such only as are expressly enumerated in the constitution, and that the United States in Congress assembled, shall not have power to enact laws, which shall alter the laws of descent and distribution of the effects of deceased persons, the titles of lands or goods, or the regulation of contracts in the individual states.

XXXIX.

NEW ENGLAND AND VIRGINIA RATIFYING CONVENTIONS, JANUARY-JUNE 1788

The deadlock in Massachusetts was finally broken by a compromise. In exchange for "ratification now," the Federalists promised that they would introduce "amendments later." The debates of the Massachussetts Ratification Convention between January 9, 1788 and February 6, 1788 can be found in Elliot's *Debates* (II: 1-183). Reproduced below are the nine proposed amendments. See Elliot's *Debates* (II: 176-178), on whom we rely, Kurland and Lerner (I: 461-462), and Schwartz (III:. 712-714).

The New Hampshire Ratifying Convention proposed twelve amendments; the first nine were virtually identical to those proposed by the Massachusetts Ratifying Convention. Consequently, we have reproduced only the last three proposals and the closing injunction. We have followed the version in Tansill (1026). See also Schwartz (IV: 760-761).

The evenly divided Virginia Ratifying Convention met from 2 June to 27 June 1788. The Antifederalists, led by Patrick Henry and George Mason, attempted to make ratification conditional upon prior adoption of amendments. James Madison and Edmund Randolph, however, secured ratification along the lines of the Massachusetts Compromise. We have reproduced the twenty amendment proposals from the Wythe Committee to alter the structure and powers of the new government along with the separate, and prior, proposal that the Constitution be amended to include a declaration of twenty essential rights. We have followed Elliot (III: 657-661). Also see Kurland and Lerner (I: 472-474), and Schwartz (IV: 840-845).

~

[A] Massachusetts Ratifying Convention Proposed Amendments, 6 February 1788

COMMONWEALTH OF MASSACHUSETTS.
In Convention of the Delegates of the People of the Commonwealth of Massachusetts, 1788.

The Convention, having impartially discussed and fully considered the Constitution for the United States of America, reported to Congress by the Convention of delegates from the United States of America, and submitted to us by a resolution of the General Court of the said commonwealth, passed the twenty-fifth day of October last past; and acknowledging, with grateful hearts, the goodness of the Supreme Ruler of the universe in affording the people of the United States, in the course of his providence, an opportunity, deliberately and peaceably, without fraud or surprise, of entering into an explicit and solemn compact with each other, by assenting to and ratifying a new Constitution, in order to form a more perfect union, establish justice, insure domestic tranquillity, provide for the common defence, promote the general welfare, and secure the blessing of liberty to themselves and their posterity, DO, in the name and in behalf of the people of the commonwealth of Massachusetts, assent to and ratify the said Constitution for the United States of America.

And, as it is the opinion of this Convention, that certain amendments and alterations in the said Constitution would remove the fears and quiet the apprehensions of many of the good people of the commonwealth, and more effectually guard against an undue administration of the federal government, the Convention do therefore recommend that the following alterations and provisions be introduced into the said Constitution:—

First. That it be explicitly declared, that all powers not expressly delegated by the aforesaid Constitution are reserved to the several states, to be by them exercised.

Secondly. That there shall be one representative to every thirty thousand persons, according to the census mentioned in the Constitution, until the whole number of representatives amounts to two hundred.

Thirdly. That Congress do not exercise the powers vested in them by the 4th section of the 1st article, but in cases where a state shall neglect or refuse to make the regulations therein mentioned, or shall make regulations subversive of the rights of the people to a free and equal representation in Congress, agreeably to the Constitution.

Fourthly. That Congress do not lay direct taxes, but when the moneys arising from the impost and excise are insufficient for the public exigencies, nor then, until Congress shall have first made a requisition upon the states, to assess, levy, and pay their respective proportion of such requisitions, agreeably to the census fixed in the said Constitution, in such way and manner as the legislatures of the states shall think best, and, in such case, if any state shall neglect or refuse to pay its proportion, pursuant to such requisition, then Congress may assess and levy such state's proportion, together with interest thereon, at the rate of six per cent. per annum, from the time of payment prescribed in such requisition.

Fifthly. That Congress erect no company with exclusive advantages of commerce.

Sixthly. That no person shall be tried for any crime, by which he may incur an infamous punishment, or loss of life, until he be first indicted by a grand jury, except in such cases as may arise in the government and regulation of the land and naval forces.

Seventhly. The Supreme Judicial Federal Court shall have no jurisdiction of causes between citizens of different states, unless the matter in dispute, whether it concern the realty or personalty, be of the value of three thousand dollars at the least; nor shall the federal judicial powers extend to any action between citizens of different states, where the matter in dispute, whether it concern the realty or personalty, is not of the value of fifteen hundred dollars at the least.

Eighthly. In civil actions between citizens of different states, every issue of fact, arising in actions at common law, shall be tried by a jury, if the parties, or either of them, request it.

Ninthly. Congress shall at no time consent that any person holding an office of trust or profit, under the United States, shall accept of a title of nobility, or any other tide or office, from any king, prince, or foreign state.

And the Convention do, in the name and in the behalf of the people of this commonwealth, enjoin it upon their representatives in Congress, at all times, until the alterations and provisions aforesaid have been considered, agreeably to the 5th article of the said Constitution, to exert all their influence, and use all reasonable and legal methods, to obtain a ratification of the said alterations and provisions, in such manner as is provided in the said article.

And, that the United States, in Congress assembled, may have due notice of the assent and ratification of the said Constitution by this convention, it is

Resolved, That the assent and ratification aforesaid be engrossed on parchment, together with the recommendation and injunction aforesaid, and with this resolution; and that his excellency, JOHN HANCOCK, President, and the Hon. WILLIAM CUSHING, Esq., Vice-President of this Convention, transmit the same, countersigned by the Secretary of the Convention, under their hands and seals, to the United States in Congress assembled.

[B] New Hampshire Ratifying Convention Proposed Amendments, 21 June 1788

Tenth,

That no standing Army shall be Kept up in time of Peace unless with the consent of three fourths of the Members of each branch of

Congress, nor shall Soldiers in Time of Peace be quartered upon private Houses without the consent of the Owners.——

Eleventh

Congress shall make no Laws touching Religion, or to infringe the rights of Conscience——

Twelfth

Congress shall never disarm any Citizen unless such as are or have been in Actual Rebellion.——

And the Convention Do. In the Name & behalf of the People of this State enjoin it upon their Representatives in Congress, at all Times untill the alterations and provisions aforesaid have been Considered agreeably to the fifth Article of the said Constitution to exert all their Influence & use all reasonable & Legal methods to obtain a ratification of the said alterations & Provisions, in such manner as is provided in the said article——And That the United States in Congress Assembled may have due notice of the assent & Ratification of the said Constitution by this Convention.——It is resolved that the Assent & Ratification aforesaid be engrossed on Parchment, together with the Recommendation & injunction aforesaid & with this Resolution——And that John Sullivan Esquire President of Convention, & John Langdon Esquire President of the State Transmit the same Countersigned by the Secretary of Convention & the Secretary of the State under their hands & Seals to the United States in Congress Assembled.——

[C] Virginia Ratifying Convention, 27 June 1788

MR. WYTHE reported, from the committee appointed, such *amendments* to the proposed Constitution of government for the United States as were by them deemed necessary to be recommended to the consideration of the Congress which shall first assemble under the said Constitution, to be acted upon according to the mode prescribed in the 5th article thereof; and he read the same in his place, and afterwards delivered them in at the clerk's table, where the same were again read, and are as follows:—

"That there be a declaration or bill of rights asserting, and securing from encroachment, the essential and unalienable rights of the people, in some such manner as the following:—

"1st. That there are certain natural rights, of which men, when they form a social compact, cannot deprive or divest their posterity; among which are the enjoyment of life and liberty, with the means of acquiring, possessing, and protecting property, and pursuing and obtaining happiness and safety.

"2d. That all power is naturally invested in, and consequently derived from, the people; that magistrates therefore are their *trustees* and *agents*, at all times amenable to them.

"3d. That government ought to be instituted for the common benefit, protection, and security of the people; and that the doctrine of non-resistance against arbitrary power and oppression is absurd, slavish, and destructive to the good and happiness of mankind.

"4th. That no man or set of men are entitled to separate or exclusive public emoluments or privileges from the community, but in consideration of public services, which not being descendible, neither ought the offices of magistrate, legislator, or judge, or any other public office, to be hereditary.

"5th. That the legislative, executive, and judicial powers of government should be separate and distinct; and, that the members of the two first may be restrained from oppression by feeling and participating the public burdens, they should, at fixed periods, be reduced to a private station, return into the mass of the people, and the vacancies be supplied by certain and regular elections, in which all or any part of the former members to be eligible or ineligible, as the rules of the Constitution of government, and the laws, shall direct.

"6th. That the elections of representatives in the legislature ought to be free and frequent, and all men having sufficient evidence of permanent common interest with, and attachment to, the community, ought to have the rights of suffrage; and no aid, charge, tax, or fee, can be set, rated, or levied, upon the people without their own consent, or that of their representatives, so elected; nor can they be bound by any law to which they have not, in like manner, assented, for the public good.

"7th. That all power of suspending laws, or the execution of laws, by any authority, without the consent of the representatives of the people in the legislature, is injurious to their rights, and ought not to be exercised.

"8th. That, in all criminal and capital prosecutions, a man hath a right to demand the cause and nature of his accusation, to be confronted with the accusers and witnesses, to call for evidence, and be allowed counsel in his favor, and to a fair and speedy trial by an impartial jury of his vicinage, without whose unanimous consent he cannot be found guilty, (except in the government of the land and naval forces;) nor can he be compelled to give evidence against himself.

"9th. That no freeman ought to be taken, imprisoned, or disseized of his freehold, liberties, privileges, or franchises, or outlawed, or exiled, or in any manner destroyed, or deprived of his life, liberty, or property, but by the law of the land.

"10th. That every freeman restrained of his liberty is entitled to a remedy, to inquire into the lawfulness thereof, and to remove the same, if unlawful, and that such remedy ought not to be denied not delayed.

"11th. That, in controversies respecting property, and in suits between man and man, the ancient trial by jury is one of the greatest securities to the rights of the people, and to remain sacred and inviolable.

"12th. That every freeman ought to find a certain remedy, by recourse to the laws, for all injuries and wrongs he may receive in his person, property, or character. He ought to obtain right and justice freely, without sale, completely and without denial, promptly and without delay, and that all establishments or regulations contravening these rights are oppressive and unjust.

"13th. That excessive bail ought not to be required, nor excessive fines imposed, nor cruel and unusual punishments inflicted.

"14th. That every freeman has a right to be secure from all unreasonable searches and seizures of his person, his papers, and property; all warrants, therefore, to search suspected places, or seize any freeman, his papers, or property, without information on oath (or affirmation of a person religiously scrupulous of taking an oath) of legal and sufficient cause, are grievous and oppressive; and all general warrants to search suspected places, or to apprehend any suspected person, without specially naming or describing the place or person, are dangerous, and ought not to be granted.

"15th. That the people have a right peaceably to assemble together to consult for the common good, or to instruct their representatives; and that every freeman has a right to petition or apply to the legislature for redress of grievances.

"16th. That the people have a right to freedom of speech, and of writing and publishing their sentiments; that the freedom of the press is one of the greatest bulwarks of liberty, and ought not to be violated.

"17th. That the people have a right to keep and bear arms; that a well-regulated militia, composed of the body of the people trained to arms, is the proper, natural, and safe defence of a free state; that standing armies, in time of peace, are dangerous to liberty, and therefore ought to be avoided, as far as the circumstances and protection of the community will admit; and that, in all cases, the military should be under strict subordination to, and governed by, the civil power.

"18th. That no soldier in time of peace ought to be quartered in any house without the consent of the owner, and in time of war in such manner only as the law directs.

"19th. That any person religiously scrupulous of bearing arms ought to be exempted, upon payment of an equivalent to employ another to bear arms in his stead.

"20th. That religion, or the duty which we owe to our Creator, and the manner of discharging it, can be directed only by reason and conviction, not by force or violence; and therefore all men have an equal, natural, and unalienable right to the free exercise of religion, according to the dictates of conscience, and that no particular religious sect or society ought to be favored or established, by law, in preference to others."

AMENDMENTS TO THE CONSTITUTION.

"1st. That each state in the Union shall respectively retain every power, jurisdiction, and right, which is not by this Constitution delegated to the Congress of the United States, or to the departments of the federal government.

"2d. That there shall be one representative for every thirty thousand according to the enumeration or census mentioned in the Constitution until the whole number of representatives amounts to two hundred; after which, that number shall be continued or increased, as Congress shall direct, upon the principles fixed in the Constitution, by apportioning the representatives of each state to some greater number of people, from time to time, as population increases.

"3d. When the Congress shall lay direct taxes or excises, they shall immediately inform the executive power of each state, of the quota of such state, according to the census herein directed, which is proposed to be thereby raised; and if the legislature of any state shall pass a law which shall be effectual for raising such quota at the time required by Congress, the taxes and excises laid by Congress shall not be collected in such state.

"4th. That the members of the Senate and House of Representatives shall be ineligible to, and incapable of holding, any civil office under the authority of the United States, during the time for which they shall respectively be elected.

"5th. That the journals of the proceedings of the Senate and House of Representatives shall be published at least once in every year, except such parts thereof, relating to treaties, alliances, or military operations, as, in their judgment, require secrecy.

"6th. That a regular statement and account of the receipts and the expenditures of public money shall be published at least once a year.

"7th. That no commercial treaty shall be ratified without the concurrence of two thirds of the whole number of the members of the

Senate; and no treaty ceding, contracting, restraining, or suspending, the territorial rights or claims of the United States, or any of them, or their, or any of their rights or claims to fishing in the American seas, or navigating the American rivers, shall be made, but in cases of the most urgent and extreme necessity; nor shall any such treaty be ratified without the concurrence of three fourths of the whole number of the members of both houses respectively.

"8th. That no navigation law, or law regulating commerce, shall be passed without the consent of two thirds of the members present, in both houses.

"9th. That no standing army, or regular troops, shall be raised, or kept up, in time of peace, without the consent of two thirds of the members present, in both houses.

"10th. That no soldier shall be enlisted for any longer term than four years, except in time or war, and then for no longer term than the continuance of the war.

"11th. That each state respectively shall have the power to provide for organizing, arming, and disciplining its own militia, whensoever Congress shall omit or neglect to provide for the same. That the militia shall not be subject to martial law, except when in actual service, in time of war, invasion, or rebellion; and when not in the actual service of the United States, shall be subject only to such fines, penalties, and punishments, as shall be directed or inflicted by the laws of its own state.

"12th. That the exclusive power of legislation given to Congress over the federal town and its adjacent district, and other places, purchased or to be purchased by Congress of any of the states, shall extend only to such regulations as respect the police and good government thereof.

"13th. That no person shall be capable of being President of the United States for more than eight years in any term of sixteen years.

"14th. That the judicial power of the United States shall be vested in one Supreme Court, and in such courts of admiralty as Congress may from time to time ordain and establish in any of the different states. The judicial power shall extend to all cases in law and equity arising under treaties made, or which shall be made, under the authority of the United States; to all cases affecting ambassadors, other foreign ministers, and consuls; to all cases of admiralty and maritime jurisdiction; to controversies to which the Untied States shall be a party; to controversies between two or more states, and between parties claiming lands under the grants of different states. In all cases affecting ambassadors, other foreign ministers, and consuls, and those in which a state shall be a party, the Supreme Court shall have original jurisdiction; in all other cases before mentioned, the Supreme Court shall have appellate jurisdiction, as to matters of law only, except in cases of equity, and of admiralty, and maritime jurisdiction, in which the Supreme Court shall have appellate jurisdiction both as to law and fact, with such exceptions and under such regulations as the Congress shall make. [B]ut the judicial power of the United States shall extend to no case where the cause of action shall have originated before the ratification of the Constitution, except in disputes between states about their territory, disputes between person claiming lands under the grants of different states, and suits for debts due to the United States.

"15th. That, in criminal prosecutions, no man shall be restrained in the exercise of the usual and accustomed right of challenging or excepting to the jury.

"16th. That Congress shall not alter, modify, or interfere in the times, places, or manner of holding elections for senators and representatives, or either of them, except when the legislature of any state shall neglect, refuse, or be disabled, by invasion or rebellion, to prescribe the same.

"17th. That those clauses which declare that Congress shall not exercise certain powers, be not interpreted, in any manner whatsoever, to extend the powers of Congress; but that they be construed either as making exceptions to the specified powers where this shall be the case, or otherwise, as inserted merely for greater caution.

"18th. That the laws ascertaining the compensation of senators and representatives for their services, be postponed, in their operation, until after the election of representatives immediately succeeding the passing thereof; that excepted which shall first be passed on the subject.

"19th. That some tribunal other than the Senate be provided for trying impeachments of senators.

"20th. That the salary of a judge shall not be increased or diminished during his continuance in office, otherwise than by general regulations of salary, which may take place on a revision of the subject at the stated periods of not less than seven years, to commence from the time such salaries shall be first ascertained by Congress."

XL.

JEFFERSON-MADISON CORRESPONDENCE I, OCTOBER 1787-JULY 1788

James Madison's two letters to Thomas Jefferson, are from *Letters of James Madison* (I: 376-378 and 404-406). See also Schwartz (IV: 724-726, 850-851), and Kurland and Lerner (I: 644-647). For Jefferson's two letters to Madison, we have relied on Jefferson's *Writings* (II: 329-328, 445-447). See also Schwartz (III: 605-608), Kurland and Lerner (I: 456-457, 476-478), and Koch, *Selected Writings* (436-441, 450-452). Banning's *Jefferson and Madison* (132-149) contains an edited version of three of the letters.

~

[A] Jefferson to Madison

PARIS, December 20, 1787.

I will now tell you what I do not like. First, the omission of a bill of rights, providing clearly, and without the aid of sophism, for freedom of religion, freedom of the press, protection against standing armies, restriction of monopolies, the eternal and unremitting force of the habeas corpus laws, and trials by jury in all matters of fact triable by the laws of the land, and not by the law of nations. To say, as Mr. Wilson does, that a bill of rights was not necessary, because all is reserved, in the case of the general government which is not given, while in the particular ones, all is given which is not reserved might do for the audience to which it was addressed; but is surely a *gratis dictum*, the reverse of which might just as well be said; and it is opposed by strong inferences from the body of the instrument, as well as from the omission of the clause of our present Confederation which had made the reservation in express terms. It was hard to conclude, because there has been a want of uniformity among the States as to the cases triable by jury, because some have been so incautious as to abandon this mode of trial in certain cases, therefore, the more prudent States shall be reduced to the same level of calamity. It would have been much more just and wise to have concluded the other way, that as most of the States had preserved with jealousy this sacred palladium of liberty,[4] those who had wandered, should be brought back to it; and to have established general right instead of general wrong. For I consider all the ill as established, which may be established. I have a right to nothing, which another has a right to take away; and Congress will have a right to take away trials by jury in all civil cases.[5] Let me add, that a bill of rights is what the people are entitled to against every government on earth, general or particular; and what no just government should refuse, or rest on inference.

---

[4]Kurland and Lerner (I: 457) have the following: "most of the States had judiciously preserved this palladium."

[5]Kurland and Lerner omit this sentence from the text.

[B] Madison to Jefferson

ORANGE, April 22d, 1788.

The proposed Constitution still engrosses the public attention. The elections for the Convention here are but just over and promulged. From the returns, (excepting those from Kentucky, which are not yet known,) it seems probable, though not absolutely certain, that a majority of the members elect are friends to the Constitution. The superiority of abilities, at least seems to lie on that side. The characters of most note which occur to me are marshaled thus: For the Constitution, Pendleton, Wythe, Blair, Innes, Marshall, Doctor W. Jones, G. Nicholas, Wilson Nicholas, Gabl Jones, Thomas Lewis, F. Corbin, Ralph Wormley Jr., White of Frederick, General Gates, General A. Stephens, Archibald Stuart, Zachy Johnson, Doctor Stuart, Parson Andrews, H. Lee, Jr., Bushrod Washington, considered as a young gentleman of talents; against the Constitution, Mr. Henry, Mason, Harrison, Grayson, Tyler, M. Smith, W. Ronald, Lawson, Bland, Wm. Cabell, Dawson.

The Governor is so temperate in his opposition, and goes so far with the friends of the Constitution, that he cannot properly be classed with its enemies. Monroe is considered by some as an enemy; but I believe him to be a friend.[6] There are other individuals of weight whose opinions are unknown to me. R. H. Lee is not elected. His brother, F. L. Lee, is a warm friend to the Constitution, as I am told; but, also, is not elected. So are John and Mann Page.

The adversaries take very different grounds of opposition. Some are opposed to the substance of the plan; others, to particular modifications only. Mr. Henry is supposed to aim at disunion. Col. Mason is growing every day more bitter and outrageous in his efforts to carry his point, and will probably, in the end, be thrown by the violence of his passions into the politics of Mr. Henry. The preliminary question will be, whether previous alterations shall be insisted on or not. Should this be carried in the affirmative, either a conditional ratification or a proposal for a new Convention will ensue. In either event, I think the Constitution and the Union will be both endangered. It is not to be expected that the States which have ratified will reconsider their determinations, and submit to the alterations prescribed by Virginia. And if a second Convention should be formed, it is as little to be expected that the same spirit of compromise will prevail in it as produced an amicable result to the first. It will be easy, also, for those who have latent views of disunion, to carry them on

---

[6]Schwartz (IV: 847) adds "though a cool one."

under the mask of contending for alterations, popular in some, but inadmissible in other parts of the United States.

[C] Madison to Jefferson

NEW YORK, 24th July, 1788.

I returned here about ten days ago from Richmond, which I left a day or two after the dissolution of the Convention. The final question on the new Government was put on the 25th of June. It was two-fold: 1. Whether previous amendments should be made a condition of ratification. 2. Directly on the Constitution, in the form it bore. On the first, the decision was in the negative, 88 being no, 80 only ay. On the second and definitive question, the ratification was affirmed by 89 ayes aganst 79 noes. A number of alterations were then recommended to be considered in the mode pointed out in the Constitution itself. The meeting was remarkably full; two members only being absent and those known to be on the opposite sides of the question. The debates, also, were conducted on the whole with a very laudable moderation and decorum, and continued until both sides declared themselves ready for the question. And it may be safely concluded that no irregular opposition to the System will follow in that State, at least with the countenance of the leaders on that side. What local eruptions may be occasioned by ill-timed or rigorous executions of the Treaty of peace against British debtors, I will not pretend to say. But although the leaders, particularly Henry and Mason, will give no countenance to popular violences, it is not to be inferred that they are reconciled to the event, or will give it a positive support. On the contrary, both of them declared they could not go that length, and an attempt was made under their auspices to induce the minority to sign an address to the people, which, if it had not been defeated by the general moderation of the party, would probably have done mischief.

Among a variety of expedients employed by the opponents to gain proselytes, Mr. Henry first, and after him Col^{o}. Mason, introduced the opinions expressed in a letter from a correspondent, (Mr. Donald or Skipwith, I believe,) and endeavored to turn the influence of your name even against parts of which I knew you approved. In this situation, I thought it due to truth, as well as that it would be most agreeable to yourself, and accordingly took the liberty to state some of your opinions on the favorable side. I am informed that copies or extracts of a letter from you were handed about at the Maryland Convention, with a like view of impeding the ratification.

New Hampshire ratified the Constitution on the 20th ult., and made the ninth State. The votes stood 57 for, and 46 against the measure. South Carolina had previously ratified by a very great majority. The

Convention of North Carolina is now sitting. At one moment, the sense of that State was considered as strongly opposed to the system. It is now said that the time has been for some time turning, which, with the example of other States, and particularly of Virginia, prognosticates a ratification there also. The Convention of New York has been in Session ever since the 17th ultimo, without having yet arrived at any final vote. Two-thirds of the members assembled with a determination to reject the Constitution, and are still opposed to it in their hearts. The local situation of New York, the number of ratifying States, and the hope of retaining the federal Government in this City, afford, however, powerful arguments to such men as Jay, Hamilton, the Chancellor, Duane and several others; and it is not improbable that some form of ratification will yet be devised, by which the dislike of the opposition may be gratified, and the State, notwithstanding, made a member of the new Union.

[D] Jefferson to Madison

PARIS, July 31, 1788.

I sincerely rejoice at the acceptance of our new constitution by nine States. It is a good canvas, on which some strokes only want retouching. What these are, I think are sufficiently manifested by the general voice from north to south, which calls for a bill of rights. It seems pretty generally understood, that this should go to juries, habeas corpus, standing armies, printing, religion and monopolies. I conceive there may be difficulty in finding general modifications of these, suited to the habits of all the States. But if such cannot be found, then it is better to establish trials by jury, the right of habeas corpus, freedom of the press and freedom of religion, in all cases, and to abolish standing armies in time of peace, and monopolies in all cases, than not to do it in any. The few cases wherein these things may do evil, cannot be weighed against the multitude wherein the want of them will do evil. In disputes between a foreigner and a native, a trial by jury may be improper. But if this exception cannot be agreed to, the remedy will be to model the jury by giving the *mediatas linguae*, in civil as well as criminal cases. Why suspend the habeas corpus in insurrections and rebellions? The parties who may be arrested, may be charged instantly with a well defined crime; of course, the judge will remand them. If the public safety requires that the government should have a man imprisoned on less probable testimony, in those than in other emergencies, let him be taken and tried, retaken and retried, while the necessity continues, only giving him redress against the government, for damages. Examine the history of England. See how few of the cases of the suspension of the habeas corpus law, have been worthy of that suspension. They have been either real treasons wherein the parties might as well have been charged at once, or sham plots, where it was shameful they should ever have been suspected. Yet for the few cases wherein the suspension of the habeas corpus has done real good, that operation is now become habitual, and the minds of the nation almost prepared to live under its constant suspension. A declaration, that the federal government will never restrain the presses from printing any thing they please, will not take away the liability of the printers for false facts printed. The declaration, that religious faith shall be unpunished, does not give impunity to criminal acts, dictated by religious error. The saying there shall be no monopolies, lessens the incitements to ingenuity, which is spurred on by the hope of a monopoly for a limited time, as of fourteen years; but the benefit even of limited monopolies is too doubtful, to be opposed to that of their general suppression. If no check can be found to keep the number of standing troops within safe bounds, while they are tolerated as far as necessary, abandon them altogether, discipline well the militia, and guard the magazines with them. More than magazine guards will be useless, if few, and dangerous, if many. No European nation can ever send against us such a regular army as we need fear, and it is hard if our militia are not equal to those of Canada or Florida. My idea then, is, that though proper exceptions to these general rules are desirable and probably practicable, yet if the exceptions cannot be agreed on, the establishment of the rules, in all cases, will do ill in very few. I hope, therefore, a bill of rights will be formed to guard the people against the federal government, as they are already guarded against their State governments, in most instances.

XLI.

JEFFERSON-MADISON CORRESPONDENCE II, OCTOBER 1788-MARCH 1789

The two letters from James Madison to Thomas Jefferson are from *Letters* (I: 423-427 and 441-443). See also Schwartz (V: 992-994), Kurland and Lerner (I: 447-448), and Banning, *Jefferson and Madison* (150-153). The letter from Jefferson to Madison can be found in Jefferson *Writings* (III: 3-5). See also Kurland and Lerner (I: 479), Koch, *Selected Writings* (462-464), and Banning (156-158).

~

[A] Madison to Jefferson

NEW YORK, October 17th, 1788.

The little pamphlet herewith inclosed will give you a collective view of the alterations which have been proposed by the State Conventions for the new Constitution. Various and numerous as they appear, they certainly omit many of the true grounds of opposition. The articles relating to Treaties, to paper money, and to contracts, created more enemies than all the errors in the system, positive and negative, put together.

It is true, nevertheless, that not a few, particularly in Virginia, have contended for the proposed alterations from the most honorable and patriotic motives; and that among the advocates for the Constitution there are some who wish for further guards to public liberty and individual rights. As far as these may consist of a constitutional declaration of the most essential rights, it is probable they will be added; though there are many who think such addition unnecessary, and not a few who think it misplaced in such a Constitution. There is scarce any point on which the party in opposition is so much divided as to its importance and its propriety. My own opinion has always been in favor of a bill of rights, provided it be so framed as not to imply powers not meant to be included in the enumeration. At the same time, I have never thought the omission a material defect, nor been anxious to supply it even by *subsequent* amendment, for any other reason than that it is anxiously desired by others. I have favored it because I supposed it might be of use, and if properly executed, could not be of disservice.

I have not viewed it in an important light—1. Because I conceive that in a certain degree, though not in the extent argued by Mr. Wilson, the rights in question are reserved by the manner in which the federal powers are granted. 2. Because there is great reason to fear that a the most essential rights could not be obtained in the requisite latitude. I am sure that the rights of conscience in particular, if submitted to public definition, would be narrowed much more than they are likely ever to be by an assumed power. One of the objections in New England was, that the Constitution, by prohibiting religious tests, opened a door for Jews, Turks, and infidels. 3. Because the limited powers of the federal Government, and the jealousy of the subordinate Governments, afford a security which has not existed in the case of the State Governments, and exists in no other. 4. Because experience proves the inefficacy of a bill of rights on those occasions when its controul is most needed. Repeated violations of these parchment barriers have been committed by overbearing majorities in every State.

In Virginia, I have seen the bill of rights violated in every instance where it has been opposed to a popular current. Notwithstanding the explicit provision contained in that instrument for the rights of conscience, it is well known that a religious establishment would have taken place in that State, if the Legislative majority had found, as they expected, a majority of the people in favor of the measure; and I am persuaded that if a majority of the people were now of one sect, the measure would still take place, and on narrower ground than was then proposed, notwithstanding the additional obstacle which the law[7] has since created.

Wherever the real power in a Government lies, there is the danger of oppression. In our Governments the real power lies in the majority of the community, and the invasion of private rights is *chiefly* to be apprehended, not from acts of Government contrary to the sense of its constituents, but from acts in which the Government is the mere instrument of the major number of the Constituents. This is a truth of great importance, but not yet sufficiently attended to; and is probably more strongly impressed on my mind by facts and reflections suggested by them than on yours, which has contemplated abuses of power issuing from a very different quarter. Wherever there is an interest and power to do wrong, wrong will generally be done, and not less readily by a powerful and interested party than by a powerful and interested prince. The difference, so far as it relates to the superiority of republics over monarchies, lies in the less degree of probability that interest may prompt abuses of power in the former than in the latter; and in the security in the former against oppression of more than the smaller part of the Society, whereas, in the latter, it may be extended in a manner to the whole.

The difference, so far as it relates to the point in question—the efficacy of a bill of rights in controuling abuses of power—lies in this: that in a monarchy the latent force of the nation is superior to that of the Sovereign, and a solemn charter of popular rights must have a great effect as a standard for trying the validity of public acts, and a signal for rousing and uniting the superior force of the community; whereas, in a popular Government, the political and physical power may be considered as vested in the same hands, that is, in a majority of the people, and, consequently, the tyrannical will of the Sovereign is not to be controuled by the dread of an appeal to any other force within the community.

What use, then, it may be asked, can a bill of rights serve in popular Governments? I answer, the two following, which, though less

---

[7] The bill of Religious freedom.

essential than in other Governments, sufficiently recommend the precaution: 1. The political truths declared in that solemn manner acquire by degrees the character of fundamental maxims of free Government, and as they become incorporated with the National sentiment, counteract the impulses of interest and passion. 2. Although it be generally true, as above stated, that the danger of oppression lies in the interested majorities of the people rather than in usurped acts of the Government, yet there may be occasions on which the evil may spring from the latter source; and on such, a bill of rights will be a good ground for an appeal to the sense of the community. Perhaps, too, there may be a certain degree of danger, that a succession of artful and ambitious rulers may, by gradual and well-timed advances, finally erect an independent Government on the subversion of liberty. Should this danger exist at all, it is prudent to guard against it, especially when the precaution can do no injury.

At the same time, I must own that I see no tendency in our Governments to danger on that side. It has been remarked that there is a tendency in *all* Governments to an augmentation of power at the expence of liberty. But the remark, as usually understood, does not appear to me well founded. Power, when it has attained a certain degree of energy and independence, goes on generally to further degrees. But when below that degree, the direct tendency is to further degrees of relaxation, until the abuses of liberty beget a sudden transition to an undue degree of power. With this explanation the remark may be true; and in the latter sense only is it, in my opinion, applicable to the Governments in America. It is a melancholy reflection that liberty should be equally exposed to danger whether the Government have too much or too little power, and that the line which divides these extremes should be so inaccurately defined by experience.

Supposing a bill of rights to be proper, the articles which ought to compose it admit of much discussion. I am inclined to think that *absolute* restrictions in cases that are doubtful, or where emergencies may overrule them, ought to be avoided. The restrictions, however strongly marked on paper, will never be regarded when opposed to the decided sense of the public; and after repeated violations, in extraordinary cases will lose even their ordinary efficacy. Should a Rebellion or insurrection alarm the people as well as the Government, and a suspension of the Habeus Corpus be dictated by the alarm, no written prohibitions on earth would prevent the measure. Should an army in time of peace be gradually established in our neighborhood by Britain or Spain, declarations on paper would have as little effect in preventing a standing force for the public safety. The best security against these evils is to remove the pretext for them.

With regard to monopolies, they are justly classed among the greatest nuisances in Government. But is it clear that, as encouragements to literary works and ingenious discoveries, they are not too valuable to be wholly renounced? Would it not suffice to reserve in all cases a right to the public to abolish the privilege, at a price to be specified in the grant of it? Is there not, also, infinitely less danger of this abuse in our Governments than in most others? Monopolies are sacrifices of the many to the few. Where the power is in the few, it is natural for them to sacrifice the many to their own partialities and corruptions. Where the power, as with us, is in the many, not in the few, the danger can not be very great that the few will be thus favored. It is much more to be dreaded that the few will be unnecessarily sacrificed to the many.

[B] Madison to Jefferson

PHILADELPHIA, DEC[r] 8, 1788.

Notwithstanding the formidable opposition made to the new federal Government, first, in order to prevent its adoption, and since, in order to place its administration in the hands of disaffected men, there is now both a certainty of its peaceable commencement in March next, and a flattering prospect that it will be administered by men who will give it a fair trial. General Washington will certainly be called to the Executive department. Mr. Adams, who is pledged to support him, will probably be the vice President. The enemies to the Government, at the head and the most inveterate of whom is Mr. Henry, are laying a train for the election of Governor Clinton, but it cannot succeed unless the federal votes be more dispersed than can well happen. Of the seven States which have appointed their Senators, Virginia alone will have anti-federal members in that branch. Those of New Hampshire are President Langdon and Judge Bartlett; of Massachusetts, Mr. Strong and Mr. Dalton; of Connecticut, Doctor Johnson and Mr. Ellesworth; of New Jersey, Mr. Patterson and Mr. Elmer; of Pennsylvania, Mr. R. Morris and Mr. McClay; of Delaware, Mr. George Reed and Mr. Bassett; of Virginia, Mr. R. H. Lee and Col. Grayson. Here is already a majority of the ratifying States on the side of the Constitution. And it is not doubted that it will be reinforced by the appointments of Maryland, South Carolina, and Georgia. As one branch of the Legislature of New York is attached to the Constitution, it is not improbable that one of the Senators from that State also will be added to the majority.

In the House of Representatives the proportion of anti-federal members will of course be greater, but cannot, if present appearances are to be trusted, amount to a majority, or even a very formidable minority. The election for this branch has taken place as yet no where except in Pennsylvania, and here the returns are not yet come in from all the Counties. It is certain, however, that seven out of the eight, and probable that the whole eight, representatives will bear the federal stamp. Even in Virginia, where the enemies to the Government form 2/3 of the *legislature,* it is computed that more than half the number of Representatives, who will be elected by the *people*, formed into districts for the purpose, will be of the same stamp. By some, it is computed that seven out of the ten allotted to that State will be opposed to the politics of the present Legislature.

The questions which divide the public at present relate—1. To the extent of the amendments that ought to be made to the Constitution. 2. To the mode in which they ought to be made. The friends of the Constitution, some from an approbation of particular amendments, others from a spirit of conciliation, are generally agreed that the system should be revised. But they wish the revisal to be carried no farther than to supply additional guards for liberty, without abridging the sum of power transferred from the States to the general Government, or altering previous to trial the particular structure of the latter, and are fixed in opposition to the risk of another Convention, whilst the purpose can be as well answered by the other mode provided for introducing amendments. Those who have opposed the Constitution are, on the other hand, zealous for a second Convention and for a revisal, which may either not be restrained at all, or extend at least as far as alterations have been proposed by any State. Some of this class are, no doubt, friends to an effective Government, and even to the substance of the particular Government in question. It is equally certain that there are others who urge a second Convention with the insidious hope of throwing all things into confusion, and of subverting the fabric just established, if not the Union itself. If the first Congress embrace the policy which circumstances mark out, they will not fail to propose, of themselves, every desirable safeguard for popular rights; and by thus separating the well-meaning from the designing opponents, fix on the latter their true character, and give to the Government its due popularity and stability.

[C] Jefferson to Madison

PARIS, March 15, 1789

Your thoughts on the subject of the declaration of rights in the letter of October the 17th, I have weighed with great satisfaction. Some of them had not occurred to me before, but were acknowledged just in the moment they were presented to my mind. In the arguments in favor of a declaration of rights, you omit one which has great weight with me;

the legal check which it puts into the hands of the judiciary. This is a body, which, if rendered independent, and kept strictly to their own department, merits great confidence for their learning and integrity. In fact, what degree of confidence would be too much, for a body composed of such men as Wythe, Blair, and Pendleton? On characters like these, the "*civium ardor prava jubentium*"[8] would make no impression. I am happy to find that, on the whole, you are a friend to this amendment. The declaration of rights is, like all other human blessings, alloyed with some inconveniences, and not accomplishing fully its object. But the good of this instance vastly overweighs the evil. I cannot refrain from making short answers to the objections which your letter states to have raised. 1. That the rights in question are reserved by the manner in which the federal powers are granted. Answer. A constitutive act may, certainly, be so formed, as to need no declaration of rights. The act itself has the force of a declaration, as far as it goes; and if it goes to all material points, nothing more is wanting. In the draught of a constitution which I had once a thought of proposing in Virginia, and printed afterwards, I endeavored to reach all the great objects of public liberty, and did not mean to add a declaration of rights. Probably the object was imperfectly executed; but the deficiencies would have been supplied by others, in the course of discussion. But in a constitutive act which leaves some precious articles unnoticed, and raises implications against others, a declaration of rights becomes necessary, by way of supplement. This is the case of our new federal Constitution. This instrument forms us into one State, as to certain objects, and gives us a legislative and executive body for these objects. It should, therefore, guard us against their abuses of power, within the field submitted to them. 2. A positive declaration of some essential rights could not be obtained in the requisite latitude. Answer. Half a loaf is better than no bread. If we cannot secure all our rights, let us secure what we can. 3. The limited powers of the federal government, and jealousy of the subordinate governments, afford a security which exists in no other instance. Answer. The first member of this seems resolvable into the first objection before stated. The jealousy of the subordinate governments is a precious reliance. But observe that those governments are only agents. They must have principles furnished them, whereon to found their opposition. The declaration of rights will be the text, whereby they will try all the acts of the federal government. In this view, it is necessary to the federal government also; as by the same text they may try the opposition of the subordinate governments. 4. Experience proves the inefficacy of a

---

[8] "The wayward zeal of the ruling citizens," Koch, 462.

bill of rights. True. But though it is not absolutely efficacious under all circumstances, it is of great potency always, and rarely inefficacious. A brace the more will often keep up the building which would have fallen, with that brace the less. There is a remarkable difference between the characters of the inconveniencies which attend a declaration of rights, and those which attend the want of it. The inconveniences of the declaration are, that it may cramp government in its useful exertions. But the evil of this is short-lived, moderate and reparable. The inconveniencies of the want of a declaration are permanent, afflicting and irreparable. They are in constant progression from bad to worse. The executive, in our governments, is not the sole, it is scarcely the principal object of my jealousy. The tyranny of the legislatures is the most formidable dread at present, and will be for many years. That of the executive will come in its turn; but it will be at a remote period. I know there are some among us, who would now establish a monarchy. But they are inconsiderable in number and weight of character. The rising race are all republicans. We were educated in royalism; no wonder if some of us retain that idolatry still. Our young people are educated in republicanism; an apostacy from that to royalism, is unprecedented and impossible. I am much pleased with the prospect that a declaration of rights will be added; and hope it will be done in that way which will not endanger the whole frame of the government, or any essential part of it.

XLII.

JAMES MADISON ARGUES FOR CONSTITUTIONAL AMENDMENTS, 8 JUNE 1789

We have reproduced James Madison's remarks on 8 June 1789, during the first session of the First Congress, from *Annals of Congress* (I: 424-450). Madison was interrupted on three separate occasions; the concerns of his colleagues are summarized in square parenthesis. See also Kurland and Lerner (I: 479-484) for a condensed version of Madison's June 8th speech. A more complete account of the June 8th debate can be found in Kurland and Lerner (V: 20-32) and Schwartz (V: 1016-1043).

~

MONDAY, 8 June 1789

AMENDMENTS TO THE CONSTITUTION

Mr. MADISON.——I am sorry to be accessary to the loss of a single moment of time by the House. If I had been indulged in my motion, and we had gone into a Committee of the Whole, I think we might have rose, and resumed the consideration of other business before this time; that is, so far as it depended on what I proposed to bring forward. As that mode seems not to give satisfaction, I will withdraw the motion, and move you, sir, that a select committee be appointed to consider and report such amendments as are proper for Congress to propose to the Legislatures of the several States, comformably to the fifth article of the Constitution.

I will state my reasons why I think it proper to propose amendments; and state the amendments themselves, so far as I think they ought to be proposed. If I thought I could fulfil the duty which I owe to myself and my constituents, to let the subject pass over in silence, I most certainly should not trespass upon the indulgence of this House. But I cannot do this; and am therefore compelled to beg a patient hearing to what I have to lay before you. And I do most sincerely believe, that if Congress will devote but one day to this subject, so far as to satisfy the public that we do not disregard their wishes, it will have a salutary influence on the public councils, and prepare the way for a favorable reception of our future measures. It appears to me that this House is bound by every motive of prudence, not to let the first session pass over without proposing to the State Legislatures, some things to be incorporated into the Constitution, that will render it as acceptable to the whole people of the United States, as it has been found acceptable to a majority of them. I wish, among other reasons why something should be done, that those who have been friendly to the adoption of this Constitution, may have the opportunity of proving to those who were opposed to it that they were as sincerely devoted to liberty and a Republican Government, as those who charged them with wishing the adoption of this Constitution in order to lay the foundation of an aristocracy or despotism. It will be a desirable thing to extinguish from the bosom of every member of the community any apprehensions that there are those among his countrymen who wish to deprive them of the liberty for which they valiantly fought and honorably bled. And if there are amendments desired of such a nature as will not injure the Constitution, and they can be ingrafted so as to give satisfaction to the doubting part of our fellow-citizens, the friends of the

Federal Government will evince that spirit of deference and concession for which they have hitherto been distinguished.

It cannot be a secret to the gentlemen in this House, that, notwithstanding the ratification of this system of Government by eleven of the thirteen United States, in some cases unanimously, in others by large majorities; yet still there is a great number of our constituents who are dissatisfied with it; among whom are many respectable for their talents and patriotism, and respectable for the jealousy they have for their liberty, which, though mistaken in its object, is laudable in its motive. There is a great body of the people falling under this description, who at present feel much inclined to join their support to the cause of Federalism, if they were satisfied on this one point. We ought not to disregard their inclination, but, on principles of amity and moderation, conform to their wishes, and expressly declare the great rights of mankind secured under this Constitution. The acquiescence which our fellow citizens show under the Government, calls upon us for a like return of moderation. But perhaps there is a stronger motive than this for our going into a consideration of the subject. It is to provide those securities for liberty which are required by a part of the community; I allude in a particular manner to those two States who have not thought fit to throw themselves into the bosom of the Confederacy. It is a desirable thing, on our part as well as theirs, that a re-union should take place as soon as possible. I have no doubt, if we proceed to take those steps which would be prudent and requisite at this juncture, that in a short time we should see that disposition prevailing in those States that are not come in, that we have seen prevailing in those States which have embraced the Constitution.[9]

But I will candidly acknowledge, that, over and above all these considerations, I do conceive that the Constitution may be amended; that is to say, if all power is subject to abuse, that then it is possible the abuse of the powers of the General Government may be guarded against in a more secure manner than is now done, while no one advantage arising from the exercise of that power shall be damaged or endangered by it. We have in this way something to gain, and, if we proceed with caution, nothing to lose. And in this case it is necessary to proceed with caution; for while we feel all these inducements to go into a revisal of the Constitution, we must feel for the Constitution itself, and make that revisal a moderate one. I should be unwilling to see a door opened for a re-consideration of the whole structure of the

---

[9]Kurland and Lerner (I: 480) have "we have seen prevailing [in] those states which are." The phrase "have embraced the Constitution" is omitted.

Government—for a re-consideration of the principles and the substance of the powers given; because I doubt, if such a door were opened, we should be very likely to stop at that point which would be safe to the Government itself. But I do wish to see a door opened to consider, so far as to incorporate those provisions for the security of rights, against which I believe no serious objection has been made by any class of our constituents: such as would be likely to meet with the concurrence of two-thirds of both Houses, and the approbation of three-fourths of the State Legislatures. I will not propose a single alteration which I do not wish to see take place, as intrinsically proper in itself, or proper because it is wished for by a respectable number of my fellow-citizens; and therefore I shall not propose a single alteration but is likely to meet the concurrence required by the Constitution. There have been objections of various kinds made against the Constitution. Some were levelled against its structure, because the President was without a council; because the Senate, which is a legislative body, had judicial powers in trials on impeachments; and because the powers of that body were compounded in other respects, in a manner that did not correspond with a particular theory; because it grants more power than is supposed to be necessary for every good purpose, and controls the ordinary powers of the State Governments. I know some respectable characters who opposed this Government on these grounds; but I believe that the great mass of the people who opposed it, disliked it because it did not contain effectual provision against the encroachments on particular rights, and those safeguards which they have been long accustomed to have interposed between them and the magistrate who exercised the sovereign power: nor ought we to consider them safe, while a great number of our fellow-citizens think these securities necessary.

It has been a fortunate thing that the objection to the Government has been made on the ground I stated; because it will be practicable, on that ground, to obviate the objection, so far as to satisfy the public mind that their liberties will be perpetual, and this without endangering any part of the Constitution, which is considered as essential to the existence of the Government by those who promoted its adoption.

The amendments which have occurred to me, proper to be recommended by Congress to the State Legislatures, are these:

First. That there be prefixed to the Constitution a declaration, that all power is originally vested in, and consequently derived from, the people.

That Government is instituted and ought to be exercised for the benefit of the people; which consists in the enjoyment of life and liberty, with the right of acquiring and using property, and generally of pursuing and obtaining happiness and safety.

That the people have an indubitable, unalienable, and indefeasible right to reform or change their Government, whenever it be found adverse or inadequate to the purposes of its institution.[10]

Secondly. That in article 1st, section 2, clause 3, these words be struck out, to wit: "The number of Representatives shall not exceed one for every thirty thousand, but each State shall have at least one Representative, and until such enumeration shall be made;" and in place thereof be inserted these words, to wit: "After the first actual enumeration, there shall be one Representative for every thirty thousand, until the number amounts to——, after which the proportion shall be so regulated by Congress, that the number shall never be less than——, nor more than——, but each State shall, after the first enumeration, have at least two Representatives; and prior thereto."

Thirdly. That in article 1st, section 6, clause 1, there be added to the end of the first sentence, these words, to wit: "But no law varying the compensation last ascertained shall operate before the next ensuing election of Representatives."

Fourthly. That in article 1st, section 9, between clauses 3 and 4, be inserted these clauses, to wit: The civil rights of none shall be abridged on account of religious belief or worship, nor shall any national religion be established, nor shall the full and equal rights of conscience be in any manner, or on any pretext, infringed.

The people shall not be deprived or abridged of their right to speak, to write, or to publish their sentiments; and the freedom of the press, as one of the great bulwarks of liberty, shall be inviolable.

The people shall not be restrained from peaceably assembling and consulting for their common good; nor from applying to the legislature by petitions, or remonstrances for redress of their grievances.

The right of the people to keep and bear arms shall not be infringed; a well armed and well regulated militia being the best security of a free country: but no person religiously scrupulous of bearing arms shall be compelled to render military service in person.

No soldier shall in time of peace be quartered in any house without the consent of the owner; nor at any time, but in a manner warranted by law.

No person shall be subject, except in cases of impeachment, to more than one punishment, or one trial for the same offence; nor shall be compelled to be a witness against himself; nor be deprived of life, liberty, or property, without due process of law; nor be obliged to

---

[10]Kurland and Lerner (I: 480) omit Madison's second and third propositions.

relinquish his property, where it may be necessary for public use, without a just compensation.

Excessive bail shall not be required, nor excessive fines imposed, nor cruel and unusual punishments inflicted.

The rights of the people to be secured in their persons, their houses, their papers, and their other property, from all unreasonable searches and seizures, shall not be violated by warrants issued without probable cause, supported by oath or affirmation, or not particularly describing the places to be searched, or the persons or things to be seized.

In all criminal prosecutions, the accused shall enjoy the right to a speedy and public trial, to be informed of the cause and nature of the accusation, to be confronted with his accusers, and the witnesses against him; to have a compulsory process for obtaining witnesses in his favor; and to have the assistance of counsel for his defence.

The exceptions here or elsewhere in the Constitution, made in favor of particular rights, shall not be so construed as to diminish the just importance of other rights retained by the people, or as to enlarge the powers delegated by the Constitution; but either as actual limitations of such powers, or as inserted merely for greater caution.

Fifthly. That in article 1st, section 10, between clauses 1 and 2, be inserted this clause, to wit:

No State shall violate the equal rights of conscience, or the freedom of the press, or the trial by jury in criminal cases.

Sixthly. That, in article 3d, section 2, be annexed to the end of clause 2d, these words, to wit:

But no appeal to such court shall be allowed where the value in controversy shall not amount to —— dollars: nor shall any fact triable by jury, according to the course of common law, be otherwise re-examinable than may consist with the principles of common law.

Seventhly. That in article 3d, section 2, the third clause be struck out, and in its place be inserted the clauses following, to wit:

The trial of all crimes (except in cases of impeachments, and cases arising in the land or naval forces, or the militia when on actual service, in time of war or public danger) shall be by an impartial jury of freeholders of the vicinage, with the requisite of unanimity for conviction, of the right with the requisite of unanimity for conviction, of the right of challenge, and other accustomed requisites; and in all crimes punishable with loss of life or member, presentment or indictment by a grand jury shall be an essential preliminary, provided that in cases of crimes committed within any county which may be in possession of an enemy, or in which a general insurrection may prevail, the trial may by law be authorized in some other county of the same State, as near as may be to the seat of the offence.

In cases of crimes committed not within any county, the trial may by law be in such county as the laws shall have prescribed. In suits at common law, between man and man, the trial by jury, as one of the best securities to the rights of the people, ought to remain inviolate.

Eighthly. That immediately after article 6th, be inserted, as article 7th, the clauses following, to wit:

The powers delegated by this Constitution are appropriated to the departments to which they are respectively distributed: so that the Legislative Department shall never exercise the powers vested in the Executive or Judicial, nor the Executive exercise the powers vested in the Legislative or Judicial, nor the Judicial exercise the powers vested in the Legislative or Executive Departments.

The powers not delegated by this Constitution, nor prohibited by it to the states, are reserved to the States respectively.

Ninthly. That article 7th, be numbered as article 8th.

The first of these amendments, relates to what may be called a bill of rights. I will own that I never considered this provision so essential to the Federal Constitution as to make it improper to ratify it, until such an amendment was added; at the same time, I always conceived, that in a certain form, and to a certain extent, such a provision was neither improper nor altogether useless. I am aware that a great number of the most respectable friends to the Government, and champions for republican liberty, have thought such a provision not only unnecessary, but even improper, nay, I believe some have gone so far as to think it even dangerous. Some policy has been made use of, perhaps, by gentlemen on both sides of the question: I acknowledge the ingenuity of those arguments which were drawn against the Constitution, by a comparison with the policy of Great Britain, in establishing a declaration of rights; but there is too great a difference in the case to warrant the comparison: therefore, the arguments drawn from that source were in a great measure inapplicable. In the declaration of rights which that country has established, the truth is, they have gone no farther than to raise a barrier against the power of the Crown; the power of the Legislature is left altogether indefinite. Although I know whenever the great rights, the trial by jury, freedom of the press, or liberty of conscience, came in question in that body, the invasion of them is resisted by able advocates, yet their Magna Charta does not contain any one provision for the security of those rights, respecting which the people of America are most alarmed. The freedom of the press and rights of conscience, those choicest privileges of the people, are unguarded in the British Constitution.

But although the case may be widely different, and it may not be thought necessary to provide limits for the legislative power in that country, yet a different opinion prevails in the United States. The people of many States, have thought it necessary to raise barriers against power in all forms and departments of Government, and I am inclined to believe, if once bills of rights are established in all the States as well as the Federal Constitution, we shall find, that, although some of them are rather unimportant, yet, upon the whole, they will have a salutary tendency. It may be said, in some instances, they do no more than state the perfect equality of mankind. This, to be sure, is an absolute truth, yet it is not absolutely necessary to be inserted at the head of a Constitution.

In some instances they assert those rights which are exercised by the people in forming and establishing a plan of Government. In other instances, they specify those rights which are retained when particular powers are given up to be exercised by the Legislature. In other instances, they specify positive rights, which may seem to result from the nature of the compact. Trial by jury cannot be considered as a natural right, but a right resulting from a social compact, which regulates the action of the community, but is as essential to secure the liberty of the people as any one of the pre-existent rights of nature. In other instances, they lay down dogmatic maxims with respect to the construction of the Government; declaring, that the Legislative, Executive, and Judicial branches, shall be kept separate and distinct. Perhaps the best way of securing this in practice is, to provide such checks as will prevent the encroachment of the one upon the other.

But, whatever may be the form which the several States have adopted in making declarations in favor of particular rights, the great object in view is to limit and qualify the powers of Government, by excepting out of the grant of power those cases in which the Government ought not to act, or to act only in particular mode. They point these exceptions sometimes against the abuse of the Executive power, sometimes against the Legislative, and, in some cases, against the community itself; or, in other words, against the majority in favor of the minority.

In our Government it is, perhaps, less necessary to guard against the abuse in the Executive Department than any other; because it is not the stronger branch of the system, but the weaker. It therefore must be levelled against the Legislative, for it is the most powerful, and most likely to be abused, because it is under the least control. Hence, so far as a declaration of rights can tend to prevent the exercise of undue power, it cannot be doubted but such declaration is proper. But I confess that I do conceive, that in a Government modified like this of the United States, the great danger lies rather in the abuse of the community than in the Legislative body. The prescriptions in favor of liberty ought to be levelled against that quarter where the greatest danger lies, namely, that which possesses the highest prerogative of power. But this is not found in either the Executive or Legislative departments of Government, but in the body of the people, operating by the majority against the minority.

It may be thought all paper barriers against the power of the community are too weak to be worthy of attention. I am sensible they are not so strong as to satisfy gentlemen of every description who have seen and examined thoroughly the texture of such a defence; yet, as they have a tendency to impress some degree of respect for them, to establish the public opinion in their favor, and rouse the attention of the whole community, it may be one means to control the majority from those acts to which they might be otherwise inclined.

It has been said, by way of objection to a bill of rights, by many respectable gentlemen out of doors, and I find opposition on the same principles likely to be made by gentlemen on this floor, that they are unnecessary articles of a Republican Government, upon the presumption that the people have those rights in their own hands, and that is the proper place for them to rest. It would be a sufficient answer to say, that this objection lies against such provisions under the State Government, as well as under the General Government; and there are, I believe, but few gentlemen who are inclined to push their theory so far as to say that a declaration of rights in those cases is either ineffectual or improper. It has been said, that in the Federal Government they are unnecessary, because the powers are enumerated, and it follows, that all that are not granted by the Constitution are retained; that the Constitution is a bill of powers, the great residuum being the rights of the people; and, therefore, a bill of rights cannot be so necessary as if the residuum was thrown into the hands of the Government. I admit that these arguments are not entirely without foundation; but they are not conclusive to the extent which has been supposed. It is true, the powers of the General Government are circumscribed, they are directed to particular objects; but even if Government keeps within those limits, it has certain discretionary powers with respect to the means, which may admit of abuse to a certain extent, in the same manner as the powers of the State Governments under their constitutions may to an indefinite extent; because in the Constitution of the United States, there is a clause granting to Congress the power to make all laws which shall be necessary and proper for carrying into execution all the powers vested in the Government of the United States, or in any department or officer thereof; this enables them to fulfil every purpose for which the Government was established. Now, may not laws be considered necessary and proper by Congress, (for it is them who are to judge of the necessity and propriety to accomplish those special purposes which they may have in contemplation,) which laws in themselves are neither necessary or proper; as well as improper laws could be enacted by the State Legislatures, for fulfilling the more extended objects of those Governments? I will state an instance, which I think in point, and proves that this might be the case. The General Government has a right to pass all laws which shall be necessary to collect its revenue; the means for enforcing the collection are within the direction of the Legislature: may not general warrants be considered necessary for this purpose, as well as for some purposes which it was supposed at the framing of their constitutions the State Governments had in view? If there was reason for restraining the State Governments from exercising this power, there is like reason for restraining the Federal Government.

It may be said, indeed it has been said, that a bill of rights is not necessary, because the establishment of this Government has not repealed those declarations of rights which are added to the several State constitutions; that those rights of the people which had been established by the most solemn act, could not be annihilated by a subsequent act of that people, who meant and declared at the head of the instrument, that they ordained and established a new system, for the express purpose of securing to themselves and posterity the liberties they had gained by an arduous conflict.

I admit the force of this observation, but I do not look upon it to be conclusive. In the first place, it is too uncertain ground to leave this provision upon, if a provision is at all necessary to secure rights so important as many of those I have mentioned are conceived to be, by the public in general, as well as those in particular who opposed the adoption of this Constitution. Beside some States have no bills of rights, there are others provided with very defective ones, and there are others whose bills of rights are not only defective, but absolutely improper; instead of securing some in the full extent which republican principles would require, they limit them too much to agree with the common ideas of liberty.

It has been objected also against a bill of rights, that, by enumerating particular exceptions to the grant of power, it would disparage those rights which were not placed in that enumeration; and it might follow by implication, that those rights which were not singled out, were intended to be assigned into the hands of the General Government, and were consequently insecure. This is one of the most plausible arguments I have ever heard urged against the admission of a bill of rights into this system; but, I conceive, that may be guarded against. I have attempted it, as gentlemen may see by turning to the last clause of the fourth resolution.

It has been said that it is unnecessary to load the Constitution with this provision, because it was not found effectual in the constitution of the particular States. It is true, there are a few particular States in which some of the most valuable articles have not, at one time or other, been violated; but does it not follow but they may have, to a certain degree, a salutary effect against the abuse of power. If they are incorporated into the Constitution, independent tribunals of justice will consider themselves in a peculiar manner the guardians of those rights; they will be an impenetrable bulwark against every assumption of power in the Legislative or Executive; they will be naturally led to resist every encroachment upon rights expressly stipulated for in the Constitution by the declaration of rights. Besides this security, there is a great probability that such a declaration in the federal system would be enforced; because the State Legislatures will jealously and closely watch the operations of this Government, and be able to resist with more effect every assumption of power, than any other power on earth can do; and the greatest opponents to a Federal Government admit the State Legislatures to be sure guardians of the people's liberty. I conclude, from this view of the subject, that it will be proper in itself, and highly politic, for the tranquility of the public mind, and the stability of the Government, that we should offer something, in the form I have proposed, to be incorporated in the system of Government, as a declaration of the rights of the people.[11]

In the next place, I wish to see that part of the Constitution revised which declares that the number of Representatives shall not exceed one for every thirty thousand persons, and allows one Representative to every State that ranks below that proportion. If we attend to the discussion of this subject, which has taken place in the State conventions, and even in the opinion of the friends to the Constitution, an alteration here is proper. It is the sense of the people of America, that the number of Representatives ought to be increased, but particularly that it should not to be left in the discretion of the Government to diminish them, below that proportion which is certainly in the power of the Legislature, as the Constitution now stands; and they may, as the population of the country increases, increase the House of Representatives to a very unwieldly degree. I confess I always thought this part of the Constitution defective, though not dangerous; and that it ought to be particularly attended to whenever Congress should go into the consideration of amendments.

There are several minor cases enumerated in my proposition, in which I wish also to see some alteration take place. That article which

[11] Kurland and Lerner (I: 484) omit the next two paragraphs.

leaves it in the power of the Legislature to ascertain its own emolument, is one to which I allude. I do not believe this is a power which, in the ordinary course of Government, is likely to be abused. Perhaps of all the powers granted, it is the least likely to abuse; but there is a seeming impropriety in leaving any set of men without control to put their hand in the public coffers, to take out money to put in their own pockets; there is a seeming indecorum in such power, which leads me to propose a change. We have a guide to this alteration in several of the amendments which the different conventions have proposed. I have gone, therefore, so far as to fix it, that no law varying the compensation, shall operate until there is a change in the Legislature; in which case it cannot be for the particular benefit of those who are concerned in determining the value of the service.

I wish, also, in revising the Constitution, we may throw into that section, which interdicts the abuse of certain powers in the State Legislatures, some other provisions of equal if not greater importance than those already made. The words, "No state shall pass any bill of attainder, *ex post facto* law," &c., were wise and proper restrictions in the Constitution. I think there is more danger of those powers being abused by the State Governments than by the Government of the United States. The same may be said of other powers which they possess, if not controlled by the general principle, that laws are unconstitutional which infringe the rights of the community. I should, therefore, wish to extend this interdiction, and add, as I have stated in the 5th resolution, that no State shall violate the equal right of conscience, freedom of the press, or trial by jury in criminal cases; because it is proper that every Government should be disarmed of powers which trench upon those particular rights. I know, in some of the State constitutions, the power of the Government is controlled by such a declaration; but others are not. I cannot see any reason against obtaining even a double security on those points; and nothing can give a more sincere proof of the attachment of those who opposed this Constitution to these great and important rights, than to see them join in obtaining the security I have now proposed; because it must be admitted, on all hands, that the State Governments are as liable to attack these invaluable privileges as the General Government is, and therefore ought to be as cautiously guarded against.

I think it will be proper, with respect to the judiciary powers, to satisfy the public mind on those points which I have mentioned. Great inconvenience has been apprehended to suitors from the distance they would be dragged to obtain justice in the Supreme Court of the United States, upon an appeal on an action for a small debt. To remedy this, declare, that no appeal shall be made unless the matter in controversy amounts to a particular sum; this, with the regulations respecting jury trials in criminal cases, and suits at common law, it is to be hoped, will quiet and reconcile the minds of the people to that part of the Constitution.

I find, from looking into the amendments proposed by the State conventions, that several are particularly anxious that it should be declared in the Constitution, that the powers not therein delegated, should be reserved to the several States. Perhaps other words may define this more precisely than the whole of the instrument now does.[12] I admit they may be deemed unnecessary; but there can be no harm in making such a declaration, if gentlemen will allow that the fact is as stated. I am sure I understand it so, and do therefore propose it.

These are the points on which I wish to see a revision of the Constitution take place. How far they will accord with the sense of this body, I cannot take upon me absolutely to determine; but I believe every gentleman will readily admit that nothing is in contemplation, so far as I have mentioned, that can endanger the beauty of the Government in any one important feature, even in the eyes of its most sanguine admirers. I have proposed nothing that does not appear to me as proper in itself, or eligible as patronised by a respectable number of our fellow-citizens; and if we can make the Constitution better in the opinion of those who are opposed to it, without weakening its frame, or abridging its usefulness in the judgment of those who are attached to it, we act the part of wise and liberal men to make such alterations as shall produce that effect.

Having done what I conceived was my duty, in bringing before this House the subject of amendments, and also stated such as I wish for and approve, and offered the reasons which occurred to me in their support, I shall content myself, for the present, with moving "that a committee be appointed to consider of and report such amendments as ought to be proposed by Congress to the Legislatures of the States, to become, if ratified by three-fourths thereof, part of the Constitution of the United States." By agreeing to this motion, the subject may be going on in the committee, while other important business is proceeding to a conclusion in the House. I should advocate greater dispatch in the business of amendments, if I was not convinced of the absolute necessity there is of pursuing the organization of the Government; because I think we should obtain the confidence of our fellow-citizens,

---

[12]Kurland and Lerner (I: 484) have "Perhaps words which may define this more precisely, than the whole of the instrument now does, may be considered superfluous."

in proportion as we fortify the rights of the people against the encroachments of the Government.

[Jackson, Elbridge Gerry, Samuel Livermore, Sherman, Thomas Sumter, and Vining debated the merits of sending Madison's proposals to a select committee.]

Mr. MADISON found himself unfortunate in not satisfying gentlemen with respect to the mode of introducing the business; he thought, from the dignity and the peculiarity of the subject, that it ought to be referred to a Committee of the Whole. He accordingly made that motion first, but finding himself not likely to succeed in that way, he had changed his ground. Fearing again to be discomfited, he would change his mode, and move the propositions he had stated before, and the House might do what they thought proper with them. He accordingly moved the propositions by way of resolutions to be adopted by the House.

[After a brief discussion, "Mr. MADISON'S propositions were ordered to be referred to a Committee of the Whole on the State of the Union."]

XLIII.

CONGRESSIONAL HISTORY OF THE BILL OF RIGHTS, 8 JUNE 1789-15 DECEMBER 1791

On 21 July, the House sent Madison's proposals to a select committee. Our first entry is the 28 July 1789 Report of the House Select Committee on Amendments. We have relied on *Documentary History of the Constitution of the United States* (V: 186-189). The second entry contains the House debates on the Select Committee Report between 13 and 24 August. These selections show that Madison was ultimately unsuccessful in his attempt to 1) "interweave" the proposed amendments into the body of the Constitution and 2) alter the Preamble of the Constitution to incorporate, expressly, the principles of the Declaration of Independence. He was successful, however, in limiting the scope of the amendments to a declaration of rights. We have relied on the *Annals of Congress* (I: 704-780). The third entry reproduces the seventeen amendments passed by the House and sent to the Senate. We have relied on *Documentary History of the Constitution of the United States* (V: 193-197). The Senate reduced the number to twelve, and a six-member joint Conference Committee ironed out the remaining differences. Our fourth entry reproduces the twelve amendments submitted by the Congress to the States for approval following the version found in Tansill (1063-1065). We have included Tansill's final footnote summarizing the decisions of the state legislatures and added, in square parentheses, the date, and order in which each state ratified the Bill of Rights. Tansill, following Elliot's *Debates* (I: 339-340), includes Kentucky as a non-ratifying state and does not indicate that Vermont was the tenth state to ratify on November 3, 1791. Massachusetts, Connecticut, and Georgia ratified on March 2, 1939 during the sesquicentennial celebrations. Our final entry reproduces the first ten amendments from Tansill (1066-1067). See Kurland and Lerner (I: 485-494, V: 32-43) for summaries of reports, debates, and the legislative history of the amendments. Schwartz (V: 983-1204) contains extensive coverage of the House and Senate discussions and decisions. See also Edward Dumbauld, *The Bill of Rights and What it Means Today* for highlights, and Linda Grant DePauw, *Documentary History of the First Federal Congress, 1789-1791* (Baltimore: Johns Hopkins University Press, 1972), for the complete account of the legislative history.

~

[A] Report of the House Select Committee, 28 July 1789

MR. VINING, *from the Committee of eleven, to whom it was referred to take the subject of* AMENDMENTS *to the* CONSTITUTION *of the* UNITED STATES, *generally into their consideration, and to report therupon, made a report, which was read, and is as followeth:*

In the introductory paragraph before the words, "*We the people,*" add, "Government being intended for the benefit of the people, and the rightful establishment thereof being derived from their authority alone."

ART. I, SEC. 2, PAR. 3—Strike out all between the words, "*direct*" and "*and until such,*" and instead thereof insert, "After the first enumeration there shall be one representative for every thirty thousand until the number shall amount to one hundred; after which the proportion shall be so regulated by Congress that the number of Representatives shall never be less than one hundred, nor more than one hundred and seventy-five, but each State shall always have at least one Representative."

ART. I, SEC. 6—Between the words, "*United States,*" and "*shall in all cases,*" strike out "*they,*" and insert, "But no law varying the compensation shall take effect until an election of Representatives shall have intervened. The members."

ART. I, SEC. 9—Between PAR. 2 and 3 insert, "No religion shall be established by law, now shall the equal rights of conscience be infringed."

"The freedom of speech, and of the press, and the right of the people peaceably to assemble and consult for their common good, and to apply to the government for redress of grievances, shall not be infringed."

"A well regulated militia, composed of the body of the people, being the best security of a free State, the right of the people to keep and bear arms shall not be infringed, but no person religiously scrupulous shall be compelled to bear arms."

"No soldier shall in time of peace be quartered in any house without the consent of the owner, nor in time of war but in a manner to be prescribed by law."

"No person shall be subject, except in case of impeachment, to more than one trial or one punishment for the same offence, nor shall be compelled to be a witness against himself, nor be deprived of life, liberty, or property without due process of law; nor shall private property be taken for public use without just compensation."

"Excessive bail shall not be required, nor excessive fines imposed, nor cruel and unusual punishment inflicted."

"The right of the people to be secure in their person, houses, papers and effects, shall not be violated by warrants issuing, without probable cause supported by oath or affirmation, and not particularly describing the places to be searched, and the persons or things to be seized."

"The enumeration in this Constitution of certain rights shall not be construed to deny or disparage others retained by the people."

ART. 1, SEC. 10, between the 1st and 2d PAR. insert, "No State shall infringe the equal rights of conscience, nor the freedom of speech, or of the press, nor of the right of trial by jury in criminal cases."

ART. 3, SEC. 2, add to the 2d PAR. "But no appeal to such court shall be allowed, where the value in controversy shall not amount to one thousand dollars; nor shall any fact, triable by a Jury according to the course of the common law, be otherwise re-examinable than according to the rules of common law."

ART. 3, SEC. 2—Strike out the whole of the 3d paragraph, and insert— "In all criminal prosecutions the accused shall enjoy the right to a speedy and public trial, to be informed of the nature and cause of the accusation, to be confronted with the witnesses against him, to have compulsory process for obtaining witnesses in his favor, and to have the assistance of counsel for his defence."

"The trial of all crimes (except in cases of impeachment, and in cases arising in the land or naval forces, or in the militia, when in actual service in time of war or public danger) shall be by an impartial jury of freeholders of the vicinage, with the requisite of unanimity for conviction, the right of challenge and other accustomed requisites; and no person shall be held to answer for a capital, or otherwise infamous crime, unless on a presentment or indictment by a Grand Jury; but if a crime be committed in a place in the possession of an enemy, or in which an insurrection may prevail, the indictment and trial may by law be authorized in some other place within the same State; and if it be committed in a place not within a State, the indictment and trial may be at such lace or places as the law may have directed."

"In suits at common law the right of trial by jury shall be preserved."

"Immediately after ART. 6, the following to be inserted as ART. 7:"

"The powers delegated by this Constitution to the government of the United States, shall be exercised as therein appropriated, so that the Legislative shall never exercise the powers vested in the Executive or the Judicial; nor the Executive the powers vested in the Legislative or Judicial; nor the Judicial the powers vested in the Legislative or Executive."

"The powers not delegated by this Constitution, nor prohibited by it to the States, are reserved to the States respectively."

ART. 7 to be made ART. 8.

[B] House Debates Select Committee Report, 13-24 August 1789

THURSDAY, August 13

The House then resolved itself into a Committee of the Whole, Mr. BOUDINOT in the Chair, and took the amendments under consideration. The first article ran thus: "In the introductory paragraph of the Constitution, before the words 'We the people,' add 'Government being intended for the benefit of the people, and the rightful establishment therof being derived from their authority alone.'"

MR. SHERMAN.—I believe, Mr. Chairman, this is not the proper mode of amending the Constitution. We ought not to interweave our propositions into the work itself, because it will be destructive of the whole fabric. We might as well endeavor to mix brass, iron, and clay, as to incorporate such heterogeneous articles, the one contradictory to the other. Its absurdity will be discovered by comparing it with a law. Would any Legislature endeavor to introduce into a former act a subsequent amendment, and let them stand so connected? When an alteration is made in an act, it is done by way of supplement; the latter act always repealing the former in every specified case of difference.

Besides this, sir, it is questionable whether we have the right to propose amendments in this way. The Constitution is the act of the people, and ought to remain entire. But the amendments will be the act of the State Governments. Again, all the authority we possess is derived from that instrument; if we mean to destroy the whole, and establish a new Constitution, we remove the basis on which we mean to build. For these reasons, I will move to strike out that paragraph and substitute another.

The paragraph proposed was to the following effect:

Resolved, by the Senate and House of Representatives of the United States in Congress assembled, That the following articles be proposed as amendments to the Constitution, and when ratified by three-fourths of the State Legislatures, shall become valid to all intents and purposes, as part of the same.

Under this title, the amendments might come in nearly as stated in the report, only varying the phraseology so as to accommodate them to a supplementary form.

Mr. MADISON.—Form, sir, is always of less importance than the substance; but on this occasion I admit that form is of some consequence, and it will be well for the House to pursue that which, upon reflection, shall appear to be the most eligible. Now it appears to me, that there is a neatness and propriety in incorporating the amendments into the Constitution itself; in that case, the system will remain uniform and entire; it will certainly be more simple when the amendments are interwoven into those parts to which they naturally belong, than it will if they consist of separate and distinct parts. We shall then be able to determine its meaning without references or comparison; whereas, if they are supplementary, its meaning can only be ascertained by a comparison of the two instruments, which will be a very considerable embarrassment. It will be difficult to ascertain to what parts of the instrument the amendments particularly refer; they will create unfavorable comparisons; whereas, if they are placed upon the footing here proposed, they will stand upon as good foundation as the original work. Nor is it so uncommon a thing as gentlemen suppose; systematic men frequently take up the whole law, and, with its amendments and alterations, reduce it into one act. I am not, however, very solicitous about the form, provided the business is but well completed.

[Smith, Livermore, Vining, Clymer, Stone, Gerry, Benson, Hartley, Page, and Jackson discuss the relative merits of the two "forms" of amending the Constitution.]

Mr. SHERMAN.—If I had looked upon this question as a mere matter of form, I should not have brought it forward, or troubled the committee with such a lengthy discussion. But, sir, I contend that amendments made in the way proposed by the committee are void. No gentleman ever knew an addition and alteration introduced into an existing law, and that any part of such law was left in force; but if it was improved or altered by a supplemental act, the original retained all its validity and importance, in every case where the two were not incompatible. But if these observations alone should be thought insufficient to support my motion, I would desire gentlemen to consider the authorities upon which the two Constitutions are to stand. The original was established by the people at large, by conventions chosen by them for the express purpose. The preamble to the Constitution declares the act; but will it be a truth in ratifying the next Constitution, which is to be done perhaps by the State Legislatures, and not conventions chosen for the purpose? Will gentlemen say it is "We the people" in this case? Certainly they cannot; for, by the present Constitution, we, nor all the Legislatures in the Union together, do not possess the power of repealing it. All that is granted us by the 5th article is, that whenever we shall think it necessary, we may propose amendments to the Constitution; not that we may propose to repeal the old, and substitute a new one.

Gentlemen say, it would be convenient to have it in one instrument, that people might see the whole at once; for my part, I view no difficulty on this point. The amendments reported are a declaration of rights; the people are secure in them, whether we declare them or not; the last amendment but one provides that the three branches of Government shall each exercise its own rights. This is well secured already; and, in short, I do not see that they lessen the force of any article in the Constitution; if so, there can be little more difficulty in comprehending them whether they are combined in one, or stand distinct instruments.

[Smith, Seney, Vining, Gerry continue to discuss which mode of amending the Constitution should be adopted.]

Mr. SHERMAN.—The gentlemen who oppose the motion say we contend for matter of form; they think it nothing more. Now we say we contend for substance, and therefore cannot agree to amendments in this way. If they are so desirous of having the business completed, they had better sacrifice what they consider but a matter of indifference to gentlemen, to go more unanimously along with them in altering the Constitution.

The question on Mr. SHERMAN'S motion was now put and lost.

FRIDAY, August 14

[Representatives Smith, Gerry, Tucker, Sumter, Livermore, and Page discuss the merits of the Select Committee's first amendment proposal that "Government being intended for the benefit of the people, and the rightful establishment therof being derived from their authority alone," be included in the introductory paragraph.]

Mr. MADISON.—If it be a truth, and so self-evident that it cannot be denied—if it be recognised, as is the fact in many of the State Constitutions—and if it be desired by three important States to be added to this—I think they must collectively offer a strong inducement to the mind desirous of promoting harmony to acquiesce with the report; at least some strong arguments should be brought forward to show the reason why it is improper.

My worthy colleague says the original expression is neat and simple; that loading it with more words may destroy the beauty of the sentence; and others say it is unnecessary, as the paragraph is complete without it. Be it so in their opinion; yet still it appears important in the estimation of three States that this solemn truth should be inserted in the Constitution. For my part, sir, I do not think the association of ideas anywise unnatural; it reads very well in this place; so much so, that I think gentlemen, who admit it should come in somewhere else, will be puzzled to find a better place.

Mr. SHERMAN thought they ought not to come in this place. The people of the United States have given their reasons for doing a certain act. Here we propose to come in and give them a right to do what they did on motives which appeared to them sufficient to warrant their determination; to let them know that they had a right to exercise a natural and inherent privilege, which they have asserted in a solemn ordination and establishment of the Constitution.

Now, if this right is indefeasible, and the people have recognised it in practice, the truth is better asserted than it can be by any words whatever. The words "We the people," in the original Constitution, are as copious and expressive as possible; any addition will only drag out the sentence without illuminating it; for these reasons it may be hoped the committee will reject the proposed amendment.

The question on the first paragraph of the report was put and carried in the affirmative, twenty-seven to twenty-three.

WEDNESDAY, August 19

[The Representatives concluded their consideration of the Select Committee report and defeated attempts by Gerry and Tucker to broaden the scope of the amendments to include the structure and powers of the federal government.]

Mr. SHERMAN renewed his motion for adding the amendments to the Constitution by way of supplement.

Hereupon, ensued a debate similar to what took place in the Committee of the Whole, [see THURSDAY, August 13, above] but, on the question, Mr. SHERMAN'S motion was carried by two-thirds of the House; in consequence it was agreed to.

The first proposition of amendment [see FRIDAY, August 14, above] was rejected, because two-thirds of the members present did not support it.

[The House, as the last order of business on Saturday, August 22, directed Representatives Benson, Sherman, and Sedgwick "to arrange" the agreed upon amendments "and make a report thereof."]

MONDAY, August 24

Mr. BENSON, from the committee appointed for the purpose, reported an arrangement of the articles of amendment to the Constitution of the United States, as agreed to by the House on Friday last.

[C] House Approves Seventeen Amendments, 24 August 1789

ARTICLE THE FIRST.

After the first enumeration, required by the first Article of the Constitution, there shall be one Representative for every thirty thousand, until the number shall amount to one hundred, after which the proportion shall be so regulated by Congress, that there shall be not less than one hundred Representatives, nor less than one Representative for every forty thousand persons, until the number of Representatives shall amount to two hundred, after which the proportion shall be so regulated by Congress, that there shall not be less than two hundred Representatives, nor less than one Representative for every fifty thousand persons.

ARTICLE THE SECOND.

No law varying the compensation to the members of Congress, shall take effect, until an election of Representatives shall have intervened.

ARTICLE THE THIRD.

Congress shall make no law establishing religion or prohibiting the free exercise thereof, nor shall the rights of Conscience be infringed.

ARTICLE THE FOURTH.

The Freedom of Speech, and of the Press, and the right of the People peaceably to assemble, and consult for their common good, and to apply to the Government for a redress of grievances, shall not be infringed.

ARTICLE THE FIFTH.

A well regulated militia, composed of the body of the People, being the best security of a free State, the right of the People to keep and bear arms, shall not be infringed, but no one religiously scrupulous of bearing arms, shall be compelled to render military service in person.

ARTICLE THE SIXTH.

No soldier shall, in time of peace, be quartered in any house without the consent of the owner, nor in time of war, but in a manner to be prescribed by law.

ARTICLE THE SEVENTH.

The right of the People to be secure in their persons, houses, papers and effects, against unreasonable searches and seizures, shall not be violated, and no warrants shall issue, but upon probable cause supported by oath or affirmation, and particularly describing the place to be searched, and the persons or things to be seized.

ARTICLE THE EIGHTH.

No person shall be subject, except in case of impeachment, to more than one trial, or one punishment for the same offence, nor shall be compelled in any criminal case, to be a witness against himself, nor be deprived of life, liberty or property, without due process of law; nor shall private property be taken for public use without just compensation.

ARTICLE THE NINTH.

In all criminal prosecutions, the accused shall enjoy the right to a speedy and public trial, to be informed of the nature and cause of the accusation, to be confronted with the witnesses against him, to have compulsory process for obtaining witnesses in his favor, and to have the assistance of counsel for his defence.

ARTICLE THE TENTH.

The trial of all crimes (except in cases of impeachment, and in cases arising in the land or naval forces, or in the militia when in actual service in time of War or public danger) shall be by an Impartial Jury of the Vicinage, with the requisite of unanimity for conviction, the right of challenge, and other accostomed requisites; and no person shall be held to answer for a capital, or otherways infamous crime, unless on a presentment or indictment by a Grand Jury; but if a crime be committed in a place in the possession of an enemy, or in which an insurrection may prevail, the indictment and trial may by law be authorised in some other place within the same State.

ARTICLE THE ELEVENTH.

No appeal to the Supreme Court of the United States, shall be allowed, where the value in controversy shall not amount to one thousand dollars, nor shall any fact, triable by a Jury according to the course of the common law, be otherwise re-examinable, than according to the rules of common law.

ARTICLE THE TWELFTH.

In suits at common law, the right of trial by Jury shall be preserved.

ARTICLE THE THIRTEENTH.

Excessive bail shall not be required, nor excessive fines imposed, nor cruel and unusual punishments inflicted.

ARTICLE THE FOURTEENTH.

No State shall infringe the right of trial by Jury in criminal cases, nor the rights of conscience, nor the freedom of speech, or of the press.

ARTICLE THE FIFTEENTH.

The enumeration in the Constitution of certain rights, shall not be construed to deny or disparage others retained by the people.

ARTICLE THE SIXTEENTH.

The powers delegated by the Constitution to the government of the United States, shall be exercised as therein appropriated, so that the Legislative shall never exercise the powers vested in the Executive or Judicial; nor the Executive the powers vested in the Legislative or Judicial; nor the Judicial the powers vested in the Legislative or Executive.

ARTICLE THE SEVENTEENTH.

The powers not delegated by the Constitution, nor prohibited by it, to the States, are reserved to the States respectively.

[D] First Congress Approves Twelve Amendments, 25 September 1789

Article the first...After the first enumeration required by the first Article of the Constitution, there shall be one Representative for every thirty thousand, until the number shall amount to one hundred, after which, the proportion shall be so regulated by Congress, that there shall be not less than one hundred Representatives, nor less than one Representative for every forty thousand persons, until the number of Representatives shall amount to two hundred, after which the proportion shall be so regulated by Congress, that there shall not be less than two hundred Representatives, nor more than one Representative for every fifty thousand persons.

Article the second...No law, varying the compensation for the services of the Senators and Representatives, shall take effect, until an election of Representatives shall have intervened.

Article the third...Congress shall make no law respecting an establishment of religion, or prohibiting the free exercise thereof; or abridging the freedom of speech, or of the press; or the right of the people peaceably to assemble, and to petition the Government for a redress of grievances.

Article the fourth...A well regulated Militia, being necessary to the security of a free State, the right of the people to keep and bear Arms, shall not be infringed.

Article the fifth...No Soldier shall, in time of peace be quartered in any house, without the consent of the Owner, nor in time of war, but in a manner to be prescribed by law.

Article the sixth...The right of the people to be secure in their persons, houses, papers, and effects, against unreasonable searches and seizures, shall not be violated, and no Warrants shall issue, but upon probable cause, supported by Oath or affirmation, and particularly describing the place to be searched, and the persons or things to be seized.

Article the seventh...No person shall be held to answer for a capital, or otherwise infamous crime, unless on a presentment or indictment of a Grand Jury, except in cases arising in the land or naval forces, or in the Militia, when in actual service in time of War or public danger; nor shall any person be subject for the same offence to be twice put in jeopardy of life or limb, nor shall be compelled in any criminal case to be a witness against himself, nor be deprived of life, liberty, or property, without due process of law; nor shall private property be taken for public use without just compensation.

Article the eighth...In all criminal prosecutions, the accused shall enjoy the right to a speedy and public trial, by an impartial jury of the State and district wherein the crime shall have been committed, which district shall have been previously ascertained by law, and to be informed of the nature and cause of the accusation; to be confronted with the witnesses against him; to have compulsory process for obtaining witnesses in his favor, and to have the Assistance of Counsel for his defence.

Article the ninth...In Suits at common law, where the value in controversy shall exceed twenty dollars, the right of trial by jury shall be preserved, and no fact tried by a jury, shall be otherwise re-examined in any Court of the United States, than according to the rules of the common law.

Article the tenth...Excessive bail shall not be required, nor excessive fines imposed, nor cruel and unusual punishments inflicted.

Article the eleventh...The enumeration in the Constitution, of certain rights, shall not be construed to deny or disparage others retained by the people.

Article the twelfth...The powers not delegated to the United States by the Constitution, nor prohibited by it to the States, are reserved to the States respectively, or to the people.*

---

*The proposed amendments were transmitted to the legislatures of the several States, upon which the following action was taken:

By the State of New Hampshire.—Agreed to the whole of the said amendments, except the 2d article. [#5. January 25, 1790.]

By the State of New York.—Agreed to the whole of the said amendments, except the 2d article. [#8. March 27, 1790.]

By the State of Pennsylvania.—Agreed to the 3d, 4th, 5th, 6th, 7th, 8th, 9th, 10th, 11th, and 12th articles of amendment. [#7. March 10, 1790.]

By the State of Delaware.—Agreed to the whole of the said amendments, except the 1st article. [#6. January 28, 1790.]

By the State of Maryland.—Agreed to the whole of the said twelve amendments. [#2. December 19, 1789.]

By the State of South Carolina.—Agreed to the whole said twelve amendments. [#4. January 19, 1790.]

By the State of North Carolina.—Agreed to the whole of the said twelve amendments. [#3. December 22, 1789.]

By the State of Rhode Island and Providence Plantations.—Agreed to the whole of the said twelve articles. [#9. June 11, 1790.]

By the State of New Jersey.—Agreed to the whole of the said amendments, except the 2d article. [#1. November 20, 1789.]

By the State of Virginia.—Agreed to the whole of the said twelve articles (Elliot's *Debates*, Vol. 1. pp. 339-340.) [#11. December 15, 1791.]

No returns were made by the states of Massachusetts, Connecticut, Georgia, and Kentucky.

The amendments thus proposed became part of the constitution--the first and second of them excepted; which were not ratified by a sufficient number of the state legislatures. (*Journal of the Federal Convention*, 1819, Supplement, p. 481.)

[E] Adoption of the First Ten Amendments, 15 December 1791

ARTICLE I

Congress shall make no law respecting an establishment of religion, or prohibiting the free exercise thereof; or abridging the freedom of speech, or of the press; or the right of the people peaceably to assembly, and to petition the Government for a redress of grievances.

ARTICLE II

A well regulated Militia, being necessary to the security of a free State, the right of the people to keep and bear Arms, shall not be infringed.

ARTICLE III

No Soldier shall, in time of peace be quartered in any house, without the consent of the Owner, nor in time of war, but in a manner to be prescribed by law.

ARTICLE IV

The right of the people to be secure in their persons, houses, papers, and effects, against unreasonable searches and seizures, shall not be violated, and no Warrants shall issue, but upon probable cause, supported by Oath or affirmation, and particularly describing the place to be searched, and the persons or things to be seized.

ARTICLE V

No person shall be held to answer for a capital, or otherwise infamous crime, unless on a presentment or indictment of a Grand Jury, except in cases arising in the land or naval forces, or in the Militia, when in actual service in time of War or public danger; nor shall any person be subject for the same offence to be twice put in jeopardy of life or limb; nor shall be compelled in any criminal case to be a witness against himself, nor be deprived of life, liberty, or property, without due process of law; nor shall private property be taken for public use, without just compensation.

ARTICLE VI

In all criminal prosecutions, the accused shall enjoy the right to a speedy and public trial, by an impartial jury of the State and district wherein the crime shall have been committed, which district shall have been previously ascertained by law, and to be informed of the nature and cause of the accusation; to be confronted with the witnesses against him; to have compulsory process for obtaining witnesses in his favor, and to have the Assistance of Counsel for his defence.

ARTICLE VII

In Suits at common law, where the value in controversy shall exceed twenty dollars, the right of trial by jury shall be preserved, and no fact tried by a jury, shall be otherwise re-examined in any Court of the United States, than according to the rules of the common law.

ARTICLE VIII

Excessive bail shall not be required, nor excessive fines imposed, nor cruel and unusual punishments inflicted.

ARTICLE IX

The enumeration in the Constitution, of certain rights, shall not be construed to deny or disparage others retained by the people.

ARTICLE X

The powers not delegated to the United States by the Constitution, nor prohibited by it to the States, are reserved to the States respectively, or to the people.

Selected Bibliography of Original Sources

Adler, Mortimer. 1968. *The Annals of America, volume 1.* Chicago: Encyclopedia Britannica, Incorporated.

Allen, W.B., and Gordon Lloyd, editors. 1985. *The Essential Antifederalist.* Lanham, MD: University Press of America.

Banning, Lance. 1995. *Jefferson and Madison: Three Conversations From the Founding.* Madison: Madison House.

Blackstone, William. 1765. *Commentaries on the Laws of England.* Oxford: Clarendon Press.

Bland, Richard. 1766. *An Inquiry into the Rights of the British Colonies.* Williamsburg: Alexander Purdie.

Bloom, Sol. 1943. *History of the Formation of the Union Under the Constitution.* Washington, DC: Government Printing Office.

Bowen, Francis. 1844. "James Otis." In *The Library of American Biography.* Edited by Jared Sparks. Second series. Volume II. Boston: Little and Brown.

Boyd, Julian P. 1964. *Fundamental Laws and Constitutions of New Jersey.* Princeton: Van Nostrand.

______, editor, et al. 1950. *The Papers of Thomas Jefferson.* Princeton: Princeton University Press.

Burke, Edmund. 1899. *The Works of Edmund Burke.* Boston: Little, Brown and Company.

Bushman, Claudia L., Harold B. Hancock, and Elizabeth Moyne Homsey, editors. 1986. *Proceedings of the Assembly of the Lower Counties of Delaware 1770-1776, of the Constitutional Convention of 1776, and of the House of Assembly of the Delaware State 1776-1781.* Newark: University of Delaware Press.

Cato. 1754 . *Letters.* London: W. Wilkins, T. Woodward, J. Waltroe, and J. Peele.

Commager, Henry Steele, editor. 1968. *Documents of American History*. New York: Appleton-Century-Crofts.

Conley, Patrick T., and John P. Kaminski, editors. 1988. *The Constitution and the States: The Role of the Original Thirteen in the Framing and Adoption of the Federal Constitution.* Madison, WI: Madison House.

Cook, S. A., F. E. Adcock, and M. P. Charlesworth, editors. 1930. *The Cambridge Ancient History,* volume III. Cambridge: Cambridge University Press.

Cushing, H. A., editor. 1904. *The Writings of Samuel Adams.* New York: Putnam's.

Davis, G. R. C. 1963. *Magna Carta.* London: The Trustees of the British Museum.

Deane, Charles, editor. 1856. *History of Plymouth Plantation by William Bradford.* Boston: privately printed.

DePauw, Linda Grant, et al, editors. 1972. *Documentary History of the First Federal Congress, 1789-1791*. Baltimore: Johns Hopkins University Press.

Dumbauld, Edward. 1957. *The Bill of Rights and What It Means Today*. Norman: University of Oklahoma Press.

Elliot, Jonathan, editor. 1836. *The Debates in the Several State Conventions on the Adoption of the Federal Constitution.* Five volumes. Philadephia: J. B. Lippencott Company.

Farrand, Max, editor. 1966. *The Records of the Federal Convention of 1787*. Four volumes. New Haven: Yale University Press.

Ford, Paul Leicester, editor. 1968. *Pamphlets on the Constitution of the United States.* New York: Da Capo Press.

Ford, W. C., editor. 1904. *Journals of the Continental Congress: 1774-1789*. Washington, D.C.: Government Printing Office.

Gales, Joseph, Sr., editor. 1834. *Annals of Congress (The Debates and Proceedings in the Congress of the United States).* Washington, D.C.: Government Printing Office.

Green, T. H., and T. H. Grose. 1875. *Essays: Moral, Political, and Literary.* Two volumes. London: Longmans, Green, and Company.

Haakonssen, Knud, editor. 1994. *David Hume: Political Essays* . Cambridge: Cambridge University Press.

Hamowy, Ronald, editor. 1995. *Cato's Letters: Or Essays on Liberty, Civil and Religious, And other Important Subjects.* Indianapolis: Liberty Fund.

Handlin, Oscar, and Mary Handlin, editors. 1966. *The Popular Sources of Political Authority: Documents on the Massachusetts Constitution of 1780.* Cambridge, MA: Belknap Press of Harvard University Press.

Hening, W. W. 1823. *Statutes at Large.* Richmond: George Cochran.

Hutson, James H, editor. 1975. A *Decent Respect to the Opinions of Mankind.* Washington, D.C.: United States Printing Office.

Hume, David. 1870. *Essays, Literary, Moral, and Political.* London: Ward, Lock, and Tyler.

———. 1752. *Political Discourses.* Second edition. Edinburgh: R. Fleming.

Hunt, Gaillard, editor. 1900-1910. *The Writings of James Madison.* Nine volumes. New York: G. P. Putman's Sons.

Hyneman, Charles S., and Donald S. Lutz, editors. 1985. *American Political Writings During the Founding Era.* Two volumes. Indianapolis: Liberty Press.

Jacobson, David L., editor. 1965. *Cato's Letters.* Indianapolis: Bobbs-Merrill.

Jefferson, Thomas. 1774. *A Summary View of the Rights of British America.* Williamsburg: Clementina Rind.

Jennings, Sir Ivan. 1965. *Magna Carta and Its Influence in the World Today.* London: Her Majesty's Stationary.

Jensen, Merrill, et al, editors. 1976. *Documentary History of the Ratification of the Constitution.* Madison: State Historical Society of Wisconsin.

Katz, Stanley N., editor. 1979. *Commentaries on the Laws of England.* Chicago: University of Chicago Press.

Koch, Adrienne, and William Peden, editors. 1972. *The Life and Selected Writings of Thomas Jefferson.* New York: The Modern Library.

Kurland, Philip B., and Ralph Lerner, editors. 1987. *The Founders' Constitution.* Five volumes. Chicago: University of Chicago Press.

Leaming, Aaron, and Jacob Spicer. 1881. *New Jersey: The Grants, Concessions, and Original Constitutions of the Province of New Jersey,* second edition. Somerville, NJ: Honeyman.

Letters and Writings of James Madison. Volume I (1769-1793). Published by order of Congress. Philadelphia: J. B. Lippincott and Company [1867].

Locke, John. 1694. *Two Treatises of Government.* Second Edition. London: A. and J. Churchill.

MacDonald, William, editor. 1914. *Documentary Source Book of American History, 1606-1898.* New York: The MacMillan Company.

Maryland Historical Society. *Proceedings and Acts of the General Assembly of Maryland, 1637-1664.* Baltimore: Maryland Historical Society, 1883.

McMaster, John B., and Frederick Stone, editors. 1888. *Pennsylvania and the Federal Constitution: 1787-1788.* Lancaster, PA: The Historical Society of Pennsylvania.

Miller, Eugene F., editor. 1985. *Essays: Moral, Political, and Literary.* Indianapolis: Liberty Classics.

Montesquieu, Baron de. 1752. *The Spirit of Laws.* Translated by Thomas Nugent. Second Edition. London: J. Nourse, and P. Vaillant.

______. 1949. *The Spirit of Laws.* Translated by Thomas Nugent. New York: Hafner Publishing Company.

Otis, James. 1765. *The Rights of the British Colonies Asserted and Proved.* Second edition. London: J. Almon.

______. 1929. *Some Political Writings of James Otis.* Introduction by Charles F. Mullett. Columbia: University of Missouri Press.

Richardson, James D. 1900. *A Compilation of the Messages and Papers of the Presidents, 1787-1897.* Washington D.C.: Published by the authority of Congress.

Rutland, Robert Alan et al, editors. 1975. *The Papers of James Madison.* Chicago: University of Chicago Press.

Schwartz, Bernard, editor. 1980. *The Roots of the Bill of Rights.* Five Volumes. New York: Chelsea House Publishers.

Sidney, Algernon. 1698. *Discourses Concerning Government.* London: Booksellers of London and Westminster.

Statutes at Large, From the First year of the Reign of King James the First To The Tenth Year of the Reign of King William the Third. London. [1763].

Storing, Herbert J., editor. 1981. *The Complete Anti-Federalist.* Seven volumes. Chicago: University of Chicago Press.

Stryett, Harold, editor. 1961. *The Papers of Alexander Hamilton.* New York: Columbia University Press.

Swindler, William F., editor. 1973. *Sources and Documents of United States Constitutions.* Dobbs Ferry, NY: Oceana Publications, Incorporated.

Tansill, Charles. 1927. *Documents Illustrative of the Formation of the Union of the American States.* Washington, DC: Government Printing Office.

The Charter of Privileges. Philadelphia: Samuel Keimer [1725].

The Constitution of the State of Massachusetts, adopted 1780. With the Amendments Annexed. Printed by order of the House of Representatives. Boston: Russell and Gardner [1822].

The Petition of Right. London: printed for M. Walbancke and L. Chapman [1642].

Thorpe, F. N. 1909. *The Federal and State Constitution.* Seven Volumes. Washington, DC: Government Printing Office.

Tucker, John. 1771. *An Election Sermon.* Boston: Richard Draper.

United States. Bureau of Rolls and Library. 1894. *Documentary History of the Constitution of the United States of America, 1786-1870.* Washington, Department of State.

Veit, Helen E., Kenneth R. Bowling, and Charlene Bangs Bickford, editors. 1991. *Creating the Bill of Rights: The Documentary Record From The First Federal Congress.* Baltimore: The Johns Hopkins Press.

Warner, Stuart D., and Donald W. Livingston, editors. 1994. *David Hume: Political Writings*. Indianapolis: Hackett Publishing Company.

Washington, H. A., editor. 1853. *The Writings of Thomas Jefferson.* Nine volumes. New York: John C. Riker.

West, Thomas G., editor. 1990. *Discourses Concerning Government by Algernon Sidney.* Indianapolis: Liberty Classics.

Whitemore, W. H. 1889. *The Colonial Laws of Massachusetts.* Boston: City Council.

Willson, W. M., et al, editors. 1975. *Delaware Code Annotated, Revised 1974.* Volume I. Charlottesville, VA: The Michie Company.

Index